The New Certificate Geography Series

ADVANCED LEVEL

AUSTRALASIA

This book belongs to

The New Certificate Geography Series

ADVANCED LEVEL

AUSTRALASIA

Australia, New Zealand, the Pacific Islands and Antarctica

FOURTH EDITION

HENRY REES, M.Sc. (Econ.), Ph.D.

Principal Lecturer in Geography
St Paul's College, Rugby

MACDONALD & EVANS LTD

8 John Street, London WC1N 2HY

1975

First published February 1962
Reprinted August 1962
Second edition January 1964
Reprinted December 1965
Third edition February 1968
Reprinted November 1969
Fourth edition May 1975

©

MACDONALD & EVANS LIMITED
1975

ISBN: Hardback Edition: 0 7121 0133 0
ISBN: Paperback Edition: 0 7121 0134 9

The New Certificate Geography Series

ADVANCED LEVEL

Australasia

Africa

Europe

Latin America

Mediterranean Lands

Monsoon Asia

North America

The Soviet Union

Filmset in Photon Times 11 pt by
Richard Clay (The Chaucer Press), Ltd, Bungay, Suffolk
and printed in Great Britain by
Fletcher & Son Ltd, Norwich

GENERAL INTRODUCTION TO THE SERIES

THE study of geography in the Sixth Form has been seriously handicapped in the past through the lack of suitable textbooks. There was no shortage of advanced books at university level, and this meant that pupils who had only just ceased using elementary texts, usually general world geographies, were suddenly introduced to volumes intended for university students. The gap between the two was wide, often too wide for the immature pupil who had only recently passed geography at "O" level. The reading, understanding, and digesting of serious studies called for an outlook, comprehension and breadth of knowledge which the average first-year Sixth Former frankly did not possess. Among pupils and teachers there was a felt need for texts which would bridge the gap; for books which were not elementary nor yet abstruse but intermediate in approach, content and style; for books which were clearly arranged and which dealt with ideas and terms new to pupils beginning Sixth Form work. It is a matter of some surprise that such texts have taken so long to appear.

The aim of this new series is to produce such texts, books which are essentially intermediate and more nearly meet the requirements of the Sixth Form student who is beginning to do much work on his own. New ideas and concepts are introduced, facts and figures are as up-to-date as it is possible to make them, maps and diagrams have been kept simple and clear, and a lucid exposition aimed at. The authors hope that their efforts will satisfy both students and teachers who are searching for a readily understandable but sufficiently comprehensive text.

While the books in the series have a uniform lay-out and adopt a similar technique in exposition, it has been thought desirable to allow each author to choose his own method of geographical presentation. No attempt has been made to produce stereotyped texts. Flexibility of approach has been considered more desirable. Some continents are more amenable to treatment by regions than others; in some cases it is probably better to follow a description by countries rather than by regions; and in some instances there are special problems that need high-lighting. For these principal reasons each continental area or major world region is afforded differing treatment.

H. ROBINSON,
Geographical Editor

PREFACE TO THE FIRST EDITION

THIS book forms part of a series designed to serve the needs of students preparing for the Advanced and Scholarship levels of the various General Certificate of Education examinations. It is, however, hoped that the subject matter will appeal to the general reader and to all those who wish to know more about the two young and energetic nations whose home lies on the "other side of the world."

Any general account such as this must draw heavily on the researches of others. A short reading list appears at the end of the book as a guide to the student; but I am pleased to acknowledge here my debt to the many published works of Professor Griffith Taylor on aspects of Australia, to those of Professor C. A. Cotton on the structure of New Zealand, and to the lucid account by Professor B. J. Garnier of the climate of New Zealand. Much valuable information has been supplied by the various central government and state representatives in the United Kingdom. The photographs of Australia have been very kindly supplied by the Australian News and Information Bureau, and those of New Zealand by the High Commissioner for New Zealand.

The reader is assumed to have access to modern and detailed maps of Australasia. The most valuable are those in the new edition of *The Times Atlas*; but two useful maps may be obtained for a few shillings in Bartholomew's World Series.

If this book helps in some small way to strengthen the bonds of friendship between Australia, New Zealand and the United Kingdom its writing will have been worth while.

HENRY REES

December 1961

PREFACE TO THE FOURTH EDITION

DURING the seven years that have elapsed since the publication of the third edition important advances have taken place in the economy of Australasia. Surges in mining activity have transformed many hitherto sparsely peopled districts; oil and natural gas have been discovered and utilised; progress has been made in almost every branch of farming.

All of the Australian States now publish their individual year books, which provide valuable additional source material for geographical study. For this edition I have drawn also on the accounts published in the Australian and New Zealand geographical journals during the last ten years or so; acknowledgments are made to these new sources in the notes at the end of the chapters.

The result is a substantially enlarged text, to which has been added seventy new illustrations and seventy additional tables. Needless to say, the student is not expected to memorise all this data; but he will now find more material from which he can select for the purpose in hand. It should be noted that, in some tables, the totals given do not necessarily agree with the apparent mathematical totals, owing to the rounding of figures.

I should like to thank the publishers for their continued co-operation in the production of this enlarged edition of *Australasia*.

HENRY REES

January 1975

CONTENTS

ix

PART TWO

NEW ZEALAND AND THE PACIFIC ISLANDS

LIST OF ILLUSTRATIONS

LIST OF TABLES

PART ONE

AUSTRALIA

Chapter I

DISCOVERY, EXPLORATION AND POLITICAL BEGINNINGS

THE DISCOVERY OF AUSTRALIA

WHO discovered Australia? Like many a simple question, it admits of no simple answer.

One of the most intriguing features of the history of exploration is the belief in the existence of a great southern continent awaiting discovery. Its name, indeed (from the Latin "auster," or "south wind"), preceded its discovery. Ptolemy drew it on his world map, in the middle of the second century A.D. In later centuries the classical geographers were forgotten; but the idea was revived in the later Middle Ages. Ortelius included it in his world map of 1564; and Mercator, arguing that the symmetry of the earth demanded such a land, marked a vast antarctic continent in his map of 1587.

It is highly likely that during the centuries before the European discovery of Australia the continent was visited from time to time by peoples from south-eastern Asia. Marco Polo hints at knowledge of a great land lying in the ocean to the south. There is also a very strong possibility that Chinese navigators visited, perhaps even circum-navigated, Australia. The great Chinese admiral, Cheng Ho, made several protracted voyages into the Indian Ocean, reaching as far west as Aden and Mogadishu in Somalia, during the early part of the fifteenth century. On one of his great voyages a storm dispersed his armada and part of it was blown southwards, making, it is thought, a landfall on the Australian continent. Recent archaeological finds of a Chinese charac-ter, such as the Chinese altar unearthed near Darwin, give a measure of credence to what otherwise might appear to be a fanciful conjecture. However it may be, any Chinese discovery was of no real moment in the history of Australian discovery and exploration, for it was never fol-lowed up and did not lead so far as we know to any further Chinese endeavour in Australian waters or to any Chinese settlement of a permanent character on the mainland.

The real extent of the southern continent was not known till 1770, and the lateness of its discovery may be attributed to two facts: it lay off the route to the spice islands; and when its chance discovery was made, the earliest parts to be seen included the barren, uninviting west coast.

THE EARLY DUTCH NAVIGATORS

The charting of the north and west coasts was almost entirely the work of the Dutch, and for this they were particularly well fitted. After the foundation of the Dutch East India Company in 1602 they possessed trading posts in Java and the Moluccas—useful bases from which to explore the seas to the south. The Dutch were skilled and fearless navigators; their charts were carefully drawn, and each new discovery was soon made available for other mariners by an organisation in Amsterdam.

There seems little doubt that the first European to chart any portion of the Australian coast was a Dutch mariner, Willem Janszoon, who set sail in 1605 from Bantam in western Java on a voyage of discovery. In his little ship *Duyfken* (Little Dove), Janszoon coasted along the southern shores of New Guinea, then turned south, crossed the Torres Strait (which he thought to be an inlet) and cruised along the eastern shore of the Gulf of Carpentaria. Some of his men landed, but hostile natives turned them back. Janszoon christened this place Cape Keerweer ("turn again"), and so it remains today (lat. 14° S., long. 141° 30′ E.). It is quite clear from the *Duyfken*'s chart that this is the north-west shore of the Cape York Peninsula.[1] But Janszoon returned, thinking that the coast he had discovered was merely a prolongation of New Guinea, and unaware that he had stumbled upon a new continent. It was not long before the western shores were discovered and charted; but the narrow Torres Strait, separating Australia from New Guinea, did not find its way on to the maps for a century and a half, and the result was to give a peculiar westward twist to the land where now is the Cape York Peninsula.

In 1611 the Dutch navigators began to make use of the steady west winds, as opposed to the monsoons, on their journeys from the Cape to Java; they therefore sailed farther south and then farther east than formerly, and it was this new route which led some of them to reach unexpectedly the west coast of Australia. In 1616 Dirk Hartog, in the *Eendraght*, struck its most westerly portion (in lat. 26° S.) and has left his name there in Dirk Hartog Island; in 1619 Jan Edels chanced upon the peninsula immediately to the south, formerly known as Edel Land; and in 1622 the *Leeuwin* (Lion) discovered the south-western tip of the continent, and gave her name to that cape. Only five years afterwards the south coast was charted by De Nuyts, and named Pieter Nuyts Land (though the name now survives only in Nuyts' Archipelago, at the eastern end of his exploration, immediately west of Lake Gairdner).

Thus, by 1628 a fairly complete chart of the whole of the west coast and much of the south coast of the new continent was available. These were barren shores; but the Dutch East India Company cherished the hope that further exploration might bring gold, or at least, a profitable commerce, or an easy route to Chile.

It was the task of Abel Tasman to continue the charts. He sailed from Mauritius in 1642, eastwards and then southwards, and first met with land in the southern shores of Tasmania; these he named Van Diemen's Land in honour of the Governor of the Dutch East Indies. The neighbouring coast of Australia was still a blank on the world's maps, and Tasman did not appreciate that Van Diemen's Land was an island. Continuing eastwards, he struck the western shore of South Island, New Zealand, which he named Staaten Land, after the States-General of the Netherlands. Cape Farewell and other coastal features can be plainly recognised from his chart. Tasman then entered the wide western approaches to Cook Strait: this he assumed to be a bay, and so continued northwards along the smooth western coasts of North Island, whose northerly tip he named Cape Maria Van Diemen. He left New Zealand behind him, sailed first north-east, then west, and so reached Java.

Tasman had sailed almost completely around Australia, yet he had seen nothing of its mainland. The knowledge of its north coast was still only fragmentary, and it was to repair this gap that Tasman undertook his second voyage in 1644. He carried out his task faithfully, tracing the shoreline around the Gulf of Carpentaria as far as the North-West Cape.

The shape of the new continent was becoming known; yet it was more than a century before the eastern coasts were mapped. Now, for the first time, the British Government took the initiative. Captain James Cook was chosen by the Admiralty for two tasks: ostensibly to carry a party of scientists of the Royal Society to Tahiti so that they might observe the transit of the planet Venus across the sun; secretly, to search for the unknown south-land, of which New Zealand might perhaps form part.

COOK'S VOYAGES

In August 1768 Cook sailed from Plymouth in the Whitby collier, *Endeavour*. He arrived safely in Tahiti, and the transit was successfully observed in June 1769. He had now already traversed the whole of the Atlantic and half the Pacific, but he continued westwards and reached Tasman's Staaten Land (New Zealand). He discovered the strait which Tasman had missed and gave his own name to it; furthermore, he confounded the theory that Staaten Land was part of a southern continent, by charting the whole of its 2400-mile (3860 km) coastline in a matter of six months (October 1769 till March 1770).

Sailing now westwards across the Tasman Sea, after nineteen days he came across the hitherto unknown east coast of Australia. He struck it close to Cape Howe—the most south-easterly point of the continent—and with great tenacity sailed northwards along the entire length of the east coast, charting as he went, mapping 2000 miles (3200 km) in four months and leaving behind him a string of names which are still to be seen in the atlas (Fig. 1). Botany Bay was so named from the many

new plants found there; Smoky Cape (north of Port Macquarie) from
the fires observed there; Cape Manifold (north of Rockhampton) from
the large number of high hills bordering it; Trinity Bay (north of
Cairns) because it was discovered on Trinity Sunday.

   The *Endeavour* was now hemmed in by the Great Barrier Reef; and
she struck it in August 1770. The sharp coral cut through her planks,
water poured in and was scarcely held in check by three pumps. An
ingenious device saved the ship: an old sail was covered with wool and

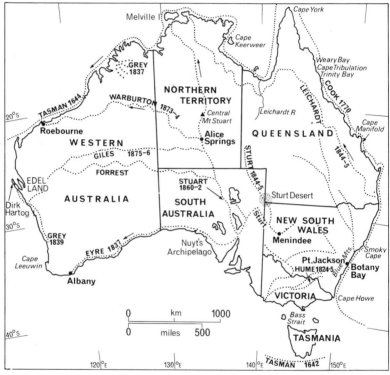

FIG. 1.—Australia: explorers' routes. The names and boundaries of the states are added
    for clarification, not being settled until 1911. The unnamed lines in New South
    Wales and Victoria are Major Thomas Mitchell's routes, 1831–46.

oakum (rope fibres), then the sailors hauled it below the ship until by
pressure the cloth was held tight against the leak. The *Endeavour*'s chart
provides a commentary on the events. Cape Tribulation and Weary Bay
are marked just south of the present Cooktown; offshore are the shoals
of the Barrier Reef, where "on these rocks the ship lay 23 hours."
Nearer the shore are Hope Islands, and beyond, Endeavour's River,
"where we repaired the ship."

Cook safely reached Cape York. Noticing some resemblance to the shores of Glamorganshire, he gave the name New South Wales to the whole of the new coast, and took possession of it in the name of King George III. Finally, making for Java, he passed through Torres Strait—the first European ship to do so since 1606—and proved that Australia was distinct from New Guinea.

Cook's first voyage had made clear the shape and size of the new continent. Only relatively small portions in the region of Bass Strait and Adelaide remained unknown. Australia was distinct from New Guinea in the north, and neither it nor New Zealand formed part of any antarctic continent still awaiting discovery. The stage was now set for colonisation and inland exploration.

BEGINNINGS OF SETTLEMENT AND EXPLORATION

Captain Cook returned to England from his first voyage in 1772; in 1783 came the end of the American War of Independence. There is a connection between the two events: the end of the American Colonies deprived the Government of a useful dumping ground for enemies of society; but Cook had already told them of a new land—a possible alternative. So it was that the first colonisation of Australia was by convicts.

In 1787 Captain Arthur Philip (destined to become the first Governor of New South Wales) set out for Australia, leading a fleet of eleven vessels. Six of his ships carried convicts (550 men and 230 women); three carried provisions, including 44 sheep, and the remaining two were warships.

The voyage took eight months. Captain Philip made straight for Botany Bay; but it was a disheartening spectacle of shallow water, sand and swamp. He searched farther north, and entered Port Jackson, which Cook had reported to be a small bay. Its entrance, true, was small; but this opened out into a wide expanse of water, full of inlets and coves. In one of these bays, where a fresh stream issued from a thick wood, Philip planted his first settlement. The inlet formed a magnificent harbour, sheltered and deep, perhaps the finest in the world; here the city of Sydney was founded, and named after the Colonial Secretary who had begun the enterprise.

For twenty-five years the settlers confined their operations to the coastal tract. Fifty miles inland lay the Blue Mountains, more than 3000 feet (2743 m) high, seamed with deep bottle-necked valleys and gorges, and presenting a formidable barrier (even today they are penetrated by only a single railway). But in 1813 a severe drought emphasised the need for new pastures, and a difficult route across the mountains was discovered, to reveal the fertile Bathurst Plains beyond. Sheep and cattle were driven along it, the Government built a road, and in 1815 the town of Bathurst was founded.

But the stream here flowed northwards—whither? River after river was seen, all flowing northwards or westwards. Did they flow right across the continent to the north-west coast? Or enter a great inland sea? It took fifteen years or more to solve the problem, and the work was largely carried out by three men. Hamilton Hume, a young colonist, discovered the Murray and Murrumbidgee rivers; Captain Charles Sturt found the Darling and reached its mouth in Lake Alexandrina (1830); and Major Thomas Mitchell, Surveyor-General of New South Wales, in three long journeys mapped the Lachlan, the Loddon, the Goulburn (Fig. 29), and Wimmera rivers and laid the foundation of Bourke. He had traversed some of the most fertile and attractive parts of Victoria, "a country ready for the immediate reception of civilised man, and destined perhaps to become eventually a portion of a great empire."[2]

POLITICAL DEVELOPMENT

POLITICAL BEGINNINGS

The name "New South Wales," as we have seen, was given by Cook to the whole of the eastern coast, so that this territory, based on the settlement at Sydney, was the parent colony. From 1810 to 1821 its governor was Lachlan Macquarie, who encouraged the rearing of sheep on the Bathurst Plains, and thus laid the foundation of a leading industry; his name is commemorated in those of two rivers. With the gradual spread of settlement the more outlying parts of this large region were granted independent status.

First to emerge was Tasmania (till 1853 known as Van Diemen's Land). French navigators had been busy charting its shores during the eighteenth century. The English authorities in New South Wales regarded these activities with suspicion, and, to forestall any attempt at French settlement, sent out colonising parties in 1803. At first progress was slow: the aborigines were hostile and the immigrants included many convicts. But in 1825 Van Diemen's Land was made independent of New South Wales; by 1830 large areas in the north-west had been taken up for sheep rearing, and by 1835 there were 40,000 people in the island. Transportation was abolished in 1853; in the same year a representative parliament was introduced and the name of the colony was changed to Tasmania.

Western Australia differs from the other states in that it never had any close links in early times with New South Wales. It, too, owed its beginnings to the fear of possible French colonisation: military garrisons were first established at Melville Island on the north coast, and at Albany and Perth (1829). The home Government encouraged settlers, and within six years Bunbury and Albany were established and the upper Swan river district occupied. In 1839 the population numbered 2150; but the colony was making little headway and requested the help of convict labour. The convicts seem to have set Western Australia on the road to self-government: the first ship-load arrived in 1850, when the colony numbered 6000 people; two years after the end of transportation (the system ended in 1868) convict and free settlers together numbered 25,000, and a partially representative government was conceded. There were now 690,000 sheep and 45,000 cattle in Western Australia. But the real advance came with the discovery of rich gold-fields after 1887: between that year and the end of the century the population quadrupled (from 42,000 to 180,000), the area under crops trebled, and the railway mileage increased eightfold (from 168 to 1355 miles (270 to 2181 m)).

South Australia owes its existence largely to Sturt, who, when voyaging down the Murray river in 1830, noticed good pasture land along its lower course. In 1834 the Parliament at Westminster set up a body of colonisation commissioners; the first settlers arrived in 1836 and the colony was formally proclaimed under a gum tree. Settlement was stimulated by the discoveries of copper in 1842 and 1845. Some of the population was attracted away into the neighbouring colony when gold was discovered in Victoria; but South Australia was soon found to be suited to the production of grain and fruit to feed the many gold-diggers.

The colony of Victoria was established fifteen years after the proclamation of South Australia. Part of its coast had been sighted by Cook in 1770, and in 1797 Mr Bass, a naval surgeon, discovered the strait which bears his name. Three years later the south coast of what is now Victoria was charted, and the Melbourne district and Port Philip harbour were first surveyed in 1802.

Settlement, however, did not begin until about 1835, by which time, as we have seen, Tasmania was fairly well occupied. Sheep and cattle farmers then crossed from Tasmania to begin operations on the mainland, and the Government of New South Wales sent out a resident magistrate for the district. There was a steady immigration from Great Britain and the population grew rapidly from 3500 in 1838 to 11,700 in 1841 and 32,900 in 1846. In the following year Melbourne was granted the status of a city; but the district was still governed from Sydney. Agitation grew in favour of separation, and in 1851, when the population was 77,400, the Colony of Victoria was proclaimed. A few weeks later gold was discovered, and heralded a new wave of immigration. Within three years the population trebled, to reach 236,800; and the new colony was firmly established.

Queensland was the last colony to emerge. A site for a new penal colony was needed, and the Moreton Bay area was accordingly explored. In 1823 the Brisbane river was discovered, and named after the then Governor of New South Wales. The convict settlement was established; but within 20 years the convicts had been withdrawn to Sydney, the land had been declared open for free settlers and farmers were pasturing their stock beyond the Darling Downs. From only 200 people in 1841, the number grew to 540 in 1844 and to 1867 in 1846. By

1849 there were 72,000 cattle there and more than a million sheep. Ten years later, when the population had grown to about 26,000, the Colony of Queensland was proclaimed.

Owing to its small population (about 37,000) Northern Territory has not become a self-supporting state, but like its counterpart in Canada (with a comparable population) is administered by the Federal Government.

INTERIOR EXPLORATION

EXPLORATION IN THE CENTRE AND WEST (Fig. 1)

In the mapping of the south-western coastlands much of the credit is due to Lieutenant Grey, who made his journeys in 1837–39. During 1837 he discovered the Prince Regent and Glenelg rivers in the far north (long. 125° E.); then, two years later, he sailed to Shark's Bay. There misfortune overtook him: first a hurricane destroyed most of his stores; then both of his boats were wrecked and his party had to *walk* the 300 miles (483 km) back to Perth. During the long journey they discovered the Murchison, Greenough, Irwin and other rivers, and mapped parts of the Victoria and Darling Ranges.

The same year saw the beginning of the explorations of Edward John Eyre, who operated a sheep farm north of Adelaide. He discovered the Broughton river, which flows westwards into Spencer's Gulf, and surveyed part of the Flinders Range; from Mount Eyre (later named after him) he was the first to view Lake Torrens. He followed the Flinders range to its northern terminus ("Mount Hopeless"), where he saw nothing but desolate salt lake and marsh stretching before him; thinking that it was still Lake Torrens which curved round in a great semicircle so as to bar all progress, he turned back. He had probably seen Lake Eyre, to which his name was later given.

Eyre next conceived the idea of crossing the continent by following the south coast from east to west. Starting in 1841 from the head of Spencer's Gulf, he covered the first 250 miles (402 km) into the desert. But four of his best horses had already been lost, and Eyre now had to send back half of his companions. With ten horses, six sheep and provisions for nine weeks the party pressed on, now reduced to five men. When they were still 650 miles (1046 km) from their destination the overseer was murdered and two natives deserted; Eyre was now left with only his servant and three weeks' supplies. They were travelling over a porous limestone region and had 150 miles (241 km) to go before they could replenish their water bags. On they struggled for another month; then, almost by a miracle, they were able to attract the attention of a whaling ship, and they were saved.

They rested on board for a fortnight, then continued their journey, arriving three weeks later at Albany. The expedition of 1209 miles (1946 km) had occupied more than a year. It had proved that no river entered the Great Australian Bight, and that most of the region would never be suitable for settlement.

The southern coast was now known, but the heart of the continent was as yet unexplored, and this task was taken up by Sturt in 1844 and 1845. Sturt left the Darling at Menindee, struck north-westwards, and passed Lake Frome. He carried his boat with him, for he felt that there must be a great inland sea here. At Depot Glen, near Mount Poole (north-east of Lake Frome), he waited *six months* for a rainstorm to provide him with water in advance; then he continued to the north-west. He passed endless ridges of sand, then a plain thickly covered with fragments of quartz; he found a lowland covered with the sharp-pointed spinifex grass, and a creek which petered out in the desert; and he saw wave after wave of red sandy ridges without a blade of grass. This is Sturt's Desert—one of the driest regions of the continent.

THE TRANSCONTINENTAL JOURNEYS

During these same years the German naturalist Leichhardt was busy exploring in eastern Queensland—a very different country, of dense forests and innumerable streams. His object was to discover a route which might link Brisbane with Arnhem Land. He passed successively through the valleys of the Fitzroy (Fig. 68), Burdekin, Lynd and Mitchell rivers, then skirted the southern shore of the Gulf of Carpentaria (where his name is commemorated in the Leichhardt river). Finally, he reached Port Essington, north-east of Darwin; he had travelled 3000 miles (4828 km) in four months and had discovered much valuable farmland. This was only the first of a series of transcontinental journeys which made it possible to map the centre and western half of the continent.

In 1858 and 1859 J. M. Stuart explored the district of Lakes Eyre, Gairdner and Torrens; he then set out on a traverse of the entire continent from south to north.[3] He departed from Adelaide in 1860 and passed through the hitherto unknown country to the west of Lake Eyre. He was farther inland than previous explorers, yet he found the land better watered: fortunately he had struck the line of springs where artesian water reaches the surface. In the region of the Macdonnell Ranges he found deep permanent pools; he passed a mountain near the centre of the continent, and this has been named, after him, Mount Stuart. He was forced back twice—first by hostile natives, then by impenetrable scrub; but he was not to be beaten. At the third attempt, in 1862, he came across a creek (Daly Waters), then reached the Adelaide river and so came to the sea.

Stuart's journeys were of great practical value to his countrymen. He had discovered a permanent route from north to south. Within ten years the overland telegraph line had been laid along it and maintenance stations established at several points; later for part of its line it was followed by a railway, and today the Stuart Highway follows its entire length. The corridor established by John McDouall Stuart still forms the backbone or economic lifeline of Northern Territory.

The permanent settlements along the telegraph line now provided explorers with useful bases from which to attack the last remaining blank on the map. Apart from a narrow belt fringing the south and west coasts, the whole of the land west of Stuart's route was quite unknown. Within a few years (1872–75) no fewer than five traverses were made in different latitudes—by Ernest Giles (who made two journeys), Gosse, Colonel Warburton and J. Forrest. Some of these explorers travelled with the aid of camels.

Warburton left Alice Springs in 1873 and journeyed for eight months through almost complete desert, reaching the coast at Roebourne (long. 117° E.): all but three of his seventeen camels died on the way. Giles, in 1875, made a traverse farther south, and on one occasion had to journey 325 miles (523 km) before finding a spring. All reported a land of sand hills, scrub and spinifex, in which water was almost completely absent—a land with no possibilities for settlement. There remained many details to be filled in, but by 1875 the main features of Australia were known.

NOTES

1. It is reproduced by R. A. Skelton, "The Dutch Quest of the Southland in the 17th Century," *Geog. Mag.*, May 1955, p. 29.

2. Quoted in J. N. L. Baker, *A History of Geographical Discovery and Exploration*, London, 1937.

3. Stuart's journeys are described more fully in Chapter XI.

STUDY QUESTIONS

1. Describe shortly the part played by Dutch mariners in the charting of the Australian coasts. Which place names have survived from this period?

2. On a map of the world plot the course taken by Captain Cook in his first voyage.

3. Compare the contributions of Sturt and Stuart respectively in the exploration of the Australian interior.

4. Attempt a summary description of the physical and human geography of Australia as it was known in 1850.

5. Contrast the early political development of Western Australia with that of New South Wales.

Chapter II

THE PHYSICAL BACKGROUND

STRUCTURE AND RELIEF

BROADLY speaking, Australia contains three structural divisions: the Eastern Highlands, the Western Plateau and, between them, the Central Lowlands.

But behind this apparent simplicity there lie traps for the unwary student whose knowledge of physical geography is based upon that of the British Isles or North America. A serious difficulty is the lack of any obvious connection between the geological age of a rock and its physical character. In the British Isles, for instance, when we speak of the Carboniferous Limestone, the Millstone Grit, the Oxford Clay or the Permian rocks, we think not only of a geological age but also of a rock with a distinct character which we recognise in the personality of the region.

In Australia, however, the sedimentary rocks are almost all of marine or fresh-water origin and are distinguished by their fossils rather than by their physical character; the Australian Carboniferous rocks do not contain coal—which is to be found in strata of widely differing age, from Permian to Tertiary; the Cretaceous rocks do not contain chalk; and the Tertiary strata (in contrast to those of the London Basin) are not usually of clay. To complicate matters further, great lava outpourings have taken place in many different periods, and there is clear evidence of several distinct ice ages.

THE EASTERN HIGHLANDS

The name "Great Dividing Range" is applied to the hilly country which everywhere rises from the eastern coast of the continent. A more accurate term, however, is "Eastern Highlands," for they are not a true range of folded mountains such as the Rockies, Andes or Alps. Mount Kosciusko, their highest point, is less than half as high as Mont Blanc (Kosciusko: 7328 feet (2241 m), Mont Blanc: 15,781 feet (4810 m)); and instead of the soaring peaks of the Alpine ranges, they present a series of plateau blocks.

Their nearest relatives, in fact, are the now isolated plateau blocks of Europe: the Meseta of Spain, the Central Plateau of France, the Rhine blocks and the Bohemian Plateau. Like these, the Eastern Highlands are composed of rocks of many different periods, from Precambrian to Carboniferous, and are flanked by younger deposits. At the close of the Carboniferous period great thicknesses of accumulated sediments were

raised up into folds, the pressure coming from the east. A long period of
quiet followed, during which the new folds were attacked by rivers and
gradually levelled off to form a peneplain; finally, in Tertiary times, the
denuded stumps were raised, almost as a single mass, and great outpourings of lava took place, burying in many parts the older landscape.
Otherwise, the Alpine earth storm passed Australia by, though it
modified profoundly the landscape of New Zealand.

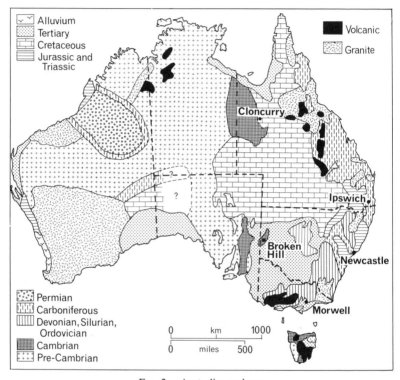

Fig. 2.—Australia: geology.

Today the Eastern Highlands form a plateau whose main surface is
largely untouched by the present drainage system. Only on its edges are
the rivers actively eroding their valleys: here there are deep gorges (such
as those near Katoomba, west of Sydney) and waterfalls and rapids
(such as the Barron Falls, west of Cairns).

Granite masses and old lava flows occupy much of the surface (Fig.
2). The granite bosses represent the cores of former upfolds, and extend
the whole length of the highland zone, never very far from the coast.
They form the Coast Range in the Cape York Peninsula; the Gregory
Range, west of Townsville; the Bunya Mountains and the New England

TABLE 1
Geological time-scale

Era	System/Period	Age (approximately in millions of years)	Life forms (based on fossil evidence)	Resources — Metal	Coal	Water	Geological events
QUATERNARY	Holocene	1	Man (homo sapiens emerges about 40,000 years ago)			Some	Sub-aerial erosion during the Quaternary era resulted in a significant lowering of the land surface.
	Pleistocene						
TERTIARY OR CAINOZOIC	Pliocene	15	Emergence of Man		Rich	Some	Near the close of the Tertiary era the Eastern Highlands and the Western Plateau suffered slight uplift. In Miocene times extensive lava flows occurred along the eastern coastal areas. By the beginning of the Tertiary era most of the land surface had been reduced almost to a peneplain.
	Miocene	35	Mammals dominant creatures			Some	
	Oligocene	50	Flowering plants			Some	
	Eocene	70	Emergence of earliest primates			Some	
SECONDARY OR MESOZOIC	Cretaceous	100	Modern type plants appear		Some	Rich	Inland seas covered the geosynclinal trough between the Eastern Highlands and the Western Plateau. Vast series of sands were laid down. During Mesozoic times proto-Australia probably severed its land connections with both south-eastern Asia and N.Z.
	Jurassic	130	First primitive birds		Rich	Rich	
	Triassic	170	Reptiles very abundant		Rich		
PRIMARY OR PALAEOZOIC	Permian	200	Amphibians and primitive types of plants	Some	Rich		During Permian times coal deposits were laid down. The mountains of eastern Australia were raised at the close of the Carboniferous period. In Silurian times all Australia, except Victoria, was dry land. In Cambrian times a great sea separated the western shield from the land to the east.
	Carboniferous	250	}	Some			
	Devonian	350	Primitive fishes	Rich			
	Silurian	450	Spineless creatures	Some			
	Ordovician	500	First definite fossils attested				
	Cambrian	600					
PRECAMBRIAN	Numerous series of rocks, subsequently greatly altered, laid down over a long period	2500–3000	Virtually no fossil evidence	Rich mineral concentrations			The western shield, which now forms the Western Plateau, came into being.

Range, astride the Queensland–New South Wales border; and the Australian Alps—the highest land in the continent. Intervening portions of the highlands are formed of the older sedimentary rocks: thus the Blue Mountains, which rise to the west of Sydney, are of Triassic Hawkesbury Sandstone, and the plateaus generally between latitudes 21° and 32° S. are of varied strata, ranging in age from the Permian to the Devonian periods.

The granite masses do not now form the water-parting, though, as we shall see later, the river systems suggest that they may formerly have done so. The present-day watershed mainly follows a series of lava flows, usually to the west of the line of granites. It is a complicated water-parting: close to the shore at Cairns, well inland at the Tropic, doubling back around the Hunter river. Australia suffers a major handicap in that so little of her surface faces the prevailing easterly winds, and is watered by them, while so much of her surface is in the lee of the Eastern Highlands, and suffers from drought.

While the highlands themselves are composed of granite, volcanic rocks and older sedimentaries, they are bordered by newer strata ranging in age from Permian to Tertiary. These newer rocks contain the most valuable coalfields of the continent.

Chief among them is the Permo-Carboniferous coal basin of New South Wales, which extends for 200 miles (322 km) along the coast (roughly from Newcastle to Jervis Bay) and widens to 100 miles (161 km) inland. The main coalfield of Queensland—that of the Dawson and Mackenzie districts in the south-east of the State—is in rocks of the same period, as is that of Tasmania. But Triassic coals are worked at Ipswich in Queensland, in Victoria (about 60 miles (96·5 km) south-east of Melbourne) and near to the eastern coast of Tasmania. There are Cretaceous coals along the Queensland coasts north of Rockhampton, and Tertiary lignites in Victoria: here, in the Latrobe valley of Gippsland (90 miles (145 km) E.S.E. of Melbourne), a remarkable deposit of brown coal 780 feet (237 m) thick is known to exist.

The eastward-flowing rivers are the most reliable in the continent. By English standards these are very large. We have already noticed that near the Tropic the water-parting retreats from the coast: here are the basins of the Burdekin and the Mackenzie (Fig. 3). Each covers an area of about 55,000 square miles (142,450 km^2)—larger than the whole of England, whose area is 50,874 square miles (131,763 km^2). The rivers of New South Wales are not quite of this order; but the Hawkesbury, 330 miles (531 km) long, is almost the length of the Trent and Severn combined, and is navigable for 70 miles (113 km); and the drainage basin of the Hunter is twice as large as that of the Thames.

Professor Griffith Taylor has drawn attention to some peculiarities in the courses of many of these rivers.[1] In some cases the headstreams begin by flowing away from the coast, then make elbow bends and flow towards the coast; this is well seen in the upper Dawson. In other cases the tributaries join the main stream at sharp angles, so that the main stream looks as if it ought to flow uphill; this may be seen in the headstreams of the Burnett river, which reaches the sea north of Maryborough. To explain these abnormal features Professor Taylor advances the interesting suggestion that during Pliocene times the

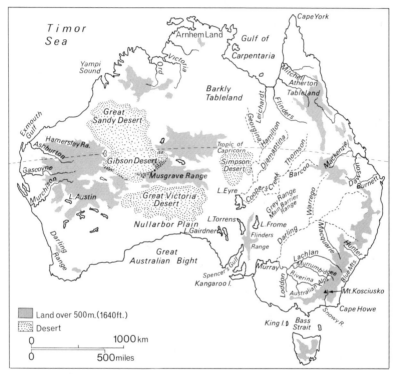

FIG. 3—Australia: physical. All the lakes indicated are salty; many of them are seasonally dry, and so, too, are many of the "rivers" (especially those shown dotted).
The names of some of the smaller features will be found on the regional maps.

earth's surface was crumpled to form a wave, whose crest moved westwards, so shifting the water-parting farther inland. As a result, the streams flowing west lost their heads, which were added to those flowing east; and in the process some of the headstreams actually reversed their flow. It is an example of river capture on the grand scale.

THE CENTRAL LOWLANDS

The name "Central Lowlands" describes this division only approxi-
mately, for much of the region lies well to the east of the centre of the continent, and it includes well-defined upland areas. Two ridges of hilly

country extend to join the Eastern Highlands with the Western Plateau: these are the Barkly Downs in the north, which rise to more than 2000 feet (610 m), and in the south the Grey Range and the Flinders Range, the latter reaching 3000 feet (914 m). As a result, the Central Lowlands may be subdivided into three portions: a coastal lowland, draining to the Gulf of Carpentaria; the Murray–Darling lowland, draining westwards; and, between them, a large area whose water-courses are seasonally dry and drain towards the interior.

These three sub-regions correspond with distinct structural features: while the northerly and southerly portions represent part of the sea-bed in relatively late (Tertiary) times, the central region is the visible surface of a basin filled with Cretaceous sediments.

We may trace the story of the Central Lowlands back to Permian times, when a long and narrow downfold existed where now are the eastern slopes of the Great Dividing Range. This trough became filled with sands and muds, settling at the bottom of the Permian sea; at times the waters receded sufficiently to allow the growth of swamp forests. These varied deposits now form the sandstones, shales and coal seams of the eastern flanks of the Great Divide.

By Cretaceous times the crustal sagging had moved farther west, into what are now the Central Lowlands, and the eastern and western portions of the continent were separated by a sea. During tens of millions of years thousands of feet of sediments collected on the Cretaceous sea-bed: they now take the form of shales, clays, marls, limy sandstones and limestones, but, in contrast to the United Kingdom, not chalk. At one stage an ice age was in being, and glacial erratics occur up to 6 feet (2 m) in diameter.

The Cretaceous basin is still the lowest part of the continent (the surface of Lake Eyre is 35 feet (11 m) *below* sea-level); its landscape is monotonous and undulating, and broken only where the uppermost beds of sandstones have resisted erosion. The rocks are of uniform com-position over wide areas and are almost horizontally bedded. Since they include impermeable shales and clays, they are of great importance in forming the capping to what has proved to be the world's largest store of artesian water. The origin of this sub-surface water is not known precisely; but it is probably derived from the rainfall of the eastern areas: the water apparently enters the Cretaceous rocks at the out-crop of a porous horizon known as the Blythesdale braystone; it gradually percolates westwards and emerges in springs to the west of Lake Eyre, to the south of Cloncurry and elsewhere. Some in-vestigators, however, following the late Professor J. W. Gregory, main-tain that the water, at least in part, is derived from the accumulation of small quantities which are known to be present in such rocks as lava, quartz and granite.

Most of the surface of this Cretaceous basin slopes gently down towards Lake Eyre, which theoretically is the focus of the drainage over half a million square miles—theoretically, since the "lake" is usually nothing but a dry, gleaming white saltpan.

The longest water-courses are from the north-east, and in one place the Great Divide is 700 miles (1126·5 km) from the lake. From this direction the Thomson and the Barcoo unite to form Cooper's Creek, which, according to the small-scale maps, feeds Lake Eyre. It is worth noticing, however, that the 1920 edition of *The Times Atlas* shows Cooper's Creek to have disappeared entirely between the two small lakes Killamperpunna and Killalpaninna, 60 miles (97 km) east of Lake Eyre. This eloquently suggests that normally very little water reaches Lake Eyre from Cooper's Creek.

From the Mount Isa district, in the hills of northern Queensland, come the parallel streams, Georgina, Burke, Hamilton and Diamantina. These water-courses enter a great swamp ("Goyder's Lagoon"), then emerge as the Warburton river and lead to the northern end of the lake. Others, draining the Macdonnell, Musgrave and Stuart Ranges in the west, "flow" eastwards to the lake; and finally, the channel of the Frome, draining the Flinders Range to the south, enters the lake in a delta.

C. T. Madigan in 1929 found Lake Eyre quite dry and concluded that it could never fill to any appreciable extent. Examining the crust of salt, he found it to be 17 inches (432 mm) thick; he bored a hole 17 feet (5 m) deep, and this soon filled with brine almost to the surface. Madigan made his journey after some years of drought.

In September 1950 Lake Eyre was full; but such a condition seems to be quite exceptional, for study of the rainfall records suggests that the last time it happened was in 1890–91. The summer rains of 1949–50 were unusually heavy. Water swept down the hitherto dry channels of the north-west, submerging the wide flood plains north of Goyder's Lagoon, filling small lakes, breaching barriers of drifted sand, and finally entering Lake Eyre. Water filled the shallow basin to an average depth of about 7 feet (2 m) and a maximum depth in the south-east of 12 to 13 feet (3·65 m to 3·96 m). Yet by 1953 the whole lake was once more completely dry.

To the south of the Cretaceous basin is a lowland composed of Tertiary and alluvial material and occupied by the lower portions of the Murray–Darling system. Again the deposits are horizontally bedded, representing marine and river sediments, often mantled by loess. The western border of this region is formed by the Flinders Range, composed of highly folded Cambrian strata. These were raised *en bloc* in late Tertiary times (when the Eastern Highlands too were in process of formation), so sealing off Lake Frome from the sea. To the north are the Barrier Range of the Broken Hill district (formed of Cambrian and Precambrian material) and the Grey Range (Cretaceous). All these rise to a plateau level of about 1400–1500 feet (427–457 m)—evidently an old surface which was once at sea-level. To the east are the varied strata which form the Eastern Highlands.

In point of *length* the Murray–Darling must be considered among the world's greatest rivers. In favourable conditions navigation may be possible as far upstream as Walgett, nearly 1700 miles (2736 km) from the sea—three times the length of navigation on the Rhine. During times of drought, however, tributaries of the Darling cease to flow and turn into isolated muddy pools, while in times of exceptional rainfall wide areas are flooded and the streams change their courses. Below Bourke the Darling gives water to the land instead of receiving it: it flows 400 miles (644 km) without a single tributary, losing both through percolation and evaporation, gaining little from rainfall and nothing from springs. In dry years the Darling contributes little or nothing to the Murray.

The Murray suffers from the disadvantages of great variation in volume and depth, and in addition has a shallow mouth in Lake Alexandrina. With the coming of the railway, commercial navigation virtually ceased, and today only the pleasure steamer is occasionally to be seen.

North of the Great Artesian Basin a new drainage system begins, in which numerous permanent rivers pursue their parallel courses to the Gulf of Carpentaria. Their upper courses are usually developed on the older sedimentary rocks (Archaean, Cambrian or Silurian), while in their lower courses they flow across a narrow belt, thinly wooded and low lying, composed of Tertiary strata.

Forming part of the watershed to the south is the elevated Barkly Tableland, with the important mining district of Cloncurry: here the strata are almost vertical and their age is in some doubt (probably Cambrian or Precambrian). This is the easternmost extension of the great shield which forms the western half of the continent.

THE WESTERN PLATEAU

This large region is one of the stable blocks of the earth's surface, composed of old and hard rocks which may have been above the sea since Precambrian times. In this respect it may be compared with the Canadian and Baltic Shields, the Deccan of India, the Arabian and African blocks and the Plateau of Brazil. Indeed, the theory of continental drift supposes that in early Carboniferous times all these blocks were joined to form a vast single land mass. The Australian block adjoined Antarctica on the south and the Deccan on the west. Then, in late Carboniferous times this land mass began to break into fragments, which gradually drifted apart to their present positions. So (according to this theory) is explained the remarkable similarity in structure and minerals of all these regions. Australia, however, is held to have broken away first (at the beginning of the Mesozoic era), so that her fauna and flora have had sufficient time to develop their distinctive character in isolation from other continents.

The plateau presents a sharp edge to the narrow coastal lowlands—a fault scarp which is locally sufficiently prominent to be called a mountain range, such as the Darling Ranges, behind Perth. Younger formations wrap round the shield: to the west, north-west and north-east are bands of Tertiary strata; to the south is a wider, almost semicircular exposure of Tertiary rocks (the Eucla Basin); and to the east is the broad expanse of Cretaceous deposits which form the Great Artesian Basin.

The Tertiary rocks of the Eucla Basin present a distinct landscape, for their surface is composed of a porous limestone which readily absorbs any rain as soon as it falls. The coast is smooth and without harbours, and fringed with cliffs 200 feet (61 m) high. Except for occasional solution hollows, the land is level; below the surface the percolating water has dissolved away the limestone to form caves. This is the country which Eyre traversed in 1841, almost meeting with disaster. Artesian water is present, but it cannot rescue this land for settlement.

The main mass of this shield consists of gneisses and schists (two common types of metamorphic rock) and granites, with occasional sheets of ancient partly metamorphosed sediments, including clay-slate and quartzite; there are many intrusive dykes, and the rocks are highly contorted and faulted, with trend lines running generally north-west and south-east. In many parts they are rich in minerals.

This great area, more than a million square miles in extent, was worn down to a peneplain by the end of Tertiary times; then the whole was raised as a single mass to about 1200 feet (366 m) above sea-level. We now see, therefore, a monotonous, flat landscape, with broad and ill-defined valleys very much as they were at the close of Tertiary times. Only on the edges are the rejuvenated streams beginning to cut deep valleys into the shield; and even this process is restricted by lack of rainfall except in the north and the south-west.

The Macdonnell Ranges, in the centre of the continent, contain rocks of Precambrian to Silurian age. As usual, they have been sharply folded, then peneplained and finally uplifted. The strata are now almost vertical, and the more resistant bands of quartzite remain as steep ridges, which follow the fold axes—east to west. These ranges, whose highest point is Mt Heughlin (4800 feet; 1463 m), are separated by deep gorges—a feature of erosion in dry climates, where there are few tributaries to wear back the valley sides. The local creeks flow only occasionally, yet some of the gorges contain deep pools of fresh water—with fish in them.

In the central and eastern parts of the Precambrian shield the solid rocks lie hidden below wide stretches of sand dune: these comprise the Great Sandy Desert in the north, the Great Victoria Desert in the south, and between them, Gibson Desert. There may be valuable deposits of minerals beneath them, such as those which are being exploited in the dune-free western region; but if so, they have not yet been discovered.

The maps indicate many lakes in the south-western portion of the shield. These contain water (always highly salt) only after rainstorms; they are shallow, and the water soon disappears owing to seepage and evaporation. They are not arranged haphazardly, but are in lines, probably following old water-courses which existed during the damper climate of Pleistocene times. Very occasionally, after heavy rains, water from one lake will find its way into the next.

Behind Perth the shield terminates in a west-facing scarp, whose almost unbroken edge continues for 200 miles (322 km), and has been named the Darling Ranges. Not far from the scarp, about 25 miles (40 km) inland from Bunbury, a fragment of a larger sheet of Permian rocks (containing coal seams) has been let down by faults, and so has escaped erosion. This is the Collie river coalfield; it covers about 500 square miles (1295 km²), and its seams reach a total thickness of 140 feet (43 m).

It is only in the northern margins of the shield that important rivers can maintain themselves throughout the year; and even here their volume varies greatly, reflecting the predominantly summer rainfall. Raised beaches along parts of the shore suggest that the Tertiary uplift is still in progress, and river canyons point to a rejuvenation of the drainage system. Yet there are unmistakable signs of a recent sinking of the land, at least, in the Kimberley District: there the coast has been clearly drowned, resulting in long, sheltered inlets, with rocky islands off the shore.

MINERAL DEPOSITS

With a few exceptions (some of them important), the metallic minerals are usually associated with plutonic rocks: they have been concentrated from substances present in the original molten rock material, and have cooled from the molten state. Just as there is a definite order in which the minerals will separate out when a salt lake dries up, so those minerals which solidify at the highest temperatures tend to be found nearest the source of molten rock—the present granite boss. The ideal sequence, beginning with the minerals nearest to the granite, is as follows: tin and tungsten, gold, copper, zinc, lead, gold and silver, antimony, mercury.

Mineral deposits may also be formed, however, when solutions ascend from the molten rock material through cracks in the overlying rocks; these are veins, and there is then no regular arrangement of the different ores. Again, rivers may transport minerals from their parent rock and sort them by gravity from the lighter sand, gravel or clay.

All cases require the presence of a mass of granite or similar rock; it follows that we shall expect to find the metallic minerals in the Precambrian shield with its granitic intrusions, rather than in the

Cretaceous rocks of the Central Lowlands; and in the granitic cores of the Great Dividing Range rather than on its flanks.

The western portion of the shield is one of the most richly mineralised portions of the earth's surface. Six parallel bands may be recognised, running roughly north and south. Nearest to the coast is a zone of slates, quartzites and schists; next inland is one of gneisses and schists containing graphite, asbestos and tin; the third belt is a wide band of barren granitic rocks. Belts numbers 4 and 6 are rich in gold, but are separated by barren granites and gneisses (belt 5). Zone 6 begins on the south coast at Esperance, passes through Norseman and Kalgoorlie to Leonora and reaches the north coast at Pilbarra; it is easily seen on the map, since railways emphasise its importance. Zone 4 extends from the Philips river (150 miles (241 km) north-east of Albany), through Southern Cross and Lake Austin, to reach the upper Gascoyne and Ashburton rivers.

Away in north-west Queensland the Cloncurry district, famous for its copper, represents, as we have seen, the most easterly portion of the shield, in a region free from sand dunes, and therefore accessible to the miner.

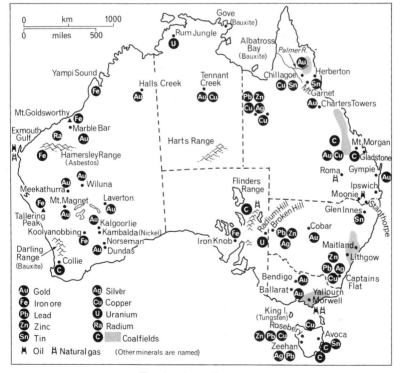

Fig. 4.—Australia: minerals.

Many mineral-bearing districts are to be found in the Eastern Highlands. From north to south they include the copper and tin deposits at Chillagoe (west of Cairns); gold at Charters Towers, Mount Morgan and Gympie (all the above are in Queensland); tin at Stanthorpe and Tingha, astride the New South Wales border; gold at several places west of the Great Divide in New South Wales, and at Ballarat and Bendigo in Victoria. In the north-west of Tasmania are ores of tin, copper, lead and silver (in the correct theoretical order, it is claimed); they may be associated with a prominent fault which crosses the region.

Two other metal-bearing regions in the south-eastern part of the continent remain to be mentioned: they are the Cobar district of central New South Wales and the Flinders Range in South Australia. Each represents the denuded crest of an upfold, where the later rocks have been stretched, weakened and removed by erosion, exposing the older rocks with their minerals (Fig. 4).

Such is the general distribution of metallic minerals in Australia. The exploitation of these deposits together with the coalfields we reserve for later study.

NOTE

1. G. Taylor, *Australia*, London, 1940, p. 50.

STUDY QUESTIONS

1. To what extent is the surface geology of the Eastern Highlands reflected in human activities?

2. Estimate the importance of artesian water in the economic life of Australia.

3. The drainage of Australia can hardly be matched in any other continent. What are its special characteristics?

4. Construct a map to indicate the relationship between the crystalline rocks of Australia and the chief mineral deposits.

5. It has been said that from the point of view of structure Australia is the enantiomorph (*i.e.* mirror-image) of South America. To what extent is this a valid assertion?

Chapter III

CLIMATE AND THE PROBLEM OF WATER SUPPLY

GENERAL FEATURES

AUSTRALIA is the dry continent.

Several elements in its build conspire to produce this condition. Like Africa alone, it has its greatest extent from east to west along the tropic. But the tropics are zones of descending air; and descending air is becoming warmer, gaining the capacity to hold water and exerting a drying influence on everything it touches—land, water or plants. Just as the Sahara is the largest desert in the northern hemisphere, so the Great Australian Desert is the largest in the southern hemisphere.

The position of Australia, astride the Tropic of Capricorn, ensures that she comes mainly under the influence of the south-east trade winds. These are moving from colder to warmer latitudes, so that, like the descending air of the tropic itself, they are by their nature drying winds. Only where they are forced to rise over hills will they become cooled sufficiently to release some of their precious moisture. But Australia, as we have seen, is not a land of lofty peaks—"the Alpine earth storm passed it by." Moreover, it is her great misfortune that the highest land lies so close to the eastern seaboard, for the well-watered land is therefore limited to the narrow eastern slopes of the Great Dividing Range.

Here the rainfall swells the many eastward-flowing streams whose water runs to waste in the Tasman Sea, while the thirsty land to the west suffers from drought. These are the thoughts behind the Snowy Mountains scheme, by which tunnels divert some of this life-giving water to the headstreams of the longer westward-flowing streams (*see* pp. 137–9).

Australia has no inland sea to temper her drought, no major gulfs or lakes to modify her climate. Europe has her Mediterranean, Asia her Caspian, North America her Hudson Bay and Great Lakes; but Australia is a compact land mass, the "lakes" of the interior are dry salt-pans or at best occasional swamps, and the Gulf of Carpentaria has little effect on climate.

The south-east trades, after having crossed the summits of the Eastern Highlands, begin to descend and revert to their normal function as agents of drought; and the more they descend, the drier is their effect. Hence the driest portion of the continent is not its centre (where there are in fact some hills) but the Lake Eyre region, which is below the level of the sea. Nevertheless, the trade winds bring drought to the whole of the centre and west of Australia, and most of it must be classed as desert.

There are two fringes, however—one in the north, the other in the south—where other winds play their part. Australia is almost as large as the United States—sufficiently big to interrupt the planetary wind system. Its great heat in summer draws the trade winds of the northern hemisphere across the equator and into the northern part of Australia, where the earth's rotation deflects them to the left; they thus appear as a north-west monsoon in summer; and conversely, a south-east monsoon blows in winter. The latter, however, merely serves to reinforce the normal south-east trades. As a result, the northern fringe of the continent has a heavy rainfall in summer (December, January, February and March) and virtually no rainfall in winter (June, July and August).

In contrast, the southern fringe of Australia comes under the influence, for part of the year at least, of the belt of westerly winds—damp at all seasons, cool in summer and mild in winter. No part of the

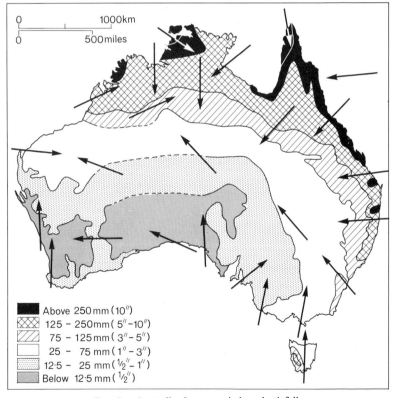

0 1000km
0 500 miles

■ Above 250 mm (10″)
⊠ 125 – 250 mm (5″–10″)
▨ 75 – 125 mm (3″–5″)
□ 25 – 75 mm (1″–3″)
▦ 12·5 – 25 mm (½″–1″)
▤ Below 12·5 mm (½″)

Fig. 5.—Australia: January winds and rainfall.

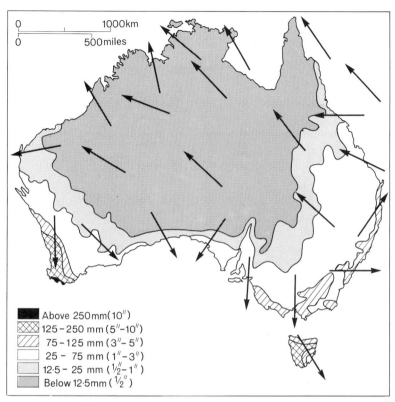

Fig. 6.—Australia: July winds and rainfall. The wind directions on this map and Fig. 5 have been deduced from a study of the 9 a.m. and 3 p.m. windroses at the appropriate centres. They indicate the most common winds, but at many stations winds from other directions are nearly as common.

mainland experiences them the whole year round, though Tasmania is sufficiently far south to do so, and in consequence her climate resembles that of the British Isles more closely than any other part of the continent. But in winter, when the westerlies, following the belt of greatest heat, shift to the north, they strike the southern tips of the mainland and bring winter rain to the two districts which face them—those around Perth and Adelaide (Figs 5 and 6).

This picture of the shifting wind belts is a little simplified, for, as we have seen, Australia is sufficiently large to develop its own pressure systems. A high-pressure system in the winter results in out-blowing winds, which in the southern hemisphere are deflected to the left, so that an anticlockwise circulation tends to develop; conversely, in summer there is a low-pressure system, with a clockwise circulation.

In detail, too, we must notice the existence of several kinds of local winds. Destructive revolving storms similar to those of the West Indies and the China Sea are a scourge of the tropical western coasts of Western Australia and of the eastern coasts of Queensland. They occur during the hottest season, when one or more may be expected each year. These tropical cyclones appear to be nothing more than particularly intense representatives of the normal depressions of these latitudes. Those of Western Australia (known as Willy Willies) originate in the Timor Sea and strike the coast generally between Condon and Fortescue: they are welcomed inland on account of the rain which they bring. Those of Queensland originate in the Fiji region and strike the shore near Cairns. In both regions the disturbances tend to move south-westwards until they strike the coast, when they are most dangerous. They then curve round to move in a south-easterly direction and at the same time become weaker. During the passage of a Queensland hurricane 6 inches (152 mm) of rain has been known to fall in twenty-four hours.

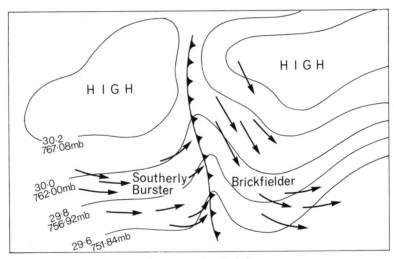

FIG. 7.—Two local winds.

Brickfielders and *Southerly Bursters* (or *Busters*) are strong local winds which are experienced, particularly in spring and summer, in the south-eastern portion of the continent. They are associated with the deep trough of low pressure which often separates a pair of anticyclones as they pass over the continent (Fig. 7). Strong northerly winds are experienced in the front of the trough, bringing with them the hot and dust-laden air of the desert to Adelaide or Melbourne: this is the Brickfielder of Victoria. When the barometer begins to rise again the wind suddenly changes into a south wind, perhaps with gale force; the temperature drops 20° and an icy rain falls in torrents. This is the Southerly Burster of New South Wales: here the Kosciusko Range seems to form a barrier to the free movement of pressure systems—a barrier which is overcome suddenly and with great violence.

More pleasant are the land-and-sea breezes which are characteristic of parts of the coast. At Perth in the afternoon (when the air over the land has been warmed and is rising) there are frequently invigorating W.S.W. breezes from the sea; conversely, in the early morning (about 3 a.m.) when the land is cold, an easterly wind blows from land to sea. The same sort of thing is true of Adelaide. These breezes add greatly to human comfort; but they remind us that the idea of a prevailing wind is at times largely theoretical.

TEMPERATURES

Australia is not only the dry continent: with a little qualification we may call it also the hot continent.

North of the Tropic of Capricorn almost everywhere has mean summer temperatures higher than 26° C or 80° F (Fig. 8). As we may expect, the greatest heat is found near the tropic and far from onshore winds. The Pilbarra district, near the north-west coast, is one of the hottest parts of the continent: here the mean temperatures for December, January and February are over 32° C (90° F); and at Marble Bar (100 miles (160 km) farther east) a maximum of over 49° C (121° F) has been recorded, while the mean *minimum* for January is 26° C (79° F). These temperatures are not far short of those of the Sahara—the hottest place on earth. Similar conditions are found in the heart of the Australian deserts, as we learn from Sturt's accounts of his journeys. On one occasion he hung a thermometer on a tree, shaded from both sun and wind; it was graduated up to 53° C (127° F), yet the mercury rose until it burst the tube. The desert sand was so hot that a match which fell on to it burst into flame instantly.

This great heat is accompanied by an extremely dry atmosphere.

"The lead dropped out of our pencils, our signal rockets were entirely spoiled; our hair, as well as the wool on the sheep, ceased to grow, and our nails became as brittle as glass."

Calculations based on the drying of Lake Eyre in 1951 gave an evaporation rate of 94 inches (2387 mm) for the calendar year in that district.

But with clear skies and a dry atmosphere the heat of the day quickly escapes, and at night temperatures are exceptionally low; thus the average monthly temperature is little guide to the actual temperature to be expected. At Alice Springs (almost on the tropic) there are 7° of frost on most winter nights.

On the north coasts the summer rains temper the heat, so that while Nullagine (south of Marble Bar) has a mean annual range of about 20° C (35·3° F), Darwin has one of only 5° C (9° F), and its highest temperatures are recorded in October (mean monthly temperature: 30° C; 86° F), just before the rains set in.

Almost everywhere, both in summer and in winter, the influence of latitude on the distribution of temperature is clear, and the isotherms trend east and west. Only near the coasts does the ocean exercise its moderating effect. The coolest places in summer are Tasmania and the Australian Alps, with mean monthly temperatures of 10–15° C (50–

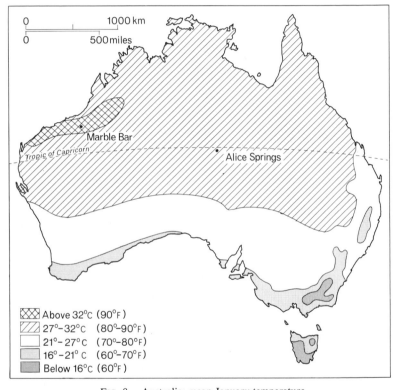

FIG. 8.—Australia: mean January temperature.

60° F): here altitude combines with latitude to reduce the temperatures.

In winter Australia is the complete contrast to Canada, for while the whole of Canada has average winter temperatures of below freezing point, in Australia such conditions are limited to one or two plateau tops in the south-east (Fig. 8). At Sydney snow is seen only about once in a lifetime; indeed, apart from the highlands of the south-east snow is hardly ever seen in Australia. Permanent snow is limited to a small portion of the Kosciusko massif.

Even south of the Tropic of Capricorn the average winter (July) temperature is rarely less than 9° C (48° F)—that is, at least 9° F

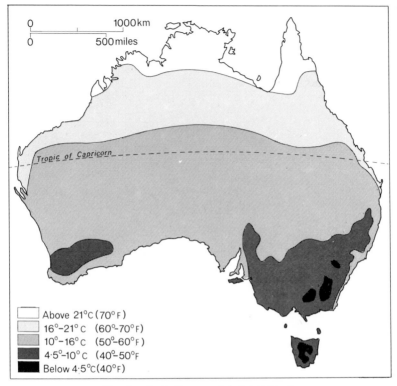

Above 21°C (70°F)
16°–21°C (60°–70°F)
10°–16°C (50°–60°F)
4·5°–10°C (40°–50°F
Below 4·5°C (40°F)

FIG. 9.—Australia: mean July temperature.

warmer than that of London. North of the tropic, places such as Townsville, Cloncurry and Port Hedland have *winter* temperatures which approximate to the *summer* temperatures in London (18° C; 64° F). Places farther north are uncomfortably warm, even in winter (Fig. 9).

RAINFALL

Where water is scarce it becomes a controlling element in settlement; the distribution of rainfall is therefore the clue to much of the geography of Australia.

DISTRIBUTION

The map of annual rainfall presents a very regular and simple picture: the isohyets form concentric semicircles centred on Lake Eyre, and the amount of rainfall diminishes inland. But this apparent simplicity hides the fact that over much of the continent the rainfall is seasonal. In the north it is monsoonal in type, arriving mainly in summer; to the south it is mainly cyclonic, and is brought by the westerly drift of air (the anti-trades). Between the two, the eastern coast receives some rain at all seasons, and includes the wettest part of the continent (Fig. 10).

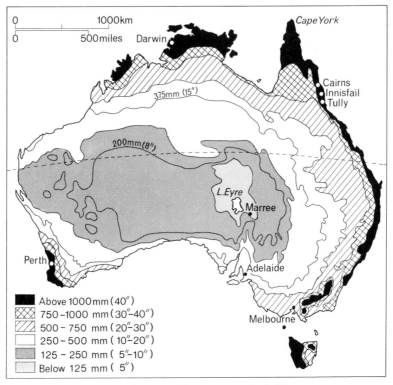

FIG. 10.—Australia: mean annual rainfall.

A vast area—more than a million square miles—in the centre and west of Australia receives less than 10 inches (254 mm) of rainfall a year: this accounts for more than one-third of the continent. Not only is the rainfall low in the interior—it is unreliable, and there are wide departures from the offical average. Thus, at Windorah (below the junction of the Thomson and Barcoo rivers) the mean annual rainfall (m.a.r.) is 10·05 inches (255 mm); yet 19·6 inches (498 mm) fell during the single month of March 1950! At Marree (south of Lake Eyre) the m.a.r. is 5·6 inches (142 mm), yet 16 inches (406 mm) fell during 1950. This district around Lake Eyre, with a m.a.r. of about 5 inches (125 mm), seems to be the driest part of the continent.

In the monsoon region of the north the seasons are sharply divided from each other. The dry (winter) season lasts from May until

TABLE 2
Temperature and rainfall figures for selected stations

Station	Latitude South	Location	Height (Metres)	Height (Feet)	Temp °C Mean monthly Jan	Temp °C Mean monthly July	Temp °C Mean annual Min	Temp °C Mean annual Max	Temp °F Mean monthly Jan	Temp °F Mean monthly July	Temp °F Mean annual Min	Temp °F Mean annual Max	Precip Millimetres Spring	Precip Millimetres Summer	Precip Millimetres Autumn	Precip Millimetres Winter	Precip Millimetres Annual total	Precip Inches Spring	Precip Inches Summer	Precip Inches Autumn	Precip Inches Winter	Precip Inches Annual total
Darwin	12	Coastal	31	100	29	25	23	33	84	77	74	91	183	975	371	8	1540	7.2	38.4	14.6	0.3	60.5
Wyndham	15	Coastal	6	20	31	25	25	34	88	76	76	93	66	467	147	8	680	2.6	18.3	5.8	0.3	27.0
Cairns	17	Coastal	5	15	28	21	20	30	82	70	68	85	193	1118	860	155	2247	7.6	40.7	34.0	6.1	88.4
Alice Springs	24	Inland	580	1900	28	12	13	29	83	53	55	84	53	122	66	33	274	2.1	4.8	2.6	1.3	10.8
Kalgoorlie	31	Inland	380	1250	26	11	12	26	79	52	54	78	43	46	81	74	244	1.7	1.8	3.2	2.9	9.6
Brisbane	27	Coastal	43	140	25	16	16	26	77	60	60	78	208	442	312	180	1440	8.2	17.6	12.3	7.1	45.2
Sydney	34	Coastal	43	140	22	12	12	21	71	53	53	70	216	272	312	320	1200	8.5	10.7	15.7	12.6	47.2
Broken Hill	32	Inland	310	1000	26	10	12	25	78	50	53	76	56	61	56	68	242	2.2	2.4	2.2	2.7	9.5
Albury	36	Inland	162	530	24	8	8	23	75	47	47	74	178	130	165	231	700	7.0	5.1	6.5	9.1	27.7
Melbourne	38	Coastal	36	120	20	10	10	20	67	49	50	67	183	150	168	147	650	7.2	5.9	6.6	5.8	25.5
Adelaide	35	Coastal	43	140	23	11	12	23	74	52	55	73	124	64	168	211	540	4.9	2.5	5.5	8.3	21.2
Perth	32	Coastal	62	200	23	13	13	23	74	55	55	74	165	36	190	492	880	6.5	1.4	7.5	19.5	34.9
Hobart	43	Coastal	56	180	17	8	8	17	62	46	47	62	173	137	140	158	600	6.8	5.4	5.5	6.2	23.7

September: the south-easterly winds are blowing, the skies are clear and the average temperatures are about 25° C (in the upper 70s F)—for example, at Cape York and Darwin. Then, from September onwards, the mean temperatures rise to about 30° C (into the 80s F) and the *maxima* over 32° C (into the 90s F). The south-east trades become weaker, thunder is in the air and by November the north-west monsoon has set in. From December to March it rains almost every day; the air is moist and the unpleasant humid heat of the equator is experienced. Then in April the rains cease and the dry south-easterly winds return. For a monsoon region, the total rainfall at Darwin, 60·5 inches (1540 mm) is not excessive. At Cape York it amounts to 82 inches (2080 mm).

The true monsoon region extends along the east coast about as far south as Cairns; beyond is a region of transition, with a summer maximum of rainfall, but with an appreciable fall in the winter too. Still farther south the trade winds are experienced the whole year through, and the rainfall is more or less uniformly distributed throughout the year.

The heaviest rainfall of the continent occurs on the southern fringe of the monsoon region, where the summits of the Atherton Tableland are very close to the sea. This is the highest land in Queensland—more than 5000 feet (1524 m) above sea-level—and here the mean annual rainfall is over 140 inches (3556 mm) per annum. The actual wettest place in Australia appears to be Tully, in this coastal district of Queensland, which receives an average of 179 inches (4546 mm) per annum.

But on the whole of the east coast sudden downpours occur, and the actual rainfall of any given year may be very different from the theoretical average. Harvey Creek has experienced as much as 255 inches (6477 mm) in a year, and many places have recorded 20 inches (540 mm) in a single day. Such enormous totals are fortunately extremely rare; but when they do occur disastrous floods follow in their wake. Thus, at Richmond (30 miles (48 km) north-west of Sydney) the Hawkesbury river has been known to rise 50 and 60 feet (15 to 18 metres) above its normal level; in 1806 the Hawkesbury floods rose to the phenomenal height of 93 feet (28 metres)!

Inland the rainfall diminishes rapidly. Suppose we follow the boundary between Queensland and New South Wales westwards into the interior. A small area on the coast receives more than 70 inches (1778 mm) of rainfall per annum; but in the space of only 35 miles (56 km) it has dropped to 40 inches (1016 mm). Then, at fairly equal intervals of about 75 miles (120 km) the total sinks successively to 30, 25, 20 and 15 inches (762, 635, 508 and 380 mm). We are not quite half-way to the border of South Australia; but beyond lies semi-desert.

The trade winds blow over Victoria only in summer, when they have swung to the south; in winter their place is taken by the westerly winds, then at their most northerly extent. The hills here are the highest in the continent and receive more than 50 inches (1270 mm) per annum. At Melbourne the winter rainfall typical of Mediterranean regions is beginning to appear, and at Adelaide more than two-thirds of the total rainfall occurs in the six winter months. A similar climate is found around Perth, in the south-western tip of the continent. The Perth and Adelaide districts, with their mild winters, cool sea breezes in summer and abundant sunshine throughout the year, have perhaps the finest climate in Australia.

It is clear that the mean annual rainfall totals do not in themselves give an adequate picture of the actual conditions, and recently an attempt has been made to devise a more appropriate index: this is the concept of *rainfall intensity*.[1] In its simplest form it is the average amount of rainfall for each rainy day, and is calculated by dividing the mean annual rainfall by the number of rain days (a rain day is defined conventionally as one on which a rainfall of at least $0 \cdot 01$ inch ($0 \cdot 254$ mm) is recorded). For this purpose the rainfall is conveniently expressed in "points," where 100 points equals one inch ($2 \cdot 54$ mm) of rainfall.

Rainfall intensity is an element of considerable geographical significance; it is mainly responsible for the volume of runoff, and so needs to be considered carefully in the design of bridges, dams, drains and irrigation channels. Maps of rainfall intensity indicate a broad correlation with total rainfall, but there are specific regions subject to tropical storms where there are unusually high intensities.

The greatest intensities are found in eastern Queensland, with its high rainfall and its liability to tropical cyclones. The record appears to be held by Reid river, near Townsville, with $98 \cdot 9$ points per rain day (p.p.r.d.); Innisfail is not far short, with $93 \cdot 4$ p.p.r.d. Convectional thunder-storms in the lands south and west of the Gulf of Carpentaria probably give high intensities, but the information is not sufficiently complete to provide an accurate picture. In the north-west of Western Australia, around Broome, the tropical storms known as Willy Willies result in high intensities in spite of the fact that the mean annual rainfall is only 10 to $12\frac{1}{2}$ inches (250 to 320 mm).

The concept of rainfall intensity has its value as a supplement to maps of "crude" rainfall, but in certain areas such as southern and western Tasmania and the Tablelands of New South Wales it has its shortcomings. These districts are subject to drizzle, which inflates the number of rain days and as a result the average level of intensity is reduced although the actual intensity on the really wet days may be very high.

THE EVIDENCE OF PAST CLIMATIC CHANGE

Evidence provided by fossils indicates that in late Tertiary (Pliocene) times central Australia was well watered and supported a luxuriant vegetation. Giant herbivorous marsupials lived on the margins of former lakes and swamps where there is now nothing but desert: there was a very large running bird, an enormous kangaroo and a wombat-like creature as big as a rhinoceros.

It seems clear that the existing Lake Eyre basin with its innumerable salt flats, together with Lakes Torrens and Frome were formerly occupied by an inland sea. There is widespread evidence in the world of a reduction in low-level air temperatures by several degrees during the last 70,000 years—which corresponded with the maximum advance of the ice-sheets of the northern hemisphere. This reduction in temperature affected not only north-west Europe and the Great Lakes but also the sub-tropical Mojave desert (southern California) and equatorial Colombia. It is reasonable to suppose that Australia too experienced a fall in temperature during this period.

Many of the streams of eastern Australia must be classed as "misfits": their wide and deep valleys can have been excavated only by far larger rivers at some time in the past. This evidence agrees with that provided by the shrunken lakes and salt-pans of the centre, together with fossil evidence, to suggest that large parts of Australia have suffered a reduction in rainfall. It has been estimated that when the ancestor of Lake Eyre was at its maximum size, the temperature was 8 or 10 degrees Centigrade (46 to 50° F) lower, and the rainfall was double its present annual total.[2]

THE PROBLEM OF WATER SUPPLY

The phenomena of climate lead logically and naturally to the problem of water supply.

Geography is the study of Man in relation to his environment, and over much of the continent of Australia the vital part of his environment is water supply. Whether he works in the goldfields of Western Australia, in the cattle lands of Northern Territory and north-west Queensland or in the vineyards of South Australia, the limiting factor to settlement and production is the available water.

Nature sets the stage. She has provided abundant rainfall (at times too abundant) only on the eastern fringe. Farther west the rivers are intermittent, the lakes are dry or salty, though in many parts there are useful supplies of water below the ground. But Man can adapt nature, and in Australia much of his effort is directed to the problem of how to improve his natural supply of water.

Essentially it is a problem for the civil engineer—how to move water? It must be lifted to the surface from the porous strata below the ground; or it must be moved in pipes or in channels to places where there is a greater need for it. But the scientist too has his place, and attacks the problem from two angles: he attempts to "make rain" and he tries to convert salt water into fresh. The details of water supply schemes will be studied in their regional context; here, at the risk of slight repetition, we draw attention to their general character.

Cumulus clouds (say the rain-makers) may be persuaded to drop their moisture by two alternative methods. One can generate on the ground a smoke consisting of particles of silver iodide: these, carried aloft by air currents, provide tiny nuclei around which the water droplets condense to form rain. Alternatively, the rain-maker ventures aloft in an aircraft, and having chosen a suitable cloud, he discharges into it particles of dry ice. These reduce the temperature of the water droplets so that they form crystals of ice which turn into rain.

A recent example, reported in June 1973, is of some interest. To combat a long drought and reduce the risk of forest fire the Victorian Government used two specially equipped aircraft from a base near Melbourne to seed clouds with a solution of silver iodide in acetone. The chemical was supplied by the Commonwealth Scientific and Industrial Research Organisation, which carries out substantial research into artificial rain-making. "Some useful falls of rain have been secured."[3]

The preparation of fresh water by distillation from sea-water clearly also has its limitations. The principle is simple: if brine is heated, its water is converted into steam, but the salt remains behind; if the steam is then cooled, the resulting water will be "fresh," if a trifle "flat." Distillation plant is suitable for use on submarines, and in coastal deserts where there are rich mineral deposits. It is used on the phosphate

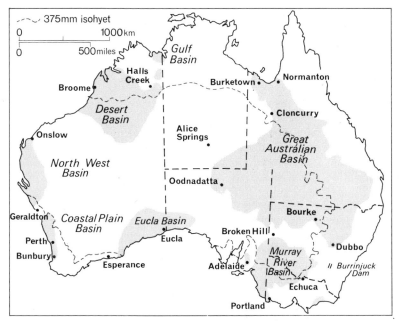

FIG. 11.—Australia: artesian basins. The 15-inch (375-mm) isohyet suggests the area in which surface water is deficient.

island of Nauru in the Pacific, where there are no streams (p. 416); but it is too slow and expensive to make any major contribution to solving the water problems of Australia.

We turn then to the contributions of the civil engineer. Australia is indeed fortunate in that below much of the area where the rainfall is marginal there are supplies of artesian or sub-artesian water. The artesian basins of Australia are indicated in Fig. 11, and Table 3, and some details of the Great Artesian Basin are given below (pp. 207–10). Here we may observe that artesian water has its limitations too: it is expensive to tap; it is generally unsuitable in quality and deficient in quantity for irrigation; and its output is declining.

TABLE 3
The principal artesian basins

Name	Geological age	Area (in square km)	Depth of water (in metres)	Quality of water
Great Basin	Cretaceous–Jurassic	1,430,000	Down to 2100	Saline
Desert Basin	Permian	338,000	60–900	Suitable for stock
Murray Basin	Miocene	278,000	30–270	Saline
Eucla Basin	Pliocene–Miocene	177,000	90–600	Saline
North-west Basin	Permian	104,000	120–1200	Saline but suitable for stock
Coastal Plain Basin	Jurassic	26,000	60–750	Potable

The total flow from the Great Artesian Basin in 1914 was estimated at 350 million gallons per day; by 1954 it had dropped to 230 million gallons; and it seems that if supplies are to be conserved the consumption must be further reduced to 110 million gallons a day. Nevertheless, with the help of artesian water many marginal areas have been opened up for grazing, and the flowing artesian bore or the spinning vanes of the wind pump are familiar sights in the cattle and sheep stations of the "outback" (Figs. 78 and 79).

For irrigation, however, water must be moved in larger quantities than either the vertical pump or the artesian bore can provide. This usually implies first the storing of water by means of a weir or dam, and then the construction of canals or pipelines to transport the water. Thus the Burrinjuck Dam (p. 168) stores the water of the upper Murray river for use in the irrigation ditches which are nearly 300 miles (482 km) downstream, while the dam at Mundaring, east of Perth, provides water for the 346-mile (557-km) pipeline to the Kalgoorlie goldfields (p. 264).

One notable conservation scheme has not involved the transport of water, but rather the prevention of water pollution. This is the 12-mile barrage at the mouth of the Murray river (p. 237) which was completed during the early years of the Second World War. Formerly the sea-water, driven by tide and wind, seeped upstream, fouling the springs, killing the vegetation, initiating erosion on the banks and ruining the pastures. After ten years the beneficial effects of the barrage are plain to see: cattle and sheep now drink the lake water, the farmers can look forward once more to the future and there is irrigation water sufficient for 10,000 acres (4046 ha) of cattle pastures and market gardens.

More enterprising still are the projects which aim at river diversion on the grand scale. Of these, the greatest is the Snowy Mountains scheme, where 80 miles (128 km) of tunnels are being constructed to divert the headwaters of the Snowy and Murrumbidgee rivers across the Great Dividing Range.

Water conservation will always be in the news in Australia. The Channel Country of south-western Queensland has had its share of projects. It consists of a flat tract of land where the Barcoo and Diamantina rivers have a slope of less than 1 foot each mile, and branch into a network of channels. About one year in four, heavy rain in the upper reaches of the rivers floods the Channel Country for several weeks to a depth of about 1 foot. Many thousands of cattle fatten themselves on the resulting growth of lush pasture.

A plan submitted to the Federal Government in the summer of 1960 urged that by diverting some of the rivers of north Queensland, con-trolled flooding of this area could be achieved. It proposed in addition a new 900-mile (1449-km) bitumen road from Bourke to Mount Isa (so linking Darwin by road to Sydney), with a water pipeline to run beside it. The effects (it was claimed) would be twofold: cattle losses due to drought would be reduced to negligible proportions over a wide region; and the beef production of western Queensland would be doubled.

Schemes such as these need to be examined very carefully, for in water conservation there is no simple or accurate way of estimating either the costs or the expected benefits.

NOTES

1. J. N. Jennings, "Two Maps of Rainfall Intensity in Australia," *Australian Geographer*, Vol. X, No. 4 (1967).

2. G. H. Dury, "Climatic Change as a Geographical Backdrop," *Australian Geographer*, Vol. X, No. 4 (1967).

3. *News from Victoria, Australia*, Victoria Promotion Committee, Bush House, London, June 1973.

STUDY QUESTIONS

1. "The predominantly dry climate of Australia is primarily a result of its orientation." In your imagination rotate the continent through 90° so that the

Great Australian Bight faces east: what would be the climate of this hypothetical continent?

2. Explain concisely: Brickfielder, Willy Willy, Southerly Burster.

3. Locate (a) the wettest place, (b) the driest place, (c) the hottest place in Australia, and examine the reasons for their pre-eminence.

4. Divide Australia into climatic regions and describe shortly the characteristics of each.

5. Examine the phenomena of land and sea breezes in Australia.

6. To what extent can the rainfall of Australia be explained by the migration of the wind belts?

7. Discuss the problem of water supply in Australia. Describe some recent projects designed to improve water supplies.

Chapter IV

VEGETATION AND ANIMALS

NATURAL VEGETATION

GENERAL FEATURES

To those who dwell in the northern hemisphere, where plants and animals can roam more or less freely over vast distances, it is climate which appears as the chief or even the sole element which determines the distribution of plants, and hence of animals.

In contrast, Australia is an island continent, and one which, moreover, has been separated from other land masses over a considerable geological time; here climate alone cannot explain completely the existence and distribution of fauna and flora. In each, indeed, Australia is unique and of exceptional interest to those whose experience is drawn from other lands.

Considering vegetation, Australia is the continent of eucalypts. With only one or two exceptions these are found in nature nowhere else on earth; yet in Australia they are spread over almost the entire continent: their 400 or 500 species range through exceedingly diverse types, from dwarfs to giants and from moisture-loving to drought-resistant species. In the deserts of the centre and west, wherever anything will grow at all, there you will find a eucalypt.

What are the distinguishing marks of this peculiar plant? The name springs from the Greek, meaning "well covered," and refers to the fact that the flower petals cling together to form a protective cap. In this way, insulated from the elements, the eucalypt can adapt itself to varied climatic conditions. While the tree grows well in moist atmospheres, it is particularly protected from drought. The bluish, waxy leaves are turned edge-on to the sun and interrupt less light and heat than the normal horizontally placed leaf. A fine film of oil covers the surface of the leaf, secreted from glands within, and it is from the leaf that the fragrant eucalyptus oil is distilled—perhaps the most powerful antiseptic of its kind. All eucalypts are evergreen, which enables them to make the greatest use of the occasional shower.

Eucalypts grow rapidly, and, given sufficient moisture, to a great height; in fact, the tallest known tree in the world is a eucalypt—*E. amygdalina*—which has been known to reach a height of 480 feet (147 m). Typically the eucalypt has a tall, straight trunk which soars up without branches to a great height and then spreads out rather like a feather duster. Extremely tolerant of drought, they are dwarfed where rainfall is low, and their roots may absorb so much of the moisture present in the ground that no other herbage can exist (this feature of the tree explains why it is sometimes planted to aid in draining swamps, as, for example, in the Pontine Marshes of central Italy).

The timber of eucalypts is often extremely durable, and is used for piles, paving blocks and railway sleepers. Jarrah of the south-western corner of the continent and ironbark of the east coast uplands are resistant to marine organisms such as the shipworm (teredo), which will bore into most other timbers. Much of the eucalyptus timber is very heavy, and tough; thus, the Karri of the south-west is 31 per cent stronger than English oak, and while oak has a specific gravity of 0·99, Australian tallowwood has one of 1·23, red ironbark, 1·22, grey iron-bark, 1·18, and jarrah, 1·12.

The bark of the eucalypt is of some interest: it is often shed annually, curling off in long rolls rather like brown cardboard, and it is frequently valued for its tannin content. The bark offers a useful guide to classifi-cation. The Stringybark, with its brown, loose and fibrous bark, prefers the moist, cool plateaus of the south-east; the Ironbark, with its dark and deeply furrowed bark, grows best in the clay soils of the east, and so does the box, with its greyish, rough bark. The gum, properly speaking, has a pale, smooth bark; but all eucalypts are colloquially called gum trees, from the resinous exudation from their bark.

Apart from the eucalypts, one other family of plants is widespread in Australia: this is the acacia, which is found scattered over other warm regions of the earth, including India, Africa and Central and South America. Like the eucalypts, there are many species of acacia, and they too with their down-hanging leaves, are adapted to withstand drought. But they do not attain the great height of the eucalypt, their tallest members rising to 50 or 60 feet (15 or 18 m). The characteristic golden globular clusters of blooms or flower spike of the acacia (or wattle) is the national flower of Australia.

VEGETATION ZONES

Geographers differ widely regarding the proper division of the con-tinent into vegetation zones. One has only to compare, for example, the maps drawn by Professor Taylor,[1] Professor Privat-Deschanel [2] and the Australian National Travel Association.[3] These differ not only in detail but also in matters of general principle. Much of the difficulty in delimiting vegetation regions results from the fact that we are dealing with a large continent in which differences in elevation are compara-tively slight: it follows, then, that the climatic changes are gradual and that the boundaries of plant regions become blurred.

Here we mention only the major distributions, and the differences in detail need not concern us.

Forest. All authorities agree on the existence of a belt of monsoonal vegetation along the northern and north-eastern fringes of the continent, remarkably similar to that of New Guinea and Malaya. The finest examples of tropical monsoon forest are to be found in the region of highest rainfall—the seaward slopes of the Atherton Plateau; but the monsoon belt extends as far south as Brisbane.

In this region the constant heat and the humid atmosphere (which is experienced in places even in the so-called dry winter) favour the growth of dense virgin evergreen forests of tall trees whose crowns touch and combine to prevent the sunlight from reaching the ground. Cycads are common: they are descendants of plants which lived 260 million years ago in the coal forests of Europe; and there are many palms. Typical forms include orchids, figs, rhododendrons and the wild banana. Lianes lace the trees together, and a variety of ferns occupies the forest floor. The coast is fringed with mangroves.

The monsoon vegetation is succeeded southwards by a coastal belt of temperate (sometimes called subtropical) forest. While the eucalypt is rare or absent from the monsoon region, here it is dominant, though it is accompanied by acacias. Where the rainfall is abundant the trees here too are closely packed. The giant *Eucalypt amygdalina* is found in the Gippsland district of Victoria.

Three storeys may be recognised in these forests: the uppermost is formed by the crowns of the tall eucalypts, 300–400 feet (90–120 m) above the ground; much closer to the soil is the middle storey, formed of the crowns of tree ferns, 30–40 feet (9–12 m) high; and the lowest storey is composed of the many creeping and climbing plants together with ground ferns. These Australian forests lack, perhaps, the freshness of an English spring and the multicoloured tints of autumn; their beauty lies in their ever-present fragrant perfumes and their magnificent blooms, such as the crimson waratah, the orange clusters of grevillea and the blue spheres of oleocarpus. In western Tasmania the eucalypts and acacias are replaced by forests of evergreen beech, similar to those of South America in the corresponding latitude.

Bush. To the west the forests thin out gradually, until they become limited to narrow belts fringing the water-courses or surrounding the water holes. The eucalypts become gnarled and wrinkled; the acacias become thin and bare, but bristle with spines. Shrubs and trees stand isolated: they include the brigalow, with its silvery leaves; the pepper tree, with its lacy, scented foliage; the wattle, with its bunches of golden blossom; the grass tree, with waving tresses and a short, scaly stem; and perhaps most peculiar of all, the bottle tree, which, with a store of water in its swollen trunk, possesses the shape and performs the function of a bottle.

In dry seasons hardly a herb is to be seen among the trees and shrubs; in wet seasons there is a sea of waving kangaroo grass: hence the conflicting reports brought back by many of the early explorers, both here and in the deserts. This is the Australian bush—the background to so much of the history of settlement. Today large portions of it in Queensland and New South Wales form grazing lands.

There are wide areas of saline soils, where grass cannot survive, and here thrives the saltbush (*Atriplex*). This is a low, flesh-leaved shrub, bluish in colour on account of the minute crystals of salt which it contains: these have enabled it to resist drought to an extraordinary degree. Fortunately it is palatable and nourishing to sheep; but when severely grazed it requires several seasons to recover. Saltbush is found extensively in the north-western parts of New South Wales and in much of South Australia.

Scrub. Intermediate between the bush and the desert are the various types of scrub, which are developed to an unusual degree in Australia. There are three principal formations: mallee (in the south and south-west), mulga (in the centre and west) and brigalow (in the east and north-east). The first is a dwarf eucalypt; the other two are acacias.

Mallee is a species of eucalypt, 12–14 feet (about 4 m) high, with a characteristic appearance: it breaks into a dozen or so thin stems close to the ground, and these bear leaves only on the outermost branches. Mallees grow so close together that they blot out the sun from the ground below, which is bare of herbage; sometimes it is impossible to penetrate a thicket of mallee. This scrub occupies large tracts of land east of the lower Murray river, east of the Darling Ranges of Western Australia and north and east of the Eucla Basin (north of the Great Australian Bight).

Mulga is a species of acacia—perhaps the most abundant of them all. It is a hardy plant, wiry and spiny, which spreads out laterally, and is accompanied by grasses. Mulga is found in the land surrounding the Macdonnell Ranges of the centre of the continent, and east of the small North-west Artesian Basin. Brigalow is another acacia (*A. harpophylla*), thorny and highly resistant to drought, and forming dense thickets with some development of grasses. It is found on the north-eastern fringe of the desert, in the lee of the Great Dividing Range, and in the area between the Cooper and Diamantina water-courses.

Desert. The deserts include varied types of country, in most of which some form of vegetable life exists. The exceptions are the areas of "living" (*i.e.* moving) dunes, such as are found in the central portions of the Arunta Desert to the north of Lake Eyre, and the gravelly or stony areas from which the wind has removed all finer particles, such as in parts of the centre of the great western desert, and in Sturt's Stony Desert of the east (the Gibber country). Here no plant can exist.

More usually, however, there is some scattered vegetation in the deserts, consisting characteristically of the so-called spinifex (*Triodia pungens*). Dr. Marion Newbigin has pointed out that the true spinifex is a native of coastal sand dunes and ranges from Australia, through Ceylon to Japan, and that the "spinifex" of central Australia is more accurately named porcupine grass.[4] It grows in round hummocks 2 or 3 feet high, which, as the name suggests, consist of masses of needles. Their sharp points inflict serious wounds on animals—wounds which are intensified by the irritating juices of the plant. From these prickly thickets blades of coarse grass rise 5 or 6 feet (nearly 2 m) into the air. Porcupine grass helps to bind the soil together, and for three short weeks during the year, when it is in seed, it forms a nourishing food for stock. Otherwise it is not only useless, but also a menace to the traveller.

"Mediterranean" Vegetation. In the neighbourhood of Perth and Adelaide are the two regions of winter rain which in other continents bear vegetation of "Mediterranean" type. In Australia these regions have no completely distinct plant life, for the eucalypts dominate there too. As we have seen, eucalypts are adapted to thrive in widely differing types of climate, and being evergreen they can utilise the winter rain of these regions.

In the Adelaide district matters are complicated by the north-to-south grain of the country, with its faulted blocks, and by the existence of sandy soils in the lowlands. Much of it is mallee country by nature, but in the better-watered hilly districts eucalypts thrive, such as the sugar gum, stringybark and peppermint.

Around Perth, however, we have the unusual spectacle of extremely tall trees growing in dense stands; yet, owing to the small amount of shade which they cast, below them is a rich shrubby undergrowth. The tree species are arranged roughly in belts running north and south according to the intensity of rainfall. About the 20-inch (508-mm) annual isohyet is a belt of york gum; this is succeeded westwards by white gum, and then, near the 30-inch (762-mm) line, by jarrah. Farther west is a narrow strip of red gum, and on the west coast, a belt of tuart. The valuable karri is found in a comparatively restricted area near the south coast. The timber industry of these parts is considered later.

Fig. 12 is based on the official vegetation map in the *Atlas of Australian Resources*, whose compilers have drawn upon all the available descriptions and have supplemented these by ground and aerial surveys. The result is an extremely complex map which not only distinguishes 35 categories of vegetation but in addition shows the extent to which they intermingle. In Fig. 12 the number of categories has been reduced to 13 and most of the transitional areas have been left blank. Short descriptions of the terms employed are as follows:

Tropical rain forest. This consists of mainly evergreen trees whose crowns join to form an interlacing canopy draped with lianes. In a single district more than 100 species of trees may be present, many of them with Indo-Malayan affinities. The tropical rain forest is limited to the eastern coastal tracts of Queensland and the neighbouring parts of New South Wales, where the rainfall is above 60 inches (1524 mm) per annum.

Tropical woodland. A long belt of woodland stretches from the neighbourhood of Broome in Western Australia almost without a break through Northern Territory and eastern Queensland as far as the New

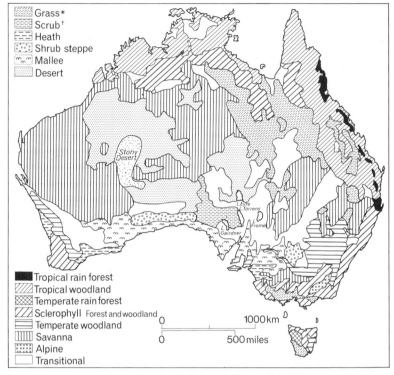

FIG. 12.—Australia: natural vegetation.

* Temperate grass in Tasmania and Victoria; elsewhere semi-arid grassland.
† In Queensland, brigalow; in South Australia, mulga.

South Wales border. The trees consist of eucalypts and acacias; they are mainly evergreen, and they are more widely spaced than in the forests, so that there is no continuous canopy.

Temperate rain forest. This type occurs chiefly in western Tasmania where the mean annual rainfall is over 50 inches (1270 mm). It differs from the tropical rain forest in the scarcity of lianes and in the small variety of species. The flora has affinities with that of New Zealand and with southern South America.

Sclerophyll forest and woodland. South of the tropic this is an evergreen forest of tall trees whose flat crowns interlace. The mean annual rainfall is in places only 35 inches (889 mm) and the species are drought-resistant; they include karri, Sydney blue gum, mountain ash and alpine ash; all are eucalypts and valuable hardwoods. North of the tropic it consists of a layer of low, evergreen trees, including mulga; in the drier parts it is confined to the margins of watercourses or to lines of springs. Light sheep grazing is possible, but overgrazing is a danger.

The rainfall in this belt ranges from 5 to 17 inches (127 to 431 mm) per annum.

Temperate woodland. Typically this clothes the western slopes of the Great Dividing Range in New South Wales. The trees are drought resistant, but owing to the lower rainfall they are more widely spaced than in the sclerophyll forest.

Savanna. Here grasses are dominant; they grow in tussocks and include some useful grazing species (wallaby grass, kangaroo grass and corkscrew grass). There are also widely scattered trees and shrubs.

Temperate grass is confined mainly to Victoria and Tasmania. It grows in tussocks, but the leaves of neighbouring tussocks intermingle to form a continuous canopy, below which is a layer of small herbs. It is found on heavy soils, which are usually richer in phosphates than the nearby woodland soils. *Semi-arid grass* occupies a wide belt astride the border between Queensland and Northern Territory and comprises most of the native grassland of the continent. It consists of an open cover of tussock grass, from which trees and tall shrubs are virtually absent, and includes Mitchell grass of the Barkly Tableland. The mean annual rainfall rises from 10 to 18 inches (254–457 mm) in the south to 25 inches (635 mm) in the north.

Scrub. Best developed in the region south-west of Lake Eyre, this consists of tall shrubs or low trees which branch close to the ground, together with a low stratum of herbs and shrubs which is continuous only after rain. The leaves are reduced and stiff or absent; species are usually non-eucalypt, and the typical example is mulga, which is readily eaten by stock. The rainfall in this region ranges between 8 and 15 inches (203 and 381 mm) per annum. In eastern Queensland the dominant plant is brigalow. The type occurs on rich, deep, black soils where the rainfall is between 17 and 35 inches (432 and 889 mm) per annum. When cleared, the scrub can be replaced by high-quality pastures.

Heath is confined to relatively small areas in the south-west corner of the continent and south of the Murray river mouth. It occurs on acid, leached, sandy soils and is of little economic value.

Shrub steppe. This vegetation is found mainly in the Nullarbor Plain and in the region of the lower Lachlan river of New South Wales. It consists of low shrubs with semi-succulent leaves which are usually covered with small hairs: it includes wallaby grass, saltbush and bluebush—the latter being typical of limestone subsoils as in the Nullarbor Plain. The rainfall is from 6 to 16 inches (152 to 406 mm) per annum, but is unreliable, and there is a long dry season. Nevertheless, the shrub steppe offers some valuable grazing for stock.

Mallee. This form of vegetation has been described above: it is largely confined to the areas of winter rainfall. The low, umbrella-shaped trees are dominant, but in the areas of lower rainfall 8–12 inches (203–304 mm) they are joined by spinifex.

Desert. In the deserts the mean annual rainfall is as low as 2–8 inches

(50–203 mm) and is very unreliable, so that some areas are dry for several consecutive years. Most of the desert is characterised by a regular pattern of parallel sand ridges: these are up to 100 feet (30 m) high, 600 yards (549 m) apart and 150 miles (240 km) long. Vegetation is present, but is sparse, consisting of seasonal grasses, herbs and low

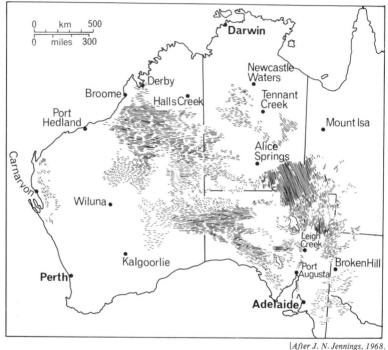

[After J. N. Jennings, 1968.

FIG. 13.—Australia: desert dunes. The mapping of the desert dunes in Australia has been completed only in the last few years, and it can now be seen that the huge anticyclonic swirl of the prevailing winds is reflected in the direction of the longitudinal dunes.

shrubs; it is found usually between the ridges. The stony desert contrasts with the sandhill desert in that its surface is hard; this, too, bears a very sparse cover of low shrubs. Its precise limits are not known.

Recent national mapping on the scale of $1 : 2\frac{1}{2}$ million has added greatly to our knowledge of the extent of the dunes and of their alignments (Fig. 13). Their directions are related to those of the dominant winds, so that fixed on the ground is a record of the surface air movements over about one-third of the continent.[5]

A huge anticyclonic swirl is evident. In the Great Victoria Desert the dunes are arranged from west to east, reflecting the westerly winds.

North and east of Lake Eyre they run from south to north, and gain a slight component from the east. By the centre of Northern Territory they are running almost due west, and achieve a true westerly direction in the Great Sandy Desert, in conformity with the so-called south-east trades.

We have already referred to the probability of a greater rainfall in the Lake Eyre basin in the past (p. 34). Strangely enough, evidence from the dunes points in an opposite direction. The dunes are now "fixed"—*i.e.*, they have a cover (often scanty), of vegetation which cannot have been present at the time of their formation. This points to an *increase* in rainfall in recent times, and suggests that the deserts have contracted.

The mode of origin of the dunes has received some recent attention.[6] Do they represent accumulations of sand piled up by the wind? Or are they residual features which stand out only because the wind has excavated the intervening hollows? In the latter case one would expect the solid floor below the hollows to be lower than that below the dunes as a result of wind erosion. Borings into the dune areas in two districts of the Simpson Desert north-east of Finke indicated no appreciable difference in the altitude of the solid floor below the dunes compared with that below the hollows, and the results therefore suggested that the dunes represent accumulations rather than residual features.

A common characteristic of the dune systems is the merging together of a pair of almost parallel longitudinal dunes to form a tuning fork shape. Where this has happened, the junction always points downwind. Crosswinds have been suggested as the cause: a crosswind would deflect the path of the more exposed of the pair so that it joined with its neighbour. Field plotting of the profiles of the dunes near the junction has revealed abnormally steep slopes on the lee side of the deflected dunes; this confirms the suggestion that the merging of dunes is the result of crosswinds.

ANIMAL LIFE

It is not the geographer's task to provide a complete survey of his chosen area: his prime concern is with man and with those elements of the natural environment which influence his life. The peculiar fauna of Australia are of interest to us on account of the light which they shed on the early separation of the continent from the other land masses; in addition, the absence of the larger carnivores (the kangaroo is vegetarian) has allowed the spread of sheep and cattle, as well as (unfortunately) the rabbit (*see* p. 50).

Living mammals are divisible into three sub-classes: the first and largest sub-class (which includes man) comprises the placentals, in which the young are born in a relatively mature state; the second comprises the monotremes, which preserve some reptilian features, in particular, hatching their young from eggs; the third comprises the marsupials, in which the young emerge as imperfectly developed embryos, and continue their growth in the mother's pouch (a kangaroo destined to be larger than a man is less than an inch long at birth).

In the placentals reproduction involves great risks to the mother; but as a compensation, a larger brain, greater intelligence and acute senses allows the animal an improved chance of survival; and it is significant that where all three sub-classes are in competition, it is the placentals which have emerged, at the expense of the monotremes and marsupials.

Fossils indicate a wide distribution of the marsupials over the earth in

[Courtesy Australian News & Information Bureau.

FIG. 14.—Duck-billed platypus. This is one of the three known representatives of the monotremes, or egg-laying mammals. It resembles birds in laying eggs and possessing webbed feet and a beak; but its body is covered with hair, it lives in a burrow and suckles its young. It attains a length of about 20 inches (510 mm).

relatively recent geological times. In the Jurassic rocks of the English Purbeck region many jaws of marsupial character have been found, and ancestors of the opossum have been discovered in the Upper Eocene of France and England. But in the Americas, Africa and Eurasia the marsupials have been unable to compete with the placentals, and are represented today by only two families—the opossums of the Americas and the rare selvas (mouse-like creatures) of South America.

Australia seems to have become an island continent before the evolution of the placentals, and here the marsupials and monotremes have not been subjected to the competition of the higher mammals. In this region are the three remaining kinds of monotreme—the duck-billed platypus (Fig. 14) and two species of spiny anteater—and here the marsupials have developed an extraordinary diversity of form and habit, analogous to those of their more advanced cousins, the placentals—hence Professor Isaiah Bowman's apt description of Australia as a "museum of archaic forms."

In the place of the rats and rabbits of western Europe are the bandicoots of Australia, living on fruits and insects, and digging burrows in the cooler and mountainous parts of the continent. The ferocious but stupid Tasmanian wolf, formerly the scourge of flocks of sheep, may be compared with the placental wolf of the temperate forests of northern Europe. Little more than 3 feet (1 m) long (excluding its tail), it is nevertheless the largest beast of prey in Australia; it has now retreated to the mountainous interior of the island, and is all but extinct (Fig. 15).

A number of fruit-eating marsupials are adapted to tree life, and resemble in their habits the lemurs of Madagascar and the East Indies: they include the flying squirrel, fitted with membranes which allow it to glide from branch to branch; the little opossum mouse (or flying mouse), sometimes kept as a schoolboy pet; and the gentle and lovable koala "bear." The marsupial mole, like its placental counterpart, lives underground and is apparently completely blind.

[*Courtesy Australian News & Information Bureau.*

FIG. 15.—Tasmanian wolf. This animal, now almost extinct, is the largest marsupial beast of prey, being 3 feet (914 mm) long excluding the tail. Its jaws are furnished with 42 formidable teeth, and in the early days of settlement it played havoc with the sheep.

The giant but vegetarian great kangaroo of the Australian grasslands is fleet of foot (his hops may be 15 feet (4 m) long and he can race at 40 m.p.h. (64 km.p.h.)), and he may perhaps be compared with the antelope of the African savannas. When sitting he is taller than a man. His favourite meal has been called kangaroo grass; but in parts of Queensland the kangaroo has so denuded the pastures that he is regarded as a pest, and there is a price on his head.

There are many relatives of the great kangaroo. The rock kangaroo is only 2 feet (600 mm) long, and his reduced hind legs allow of greater agility in rocky country; the kangaroo rat is even smaller—16 inches (400 mm) long; and in the jungle of north Queensland there lives a tree-climbing kangaroo which can leap 50 feet (15 m) to the ground.

Interesting forms of animal life have developed in the seasonally dry ponds and water-courses. The primitive lung fish, living in the Burnett and Mary rivers of north Queensland, possesses both gills and lungs, and so can live when its river dries up. Various forms of brine shrimp lay eggs that can withstand a long period of drought; and a species of crayfish burrows into the mud to such a depth that water is always present there.

Today, as in the past, Australia is indeed, not only the continent of eucalypts, but also the marsupial continent.

SOME INTRODUCED PLANTS AND ANIMALS

Wheat, lucerne, apples and sugar cane play their part in the material wealth of Australia; sheep, cattle, horses and pigs flourish in their relatively new environment. All these are considered on other pages. But not all the introduced species have met with quite the same success. Here we consider briefly the rabbit, the dingo, the camel, the buffalo and the prickly pear.

THE RABBIT

A few rabbits were among the livestock transported by the first fleet, and without natural enemies in Australia they flourished. About 1865 many rabbits were liberated when fire destroyed the fence of a warren near Castlemaine in Victoria (about 12 miles (17 km) south of Bendigo). Rabbits are notoriously quick breeders: it has been computed that one pair of rabbits theoretically could, after three years, have multiplied to 13,718,000! By 1880 the rabbits had overrun Victoria and had entered South Australia; by 1890 they had spread into Queensland; by 1900 they were in Western Australia and Northern Territory.

The rabbit reduces the stock-carrying capacity of the land by nibbling the pasture. Only the tropical pastures are largely immune from its attacks, and till recent years large tracts of sheep pasture were annually eaten bare by the rabbit. Rabbit-proof fencing is an accepted, if negative, method of control (Fig. 16); and in a desperate attempt to keep Western

[*Courtesy Australian News & Information Bureau.*

FIG. 16.—The rabbit pest. Through the middle of the picture runs a rabbit-proof fence.
To the left, every scrap of pasture has been nibbled by rabbits; but the protected
land to the right offers plenty of fodder for stock.

Australia free from the pest a thousand-mile fence was built right across
the state from Condon on the north coast to Hopetoun in the south. It
took five years to build (1902–7). But the rabbit got through, and was
noticed at York (east of Perth) in 1916.

About 1952 it was estimated that the rabbit was robbing Australia of
25 million sheep. About that time the Commonwealth Scientific and
Industrial Research Organisation began experimenting with the virus
disease, myxomatosis, which is spread among rabbits by mosquitoes,
and the rabbit pest is, it would seem, now under control. As a result, the
pastures in some areas have not only recuperated, but (as in the western
Riverina) have changed their character, for many species which the
rabbit had almost eliminated are now growing in large numbers.

THE DINGO

The dingo—half dog, half wolf—seems to have been brought to
Australia from Asia in late Pleistocene times by the ancestors of the
Australian aborigines. The dingo is very similar to the wild dog of
India: about the size of an Airedale terrier, it has erect, pointed ears and
a yellowish, sandy coloured coat. The dingo has largely forsaken man,
and lives wild (though it still aids the aboriginal hunter). Its territory
formerly was the whole of the continent; but it has now been virtually

exterminated from all but the desert fringe, chiefly along the border between Northern Territory and Queensland and that between Queensland and South Australia.

The dingo is a carnivore: for a time it lived on the rabbit, then it began to attack lambs, killing far more than it could ever eat. In the 1920s sheep stations lost many thousands of young lambs to the dingo. He does not usually attack cattle, though even they are not immune if they are weakened by drought; and the sudden howl of a dingo at night has been known to start a cattle stampede. The dingo is extremely cunning (or intelligent), and is therefore difficult to poison or trap. Large-mesh fences are erected round the pastoral properties, and in the past the State Governments have paid a bonus ranging from five shillings (25p) up to ten pounds for each dingo scalp. The general effect of the dingo has been to confine sheep rearing to the regions within the dingo-proof fences (see, for example, p. 231). In fairness, we should

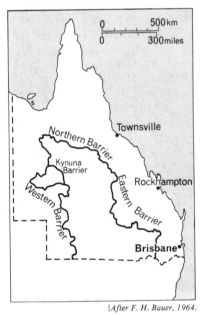

FIG. 17.—Queensland: the dingo-proof fence. This fence, 3500 miles (5600 km) long, constructed during the middle of the 1950s at a cost of over £0·5 million, keeps the dingo under reasonable control.

[After F. H. Bauer, 1964.

remember that the dingo appears to have been part ancestor of the very valuable kelpie, the sheepdog of Australia.

The problem of the dingo came to the fore during and after the Second World War when many of the fences were falling into disrepair and it had become difficult to obtain professional catchers. In the semi-desert lands to the west and in the hill country to the east of the best sheep pastures in Queensland the dingo increased in numbers and penetrated the fences. In 1952 it was estimated that the losses of sheep through dingo attacks were possibly as high as 500,000 head annually, representing in money terms about £2 million. Many farmers turned to cattle simply because the dingo made it impossible to keep sheep.[7]

In 1954 the State government decided on a bold plan, to build a dingo-proof fence 3500 miles (5635 km) long to enclose the whole of the main sheep area of Queensland, totalling 135 million acres (Fig. 17). The government specified the height of the fence, 6 feet (2 m): and the dimensions and spacing of the posts. On unleased lands the State erected and maintained it; elsewhere the State provided the netting, but the farmer erected and maintained it in return for an annual grant of £8 per mile (1·6 km).

Six inspectors have the task of examining every portion of the fence at least at six-weekly intervals. In the event, a little over one-third of the total length was adequately served by existing fences; but 768 miles (1136 km) needed repair and alteration, while 1510 miles (2431 km) needed completely new fencing. The cost of the fence, excluding posts, was £507,632. The project was financed through an annual levy on all farmers protected by the fence, in proportion to the number of sheep that they carried.

Complete extinction of the dingo within the fence is considered impracticable owing to the large areas of hilly and rough country that are enclosed: these will always form breeding grounds for the dingo. But once the animals outside the fence are prevented from entering, those that remain inside can be kept under control.

THE CAMEL

In the exploration of the interior of the continent and in the early stages of settlement the camel was invaluable. It pioneered the development of the stock routes and formed the main method of transport by which the bales of wool from the inland stations were brought to the outside world. The Stuart Highway, the lifeline of the Northern Territory, had its origin in a caravan trail known as the "Ghan," from its Afghan and Punjabi camel drivers. We have seen that the explorer Warburton relied on camels for his heroic eight-months' journey in 1875 from Alice Springs to the north-west coast. In 1913 the first furrow to mark the course of the projected railway across the Nullarbor Plain was ploughed by teams of camels.

The camel remained the chief method of transport in arid Australia until the development of the motor truck during the 1920s and early 1930s, when its downfall was rapid. Wild herds, however, maintain themselves today on land that is considered uneconomic for pastoral farming. Thus an estimated 1500 wild camels survive in the eastern fringes of Sturt's Desert, astride the border between Queensland and South Australia.

Quite out of proportion to its former utility, the camel today has a minor economic value: it is shot for the sake of its meat, which satisfies part of the growing demand for pet food from the towns of south-eastern Australia.

THE BUFFALO

During the 1820s, 1830s and 1840s a few dozen water buffaloes were taken as work animals to Fort Dundas in Melville Island and Port Essington on the Cobourg Peninsula of Arnhem Land. By 1850 both settlements had been abandoned and their animals allowed to run free. Without natural predators the buffalo herds quickly multiplied and the animals spread to the south, south-east and south-west until they occupied most of the Arnhem peninsula. South of about latitude 14° S. the slightly drier climate is less attractive to the buffalo, and west of the Stuart Highway human occupation becomes more active; but in the main part of the peninsula there are an estimated 150,000 to 200,000 head of buffalo, which represent by far the largest free-ranging herd in the world.[8] This is in spite of a long history of slaughter of the buffalo for the sake of the hide.

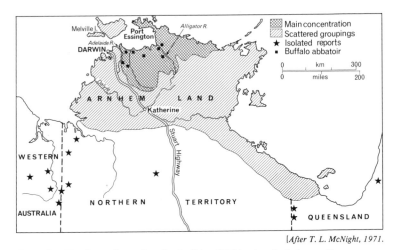

[After T. L. McNight, 1971.

Fig. 18.—Northern Australia: the buffalo. Within the shaded area there are an estimated 150,000 to 200,000 buffalo. Only recently has the potential economic value of the animal been realised.

The buffalo is a bulky animal which can weigh up to a ton. Its favoured habitat is the undulating and lightly wooded country that lies close to the streams and swamps; this allows the buffalo to move each day from the feeding grounds in order to wallow in the water or mud. It is claimed that the buffalo produces a deterioration in the environment: that he overgrazes the pasture, depletes the woodland, accelerates erosion and clogs the watercourses. Where he impinges on cattle station property he destroys fences and watertroughs and fouls the water holes.

Accordingly, in 1963 the buffalo was declared a pest, and unlimited

shooting was permitted except in a protected area: this, however, comprises the heart of the buffalo country, essentially the land between the
Adelaide and Alligator rivers (Fig. 18). The economic significance of
the buffalo is considered in Chapter XI (pp. 309–11).

THE PRICKLY PEAR

The story of the rise of the prickly pear menace and its eventual conquest
is one of the most fascinating in the development of the young dominion.

The first prickly pear was taken to Australia in 1788 by Captain
Arthur Philip himself, who collected some from Rio while on his way.
He was hoping to rear cochineal insects on them in order to supply red
dye for his soldiers' coats. The insects died, but the cactus lived on. In
1839 a single pot of prickly pear was sent from Sydney to Scone (80
miles (128 km) north-west of Newcastle) and during the next twenty
years or so prickly pear was grown as hedges around the homesteads. It
is recorded that at Chinchilla a workman was dismissed for failing to
keep the hedge watered.

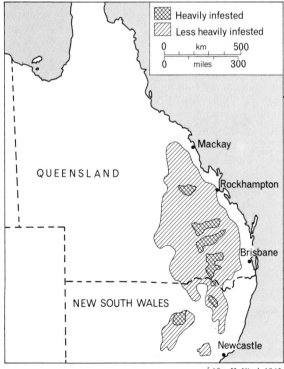

[*After H. Nicol, 1943.*

FIG. 19.—Eastern Australia: prickly pear. The map illustrates
the areas that were invaded by prickly pear at the height
of the infestation about 1925.

The prickly pear rapidly spread. By 1875 it was causing concern, by 1885, alarm; by 1895 thousands of pounds had been spent on attempts to control it; by 1905 it was seen to be a catastrophe. In 1907 the Queensland Government offered a reward of £10,000 for a satisfactory way of destroying the pest.

At the height of the infestation, in 1925, 60 million acres (24 mil. ha) were attacked by prickly pear. Four-fifths of this area was in Queensland, the remaining fifth in New South Wales (Fig. 19). It extended for a thousand miles (1600 km) from the latitude of Mackay in the north to Newcastle in the south and formed a belt ranging from 100 to 200 miles (160 to 320 km) in width from east to west; and it was spreading at the rate of a million acres a year. Half of the infected land contained a dense growth of pear in which fences were topped and all grass and herbage strangled, where stock-rearing was manifestly impossible. Where a narrow lane could be kept open the musterers wore leather armour and their horses needed leggings as a protection against the thorns. Many farmers were forced to abandon their holdings and desert their homesteads; and soon the abominable cactus was growing through the floors and through the walls.

Subsidies to farmers, free transport of arsenic, free railway passes to inventors—all proved of no avail.

From 1920 to 1925 Australian entomologists were investigating the enemies of prickly pear in its natural home, the Americas. They discovered about 150 different species of insect which bred and fed on prickly pear and other cacti; and they sent home to Australia 50 of these. Among them was a moth borer, *Cactoblastis cactorum*, which was to prove the saviour of the prickly pear country.

In 1925 2750 *Cactoblastis* egg sticks were sent from the Argentine to Queensland, and for eighteen months the insects were reared and tested in cages. They multiplied rapidly. In 1927 they were systematically liberated, and during this and the following four years 2750 *millions* of egg sticks were distributed among the prickly pear.

The success of *Cactoblastis* was immediate. By 1930 it had freed 30,000 acres (12,000 ha); a year later 500,000 acres (200,000 ha) were clear. In 1934 the last big masses of pear in Queensland were collapsing—and as the prickly pear declined so did the numbers of *Cactoblastis*, for its only food was vanishing. *Cactoblastis* ate its way through 15,000 million tons of prickly pear![9]

New homesteads were built, new pastures sown, stagnant towns revived and millions of sheep were soon grazing on land which a few years previously had been a mass of pear. In south-east Queensland, on the railway to Quilpie, is a small and obscure town named Boonarga. It lay near the centre of the infestation, and was threatened with extinction. In 1936, in recognition of the moth which saved them, the grateful inhabitants built the Cactoblastis Memorial Hall.

NOTES

1. G. Taylor, *Australia*, Methuen, 1940, p. 86.

2. P. Privat-Deschanel, *Géographie Universelle*, Tome X, Armand Colin, Paris, 1930, p. 91.

3. Australian National Travel Association, *Australia*, Melbourne, 1954, p. 7.

4. M. Newbigin, *Plant and Animal Geography*, Methuen, 1948.

5. J. N. Jennings, "A Revised Map of the Desert Dunes of Australia," *Australian Geographer*, Vol. X, No. 5 (1968).

6. J. A. Mabbutt and M. E. Sullivan, "The Formation of Longitudinal Dunes," *Australian Geographer*, Vol. X, No. 6 (1968).

7. F. H. Bauer, "Queensland's New Dingo Fence," *Australian Geographer*, Vol. IX, No. 4 (1964).

8. T. L. McNight, "Australia's Buffalo Dilemma," *Annals of the Association of American Geographers*, Vol. 61 (1971).

9. H. Nicol, *Biological Control of Insects*, Penguin Books, 1943.

STUDY QUESTIONS

1. From one of the standard atlases trace a map of the vegetation belts of Australia. For each region: (*a*) describe shortly the characteristic vegetation, and (*b*) relate the vegetation to the structure and climate.

2. How is the eucalypt adapted to the Australian environment?

3. Explain concisely: mallee, mulga, spinifex, saltbush.

4. Where are the tallest trees of Australia to be found? Is this distribution related to rainfall?

5. To what extent have the indigenous fauna and flora of Australia been replaced by introduced species?

6. Consider the rabbit, the dingo and the prickly pear in Australia. Why did they spread? Is their control complete?

Chapter V

TASMANIA

IN this and the six chapters which follow we study, one by one, the seven political divisions of Australia. In large measure these correspond with regions of distinct physical, human and economic character. The core of each state, at least, has its own "personality," though, naturally, near the political boundary there is a transitional zone where the distinguishing features of one state merge into those of its neighbour. Only the deserts, which occupy so much of the centre and west of the continent, are shared by several States and respect no political frontiers. We begin our regional studies with Tasmania, where climate and farming most nearly resemble those of the United Kingdom.

TASMANIA'S INDIVIDUALITY

With an area of 26,215 square miles (67,897 km²), Tasmania is by far the smallest of the Australian States; yet the continent is built on so vast a scale that this seemingly small island is in fact twice as large as Wales, or more than half as large again as Switzerland.

The State has many distinctive characteristics. From the point of view of fauna, Tasmania may be regarded as the sanctuary within a sanctuary; for just as many of the forms of animal life in Australia have long since become extinct in other continents, so in Tasmania there are a number of indigenous species which are not to be found on the mainland. The duck-billed platypus is more common in Tasmania than elsewhere; and there are ten different marsupials which are peculiar to the island: these include the Tasmanian "Devil" and the Tasmanian "Tiger." There are fourteen indigenous species of birds and two of reptiles, while the Tasmanian mountain shrimp, known elsewhere only in fossil times, has remained almost unaltered since Carbo-Permian times.

Tasmania is the only Australian State without a desert region—the only one where irrigation is virtually unnecessary. She lies sufficiently far south to fall within the westerly wind belt at all seasons; all the temperate crops may therefore be cultivated, and Tasmania has the largest rural population in proportion to her size among all the States. Tasmania is also the most completely mountainous State—and one of the most thoroughly mountainous islands in the world. Here are to be seen best the effects of the Pleistocene glaciation in Australia—effects which are either absent from the mainland or else present on only a small scale.

In relation to her size Tasmania is one of the most richly mineralised areas in the world, and in point of value of output per head she is the leading state of Australia in the production of minerals. Tasmania is the chief producer of tin and the second producer of copper, and makes important contributions to the Australian output of lead and zinc. Virtually the whole of Australia's tungsten is raised in Tasmania (mainly from King Island).

The mineral industries have led to the establishment of important metal-refining plants. Tasmania produces the bulk of the aluminium and refined zinc of Australia, together with large quantities of copper. These are remarkable contributions by the smallest state of the federation.

The value of the metals, concentrates and ores exported from Tasmania during 1969–70 were as follows: zinc: $A mil. 42·6; iron: $A mil. 25·3; copper: $A mil. 18·2; tin: $A mil. 16·2; lead: $A mil. 7·4; and tungsten: $A mil. 5·9.

STRUCTURE AND RELIEF

If the land were to rise 300 feet (91·4 m) relatively to the sea Bass Strait would become dry, Tasmania would be reunited to the mainland, and her relation to the rest of the continent would become plainer. A chain of mountain peaks (now represented by Wilson's Promontory and the Kent's and Furneaux Groups of islands) would then join her to the Great Dividing Range in Victoria.

Tasmania is in fact an outlying fragment of the Eastern Highlands, for faulting on a grand scale—perhaps in late Mesozoic times—has separated a heart-shaped block of old rocks from its parent mass. The Central Plateau of Tasmania is thus an excellent example of a horst: an upland region bounded by fault scarps which rise several thousand feet above the neighbouring land to the north and east. The actual separation of the island from the mainland, however, is more recent, and Bass Strait appears to date from late Tertiary or early Quaternary times.

It is believed that the core of the island consists of a mass of Archaean rocks, though these are not extensively exposed on the surface. In much of the north, north-west, west, and south-western parts there are exposures of older Palaeozoic sediments: there are Cambrian strata in the north near Latrobe, Ordovician (probably), and Silurian in the north-west, while conglomerates and quartzites of Devonian age form the West Coast Range in the south-west of the island.

These old rocks have been "stiffened" by granitic intrusions, and close to the latter are the mineral deposits for which Tasmania is famous. The most important areas, yielding tin, copper, zinc and iron, are in the north-west; but in the north-east too there are granite bosses associated with tin deposits, and the granites reappear in the rugged islands of the Furneaux Group to the north and in the Freycinet Peninsula and the neighbouring Schouten and Maria Islands. Parts of Tasmania may perhaps be compared with the south-west of England, where granite forms the rolling uplands of Dartmoor, Bodmin Moor, and the St Austell, Redruth, and Penzance areas and reappears in the Scilly Isles, and where copper and tin mining flourished a century or so ago. Cornish emigrants evidently found their way to northern Tasmania, as the place names show: for Launceston (Tasmania) is in the County of Cornwall and on the Tamar river; and it is likely that Cornishmen played some part in the early development of the mining industry there.

The whole of central and south-eastern Tasmania consists of a basin in which strata ranging in age from Carboniferous to Triassic have been deposited: these include some workable coal seams; but much of the western portion of this basin (in the central parts of the island) is occupied by great intrusive sills of greenstone or diabase, whose age is uncertain, so that the sedimentary rocks appear only as a narrow rim. On the east these greenstones present a series of striking scarps which overlook the Macquarie valley and are known locally as the Tiers.

Only in the Tamar river system are Tertiary strata to be seen; this fertile farming region is a basin in both the drainage and structural senses.

In the relief and drainage of the island there is a pronounced north-west to south-east "grain," which appears to be related to old lines of faulting. In this the structure of Tasmania is not very different from the adjacent parts of the mainland: in the Melbourne district Port Philip Bay appears to be defined by north–south faults, and not far away are the rift valleys of South Australia, with a similar trend.

We may in fact detect three mountain masses bordered or separated by three deep and roughly parallel trenches. The western coast of the island is believed (like that of the Deccan of India and southern California) to be fault-guided; bordering it are two straight and parallel mountain chains, and beyond them is a structural trough occupied by the Gordon river in the north and the upper Huon river in the south. Farther east another broad trench cuts right across the central plateau, never reaching 2000 feet (610 m) above the sea: its northern portion is drained by the Mersey and its southern by the Derwent. The Great Western Mountains, with the same alignment, separate this trough from a third longitudinal valley, occupied by the Tamar and Macquarie rivers in the north and the Coal in the south: this is the route followed by the trunk railway between Hobart and Launceston (Fig. 20).

The predominant grain of the country is well shown in the shapes of the inlets of the south-east, where the lower portions of the valleys have been drowned, and in the fine land-locked Macquarie Harbour in the west. Parts of the eastern coast are extremely steep: the South Esk rises

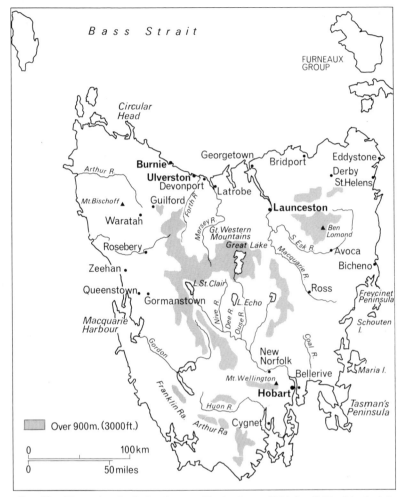

Fig. 20.—Tasmania: physical and towns. The land over 3000 feet (900 m) is shaded.

almost on the east coast, yet its water flows westwards, and has a journey of well over 100 miles (161 km) before mingling with the sea. Few, indeed, of the short eastward-flowing rivers have cut back far into the plateau: we may therefore conclude that this is land which has been uplifted only comparatively recently.

CLIMATE

In spite of its relatively small size, there are considerable differences in climate among the various regions of Tasmania. The island lies in the westerly wind belt, and the "brave west winds" are strongest in the winter half of the year, when the belt has shifted to the north. In other words, Tasmania is sufficiently near the northern fringe of the westerlies to retain a suggestion of the Mediterranean type of climate experienced in the Perth and Adelaide districts.

Virtually everywhere the rainfall is sufficient for farming (there are, however, small irrigated areas under hops in the valley bottoms of the south). The heaviest rainfall is experienced on the western slopes of the plateau, where Mount Lyell receives 116·7 inches (2964 mm) per annum; even this is surpassed by Lake Margaret, where an average of 146·5 inches (3721 mm) is reached. In contrast, the lee of the plateau receives a decidedly low rainfall: the lightest fall in Tasmania is near Ross, on the upper Macquarie river, with about 18 inches (457 mm) per annum. These rainfall limits are closely comparable with those of the United Kingdom, with a maximum of about 200 inches (5080 mm) on Snowdon summit and a minimum of 18 inches (457 mm) near Southend.

Tasmania is sufficiently far from the mainland—at its narrowest Bass Strait is about 135 miles (216 km) across—to experience a low range of temperature throughout the year. Launceston, on the north coast, has a mean annual temperature range of 11° C or 20·1° F (similar in the United Kingdom to that of Eastbourne); Hobart in the south has a range of 10° C or 16·7° F (similar to that of St Annes Head, Milford Haven).

These average figures suggest a cool and temperate climate. There are, however, occasionally severe deviations from the normal, and in February 1967 south-eastern Tasmania experienced a disastrous bushfire which threatened even the capital itself.

A moist spring had been followed by an unusually dry summer. During the three summer months only 2·37 inches (60 mm) of rain fell at Hobart, which has an average for those months of 6·47 inches (164 mm). On Tuesday, February 7th the temperature rose to exceptional heights: at 9.0 a.m. it was 30° C (86° F); at 11.25 it was 37·8° C (100° F), and at 12.15 it reached 39·3° C (102·8° F) (the record for Hobart is 40·7° C (105·2° F)).

For several days fires had been burning in the woods to the west of the city; but apparently they had been judged harmless. Then the wind gathered force, and between 1 and 3 p.m. there were a dozen gusts of 50–60 m.p.h. (80–96 km.p.h.). The fire swept through parts of south-east Tasmania, destroying 1300 buildings and killing 62 people. In the western fringe of Hobart over 400 houses were burnt and the damage would have been much greater but for the fortunate fact that the force of the wind abated.[1]

FARMING IN TASMANIA

To obtain a general view of the relative significance of the various branches of farming in the State we may compare the values of the

various farm products. Table 4 lists the chief sources of farm income
and gives their values in thousand dollars for the farming year 1969–
70.

TABLE 4

Tasmania: sources of farm income, 1969–70

Crops	Thousand dollars
Orchard fruit	17,071
Vegetables	9,723
Hay	4,217
Other stock feed	3,047
Hops	2,143
Cereals for grain	2,142
Green feed	1,018
All crops	41,824

Livestock	
Milk	21,307
Shorn wool	16,827
Cattle, slaughtered . . .	16,511
Sheep and lambs, slaughtered . .	6,464
Pigs, slaughtered	4,943
Eggs	4,652
Poultry, slaughtered . . .	913
Total livestock	72,872

In this predominantly moist climate, with ideal conditions for the
growth of lush pasture, it is not surprising to find that the most important single farm product is milk. Three other commodities vie for
second place: orchard fruits, wool and beef/veal; one of the characteristics of Tasmanian farming is that tree fruits rank very high on the
scale of farm income. The production of wool is a typical feature of
Australian farms; and in sharp contrast to the United Kingdom, the
value of the wool in Tasmania is between two and three times as great as
that of the lamb and mutton. The relatively low position held by cereals
is an effect of the damp climate, and it is barley rather than wheat that
maintains even this low status. The pattern revealed is one of specialist
agriculture where fruit and vegetables together approach three-quarters
of the total value of the crops, accompanied by an even more important
pastoral activity based mainly on milk, beef and wool.

The present pattern of farming, however, is simply the latest stage of
a lengthy period of development. What are the significant changes that
have taken place in Tasmanian farming?

During the last generation there has been a striking increase in the
area of sown pasture. In 1945 there were fewer than 500,000 acres
(202,340 ha) of sown pasture; by 1956 the area had more than doubled,
and by 1970 it had reached 1,996,000 acres (807,756 ha). This

substantial improvement in the pastures has resulted in an increase in the carrying capacity of the land, and the flocks and herds have grown steadily year by year.

The number of sheep passed the 2 million mark in 1948; ten years later it passed 3 million, and in 1966, 4 million. By 1970 the sheep flocks had reached the record size of 4,560,000. In 1950 there were 275,000 cattle in Tasmania; 10 years later the number had surpassed 375,000; and in the following decade the herds increased rapidly to reach 646,000 in 1970. Almost every branch of the pastoral industry has shown a significant expansion in output. During the decade ending in 1971 the production of meat rose from less than 50,000 to over 63,000 tons annually; the output of milk rose from 78 to 103 million gallons; of butter, from 12,000 to 15,000 tons; of cheese from only 605 tons to 5463 tons, while the exports of wool increased from 24,403 to 36,404 thousand lb.

In crop growing, Tasmania is a producer of specialities. Cereals are relatively unimportant by value, and account for only about 5 per cent of the total value of the crops. In 1969–70 hops alone equalled in value all the cereals and yet occupied less than one-fortieth of their acreage. Tasmania has long been the leading Australian State in the production of hops, and in 1970 accounted for 62 per cent of the total output. The hops are grown mainly in the New Norfolk and Hamilton districts of the Derwent valley.

Among the vegetables, potatoes and green peas rank equally in value and are well in the lead. During the 1950s and 1960s their fortunes, however, have differed: the output of potatoes has declined while that of peas has increased. The output of potatoes reached a peak in 1945, when Tasmania kept the mainland States supplied with this important food. With the reduction in their demands the Tasmanian potato crop has greatly declined both in area and quantity, though this has been accompanied by an almost doubling of the yield per acre. The production of peas, in contrast, has rapidly expanded, having risen from 20,725,000 lb (9,500,000 kg) in 1960 to 66,024,000 lb (29,700,000 kg) in 1970: they are grown for canning and deep-freezing. Both peas and potatoes are grown mainly in the north-west coastal districts of the State.

Of the orchard fruits, the apple is by far the most important, and in 1970 accounted for about 90 per cent of the total output by value. Apples constitute the chief crop of Tasmania and form a staple export of the port of Hobart; Tasmania, though the smallest State of Australia, is its leading producer of apples, and accounted for one-third of the total Australian output, from only 19 per cent of the apple-orchard land.

Apples were introduced to Tasmania by the first settlers when they arrived in the early nineteenth century. It soon became apparent that they grew quickly and yielded rich returns. The climate was more suitable than that of the mainland: Tasmania offered an assured and well distributed rainfall of 25 to 40 inches (635–1016 mm) annually; it enjoyed more than 2000 hours of sunshine during the year, and in the lowlands almost seven months free from frost.

The export trade developed rapidly during the 1850s, with shipments mainly to Victoria and New South Wales, but also to New Zealand, California, the Pacific Islands and India. In part this was to satisfy the needs of the seekers after gold in California (1849), Victoria (1851) and New Zealand (the 1860s).

Hitherto the industry had been singularly free from pests; but during the 1860s and 1870s the orchards were ravaged by the codlin moth and for a time it seemed that the whole industry faced destruction. The infestation had two permanent effects: it resulted in a concentration of apple growing in the far south, and it marked the beginning of governmental guidance in the spheres of cultivation, marketing and pest control.[2]

The 1880s and 1890s were important formative years. Pruning and spraying became normal practice in the orchards; improved varieties

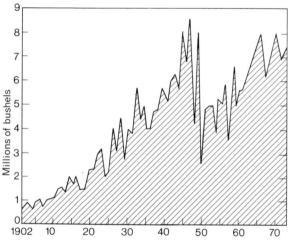

Fig. 21.—Tasmania: production of apples and pears since 1902. The general trend has been an increasing output from a declining area. Fluctuations are due to changing weather conditions; the war-time peaks were related to exceptional financial arrangements.

were planted, and the development of refrigeration opened up the distant British market to Tasmanian apples. The harvest of 164,000 bushels of 1882 grew to one of over a million bushels in 1904. About the turn of the century two-thirds of the exports went to New South Wales and most of the remainder to the United Kingdom.

Since the 1920s the trend has been towards a fluctuating but generally increasing crop from a steadily declining area; there has been a quite dramatic increase in yield, from 100 bushels to the acre in 1916 to as much as 516 bushels in 1970. Peak outputs were reached during the Second World War, but these are held to be exceptional because they were related to compensatory payments by the Commonwealth government. A post-war peak of over 8 million bushels was achieved in 1965–66, and outputs in the later 1960s have been not far below (Fig. 21).

Apple growing is a highly intensive form of cultivation. From only 5 per cent of the crop land of the State is produced 35 per cent of Tasmania's total agricultural output by value. It has resulted in a neat

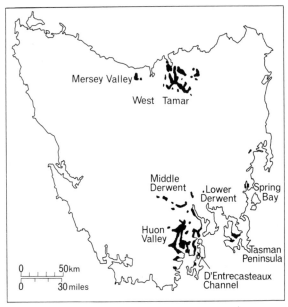

FIG. 22.—Location of the chief apple and pear orchard districts. Tasmania produces nearly one-third of the apples of Australia. About three-quarters of the crop is grown in the southern districts.

and orderly landscape of rectangular orchard plots, with their apple trees carefully pruned to the shape of inverted umbrellas, centred on white weather-boarded farmhouses together with the associated cold stores and packing sheds. About three-quarters of the orchard land is in and around the Huon valley in the south of the island; most of the remainder is in the Tamar valley in the north (Fig. 22).

Each year Tasmania exports about $3\frac{1}{2}$ million bushels of apples to the United Kingdom, Scandinavia and the East, and more than $\frac{1}{2}$ million bushels to the Australian mainland. Tasmanian apples arrive in the English greengrocers' shops from Christmas to March, in company with fruit from the mainland of Australia and from Italy. In addition, this small State ships 8 million lb (3·6 million kg) of jams and jellies, $6\frac{1}{2}$ million lb (2·9 million kg) of pulped fruit, $1\frac{1}{2}$ million lb (0·7 million kg) of dried apples, and 50,000 gallons (227,000 litres) of juices and syrups. Tasmania is the only Australian State which produces no grapes or citrus fruits. She is by far the leading State for the production of apples, and apples form 80 per cent (by value) of her total fruit production. Similarly, though the output is much smaller, Tasmania is the leading producer of small fruit in Australia (*see* Table 5).

TABLE 5

Australia: production of apples and small fruits, 1970–71

State	Apples (thousand bushels)	Small fruits (acres)
Tasmania	7,373	1,529
New South Wales	4,016	127
Victoria	5,079	835
Western Australia	3,156	25
South Australia	1,583	212
Queensland	2,025	310
Australia	23,232	3,038

THE PATTERN OF SETTLEMENT

Tasmania has a settlement structure that differs greatly from that of the mainland States. In each of these the population tends to concentrate on a well-watered coastal fringe and to thin out in a dry interior. Typically the State capital contains half or more of the total population, and the rural sector is quite small.

Tasmania differs from this type in every respect (Table 6). Its metropolitan population is not only the smallest in an absolute sense, but it forms the smallest proportion of the total among all the Australian States. Its other urban population forms a higher proportion than in any other State, and so does its rural population. In sum, compared with the other States, Tasmania has a more even balance among the three categories of population and a more even spread throughout the territory of the State.

TABLE 6

Australian States: percentage of urban and rural population, 1966

State	Metropolitan population	Other urban population	Rural population
New South Wales	57·8	28·6	13·4
Victoria	65·5	20·0	14·4
Queensland	43·2	33·6	23·1
South Australia	66·7	16·0	17·3
Western Australia	59·8	16·8	23·1
Tasmania	32·2	38·1	29·6
Australia, average	54·2	25·5	20·2

In other States the chief element that restricts the spread of settlement is drought, but in Tasmania it is the rainy, rugged and forested western third of the State that lacks population. Here the only settlements are those associated with mining, such as Rosebery and Zeehan. Elsewhere,

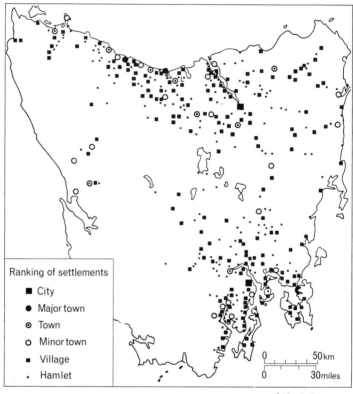

FIG. 23.—Tasmania: distribution of settlements. Tasmania has a far more even spread of settlement than any other State. Basically this may be attributed to its well-distributed rainfall. The 395 settlements shown in the diagram have been ranked as follows: 2 cities, 2 major towns, 9 towns, 20 minor towns, 171 villages and 191 hamlets.

however, there is a remarkably even scatter of hamlets, villages and towns of various rank. Tasmania more than any other Australian State offers opportunities to test the theory of central places (Fig. 23).

A study published in 1964 distinguishes six ranks in the hierarchy of Tasmanian settlements, which are grouped in accordance with the functions that they serve.[3] Of the 395 places examined, 191 are classed as hamlets and a further 171 as villages. Both are widely distributed throughout the farming districts of the north, north-east, centre and south-east. Typically the hamlet possesses only a Post Office and a telephone exchange, though in remote places the hamlet may also have a school and a general store. Most villages in addition have a church, a hall, a service station and a carrier.

The towns are subdivided into three ranks—minor towns, towns and major towns. The 20 minor towns range in population from about 800 to 2800 inhabitants; characteristically they each possess a doctor and a bank, together with a range of shopping opportunities. Many of them have developed important industries such as canning and preserving and saw-milling for the districts that they serve.

The nine fully-fledged towns range in population from 1600 to about 6000. Typically they have developed specialised shopping facilities such as furniture and jewellery, and maintain hospitals and fire brigades. In the north of Tasmania minor towns alternate with fully-fledged towns in a regular way; but in the south there are only minor towns, for all other necessary services are performed by Hobart.

There are only two major towns: Burnie (1971 population: 20,088) and Devonport (1971 population: 18,150). Both are ports on the north coast. Their shopping facilities include department stores and suppliers of such specialised goods as sewing machines and office equipment. Their services include technical colleges, offices of the Hydro-Electricity Commission and of the Supreme Court of Tasmania.

The two cities are Launceston (1971 population: 62,181) and Hobart (129,808), and they are sufficiently far apart to serve separate regions. Typical functions include a teachers' college, a museum and art gallery, a concert hall, and offices of the Commonwealth Government departments. Some specialisation however has occurred: Hobart has certain specific cultural and administrative functions, while Launceston is pre-eminently commercial. Thus Hobart houses the university and the State government and parliament, while Launceston has the State railway workshops and is the centre for the sorting and distribution of the Tasmanian mails.

THE REGIONS OF TASMANIA

On a basis of climate, geology and human activities we may distinguish five regions in Tasmania (Fig. 24), as follows: (1) the North-West, with cattle pastures and potato-fields on the lowlands and mining towns in the interior; (2) the South-West, largely virgin land; (3) the North, a region of mixed farming; (4) the Midlands or Central Plateau, with some grazing land, but of interest chiefly on account of its resources of water power; and (5) the Southern and South-Eastern Lowlands, noted for their orchards.

THE NORTH-WEST

The boundaries of the North-West may be placed as follows: on the east, from the coast midway between the Tamar and Mersey, south-west to the major water divide, and west to Macquarie Harbour. So defined, the North-West includes both the broadest extent of lowland in the island and also the highest mountain masses, with their cirques, knife-edged ridges and rounded valley profiles characteristic of glaciation.

Climatically and geologically this is a distinct region. There is a heavy rainfall throughout, reaching more than 1270 mm (50 in) per annum everywhere except for a narrow strip along the north coast; the farmer therefore concentrates on growing fodder and root crops rather than grain. The rocks include the older Palaeozoics (from Cambrian to Silurian) with granitic intrusions, and associated with the latter are the mineral deposits which have given a distinctive stamp to this portion of Tasmania. There are in addition old lava flows, and these have aided the formation of deep and friable, well-drained soils, reddish to chocolate-brown in colour. The granite masses, the reddish soils, the heavy rainfall, the rich pastures, and the tin and copper mines—all these are reminiscent of the South-West Peninsula of England.

The coastal lowlands stand in contrast with the inland plateaus. On the plateaus the heavy rainfall has encouraged the growth of tall evergreen beeches, which rise to 200 feet (61 m) above a dense undergrowth of shrubs—quite different from the eucalypt forest in other parts of the island; the lowlands include some of the most fertile and prosperous farmlands in Tasmania, and contain about one-third of its crop acreage and about one-quarter of its stock population (Fig. 24).

The farmer concentrates upon cattle, and produces both beef and milk. There are 30,000 head in the region, and half the cultivated area is used to grow forage crops to feed them. On King Island (Fig. 4), at the western entrance of Bass Strait, dairying is the chief concern, and the co-operative butter factory there produces more than 500 tons (508 t) a year. Dairying is important on the coastal lowlands generally, while the Circular Head district, near the north-west corner of the island, is noted for its production of prime beef. Each year this part of Tasmania produces about 1000 tons (1016 t) of butter and 300 tons (305 t) of cheese; it is also the chief producer of potatoes and of green peas.

This north-western coastal strip of Tasmania is the leading district in Australia for the production of vegetables for quick freezing. It is a recent development, which dates only from the Second World War. Doubtless, the mild winters favour the growth of vegetables; but equally important is the fact that the north coast of Tasmania has close trading connections with the belt of greatest population in Australia.

Two large concerns control the industry, and at the height of the season their factories at Ulverstone and Devonport employ about 1000 people. The activity is highly organised: many thousands of acres are under contract to the works, and radio-equipped cars are used to transmit reports on the progress of the crops. Frozen peas and French beans form the leading items, but many other products are frozen or canned: they include broccoli, Brussels sprouts, cauliflowers, carrots,

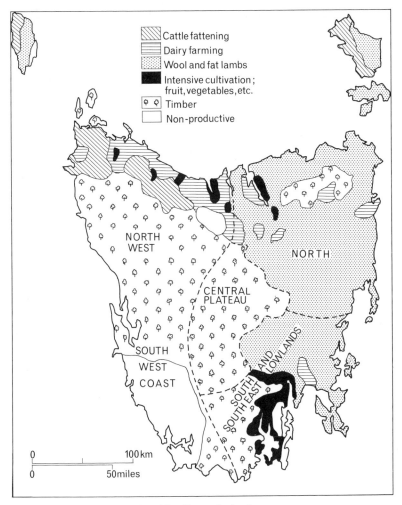

Cattle fattening
Dairy farming
Wool and fat lambs
Intensive cultivation;
fruit, vegetables, etc.
Timber
Non-productive

NORTH
WEST

NORTH

CENTRAL
PLATEAU

SOUTH
WEST
COAST

SOUTH AND LOWLANDS

SOUTH EAST

0   100 km
0   50 miles

FIG. 24.—Tasmania: land use.

broad beans, beetroots, sweet corn, swede turnips, asparagus, mush-
rooms, strawberries—and fish. Most of the produce is shipped, chiefly
to mainland Australia, through the port of Devonport.

Among the commercial centres for the region are Latrobe (with a
population of 4860 in 1968), Ulverstone (10,780) and Wynyard
(10,300); all are coastal towns and joined by rail.

Settlement in the north-west was established originally not by farming but by mining. Until the 1850s Tasmania was regarded as little
more than a convenient dumping ground for convicts. Then in 1851
gold was discovered in Victoria: there was an immediate demand for
foodstuffs of all kinds, and in the course of two years the value of

Tasmanian shipments to the mainland almost trebled. At the same time the magnet of gold attracted from the island the most active section of her population, and the number of adult males fell by nearly 50 per cent.

Nevertheless, within a generation or so, Tasmania herself was found to contain valuable minerals. In 1871 the tin deposits of Mount Bischoff were discovered; six years later gold was found at Beaconsfield; in 1884 gold-thirsty prospectors, following the trail inland, unlocked instead the famous copper deposits of Mount Lyell; and in the following year silver–lead ores were discovered at Zeehan. Three of these mining districts—Mounts Lyell, Bischoff and Zeehan—have in their time been among the most renowned in the Commonwealth.

Mount Lyell. Mount Lyell is still one of the world's great copper producers: it accounts for about 90 per cent of the output of copper in Tasmania, and about 13 per cent of the Australian total. The workings extend in a zone northwards from Gormanston for about two miles, and after 1935 the bulk of the ore was won from open-cast pits. During the early 1970s the company developed large-scale underground mining, and most of the 2·4 million tons of ore that are currently being processed annually are from this source.

The ores travel by electric tramway through a tunnel to Queenstown, about a mile distant, for concentration. This town, with a 1965 population of 4551, was built almost overnight following the Mount Lyell discoveries. It is still largely a "company town," for the works employ about 1500 people. Power is supplied by a hydro-electric installation at Lake Margaret, seven miles away. From Queenstown the concentrates pass over the company's private railway to Macquarie Harbour for shipment: they are refined at Port Kembla or in Japan.

Port Kembla is an artificial harbour 45 miles (72 km) south of Sydney, and here has been established the largest copper-manufacturing plant in Australia. The metal is cast into bars and the gold and silver elements are recovered. Close financial ties exist between the mining company in Tasmania and the manufacturing company in New South Wales; there is a two-way traffic, since New South Wales supplies the coke needed in the Queenstown furnaces.

Currently Mount Lyell is increasing its output, and this is beginning to show in the statistics:

TABLE 7

Tasmania: output of copper concentrates

			Tons
1966	.	.	55,981
1967	.	.	55,600
1968	.	.	54,600
1969	.	.	59,940
1970	.	.	84,550
1971	.	.	86,455

Twenty miles (32 km) farther north, at Rosebery, are flourishing zinc mines. Zinc has many specialist uses, for example in dental preparations and paint manufacture; but its most familiar application is for coating iron sheeting and steel wire as a protection against rust. This is particularly relevant to Australia, where there is an enormous demand for corrugated iron for farm buildings and wire netting for the fencing of properties (*see* p. 53). Australia is therefore fortunate in possessing substantial resources of zinc, and ranks as the fourth producer of this metal in the world, after the United States, Canada and the U.S.S.R.

Most of the Australian output is from New South Wales; but Tasmania produces about 9 per cent of the total, almost entirely from the Rosebery mine, at the foot of Mount Read where there are over a thousand employees. Following the completion of a new shaft in 1971, its output has doubled. The ores also yield silver, lead and copper; they are transported by rail northward to Burnie, and thence shipped for smelting to Risdon, near Hobart.

Since 1965 there have been important developments relating to tin and iron mining in the rugged north-west of Tasmania, which has witnessed a new surge of mineral activity.

From the 1870s till the late 1940s Tasmania was a significant source of tin, and the Mount Bischoff mine, which ceased to operate shortly after the Second World War, was in its day the world's greatest producer of tin. Its closure meant disaster for the town of Waratah, which shrank from 2000 to only 325 people (1965). Recently there has been a renewed interest in tin: it stems in part from the high price that the metal commands and in part from the discovery of a new and accessible body of tin estimated to contain 11 million tons at Renison Bell, about 28 miles (42 km) south of Mount Bischoff. In 1965 work began on the opening of a new mine and the erection of a mill and separation plant, while a new housing estate for the workers was constructed at Zeehan, 12 miles (19 km) farther south.

A rapid expansion in the output of concentrate has followed:

TABLE 8

Tasmania: production of tin concentrates

			Tons
1966	.	.	1,510
1967	.	.	2,352
1968	.	.	5,154
1969	.	.	8,072
1970	.	.	9,077
1971	.	.	11,415

Once again Tasmania has a flourishing tin industry, and is now the leading Australian State in the production of this mineral. In 1970–71, the assayed tin content of the total concentrate produced in Australia

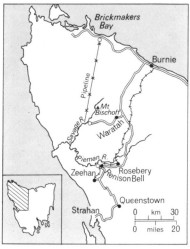

FIG. 25.—North-west Tasmania: mineral development. Mining has brought a new surge of activity to the mountainous north-west of Tasmania. Tin is being worked at Renison Bell and iron at Savage river.

[*After R. J. Soloman, 1966.*

[*Courtesy Department of Film Production, Tasmania.*

FIG. 26.—Tasmania: the Savage river iron-ore mine. Tasmania for the first time has become an important producer of iron ore. The deposits occur in remote and mountainous forested country and the concentrates are conveyed to the coast by a novel method—through a pipeline.

amounted to 8750 tons; and of this, Tasmania accounted for 5238 tons.

During the same period an important iron mining project reached fruition within the same region. The iron deposit is situated about 25 miles (40 km) by road west of Mount Bischoff (Fig. 25); its relatively low iron content of 38 per cent entails the incorporation of a pellet plant. Like the developments at Pilbara (p. 283), this project has been carried through with the help of American technology and created to supply the needs of the Japanese steel industry.

At the ore body at Savage river an open-cast mine has been inaugurated and a town and concentration plant constructed (Fig. 26). A new road links it to the Murchison Highway and Macquarie Harbour, and an airstrip on the site provides for more rapid transport. In this remote spot the problem of conveying the concentrate to a pellet plant and port has been solved in truly American fashion. A 56-mile (90-km) pipeline has been built to a spot near Brickmaker's Bay, east of Stanley on the north-west coast. Through this the finely ground concentrate is pumped in suspension in water, to reach the pellet plant. Here it is dried, rolled into balls, hardened by heat, and shipped from a new jetty in the form of pellets with an iron content of 67 per cent.[4]

Development costs have been £31 million, and a thousand men have been employed on construction work. The permanent labour force runs into hundreds and provides welcome opportunities in what was until recently a declining district. A 20-year contract with Japan provides for shipments of 2 to 3 million tons of pellets annually to a total of 60 million tons; from this the State will receive in royalties about £4½ million.

As the statistics indicate, the flow has begun:

TABLE 9

Tasmania: production of iron ore

				Tons
1967	.	.	.	—
1968	.	.	.	708,399
1969	.	.	.	1,962,849
1970	.	.	.	1,917,975
1971	.	.	.	2,158,641

Burnie. The main industrial and commercial centre for the North-West is Burnie, which, with a 1972 population of 20,000, is the third largest centre in Tasmania. The town is old by Australian standards: it was founded in 1829 as a port and settlement for the Van Diemen's Land Company. But its population numbered only 200 in 1871, when the rich deposits of tin were discovered at Mount Bischoff. Burnie became the port for the tin mines: a horse tramway was built to Waratah, and was reconstructed for stream trains in 1884. Its modern successors are the ore trains, hauled by four diesel locomotives, that transport to Burnie annually 240,000 tons of zinc, lead and copper concentrates from the Rosebery mines, 330,000 tons of iron pyrites from the mines of Rosebery and Mount Lyell and 100,000 tons of copper concentrates from Mount Lyell.

Until 1937 Burnie was basically a centre for dairy farming, potato growing and timber milling. In that year, however, paper mills were established which have grown to become the largest industrial undertaking of the district. They comprise two sawmills, a pulp mill, a hardboard mill, and two paper mills with nine paper-making machines. The total employment, about 3600 people, amounts to half the working population of the district.

In addition, Burnie is the headquarters of the largest dairy company in Tasmania, and has an important meat-freezing works. It manufactures sulphuric acid from the iron sulphide (iron pyrites) mined at Mount Lyell and Rosebery, and produces titanium pigments from ilmenite mined near Bunbury, in Western Australia (p. 276).

The port activities of Burnie are second in Tasmania only to those of Hobart. The exports consist mainly of paper, hardboard, titanium pigments and ore concentrates. The traffic is expanding. In recent years provision has been made for the increasing flow of concentrates, the growing imports of petroleum products and for the car and lorry ferries with the mainland States. A container terminal has been established. In 1972 the port was used by 420 vessels, and 1·3 million tons of cargo were handled.

THE SOUTH-WEST COAST

The South-West Coast may be defined as the land which lies to the west of the Gordon river and the Franklin and Arthur Ranges. Like the North-West, this too is a region of high mountains and heavy rainfall; but there the resemblance ends. There is practically no fringing plain: it is a wild and rugged coastline where virgin forests of sassafras, blackwood and Huon pine grow from the water's edge to the skyline. In a region 125 miles (201 km) long and 50 miles (80 km) broad there are only two small coastal settlements. There is no railway, no motor road and virtually no farming.

THE NORTH

The inland boundary of the North may be placed at the Great Western Mountains; the region therefore comprises a coastal lowland, about 100 miles (161 km) long from Latrobe to Eddystone, and 20 miles (32 km) broad; the basin of the Macquarie river, which forms a southward extension of that lowland; and a mountain mass dominated by the second highest peak in Tasmania, Ben Lomond—5010 feet (1528 m). The centre for this wide region is Launceston, situated where the Macquarie river becomes the Tamar estuary.

The lowland portions of the North are blessed with an adequate but not excessive rainfall, though exposed districts of the plateaus receive almost as much as corresponding districts in the west of the island. Thus, at Ringarooma, about 1500 feet (457 m) above sea-level, the rain gauge in 1955–56 registered 79·4 inches (1778 mm), while on the coast, only 25 miles (40 km) away, Bridport received 47·7 inches (1206 mm). The Macquarie and South Esk river basins are ringed with hills and favoured with much lower falls, and here, near Ross, is the driest spot on the island, receiving only 18 inches (457 mm) per annum on the average. 1955–56 was a wet season: 35 inches (889 mm) of rain fell in the South Esk valley, while Launceston, rather more exposed to the south-westerly winds, received 43·1 inches (1095 mm). Its mean is 28·1 inches (713 mm) per annum.

As in the North-West, about half the total crop acreage is devoted to hay and other forage crops for cattle. This region is the foremost stock-farming province of the State. All branches are represented: breeding and fattening of cattle, dairy farming, wool production and the market-ing of fat lambs, with the raising of pigs as an additional farm activity. But here too are the chief grain-growing districts of Tasmania, with the emphasis on malting barley, wheat and oats. While orchards are more typical in the south of the island, there are 3000 acres (1214 ha) under apples and pears in the Tamar valley, and another 1000 acres (405 ha) of orchard land in the sheltered Mersey valley to the west. As in the North-West, potatoes and green peas are grown, but in far smaller quantities.

The northern flanks of the plateaus contain an isolated mineral-bearing region, which supports several small settlements, such as Weldborough, Moorina and Derby; their tin was shipped from the small port of St Helens, to the east, until the silting of its lagoon-like harbour brought about its decline. Tin is still produced about 50 miles (80 km) north-east of Launceston, at Gladstone and South Mt Cameron.

The east coast has magnificent cliffs, mountains and forests, and there are several tourist resorts, such as Bicheno, Scamander and the former port of St Helens. Freycinet Peninsula, with its precipitous cliffs of red granite, its white sandy beaches and its carpets of colourful wild flowers, is reserved as a National Park.

Launceston. The focal point of the North-East is Launceston (population of urban area, 1971: 62,181)—the commercial capital for the whole of the northern part of the State, and the second city in Tasmania. Launceston stands at the head of the Tamar estuary, which is navigable for vessels of up to 4000 tons; here the North Esk meets the Macquarie, amid productive orchard land and close to some of the finest cascade and gorge scenery in Australia. The coastal plain allows easy transport by road and rail to the east and west; to the south is the Macquarie valley, followed by the trunk railway line. Launceston pos-sesses the great advantage that it faces the mainland, with which Tasmania has strong trading connections. Melbourne is 265 miles (426 km) away. Since 1900 the city has doubled its population, and it may well surpass Hobart to become the leading commercial centre of Tasmania. Launceston is an important market centre for stock, grain and wool. Its industries include sawmilling, engineering and the production of knitting yarns. Here is Australia's largest wool spinning mill—that of Messrs Paton and Baldwin—which employs 2000 people. One consideration in the choice of the site was the supply of cheap electricity.

The latest industrial development of the area has taken place nearly ten miles north of the city, on the right bank of the estuary, just south of Georgetown. Here, at Bell Bay, are the works of Comalco Aluminium Ltd. The site borders a sheltered waterway—a drowned valley—with 33 feet (10 m) of water in the approaches, so that vessels laden with bauxite can berth at the wharves adjoining the works. Cheap hydroelectric power, always of prime importance in the aluminium industry, is supplied by the Trevallyn plant, the only generating station outside the Central Plateau.

Trevallyn lies to the west of the city. The South Esk river has been dammed to form a lake three miles long, and its water passes through the intervening ridge by a $2\frac{1}{4}$-mile (3·5-km) tunnel, allowing a gross head of 415 feet (117 m) of water. Rather more than a third of the power produced is used in the aluminium works. In 1963 the capacity of the works was raised from 15,000 tons to 32,000 tons of ingots; by 1966 it had reached 56,000 tons, and by 1972, 94,000 tons. The remaining electric power serves the needs of Launceston and its growing industries. One result of the aluminium plant has been to transform the small fishing settlement of George Town (1949 population, 350) into a thriving new town of over 4000 people.

THE CENTRAL PLATEAU

This region, bounded by the major water-parting of the island on the west, and by the Great Western Mountains on the east, forms a rolling plateau whose surface lies generally more than 2000 feet (609 m) above the sea, but from which isolated summits rise to more than 4000 feet (1218 m). Sheltered by the major divide, it has a surprisingly low rainfall. Precipitation diminishes rapidly eastwards, so that most of the plateau receives less than 40 inches (1000 mm) of rain annually (on the average), and this even includes most of the Great Western Mountains.

The land is largely given over to grazing. Where crops are grown at all they consist chiefly of hay, green fodder and root crops, and these make up two-thirds of the total crop land. On the sheltered and lower southern border mixed farming is possible, with the growing of potatoes, oats and peas, together with some hops.

The chief geographical significance of the Central Plateau, however, lies not in the resources of the soil but in its possibilities for the production of hydro-electricity. Here are some of the largest fresh-water lakes of Australia; they lie for the most part above the 3000-foot (914-m) contour; they enjoy a well-distributed rainfall and they do not lose much by evaporation. Here, then, are almost ideal conditions for the development of water power, and there is hardly a stream which does not contribute to the electrical energy of the State. While the details of the development schemes are complex, one or two features have given a distinct stamp to hydro-electric power production in Tasmania.

First we must emphasise the importance of hydro-electricity to Tasmania. Until the opening of the oil-fired power station at Bell Bay in 1971 Tasmania was unique among the Australian States in basing its electricity system entirely on water power. Considered simply as an employer, the State Hydro-electric Commission occupies an important place in the economy: it ranks as the largest public corporation in

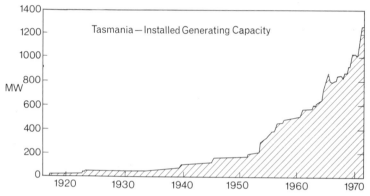

FIG. 27.—Tasmania: hydro-electric development since 1920. Tasmania is fortunate in the possession of abundant resources of water power, and has had the enterprise and skill to develop them. The graph illustrates the increasing pace of expansion in the total capacity of the power stations.

Tasmania and employs more than 5000 people. The consumption of electricity is a fair indication of the rate of economic progress of any region, and by this criterion the pace has quickened substantially since the middle 1950s (Fig. 27).

Second we notice its long history: the earliest generating station in Tasmania was at Duck Reach, near Launceston, and was opened as early as 1895. This competes with the first plant at Niagara Falls for the title of the world's first hydro-electric station. With an initial rating of 600 horse-power, its capacity was enlarged several times, and the plant ceased operating as recently as 1955, when the Trevallyn power station superseded it.

Third, we must applaud the enterprise, skill and vision of the engineers, who have not been afraid of moulding nature to their requirements. Swamps have been converted into storage basins; water from one river crosses a valley to feed another; it passes through tunnels below mountain ranges; and the same water is used again and again through turbine after turbine. The purpose of all these schemes is power development: navigation and irrigation play no part in them.

There are twenty-one generating stations in Tasmania (Table 10), and all except one (Trevallyn) are in the Central Plateau. Four main streams drain the region, and pursue their parallel courses southwards: from east to west they are the Ouse, the Dee, the Nive and the Derwent itself. Each has its generating plant. The Great Lake has been dammed and its water directed southwards by canals to the Ouse, turning on the way the turbines of the Shannon and twin Waddamana stations. Use has been made of the considerable drop in level of the middle Nive river: a canal from Pine Tier Dam leads the water gently along to a high-level plateau, where former swamps have been converted into lakes (Bronte Lagoon, Brady's Lake, Lake Binney and Tungatinah Lagoon); these have been swollen by water from the upper Ouse and Lake Echo, and so a head of a thousand feet (305 m) has been prepared. Here is Tungatinah power station: opened in 1956, it has a capacity of 125 MW. The neighbouring Tarraleah plant, with a capacity of 90 MW, utilises the run-off from the Lake St Clair catchment area. Largest of all is Poatina station (250 MW), which utilises a head of 2720 feet from the Great Lake in a single underground plant.

The last few years have witnessed a surge in the power programme: since 1966 no fewer than ten new generating stations have been opened

TABLE 10

Tasmania: hydro-electric power stations

Station				Year of completion	Head feet	Capacity MW
Poatina	.	.	.	1965	2720	250
Tungatinah	.	.	.	1956	1005	125
Tarraleah	.	.	.	1971	981	90
Cethana	.	.	.	1971	324	85
Liapootah	.	.	.	1960	361	83·7
Trevallyn	.	.	.	1955	415	80
Devils Gate	.	.	.	1969	226	60
Lemonthyme	.	.	.	1969	523	51
Waddamana B	.	.	.	1949	1127	48
Catagunya	.	.	.	1962	142	48
Fisher	.	.	.	1972	103	43·2
Meadowbank	.	.	.	1967	95	40
Wayatinah	.	.	.	1957	203	38·25
Lake Echo	.	.	.	1956	568	32·4
Wilmot	.	.	.	1971	825	30·6
Repulse	.	.	.	1968	88	28
Paloona	.	.	.	1972	103	28
Cluny	.	.	.	1967	51	17
Butlers Gorge	.	.	.	1951	184	12·2
Rowallan	.	.	.	1968	161	10
Tods Corner	.	.	.	1966	136	1·6
Under construction						
Gordon (stage 1)	.	.	.	1976	610	240

(Table 10). In 1972 the impressive Mersey–Forth power scheme of north-central Tasmania was completed. This exploits the Fisher, Mersey, Wilmot and Forth rivers by means of 7 large dams, 3 major tunnels and 7 power stations.

An important project scheduled for completion by 1976 will add a generating plant of 240 MW capacity, almost as great as the largest of the existing power stations (Poatina: 250 MW). The catchment area straddles the watershed between the Serpentine and the Huon rivers in a district of heavy rainfall (over 80 inches (2032 mm) per annum) in the south-west of the State. Three dams and a levee will impound a huge new reservoir which will be the largest in Australia, and seven or eight times as large as Tasmania's Great Lake. The power station will be built in a man-made cavern excavated from the solid rock close to the main dam (the Gordon Dam) and 610 feet (186 m) below the lake surface. No one will be employed at the power station: it will be remotely controlled from Hobart—100 miles (161 km) away!

Many varied industries are nourished by the power stations of the island. They include zinc smelting at Rosebery (on the west coast) and at Risdon (near Hobart); cement production at Railton (near Latrobe on the north coast); pulp and paper-making at Burnie (on the north coast) and near New Norfolk (close to Hobart); copper smelting at Queenstown (near Macquarie Harbour on the west coast); and the aluminium industry of the Launceston district. In relation to its size Tasmania thus ranks highly in respect of power production. About one-fifth of all the electricity used by Australian industry is consumed in this small State.

THE SOUTHERN AND SOUTH-EASTERN LOWLANDS

In the south-east of the island a number of deep and fertile river valleys, most of them tributaries of the Derwent, lead to an intricate coastline where a relative sinking of the land has drowned the valley mouths and studded the shore with rocky islands. Sheltered from the north-westerly winds, the region enjoys a low rainfall—much of it receives less than 25 inches (635 mm) per annum. Hobart, the focal centre of the region, has a mean annual rainfall of almost exactly 25 inches (635 mm), very similar in amount to that of London. But in other respects the climate is more favourable than the corresponding parts of England. In Hobart the mean temperature of the coldest month (July: 8° C; 46·6° F) is 6° F higher than that for London. It is a sunny region: in the Derwent valley one can expect nearly eight hours of sunshine a day in the summer, and four hours even in mid-winter.

The outlying valleys to the north-east and south-west are somewhat isolated and boast no railway: here agriculture is only on a small scale, and the farmers concentrate on hay, fodder crops, potatoes and vegetables. Life in the region is seen most typically in the Derwent valley, with its 14,000 (5665 ha) acres of orchard land. This is the apple

[*Courtesy Australian News & Information Bureau.*

FIG. 28.—Tasmania: apple orchards at Cygnet, in the Huon Estuary.

district of Tasmania (Fig. 28). Apple orchards are to be seen in the fertile alluvial lands of the Derwent valley, in the lowlands south of Hobart, in Tasman's Peninsula, and in North and South Bruny Island.

The fruit grower will have perhaps 15 acres (6 ha) of apple trees and an acre or two of pears; on the hillside he may plant raspberries, strawberries, blackcurrants, loganberries or gooseberries. He cultivates wheat, oats or potatoes on another 15 acres (6 ha), or he rears cattle, poultry or pigs; and his holding usually includes a large area of "bush," part of which can be improved as circumstances permit. He arranges his activities in such a way that they do not compete for labour at the peak of the apple season. He does not market his own fruit, but sends it to a central packing station, which may be organised on a co-operative basis.

While apples are the mainstay of the region, other fruits are grown in smaller quantities. Many properties are mixed farms, which include 10 or 15 acres (4 or 6 ha) of apricots or peaches, cherries or quinces. Practically all the apricots and the berry fruits are grown for processing—for canning, jam-making or for juices; and an important fruit concern (with the brand name IXL) has jam-making and canning plants in Hobart and at seven other centres in the island. Small quantities of strawberries, however, are rushed by air to the mainland.

Hobart. The centre of the South-East is Hobart. Founded in 1804, the city takes its name from Lord Hobart, Earl of Buckinghamshire, who was then Secretary of State for the Colonies. It is in a fine setting for a state capital, where the mountains overlook the sea; and the city spreads up the flanks of Mount Wellington (4166 feet; 1270 m). On the right (western) bank of the Derwent lies the port, with its docks and wharves, where the largest ocean freighters can berth at all states of the tide, to pick up cargoes of fruit, chilled meat, dairy produce or timber in readiness for a journey half-way round the world. Facing the port from the opposite shore are the sandy beaches and hotels of the seaside suburb of Bellerive.

In contrast, a few miles upstream is the industrial suburb of Risdon, where vessels from Burnie in the north-west of the island discharge their zinc concentrates for processing. Here the works of the Electrolytic Zinc Company supply the whole of the zinc requirements of Australia, leaving a margin for export to India and the United Kingdom, while their superphosphates plant produces sufficient of this fertiliser for the whole of Tasmania. This plant, which employs about 2500 people, is one of the world's largest refineries of zinc. Its establishment at Risdon was largely due to the existence of cheap electricity together with deep-water port facilities. Zinc refining gives rise to many valuable by-products, as the following table indicates:

TABLE 11

Average annual output of the Electrolytic Zinc Company of Australasia, Ltd

	Tons
Zinc	145,000
Superphosphate	150,000
Sulphuric acid	250,000
Sulphate of ammonia . . .	60,000
Die-casting alloy	10,000
Zinc sulphate	600
Cadmium	250

The port benefits from several physical advantages. A coastal submergence has resulted in a series of deep yet sheltered channels, and the chosen site was a semi-circular cove whose arms formed natural breakwaters. The approaches have never needed dredging; moreover, the tidal range is exceptionaly small—only about 2 feet—so that loading and discharging takes place at open quays.

Hobart is a general port whose trade has shown a steady increase, correlating with the expansion in the urban population (Tables 12, 13).

Much of the increase in the imports consists of consumer goods and building material. Nevertheless the port is the outlet for a region with a wide range of products, several of which figure largely in its commerce.

TABLE 12

Hobart, city and suburbs, growth in population

1961 . . .	130,236
1966 . . .	141,311
1970 (estimate) .	150,910

TABLE 13

Port of Hobart, expansion of trade

Arrivals, net tons

1960–1 . . .	1,280,000
1967–8 . . .	1,519,000
1968–9 . . .	1,598,000
1969–70 . . .	1,766,000

	Imports (tons)	Exports (tons)	Total (tons)
1949–50 . . .	554,000	320,000	874,000
1959–60 . . .	740,000	535,000	1,275,000
1969–70 . . .	757,000	694,000	1,450,000

Among the imports are zinc concentrates from Burnie (north-west Tasmania) and from Port Pirie (South Australia) for the Risdon Refinery; sugar from Queensland and New South Wales, cocoa from Ghana and concentrated milk from Burnie. The last three supply the large confectionery and chocolate works of Cadbury–Schweppes at Claremont, a northern suburb.

The chief single export by value is refined zinc; this is followed by the products of the apple orchards which cluster in the hinterland of the port. Wool remains a significant item and so do foods (other than fruit) and drinks. A number of special cargoes are handled at outlying wharves and jetties and do not appear in the city docks; thus the fruit export takes place at Geeveston on the Huon River and close to the main orchard areas. The same river at Port Huon handles the export of pelletised woodpulp. The oil storage facilities have been removed recently from the main port and the new tanker berths are at Selfs Point, $2\frac{1}{2}$ miles (3·4 km) upstream. Still higher up the Derwent River at Boyer, 20 miles (32 km) from the main port, are the wharves of the Australian Newsprint Mills Ltd. Here a rapid expansion in capacity has taken place from 27,000 tons a year in 1941 to over 200,000 tons in 1972. These mills produce nearly one-half of the total Australian requirements of newsprint.

During the 1960s important new facilities were provided in the main port on space set free by the relocation of the tanker terminal. They include passenger and vehicular ferry terminals, especially in connection with the traffic with Sydney.

Hobart is an expanding port, no matter what criteria we use to measure its trade.

The crags of Mount Wellington, snow-clad for much of the year, look down on the two cathedrals, the Government House and Parliament House, the University and the busy shops and offices and the electric trams of this thriving city of over 150,000 people. Hobart lies in the most southerly outpost of the southern continent. Farther south there is only Antarctica.

NOTES

1. R. J. Solomon and A. R. Dell, "The Hobart Bushfires of February, 1967," *Australian Geographer*, Vol. X, No. 4 (1967).

2. W. E. Goodhand, "The Growth and Development of the Tasmanian Pome Fruit Industry," *Australian Geographer*, Vol. IX, No. 1 (1963).

3. P. Scott, "The Hierarchy of Central Places in Tasmania," *Australian Geographer*, Vol. IX, No. 3 (1964).

4. R. J. Solomon, "Economic Resurgence in Tasmania's West," *Australian Geographer*, Vol. X, No. 1 (1966).

STUDY QUESTIONS

1. Examine the distinctive characteristics of Tasmania.

2. Compare the climate of Tasmania with that of Wales.

3. Write a short account of minerals and mining industries in Tasmania.

4. Make a reasoned study of the fruit industry of Tasmania.

5. Compare and contrast the sites and functions of Hobart and Launceston.

6. Discuss the physical advantages that Tasmania possesses for the development of hydro-electricity.

7. Describe and explain the distribution of population in Tasmania.

Chapter VI

VICTORIA

FROM Tasmania to Victoria is a natural transition. Both border the Bass Strait; Victoria contains part of the main mass of the Great Dividing Range, of which Tasmania forms an outlying portion; and structurally both States have much in common.

But Victoria, nevertheless, has her own distinct "personality." She is the smallest mainland State of Australia, yet she is the most densely peopled: her area of 87,884 square miles (227,619 km²) represents only 3 per cent of the total surface of Australia, while her population of 3·5 millions amounts to 27 per cent of the total for the Federation. Such statements, however, should be viewed in correct perspective. Though she is the smallest mainland State, her area is about equal to that of the United Kingdom; and her density of population (30 persons per square mile), though the highest in Australia, would be regarded as extremely low in Europe: it is in fact only a little higher than that of Norway (26 per square mile), which is the lowest in Europe.

The population of Victoria is very unevenly distributed. In the far north-west large areas are virtually uninhabited owing to drought, while other large areas in the east are too mountainous for settlement. In contrast, over two-thirds of the people are crowded together in Melbourne and its suburbs, and this proportion living in the capital city is greater than in any other State of the Commonwealth.

This is not to imply that agriculture is undeveloped. Victoria in fact is the most intensively farmed State in Australia: her annual production per acre is valued at more than twice as much in any other State. She is the leading State in the production of dried fruit and dairy products and second in the production of wheat: she produces the whole of Australia's sugar beet and three-quarters of her raisins. In addition to this concentration on farm produce, Victoria is at the same time the most heavily timbered State, with 30 per cent of her surface under forest.

The boundaries of Victoria are clear. On the south is the sea; on the north the limit follows the Murray river to its source in the Australian Alps, and then passes in a straight line to Cape Howe, the most south-easterly point of the mainland. On the west, the boundary follows meridian 141° E., which passes through largely unproductive land (owing to an error in the original survey the line lies about 2½ miles (4 km) west of that meridian). Within these borders is a province whose landscape is varied, whose surface is well watered everywhere excepting the west, and whose mountains contain some of the highest summits in the continent.

CLIMATE

Climatically, Victoria lies on the border between the trade wind and the westerly wind belts. In accordance with the theory of the wind systems we should expect to find the westerly winds in winter (May, June and July) and the south-east trades in summer (November, December and January). The facts are not quite so simple, but there is an approximation to the theoretical ideal.

Records of the morning (9.0 a.m.) winds at Melbourne show that in summer south winds are the most common, with south-westerlies coming second and with northerlies, westerlies and south-easterlies almost equally as frequent. This can fairly be described as a season of variable winds. Mount Gambier, just over the border of South Australia, lies in the same latitude, but is more exposed; here the south-easterly wind is the most frequent and is followed closely by southerly and south-westerly winds. This is what theory would lead one to expect.

As the day wears on the southerly winds become stronger, and by the afternoon (3.0 p.m.) they are quite dominant, both at Melbourne and Mount Gambier. Doubtless the explanation is that the land has by now warmed sufficiently to produce an indraught of air. The winds, then, are blowing from sea to land; but this does not necessarily imply that heavy rain is experienced in these months. In fact, the records of monthly rainfall show that summer is the dry season. Both at Melbourne and Mount Gambier the driest month is February, with January and December almost equally dry. It is merely a local application of the general rule that air which moves towards the equator is becoming warmer, and therefore retains its moisture. There is *some* rain in summer, but throughout the State there is a pronounced summer minimum of rainfall, with the sole exception of the mountainous east of Gippsland, with an even distribution of rainfall throughout the year.

In winter the dominant winds at Melbourne, both morning and afternoon, are without dispute from the north, with north-westerly and north-easterly winds well behind in frequency; at Mount Gambier the north-westerly winds are most common, followed by westerlies. These winter winds are the so-called westerlies, though at Melbourne they are definitely "northerlies." It is likely that the configuration of the land plays some part here, for Melbourne is sheltered by hills both to the north-east and north-west; and it is noticeable that winds from these directions are rare. To the north, however, lies the Kilmore Gap, and we may conclude that the wind uses this route in company with the road and railway. The "westerlies," moving from warmer to cooler regions, release their moisture, and winter is the rainy half of the year. In Melbourne the wettest month is October; elsewhere in the State it is usually June.

The mean annual rainfall ranges between 10 inches (254 mm) in the far west of Victoria to more than 60 inches (1524 mm) in parts of the north-eastern highlands. These limits enclose what is perhaps the ideal rainfall for temperate regions. Nowhere is the rainfall too light and nowhere too heavy for some form of farm or forest production.

Victoria escapes the extreme temperatures which are found in some parts of the Australian mainland, for her long coastline helps to reduce winter frosts and to temper summer heats. Maximum temperatures in summer are below 24° C (75° F) along the coasts and in the hills, though they increase to 32° C (90° F) in the far north-west. Minimum temperatures in the lowlands only rarely fall below freezing point: frost occasionally causes damage to cereals and vines, but the danger is reduced by weather forecasting, together with suitable methods of control. Only in the hills is snow to be seen for any length of time. Tornadoes are almost unknown; hail is rare; and Melbourne enjoys an average of 5·6 hours of sunshine each day throughout the year.

EARLY DEVELOPMENT

We have already seen (p. 6) that in the 1830s Thomas Mitchell discovered some of the most fertile lands of Victoria, naming it "Australia Felix." Settlement began by the establishment of sheep and cattle stations, and by the time of the first census in 1838 there were 3511 inhabitants of what was then known as the District of Port Philip. It was evidently very much the pioneer area, for to every seven or eight male inhabitants there was only one female. Immigrants were entering, however, in a steady stream. The population increased to 11,700 in 1841, to 32,900 in 1846, and to 77,400 in 1851, when Victoria became a separate colony, distinct from New South Wales.

Then in June 1851, only a few weeks later, one Hiscock discovered gold at Buninyong (now a suburb of Ballarat) and reaped a Government reward of £1000. Immediately there was a great influx of adventure-seekers. The lucky few found nuggets of gold just below the surface. The world's largest—the "Welcome Stranger" nugget—was discovered near Maryborough, 35 miles (56 km) north of Ballarat: it was covered by only an inch of soil; it contained almost two hundredweights of pure gold and was sold for £9563.

At the height of the gold rush there were 40,000 people in the Ballarat gold-diggings. By 1854 the population of Victoria had risen to 236,800 and she had become the leading producer of gold in Australia; this position she retained until she was supplanted in the 1890s by Western Australia.

While the economic development of the State was stimulated by the gold discoveries, pastoral farming and agriculture provided a sounder basis of prosperity. By 1881 the population had grown to 862,000 and the pioneer stage was over, for almost half the population were now females.

FARMING IN VICTORIA

With a total of 39 million acres (16 million ha) occupied by rural holdings, Victoria has the smallest area of farmland of all the mainland States. South Australia and New South Wales possess four times as much farmland; Western Australia has seven times and Queensland almost ten times as much as Victoria. Yet on this relatively small area devoted to farming Victoria produces more wheat than either South Australia or Western Australia, and more oats, hay, potatoes and sultanas and raisins than any other State. The Victorian sheep flocks are surpassed in size by those of New South Wales and Western Australia, and the cattle herds by those of Queensland and New South Wales; yet Victoria is the leading producer of mutton and lamb and her dairy herds yield more than half of all the milk produced in Australia (Tables 14 and 15).

TABLE 14

Australia: land in rural holdings, and output of principal crops, by State, 1970–71*

State	Land in rural holdings mil. acres	Wheat mil. bush.	Oats mil. bush.	Barley mil. bush.	Hay thou. tons	Potatoes thou. tons	Sultanas & raisins thou. tons
Victoria . .	38·9	36·9	25·7	14·0	2455	272·2	159·5
New South Wales .	171·1	110·6	25·1	18·9	1355	143·4	42·8
Queensland . .	382·3	4·4	0·5	2·7	376	108·7	—
South Australia .	162·6	29·0	8·4	32·7	743	71·4	14·8
Western Australia .	283·1	108·7	28·7	33·9	662	68·1	3·2
Tasmania . .	6·5	0·3	0·5	1·3	441	71·4	—
Australia . .	1229·7	289·9	88·9	103·6	6044	735·2	220·4

* Total figures in this and other tables may conceal non-specified areas such as production in the Northern or Federal Territories.

TABLE 15

Australia: pastoral farming, by State, 1970–71

State	Sheep thou. head	Cattle thou. head	Pigs thou. head	Milk mil. gals.	Wool mil. lb
Victoria	33,761	5,061	520	899·0	430·9
New South Wales . . .	70,605	6,494	796	276·2	692·9
Queensland	14,774	7,944	491	167·6	168·8
South Australia . . .	19,166	1,196	389	103·6	259·1
Western Australia . . .	34,709	1,781	278	54·9	350·5
Tasmania	4,517	733	113	98·1	47·8
Australia	177,792	24,373	2,590	1,600·2	1,952·2

The most valuable crop by far in Victoria is wheat: it accounts for more than one-third of the total value of all the crops and for about half their total area; and normally about 65 per cent of the output is exported (Table 16).

Almost the whole of the wheat crop is grown in the Mallee, Wimmera and Northern Districts—that is, the land of the Interior Plains south of the Murray river and west of the Goulburn: here the rainfall ranges between 20 to 30 inches (508 to 762 mm) in the south and east and about 12 inches (300 mm) annually in the north-west. One of the hazards of wheat growing is the unreliable rainfall. A severe drought in the 1967–68 season cut the crop to less than half the average output; it was followed by a bumper harvest which led to a considerable surplus above the demand for export.

A quota system was therefore devised and put into operation through the *Wheat Marketing Act*, 1969: this attempts to regulate the deliveries of wheat so as to conform with the market demands. Farmers were required to reduce their acreage of wheat, and this entailed a substantial reduction in farm incomes. The 1970–71 harvest was less than half as great as that of the previous year. In place of wheat, many farmers turned to barley, whose output rose by more than 50 per cent. The production of oats and oilseeds (rape and safflower) also showed increases; thus the general effect of the drought, as in the Canadian Prairies, has been a diversification of farm interests.

TABLE 16

Victoria: gross value and area of cultivated crops, 1969–70

Crop	Gross value mil. dollars	Area, thousand acres
Wheat	116·7	3298·3
Orchard fruits	43·4	70·9
Hay, all types	38·9	1200·0
Vegetables, excluding potatoes	24·1	56·3
Sultanas, raisins, currants	21·2	49·8
Potatoes	17·0	39·8
Tobacco	15·3	
Barley	11·0	486·6
Oats	10·5	883·7
All Crops	319·7	6312·3

The orchard area of Victoria is second only to that of New South Wales. Pears, apples, peaches and oranges (in that order) are the chief fruits grown. The orchards that are within 50 miles (80 km) or so of Melbourne concentrate on table fruits; those of the Goulburn valley produce fruit for canning, while those of the Mallee region specialise in vine and citrus fruits. The Melbourne region receives 25 to 35 inches (635 to 890 mm) of rain annually; but elaborate irrigation schemes supplement the rainfall of the Goulburn valley (mean annual rainfall, 19 inches; 483 mm) and the Mallee region (only 10 inches; 254 mm annually).

Fruit growing is an expanding branch of Victorian farming, and almost all types are showing substantial increases in output. Between 1966 and 1970 the output of pears increased from 5453 thousand bushels to 7044; that of apples from 4206 to 5331; of peaches from 2603 to 2975; and of oranges from 1012 to 1280 thousand bushels. Changes in area have been only slight, and the increases have been achieved through technical progress—in the use of improved weed-icides, high-capacity spraying units for pesticides and by the lighter pruning of apple trees.

Virtually all the commercially grown grapes of Victoria are produced in the irrigated districts of the Murray river at Mildura, Robinvale and Swan Hill. The first two enjoy high summer temperatures with abundant sunshine, and, once irrigation water is assured, are climatically ideal for grapes; Swan Hill has slightly less sunshine and lower temperatures. Most of the grapes are of sultana type and are dried; about 70 per cent of the vine fruits are exported; but during the later 1960s the output of wine more than doubled (Table 17).

TABLE 17
Victoria: area and output of vineyards

	1965–6	1969–70
Vineyard area, thousand acres	48·6	49·8
Wine made, million gallons	3·2	7·3
Sultanas, thousand cwt	1047	1276
Raisins, thousand cwt	141	65
Currants, thousand cwt	63	68

Of the vegetables, potatoes are outstanding, and represent nearly half the total both by quantity and value. No other single item approaches them. Table 18 indicates the leading products from a long and varied list.

TABLE 18
Victoria: value of output of the leading vegetable crops, 1969–70

Crop	Value of output thousand dollars
Potatoes	17,002
Tomatoes	4,138
Peas, for canning	3,375
Lettuces	2,634
Cauliflowers	2,605
Carrots	2,394
Peas, in pod	2,121
All vegetables	42,550

In 1970 the numbers of cattle, sheep and pigs in Victoria each attained a record level. This was made possible by the continued improvement of the natural pastures and by the increased conservation of fodder. Victoria now produces about 60 per cent of all the meadow hay in Australia, and in addition makes appreciable quantities of oaten hay in dry years and in dry districts. In the irrigated districts there is an important output of lucerne hay.

During the 1960s substantial increases took place in the flocks and herds of Victoria and in the output of dairy produce (Tables 19 and 20). For the first time in history the dairy farmers of Victoria and Tasmania were asked to reduce their output of butter and cheese. This policy aims to match the output to the expected reduction in demand for Australian dairy produce consequent on the entry of Britain into the Common Market. Some of the surplus milk is being fed to calves in place of bought feed; and many farmers are withholding replacements to their dairy herds by selling heifer calves for beef. In this respect the Friesian is a useful breed, for the heifer calves are suitable for either dairying or beef. Milk however remains a very important element in Victorian farming, and the State currently produces about 53 per cent of all the Australian milk.

TABLE 19

Victoria: number of livestock, in thousand head

				1961	1971
Dairy cattle	.	.	.	1,717	1,974
Beef cattle	.	.	.	1,147	3,086
Sheep	.	.	.	26,620	33,761
Pigs	.	.	.	319	520

TABLE 20

Victoria: output of dairy products

				1966	1971
Milk, million gallons	.	.	.	752	899
Butter, million lb	.	.	.	251	299
Cheese, million lb	.	.	.	58	79

A characteristic feature of sheep rearing in Victoria is the relatively large element of crossbred sheep in the flocks. In Australia as a whole merinos account for 72 per cent of the sheep flocks and crossbreds a further 15 per cent; but in Victoria the corresponding figures are 49 and 32 per cent. These details illustrate the fact that the Victorian sheep farmers have an interest in lamb and mutton in addition to wool. The wool, however, remains a vital element in the economy: its value is well above that of the wheat and is usually only a little below that of all the dairy produce of the State.

Since the middle 1950s a significant element in Victorian farming has

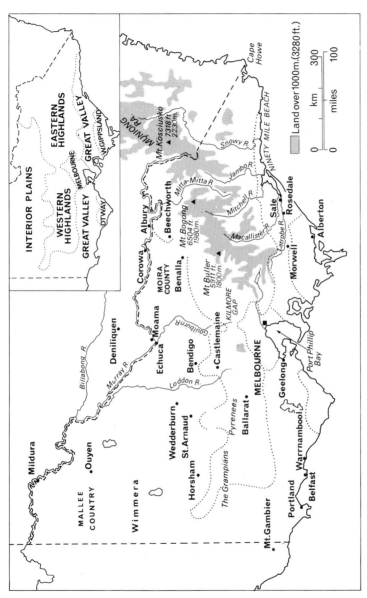

FIG. 29.—Victoria: physical features, natural regions and towns.

been the rise of the poultry industry. Chickens are efficient converters of cereals into meat and they can be multiplied rapidly: a 4 lb (1·8 kg) chicken can be reared in only nine weeks. Poultry meat, once a luxury, is now part of the normal diet. In contrast to most of the other Victorian farm products, poultry meat is largely consumed locally, and the chief producing centres are located close to the capital. A typical broiler house produces between 10 and 15 thousand chickens four times a year; and one family can raise up to 200,000 birds a year.

THE REGIONS OF VICTORIA

For the purpose of regional description we may distinguish five provinces: the hills of Otway and western Gippsland; the Great Valley; the Victorian Highlands; the interior plains; and the Melbourne district (Fig. 29).

THE HILLS OF OTWAY AND WESTERN GIPPSLAND

The hills of Otway and western Gippsland represent the remnants of a mountain system which was raised in Jurassic times. Formed of Jurassic to Carboniferous rocks, they have been so worn down that their summits now rarely reach 2000 feet (610 m) above sea-level. This is one of the few regions in the continent where the Great Dividing Range retreats from the coast sufficiently to allow the development of a relatively low and well-watered belt of land before it.

Owing to their small extent, the Gippsland and Otway ranges do not unduly restrict settlement. They receive more than 40 inches (1000 mm) of rainfall per annum and are well wooded. Here are some of the world's tallest trees, for this is the home of the famous *Eucalyptus amygdalina* (p. 39), as well as many other valuable eucalypts, such as the blue gum, white gum and mountain ash. Below the forest giants and sheltered by them are the graceful fronds of tree ferns, while a dense undergrowth of shrubs and ferns hugs the forest floor.

These timbers have been tapped by the railway and are exported from Alberton, in Gippsland; but in places the woods have been completely cleared and the land now provides sheep and cattle pastures. Today much of the woodland is managed scientifically for paper-making, with replanting where necessary, and the growing of pines to provide an admixture of softwood (to make a satisfactory brown paper it is necessary to mix long-fibred softwood with short-fibred eucalyptus wood). Pulping takes place at a mill near Morwell, close to the northern flanks of the Gippsland hills; it has an output of more than 250 tons (254 t) of kraft pulp a day.

THE GREAT VALLEY OF VICTORIA

The Great Valley. The Great Valley consists of an elongated (perhaps down-faulted) lowland, bounded to the south by the wooded hills just described and to the north by the Great Dividing Range. Port Philip Bay, which represents a drowned portion of the valley, divides it into an eastern and a western portion.

The western section derives its character from vast outpourings of lava, which took place in Tertiary times. It is a region of volcanic craters with nearly 150 lakes; some of these appear to have originated from local subsidence following the up-welling of lava, others are due to irregularities in the lava surface. These treeless, grassy plains, with their rich volcanic soils, are largely devoted to dairy farming (*see* Fig. 58, p. 160) and are well served by the railway. From such collecting centres as Camperdown and Colac (about 50 miles (80 km) west of Geelong) milk is sent eastwards to Melbourne or southwards to the ports and resorts such as Portland, Belfast and Warrnambool.

The eastern half of the Great Valley is composed of level Tertiary strata and drained by the Latrobe, Thomson, Macallister and Mitchell rivers. In geologically recent times these must have flowed independently to the sea; but a slight rise in the land, it seems, has aided the formation of the long shingle ridge known as Ninety Mile Beach, with a chain of lagoons behind it.

This is rich farmland, with orchards, vineyards, hop gardens and dairy farms, whose produce is marketed at Warragul and Sale. The rainfall is generally too high for wheat, and maize is the chief cereal, though wheat is raised in a small sheltered area around Sale. The chief interest in this district, however, lies not in its farming activities, but in the enormous deposits of brown coal which lie only a short distance below the surface.

The Latrobe Valley Brown Coal Field. The Latrobe Valley contains the largest known continuous occurrence of brown coal in the world. The field lies mainly south of the Latrobe River and the accessible deposits extend for about 40 miles (64 km) from east to west and range between 5 and 10 miles (8 and 16 km) from north to south (Figs. 30 and 31). It contains the enormous quantity of 85,000 million tons of brown coal—sufficient to last eight centuries at the current rate of working.

The deposit is of extraordinary thickness and covered by only a relatively thin layer of over-burden. At Yallourn, where most of the output is obtained at present, the "seam" averages about 200 feet (60 m) in thickness and is covered by about 40 feet (12 m) of over-burden; at Morwell, where a new cut has been opened, it is 350 to 500 feet (105–150 m) thick with about the same cover; but at Loy Yang, to the east, is the world's thickest known deposit of brown coal: it is about 760 feet (230 m) thick below an over-burden of 90 feet {27 m).

The coal ranges from Eocene to Miocene in age (about 20 to 50 million years old); it has a high moisture content but is suitable for steam-raising, conversion into electricity, for the manufacture of briquettes and for the production of high-grade metallurgical coke.

[*Courtesy Australian News & Information Bureau.*

FIG. 30.—Victoria: brown coal mining. The photograph shows part of the immense open cut at Yallourn, with one of the dredgers in operation. The "seam" is about 200 feet (60 m) in thickness.

Small-scale working of the coalfield took place in the nineteenth century but it was only after the establishment of the State Electricity Commission in 1918 that the possibilities of the field became apparent. The Commission was granted the control of a large part of the Latrobe Valley and it realised that this could become the energy centre for the whole of Victoria.

During the next few years the project was inaugurated. A 70 MW generating station was constructed; an open-cast quarry was developed

TABLE 21

Victoria: production of brown coal in 1000 tons

				Output
1939	.	.	.	3,651
1949	.	.	.	7,375
1952	.	.	.	8,104
1962	.	.	.	17,137
1964	.	.	.	19,035
1966	.	.	.	21,783
1968	.	.	.	22,971
1968–69	.	.	.	23,128
1969–70	.	.	.	23,927
1970–71	.	.	.	22,814

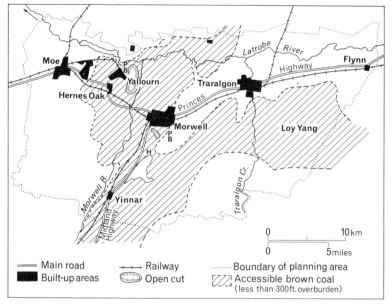

FIG. 31.—The Latrobe Valley Planning Region. The map illustrates the wide extent of the deposits of brown coal, the open cuts, and the sites of the power stations and briquette factories. Key: P, Power stations; B, Briquette factories; H, Hazelwood power station.

to feed it with fuel, and the town of Yallourn was built to supply the labour. Yallourn was planned as a garden city with detached houses, parks and pleasant tree-lined avenues round a central square. In the absence of public and private transport the town had to be placed next to the quarry.

As the demand for energy grew, the output of brown coal rapidly increased (Table 21) and by the 1950s Yallourn had reached its planned maximum population of 5000.

The coal is scooped up by the toothed buckets of enormous dredgers, produced in Germany; they are the largest of the kind in the world. One of them weighs 2200 tons and can dig 1750 tons of coal in an hour. From the open cuts the coal is moved to the local power stations and briquette factories, whose sites are shown in Fig. 31.

There are at present three generating stations in this energy centre, and a fourth is scheduled for completion during 1973. The largest of them is the Hazelwood Station, 2 miles (3·2 km) south of Morwell, which has been consistently enlarged since 1964 to attain its present size of 1600 MW. Hazelwood is the largest generating station not only in Victoria but in the whole of Australia. Its 8 huge boilers, each 200 feet (60 m) high are among the largest of their kind in the world.

Hazelwood consumes 15 million tons of brown coal annually; this is in spite of the improvements in efficiency which enable a ton of brown coal to produce twice as much power today compared with 1939. Two transmission cables from Hazelwood to Melbourne carry a load of 500 kV and constitute the highest powered lines in the southern hemisphere.

In 1970–71 Hazelwood alone produced 54 per cent of the public electricity supply of Victoria. Yallourn power station contributed 21 per cent and Morwell a further 8 per cent so that the Latrobe Valley plants based on brown coal produced 83 per cent of the State's electricity.

The local power stations are designed to burn the soft, crumbly, "raw" brown coal; but it is uneconomic to transport the fuel far in this form, and the rest is accordingly converted into briquettes; in this process the moisture content is reduced from about 66 per cent to 15 per cent and the heating value is more than trebled.

The original briquette factory, opened at Yallourn in 1925, was supplemented in 1960 by two new ones at Morwell. In 1970–71 the output of brown coal totalled 21·5 million tons, and of this, 17·4 million tons were used in the local power stations. Most of the remainder (3·8 million tons) was converted into 1·4 million tons of briquettes; and of these, 16 per cent were used for further production of electricity. Brown coal briquettes are distributed to all parts of Victoria and the State is no longer dependent on "black" coal from New South Wales.

From 1956 till 1968 brown coal briquettes were used to manufacture town gas in a plant at Morwell and in 1968–69 nearly one-third of all the town gas used in Victoria came from this source. Natural gas however, discovered in large quantities below Bass Strait (p. 111), has rendered manufactured gas obsolete; the Morwell plant closed in 1969 and the West Melbourne Gas Works followed suit in 1970.

The social and economic development of the coalfield region is guided by a comprehensive planning scheme; new industries are served by the rapid expansion of the urban areas (Table 22).

TABLE 22

The Latrobe Valley settlements: population growth

	1947	1954	1961	1965 (estimate)
Moe-Newborough . . .	2,556	12,427	15,454	17,000
Morwell	2,951	9,040	14,827	17,080
Traralgon	4,384	8,845	12,298	14,030
Yallourn and Yallourn North .	4,572	7,037	6,877	6,570
Total	14,463	37,349	49,456	54,680

Yallourn, however, has ceased to expand, for it is doomed to disappear. Its continued existence would prevent the extension of the great open-cut which now advances westwards. It is claimed that the decision is justifiable on economic and social grounds. To open a new cut would cost an additional $29 million, and from the social point of view the town is now badly sited in a polluted and industrial area. This was the only possible site in 1921 before the spread of the private car; but now that the population is far more mobile there is no necessity for workmen to live close to their factory; moreover the timber constructed houses are fifty years old and approaching the end of their span of useful life.[1]

By 1985 the hospital and the first 200 houses will need to be removed and by A.D. 2000 the whole site will be cleared. There will be no sudden exodus; for the most part houses will remain unoccupied as they fall vacant; and the Electricity Commission has undertaken to smooth the transition as far as possible.

THE VICTORIAN HIGHLANDS

The Victorian Highlands are divided by the Kilmore Gap into two unequal regions. To the east lies the main highland mass, which broadens to reach a width of about 100 miles (161 km), almost the whole width of the State. Its average height increases to more than 3000 feet (914 m), while isolated summits reach 6000 feet (1829 m). Victoria shares with New South Wales the curving ridge, known in the south as the Snowy Mountains and in the north as the Muniong Range, which forms the culmination of the Great Divide. Mount Kosciusko itself, however, lies 10 miles (16 km) within the New South Wales border. No railway or important road crosses this mountain barrier.

Geologically the highlands consist of folded and faulted Archaean and older Palaeozoic rocks, containing granitic intrusions. The granites are generally north of the present divide and are of interest in that a small mineral-bearing region is associated with them: gold is produced south of Albury (on the upper Murray river) in the district of Beechworth and Yackandandah. South of the granite intrusions lies a complicated series of block-faulted masses, which trend north and south. The faulting, which took place in Tertiary times, has left its mark in certain features of drainage; for example, a remarkable trench traverses the whole system from north to south and corresponds with a line of weakness: it is occupied by the Mitta-Mitta river flowing northwards and the Tambo flowing southwards. River capture seems to have occurred on a large scale here, the former river having beheaded the latter.

The roughly accordant summits suggest that we have here the remnants of an ancient peneplain, which, once near sea-level, has since been elevated about 6000 feet (1829 m). Here are some of the highest summits in the continent. Mount Bogong (6508 feet; 1984 m) is not far short of Kosciusko (7328 feet; 2234 m) and there are sixteen peaks of more than 5000 feet (1524 m). There are not many places in Australia which can offer winter sports to the tourist, but the dry, powdery snow attracts many visitors to such resorts at Hotham Heights, Mount Buller, Falls Creek and the Mount Buffalo National Park.

Dense forests of giant trees cover these plateaus and ranges and constitute valuable reserves of timber. Tree ferns grow in the rocky valleys, and above them rise the tall, smooth trunks of the white gum. But apart from the resorts and the mining centres the region is virtually uninhabited.

West of the Kilmore Gap the highlands present a very different scene. While the general structure is very similar to the lofty plateaus to the east, here the surface is much lower (below 2000 feet; 610 m) and the hills form no barrier to communication. There are the same granite masses, the Palaeozoic sediments and the faults. With the granites are associated the important goldfields of the Ballarat district, while the faults seem to be responsible for the steep edges of the Pyrenees (northwest of Ballarat) and the Grampians (farther west).

These, then, are no true mountains: a very indistinct divide separates the Murray tributaries from those which flow southwards. Gold mining has formed the stimulus to settlement: the forests have been cleared and the land neatly parcelled out among the farming population, and the plateau boasts one of the closest networks of railways and roads in the continent.

This western part of the Victorian Highlands includes some of the most productive land in the State. In many parts the soils have been enriched by volcanic debris, and much of the land is ideal for mixed farming. In this rather cool region potatoes and hay are more typical than the cereals, but wheat, barley and oats occupy considerable areas. Most farms rear beef and dairy cattle, and they occur in approximately equal numbers, while the density of sheep—rising in places to more than 600 per square mile—is the highest in the continent. In 1970 there were over 33 million sheep in Victoria: ten to every man, woman and child in the State; and their greatest concentration is in the western plateaus (*see* the land use map, Fig. 58, p. 160).

It was not farming, however, which brought this region its prosperity, but gold. We have already mentioned the development of the Victorian goldfields (p. 88). Today Victoria ranks well below Western Australia in the value of her gold output; but the steady annual production is a valuable asset to the State, and any increase in the price of gold acts as a stimulus to mining activity.

The gold-bearing region is of wide extent: it stretches from Ballarat as far north-west as St Arnaud, as far north as Wedderburn and as far north-east as Bendigo and Castlemaine. The alluvial workings, which devastated wide areas, have long since been superseded by deep mines and complex refining equipment. In 1851 Ballarat was the single homestead of a sheep run; today it is the third city of Victoria, with a population of 58,434 (1971).

Ballarat is the centre of the western plateau. With six railways focusing on it, the city has extensive locomotive workshops. There are metal foundries, engineering and chemical works and several establishments associated with agriculture, such as flour mills, tanneries and boot factories, bacon-curing plants and biscuit works.

THE INTERIOR PLAINS

The Interior Plains may be defined as that land which is bounded on the north by the Murray river and on the south by the 500-foot (151-m) contour. The Murray forms an effective northern limit: its broad flood plain is a barrier to communications and at only a few points does the railway cross it (an interesting exception is the short stretch of line penetrating New South Wales from Moama to Deniliquen, which brings the latter town into touch with Melbourne rather than Sydney—an example of "rail capture").

Within this region the rocks are of Tertiary or later age, level and low-lying, and representing ancient river and sea alluvium together with an admixture of wind-blown material. In late Tertiary times there was a bay in the western part of this region: it included most of the land west of the Loddon, as well as the adjoining parts of the neighbouring States. Into this bay the ancestors of the Murray, Murrumbidgee and Darling found their separate outlets. The soils are developed here upon marine sandstones or on travertine—a limy deposit which the rather low rainfall has concentrated near the surface.

The rainfall gradually diminishes northwards and westwards from 25 inches (635 mm) at Benalla (on the eastern border) through 20 inches (508 mm) to Echuca and 15 inches (380 mm) at Ouyen to just over 10 inches (254 mm) at Mildura (Fig. 29, p. 93). Consequently, while the rainfall allows temperate cereals and grapes to be cultivated successfully in the east, these can be produced in the centre and west only with the aid of irrigation. In the far west is the Mallee district, where at present there is no farming at all.

Moira county, with its productive loamy soils, may be regarded as the core of the agricultural eastern section. Here the farmer raises heavy crops of wheat and oats (for hay), together with some barley. Of the fruits, peaches are typical, while grapes flourish a little farther east, around Albury. There are about 300 sheep and 10 or 20 cattle to each square mile.

Farther west, in what was formerly mallee country, the farmers are growing grain and fruit and rearing dairy cattle. Six parallel railways thrust north-westwards into this former barren land, and 5000 miles (8040 km) of irrigation canals have rendered the farms almost independent of the rainfall.

IRRIGATION

While most of the irrigated land of Victoria lies within the boundaries of the Interior Plains, the subject of irrigation is rather complex and sufficiently important to justify separate consideration. In respect of irrigated area, Victoria and New South Wales lead all other States of the Commonwealth (Table 23).

TABLE 23

Australia: area under irrigation, by State, 1969–70, in acres

	Crops	Pasture	Total
Victoria . . .	229,448	1,238,519	1,467,967
New South Wales . . .	697,533	727,921	1,425,454
Queensland	384,429	48,317	432,746
South Australia . . .	136,150	49,808	185,958
Western Australia . . .	38,936	37,670	76,606
Tasmania	34,503	25,430	59,933

There are appreciable areas under irrigation in Queensland and smaller districts in Western Australia and Tasmania; but the chief irrigated areas lie in the south-east of the mainland and depend on the water of the Murray system (Fig. 32). The districts in New South Wales and South Australia are discussed in later chapters, but it is convenient to examine here some elements that are common to the whole region. Its physical geography sets the problem, but also suggests some of the solutions.[2]

Bordering the main irrigated districts to the south and east are the Eastern Highlands: they form a dissected plateau whose general height averages about 2000 feet (610 m) or more. Where it is crossed by the border between New South Wales and Victoria the land rises to form truly mountainous country ranging between 3000 and 6000 feet (914 and 1829 m) in altitude and rising to a summit of 7305 feet (2226 m) in Mount Kosciusko.

The highest parts experience over 80 inches (2032 mm) of rain (or the equivalent in snow) annually, but most of the plateau receives more than 25 inches (635 mm). This is normally sufficient for agriculture, though its efficiency is limited by unequal distribution throughout the year, for the region has an element of the Mediterranean climate, with a winter maximum of rainfall and a dry summer. The river flows reflect this regime, since the restricted snowfields do little to modify it. The nature of the terrain offers advantages for water conservation, for the alternation of broad basins with deep gorges provides the civil engineer with convenient possible sites for dams.

North and west of the highlands lies an extensive plain which slopes down gradually from 500 or 600 feet (152 or 183 m) above sea level at the highland edge to about 100 feet (30 m) in the far north-west. Its gradients are very slight, ranging between 1 : 1300 (four feet per mile) near the highlands to only 1 : 5300 (one foot per mile) in the north-west. Soils and temperatures are ideal for extensive and intensive farming; but the annual precipitation diminishes from 20 inches (508 mm) close to the highlands to only 10 inches (254 mm) in the north-west. Without

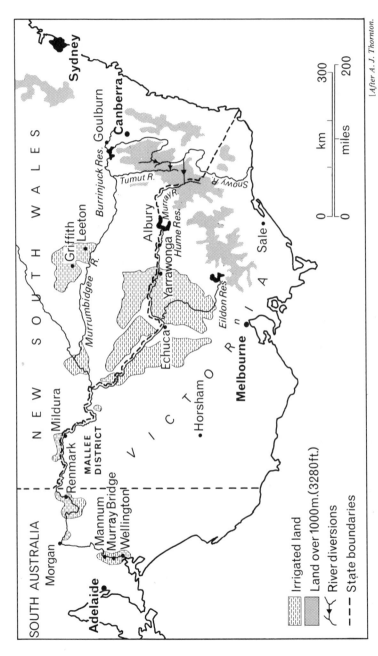

FIG. 32.——Irrigated districts in south-east Australia. Two of the areas are shown in greater detail in Fig. 61. The river diversions, which are supplying additional irrigation water to the Murray and Murrumbidgee, are indicated on a larger scale in Fig. 43.

[*After A. J. Thornton.*

irrigation the land would be suitable for wheat and sheep farming in the neighbourhood of the highlands, but for only extensive sheep grazing elsewhere.

The river systems of south-eastern Australia present problems for water conservation, in that their catchment areas are relatively small: as a result their flows are characteristically erratic. The Murray, Goulburn and Murrumbidgee are more reliable than other rivers since they rise in the heart of the highest mountain area. Even here, however, it has been necessary to construct large storage basins to smooth out the spring maximum of rainfall. Other streams such as the Lachlan and Loddon have even smaller catchment areas that experience low rainfalls.

The method of irrigation entails the construction of a dam in a gorge as close as possible to the land to be irrigated. This makes use of the maximum catchment area and stabilises the flow of the river. The river itself is then used as far as possible as the main channel for irrigation; but in order to make use of gravity to feed the water to the crops, a weir must be constructed to divert the water. Pumping is not normally necessary except in the lower reaches of the river, for example, in the Mildura district.

The three main dams and reservoirs are the Burrinjuck (Murrumbidgee river), the Hume (Murray river) and the Eildon (Goulburn river).

The first schemes to be planned were those of the Murrumbidgee river, soon after 1900. In early times State rivalries were strong, and there was a political motive to use the Murrumbidgee: it was tightly linked by rail with Sydney, so that its benefits were unlikely to accrue to any other State. The chosen dam site, at Burrinjuck, had distinct advantages: the deep and narrow gorge offered an economic project in which a large storage capacity could be contained above a relatively small dam. The floor and the walls of the gorge were of granite, which provided a strong and impermeable foundation, and offered suitable building material for the dam itself, while the site below the confluence of the Yass and Goodradigbee rivers gave a maximum catchment area upstream. Work began on the dam in 1907 and water reached the first farms in 1913.

The diversion weirs, too, need to fulfil definite requirements. The ideal site is at a narrowing of the channel so as to minimise construction costs. A firm and rocky foundation is necessary; the site must be as close as possible to the irrigable land, and it must be sufficiently high to allow the water to flow by gravity to the farms. The main diversion weirs are at Berrembed on the Murrumbidgee; at Yarrawonga on the Murray; and at Torumbarry on the Goulburn (Fig. 32).

The original object of the early dams was simply to store water from the rainy winter season into the dry summer, when it was most needed. When with the passage of time the merits of irrigation became clearer the problem of surmounting years of drought was faced. Thus the original Eildon dam of the early twentieth century stored 306,000 acre/feet of water; the new Eildon dam, completed in 1956, impounds nine times as much water. Not only has it doubled the amount of irrigation water available to the Goulburn system, but it stores the surplus water of rainy years ready to meet any deficiencies in years of drought.

We now look a little more closely at the irrigated districts within the confines of Victoria. Only a small proportion of the area of Victoria— about 2 per cent—is under irrigation; but irrigated crop lands are exceedingly productive, and they account for about 15 per cent of the farm output of the State. Nearly 90 per cent of the irrigated land is under pasture; orchard fruits, vines and vegetables share most of the remainder fairly equally, and are followed by cereals (Table 24).

TABLE 24

Victoria: chief irrigated crops, 1969–70, in 1000 acres

Orchard fruits	53·5
Vegetables	46·8
Vineyards	46·5
Cereals	19·5
All irrigated crops . . .	229·4
Irrigated pasture . . .	1238·5

What are the main features of the irrigation systems of Victoria? The great Hume dam, on the upper Murray above Albury, stores sufficient water to keep the Murray flowing for two years. With the flow thus regulated, water can be abstracted at barrages lower downstream and supplied to irrigation canals. The Yarrawonga weir, between Albury and Echuca, supplies water to 51,500 acres (20,600 ha), devoted largely to the rearing of cattle on lucerne and cultivated pastures. A second great barrage at Torumbarry irrigates 284,000 acres (133,600 ha), again, largely for pastures, but including 4300 acres (1720 ha) of grapes.

Between Echuca and Mildura are some of the most important grape-growing districts of Australia: here are 40,000 acres (16,187 ha) of vineyards, supplied with water pumped from the Murray, and concentrating almost entirely on the production of sultanas (Fig. 33). South-east of Echuca lies the largest irrigated area in the State, fed by water from the Goulburn. The reconstructed Eildon dam, completed in 1955, is the largest in Australia. About 150 miles (241 km) lower down, at Nagambie, a weir raises the water level 45 feet (14 m), to supply two main irrigation canals. These wide and straight waterways are as wide as a river of the English Fenlands; from them all the land as far north as Echuca is watered, and one broad and placid channel carries water westwards beyond the Loddon, crossing five of the six parallel railways, and reaching land which is well within the dry mallee country. Pastures

[*Courtesy Australian News & Information Bureau.*

FIG. 33.—Victoria: Mildura (aerial view). Mildura is the chief Australian centre for
dried fruits. The photograph shows vineyards, drying sheds and scattered
orchards and illustrates the severely rectangular layout of the irrigated lands.

are again dominant, but within the confines of the Goulburn scheme lie
more than half of the irrigated orchards of Victoria.

In the far north-west, and on the verge of the mallee district, lies the
irrigated area of Mildura. Here a Trust controls 45,000 acres (18,211
ha) and irrigates 18,000 (7284 ha) of them. Almost the whole of this
irrigated land grows fruit: four-fifths of it comprises grapes, and the
remainder citrus and other fruit. The precious water is led between the
rows of apple trees and into the vineyards through 168 miles (270 km)
of canals. In 1969–70 Mildura and the smaller irrigated districts of
Robinvale and Swan Hill higher upstream on the Murray produced
70,000 tons (71,120 t) of sultanas, currants and raisins. Table 25 lists

TABLE 25

*Victoria: production of principal tree fruits, 1969–70, in thousand
bushels*

Pears	7044
Apples	5331
Peaches	2975
Oranges	1280
Apricots	574
Lemons and limes . . .	164
Cherries	142
Plums and prunes . . .	132

the production of the principal tree fruits in the State, though it does not distinguish the irrigated cultivation.

Farther south is the Wimmera–Mallee system—one of the most extensive domestic and stock systems in the world. Water, drawn from reservoirs in the Grampians to the south, and supplemented from the Loddon and Goulburn, is led through 10,000 miles (16,093 km) of canals to serve 80,000 people. The scheme includes a district of pasture and soft fruits near Horsham, covering 3500 acres (1416 ha): this is being doubled in size. In all, the Wimmera–Mallee scheme covers nearly one-eighth of the area of the State.

Irrigation in Victoria is controlled by a public authority, the State Rivers and Water Supply Commission. Nevertheless, farmers who are authorised to do so may construct private storage dams on their properties to supplement the dry season flow from streams. Within the last generation the area so irrigated has increased tenfold, and now accounts for about one-seventh of all the irrigated land in the State.

But most of the irrigation in Victoria is carried out in "group" schemes, the object of which is to promote closer settlement. Here each farmer pays a fixed sum annually in return for a specific quantity of water (his "water right"), though in most seasons he can buy additional water. The main irrigation districts and systems, in order of size, are shown in the following table:

TABLE 26

Victoria: irrigation districts and their products, by area, in thousand acres, 1969–70

District	Irrigated area	Sown pasture	Lucerne and sorghum	Vines	Orchards	Market gardens
Goulburn–Loddon .	682·4	520·3	33·4	0·4	20·6	4·4
Torrumbarry .	284·1	238·4	9·6	4·3	1·8	0·8
Murray Valley .	122·0	106·4	6·9	0·1	6·6	0·3
Macallister . .	60·4	59·0	0·3	—	—	0·1
Pumped supply districts, including Mildura . .	47·6	0·3	1·2	40·3	3·0	0·1
Total, including other areas .	1389·0	1092·6	69·6	47·5	39·7	26·9

As an example of irrigation within the Goulburn–Loddon system we may instance the development of the Tongala–Stanhope district, about 20 miles (32 km) south-east of Echuca (Fig. 34).

In the middle of the nineteenth century the land was occupied by widely scattered farmsteads that formed the headquarters of pastoral properties. During the 1870s and 1880s the land was surveyed for wheat farming, based on the same system that had been developed in the Canadian Prairies and the American Mid-West. The resulting layout consisted of a grid of squares aligned north and south, and each containing 640 acres (one square mile or 2·6 km²).

But wheat farming proved a risky venture in dry years; many farms were abandoned and the land reverted to pasture. It was to retrieve this situation that irrigation was introduced, at first on a limited scale, to supply water to sheep and cattle and to small plots of fruit trees, natural

[After J. Rutherford, 1968.

Fig. 34.—Victoria: the Tongala district. This area was surveyed for settlement during the 1870s and 80s with a mile square (640 acres) (2·59 km²) as the basic unit. Irrigation was a later phase, but the square grid survives in the layout of roads.

pasture and lucerne. Then at the end of the First World War the district was selected for the resettlement of returned soldiers, and the new project was for the intensive irrigation of relatively small plots.

Tongala and Stanhope were established as commercial centres; a main irrigation channel was dug to draw water from the Goulburn, together with a storage basin—Waranga reservoir. Each settlement was surrounded by an inner zone of allotments of about 3 acres (1·2 ha); beyond were horticultural plots of about 28 acres (11·2 ha) and on the outskirts, larger dairy and mixed farms of about 68 acres (27·2 ha). The interesting feature of the layout is that through all this reorganisation the rectangular grid of the 1880s has survived, though the main irrigation channels pay little attention to it.

Mildura and its neighbouring district of Red Cliffs offer interesting contrasts in layout (Fig. 35). Here the Murray flows in a wide flood plain and pumping was necessary from the beginning to lift the water up to the potential crop land on the river terraces. The Mildura project was designed in the 1880s by the Chaffey brothers, who drew on experience

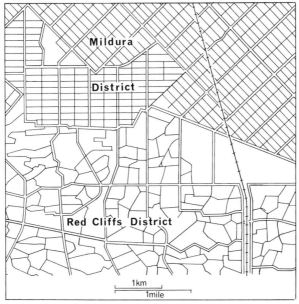

[After J. Rutherford, 1968.

FIG. 35.—Victoria: the Mildura and Red Cliffs districts. The rectangular grid of Mildura dates from the 1880s and is based on a Californian model; the pattern of Red Cliffs is of the 1920s, and is related to slight differences in relief which have conditioned the placing of irrigation ditches.

gained in California. Their plan formed a rigid grid in which rectangular blocks of about half a square mile ($1 \cdot 3$ km^2) were each subdivided into twenty plots, ten on each of the longer sides of the rectangle. This produced a large number of equal plots, each of about 10 acres (4 ha). On this rectangular pattern the water channels were superimposed, so that often the plots were cut into two or more pieces.

In the Red Cliffs project, which dates from the 1920s, the plan was quite different. Here the water channels were laid out first to take advantage of slight differences in relief; then the property boundaries were arranged in such a way that each plot was served by at least one water channel. The high cost of water at Mildura and Red Cliffs, owing to the need for pumping, has made it necessary to concentrate on crops that yield high returns: hence the emphasis on fruit rather than fodder. Normally the highest and best-drained land is devoted to the most valuable of the fruits—citrus; below them are the peaches, pears and apricots, and on the lowest levels, vines. Mildura is the commercial centre not only for Sunraysia (*i.e.* the irrigated districts of Mildura, Irymple and Red Cliffs) but also for the sheep and wheat of the Mallee country to the south.

Two other widely separated irrigation projects require to be noticed: they are the Macallister scheme in the Latrobe valley and the Millewa development in the far north-west.

The Macallister river flows into the Thomson, which is a left bank tributary of the Latrobe. The hills of Gippsland receive a high rainfall so that the Macallister river has an assured flow; but the lowland itself lies in a rain shadow and the precipitation, averaging about 24 inches (610 mm), annually, is insufficient for a stable farming system.

The irrigation district extends over 154,000 acres (62,322 ha) and includes 920 farms, in which 84,000 acres (33,993 ha) are considered suitable for irrigation. The main reservoir is at Glenmaggie, whose dam was completed in 1926; later extensions to the scheme have taken place almost continuously. Gippsland as a whole is the leading dairy district of Victoria, and it is natural that the Macallister scheme concentrates on irrigated pastures. The typical farm consists of about 130 acres (52 ha) and carries a herd of 80 to 100 milking cows.

The district enjoys several advantages. The irrigated pastures grow throughout the year: they are watered fortnightly during the summer and every three weeks at other times; the cattle therefore have no need for additional feed. There is no labour problem, for the farm is generally run by the proprietor and his family. The district is served by a co-operative research farm; three dairies collect the milk, and some of it serves the Melbourne market.

The Millewa district lies west of Mildura and includes some of the hottest and driest land in the State (Mildura: mean July temperature: 9·8° C (49·5° F); mean January temperature: 24·8° C (76·1° F); mean annual rainfall: 11·4 inches (290 mm)). Here the land has been opened up for stock rearing by the construction of more than 600 miles (965 km) of open irrigation channels fed by water from the Murray river. But open channels are subject to high losses through evaporation and seepage: these are estimated at 7500 acre/feet annually. Consequently it has been decided to replace the whole system of open channels by enclosed water pipelines.

Three advantages are anticipated from the new project: water will be constantly available to the farmer instead of being confined to the winter flood period; the saving on evaporation and seepage will result in the provision of greater quantities of water; and there will be a reduction in maintenance costs. The first supplies of piped water reached the settlement of Yarrara in 1972 and completion is anticipated in 1975. The Millewa project serves 123 properties and represents the largest rural water pipeline scheme so far undertaken in Victoria.

OIL AND NATURAL GAS

The development of indigenous oil and natural gas in Victoria has been recent, rapid and far-reaching, and in the space of a few years Victoria has become established as the leading producing State of both gas and oil.

Discoveries of gas in commercial quantities date from 1965 and oil from 1967. By the end of 1971 the energy supply of Victoria had been transformed: six oil and gas fields had been evaluated in offshore

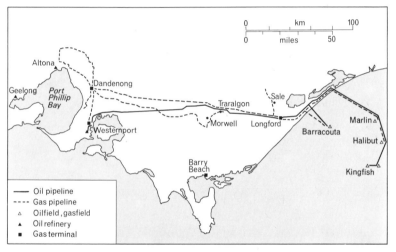

FIG. 36.—Oil and natural gas in southern Victoria. The main discoveries were made in 1965 and 1967. Victoria now supplies 65 per cent of Australia's refinery needs; the supplies of natural gas are sufficient to meet the requirements of the State for 30 years.

Gippsland, east of Bass Strait; about 94 per cent of the State's half a million gas users were being supplied with natural gas, and Victorian crude oil was accounting for 62 per cent of the whole of Australia's refinery needs.

Of the oilfields, the most southerly is known as Kingfish; the northerly is Marlin, the central, Halibut, and that to the north-west, Barracouta (Fig. 36). The last two are also gas fields. In 1970 a further field known as Snapper (north-west of Marlin) was shown to be a large commercial gas field, while Tuna to the east was declared to contain oil and gas in commercial quantities.

These fields are contained in sediments of Cretaceous and Tertiary age. Most of the wells have been drilled to between 8000 and 12,000 feet (2440 and 3658 m) below the sea bed. This represents a technical triumph over difficult physical conditions. The Kingfish platforms, for example, stand in 255 feet (78 m) of water at a distance of nearly 50 miles (80 km) from the shore; and Bass Strait has more than its share of stormy weather.

The reserves of natural gas as known at present are sufficient to supply the needs of the State for thirty years. They are shared among the fields as shown in Table 27.

TABLE 27

Victoria: estimated reserves of natural gas,
by field, in million million cubic feet

Marlin	.	.	.	3·5
Snapper		.	.	3·2
Barracouta	.	.	.	1·8
Tuna	.	.	.	0·5

To minimise the possibility of a complete breakdown in the gas supply of the State, the fields are tapped by two independent pipelines. Barracouta is served by a 30-mile (48-km) pipeline 18 inches (457 mm) in diameter, and Marlin by a 67-mile (107-km) line 20 inches (508 mm) in diameter. These convey the gas to a processing plant which was constructed in 1968–70 at Longford, on the mainland opposite the producing fields. Here varying proportions of the heavier constituents of the raw gas are removed to give a gas suitable for domestic and industrial purposes. The by-products move through a 10-inch (254-mm) pipeline 118 miles long (189 km), for further processing in a plant at Long Island Point, about 40 miles (64 km) south-east of Melbourne; and in July 1970, the first load of propane and butane—prepared from the unwanted constituents of the natural gas—was shipped for the chemical industries of Japan.

From Longford the treated gas passes westwards through a 108-mile (173-km) 30-inch (762-mm) pipeline to the terminal and distribution station at Dandenong, on the south-eastern outskirts of Melbourne. Two of the gas fields are sharing the supply roughly equally, in terms of output to the end of 1970: Marlin 15,059 million cubic feet (426·4 mil. m³), Barracouta 16,027 million cubic feet (458·3 mil. m³).

In anticipation of increased demands, the gas companies have extended and improved their distribution systems; and the sales of gas have more than doubled in the space of two years. An integrated pipeline system has been developed: Melbourne is now ringed by a new line 73 miles (117 km) in length, and new districts in the metropolitan area have been served, such as Craigieburn and Broadmeadows to the north and Mornington to the south. The Latrobe valley received natural gas in 1969, Geelong in 1971 and Ballarat and Bendigo in 1973.

Conversion to natural gas has entailed the modification of more than a million appliances in the metropolitan region: this was completed during 1970, and Melbourne became the first capital city of Australia to be converted wholly to natural gas.

Industry too is benefiting from the new form of energy. In 1971 a long-term agreement was concluded for the supply of gas to the mills at Fairfield and Maryvale (near Morwell) of the Australian Paper Manufacturers; and a new 1000 MW power station to be built at Newport, Melbourne, will be fired by natural gas.

In April 1967 oil was discovered in the Kingfish field, and later in the same year in the Halibut field. Both were declared to be of high commercial importance, and the Kingfish field was evaluated as a major oil-field by world standards. No further discovery of significance was made until 1971, when it was announced that a commercial oil and gas field had been discovered in Tuna. The oil reserves of these fields are estimated as follows: Kingfish 1060 million barrels, Halibut 440 million barrels, Tuna 84 million barrels.

Halibut has been linked by an 82-mile (131-km) 24–26-inch (609–660-mm) pipeline to a treatment plant at Longford, and delivery of the oil began in March 1970. Kingfish was then linked to the same pipeline, and its production began in April 1971. At the Longford installation the dissolved gases are removed to ensure safety in handling; the crude oil is then conveyed 117 miles (188 km) by a 28-inch (711-mm) pipeline to the storage tanks of a new shipping terminal at Long Island Point, Westernport. Dredged to a depth of 47 ft (14·4 m), this can accommodate oil tankers of up to 100,000 tons d.w.

By November 1971 the Bass Strait oilfields were producing at the rate of about 315,000 barrels a day, representing about 62 per cent of Australia's refinery requirements, and forming the peak output from the oilfields that have been so far discovered. The long-term prospects for oil, however, are not yet assured, and production at this rate, and in the absence of further discoveries, is expected to be possible for only three years.

The new terminal at Long Island Point is linked by a relatively short but high-capacity pipeline (7 miles long, 42 inch diameter; 11 km long, 1066 mm) to the neighbouring B.P. refinery at Crib Point; this refinery now receives indigenous oil by land pipeline, and at the same time it offers a second shipping terminal for the Gippsland crude oil. A further pipeline 84 miles (135 km) in length has been constructed from Long Island Point round the shores of Port Philip Bay to supply the other two local refineries, at Altona and Corio (north of Geelong). All three Victorian refineries are therefore supplied by land line, and tankers are released for shipments to refineries in other States and overseas. An associated activity is the shipment of the by-products, butane and propane: these are carried regularly in liquid form in specially constructed refrigerated carriers to Japan, in fulfilment of contracts concluded independently by Esso and the Broken Hill Proprietary Company, the partnership that has brought the whole project to fruition.

Oil and gas have brought a surge of activity to two other districts. Between 1966 and 1968 the partnership established a large marine terminal at Barry Beach, about 120 miles (190 km) south-east of Melbourne. Here the offshore platforms were fabricated and the drilling rigs and production platforms serviced. The second area is in Gippsland close to the processing plants at Longford. The nearest town is Sale, the commercial centre of eastern Gippsland, and the settlement is experiencing a burst of energy: new dwellings and shops have mushroomed and the atmosphere of the American oil industry has intruded into what was formerly a quiet country town.

THE MELBOURNE DISTRICT

At the 1971 census the population of Melbourne and its suburbs amounted to 2,388,941, while that for the whole of Victoria was 3,496,161. Over two-thirds of the population of the State, then, live in its capital. To dwellers in the Old World this is a most peculiar phenomenon; but in Australia this sort of proportion is the general rule. In the continent generally the well-watered districts are largely confined to the coasts, and in Victoria particularly the relief is such as to concentrate attention upon the site of the capital. Both arms of the Great Valley point to it; the hills of the Great Dividing Range recede to provide a lowland embayment, while the Kilmore Gap to the north allows the Murray plains to link with Melbourne. Here too is the only deep and sheltered natural harbour of the whole coast of Victoria. Nature seems to have selected this spot for the growth of a great city. Human endeavour has aided nature, and both the road system and the State railways converge upon the State capital.

While the general setting of Melbourne is admirable, the actual site has neither the mountain grandeur of Hobart nor the magnificent harbour of Sydney. The city lies astride the Yarra-Yarra, a relatively small stream which receives tributaries from all directions, and turns first south and then west to deposit its silt in Hobson's Bay, at the head of the larger and almost landlocked Port Philip Bay.

In 1836 Melbourne consisted of eight turf huts and five other buildings! But immigrants moved in, first in search of sheep pastures, and after 1851 in search of gold.

The first route-ways to be established in the neighbourhood were broad stock roads that took the easiest paths offered by the terrain. But a glance at the existing urban pattern reveals the hand of the land surveyor. Settlement has grown on a pre-existing grid of squares of side one mile and orientated on the cardinal points of the compass. This plan can be matched almost anywhere on the Canadian Prairies and the American Mid-West. It records the second stage in the development of the landscape, when the ground was divided into properties considered to be the appropriate size for extensive wheat farming.[3]

During the 1850s the population surpassed 100,000. By 1890 it had become evident that the growing city needed more room to expand, and a thriving market developed in building land. The square mile "sections" were sold by auction for subdivision for house plots, or for holding for investment. A section close to the city might be subdivided by six parallel streets each way and packed closely with houses. Elsewhere the blocks were divided up to accommodate only six or seven mansions each, intended for wealthy purchasers. Continued expansion of the city led to the subdivision of the mansion's park, though the house itself usually survived.

The latest phase of house-building has been undertaken by the State Housing Commission, and at last the rectangular grid has been abandoned, to be replaced by curving streets and the deliberate use of the cul-de-sac to give an air of quietness and seclusion.

As in London, the earliest part of the city was built over two low hills on the north side of the river. This has been laid out geometrically, with five main avenues, each 99 feet (30 m) wide, running straight from north-east to south-west. These were designed to receive the public buildings, shops and hotels. Of these, Flinders Street, which flanks the river, is closely concerned with the commerce of the port; the much photographed Collins Street is the elegant shopping centre; while Bourke Street, farther north, is perhaps the busiest in the city.

Separating these main avenues are four narrower streets, each 45 feet (14 m) wide, originally designed to act as service roads for the buildings fronting the main arteries. But the plan did not materialise: the "lanes" became occupied by warehouses and offices, and now present a rather difficult traffic problem.

Until 1920 Melbourne was the largest city in Australia, and from 1910 to 1927 it was the seat of the Commonwealth Government. Today it is still the financial centre of Australia. Its shops, offices and public buildings have been constructed in a solid, sober and prosperous style, in many cases following the classical tradition.

Parliament House crowns the more easterly of the two hills, and its massive colonnaded frontage provides a striking terminal feature of Bourke Street. Here the State legislature meets, and it was the home of the Federal Parliament until the new capital in Canberra was ready. As an ecclesiastical centre Melbourne contains both an Anglican and a Catholic cathedral; higher education is represented by the university and museum about one mile north of the central district; the Governor's residence lies in a pleasant park to the south of the river.

The rectangular street pattern makes Melbourne the most "American" of the Australian cities, and her skyline, too, reflects the skyscraper fashion. As early as 1866 the Australia Building in

Elizabeth Street rose fifteen storeys high, and other ten-storey buildings were erected in the city centre. The newest and tallest is for Imperial Chemical Industries—a great slab of aluminium and blue glass about 250 feet (66 m) high.

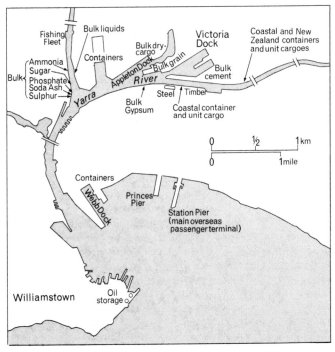

FIG. 37.—The port of Melbourne. Extensive enlargement of the dock facilities has taken place in the last few years. Swanson and Webb docks are completely new; here and elsewhere, many of the improvements are for the container traffic.

The port of Melbourne. The port of Melbourne is in Australia second only to Sydney, and includes more than thirteen miles (21 km) of wharves and piers. Remarkable to English eyes is the fact that Melbourne is virtually tideless: the average range is only 1½ feet (450 mm), and the rise at Spring Tides is only 2 feet 4 inches (650 mm). There is thus no need for enclosed basins, and the commerce of the port is handled at piers or wharves.

The largest vessels, drawing 36 feet (11 m) of water, use the piers and wharves in Port Philip Bay: there are four such berths at Station Pier, Melbourne, a fifth at Breakwater Pier, Williamstown and three in the new Webb Dock (Fig. 37).

During the 1960s radical changes took place in the character of the trade of the port, and these were matched by modifications in the methods of handling cargoes and by extensions in port facilities.

These changes in shipping techniques may be summarised as follows: firstly, the replacement of package freight by bulk cargoes; secondly, the so-called "roll-on roll-off" traffic, where cars with their passengers and lorries with their cargoes intact are transported by ship; and thirdly, the development of container traffic.

Bulk handling is more efficient than the use of individual packages. The cargo can be loaded or discharged as a continuous flow instead of intermittently by crane; conveyor belts and gravity chutes may be utilised, and in some cases, such as grain, the commodity can be treated as if it were liquid and moved by suction. Vessels designed for the carriage of specific bulk cargoes such as sugar are more efficient for that purpose than are general purpose "tramp" vessels.

In Melbourne many of the bulk cargoes are handled in the Yarra river at a series of wharves between Yarraville and Newport: here are the transit facilities for ammonia, sugar, phosphate, soda ash and sulphur (Fig. 37). Bulk grain and cement are accommodated on the north bank respectively above and below Victoria Dock, while gypsum is handled on the south bank.

Roll-on roll-off facilities do not entail extensive reconstruction of berths, but are possible only with specially designed vessels. A new cargo berth of this type has been established at North Wharf, north of Yarraville, and a passenger facility at Webb Dock, in the lowest section of the port.

The most significant developments, however, have been in the extension in container facilities. Specially built container vessels can be up to ten times as efficient as conventional vessels. They can carry greater loads through the more complete use of cargo space, and they can be loaded and discharged far more quickly. But container berths do need to be equipped with specially designed cranes, and they need large spaces for the marshalling of the containers.

Three berths in Victoria Dock, the traditional hub of the port, have been modernised for use as container terminals (Fig. 38). In addition two of the three berths in Appleton Dock, to the west, have been converted for the container traffic. Farther west again a completely new basin, Swanson Dock, has been excavated in the Yarra alluvium, and specially designed for the container trade. Its first berth was opened in 1969, and work began immediately on the construction of others. In the lowest section of the port, Webb Dock is the site of the first of the container terminals of the port, established in 1959. By 1969 two more container berths were in use, and the terminal area had been trebled.

The "container revolution" is beginning to show itself in the trade statistics. In 1969 the Port of Melbourne handled 13·2 million tons of cargo, representing an increase of 10·5 per cent over the previous year; and in 1970 the volume rose further to 14·2 million tons, representing an increase of another 7·6 per cent. Yet the number of calls made by vessels to the port has actually decreased over the two years. The trend is clear, and we may expect to see a continuation in the growth of the container traffic and further extensions to the port facilities.

[*Courtesy Australian News & Information Bureau.*

FIG. 38.—Melbourne: the Yarra river and Victoria Dock. Reclamation in the left foreground is in connection with the scheme of port extension.

Industries and trade. The industries and trade of Melbourne reflect to some extent the activities of Victoria itself, and include many links with agriculture, such as flour milling, bacon curing, brewing, tanning and the manufacture of leather and woollen goods. But, in addition, Melbourne is one of the chief industrial centres of the continent, and there are more than five thousand factories in the city.

A recent venture is the establishment by Messrs H. J. Heinz and Co. of a large food-processing and canning plant on the south-eastern outskirts of the city. A considerable Australian market exists for consumer goods, and with this in view Melbourne was chosen some years ago by General Motors–Holdens Ltd as the site for a motor-vehicle assembly plant. These works now produce 200 cars a day and supply one-third of all the Australian requirements (the engines are imported). A new Ford assembly plant, which has been constructed at Broadmeadows, a northern suburb of Melbourne, is part of a programme which aims to produce an all-Australian Ford car.

Petroleum and its products form the chief item on both the import and the export list; other imports include coal, iron and steel, tinplate, sugar and timber; other exports consist chiefly of flour and grain, frozen lamb, milk, butter and cream, preserved, pulped and dried fruit and motor cars.

Much of the manufacturing activity of the State is concentrated within a radius of 50 miles (80 km) from its capital. This includes a petro-chemical complex at Altona on the western outskirts of the city, a range of industries at Geelong in the south-west corner of Port Philip Bay and a growing district of heavy industry at Western Port.

The Altona Oil Refinery is one of the older oil installations of Australia, which came "on stream" in 1949. Since 1965 its through-put capacity has been greatly expanded, from 2·53 million tons to 4·28 million tons (1972), and the refinery now ranks as the third largest in Australia.

During the 1960s a planned industrial estate was developed next to the refinery: this is based on the use of refinery products as raw materials for further processing. Between 1960 and 1966 seven concerns set up their plants: they range in size from the Altona Petrochemical Co., which produces butadiene for the manufacture of synthetic rubber, and employs 200 people, down to Badocol Chemicals Ltd producing polystyrene insulating and packaging materials and employing only 20 people.[4]

In all, about $A66 million have been invested in this petro-chemical industry, and its total employment amounts to more than 500 people. Since these are predominantly males, an estate designed for light industry and attractive to female labour has been built nearby to give a more balanced structure to the district.

Geelong is the second city and port of Victoria. Between 1946 and 1966 it doubled its population to reach 105,000, and Geelong ranks as the fastest growing city in the State. An important group of heavy industries has developed on its northern outskirts, on land fronting the inner harbour.[5] Here on a 270-acre (109-ha) site at Corio is the Shell oil refinery. Established in 1954, it has doubled its capacity during the last seven years and is now the largest in Australia (capacity: 5·3 million tons). In the same district are a wire works, a foundry producing automobile castings, cold stores for foodstuffs and huge storage plants for wheat and wool, for Geelong is the outlet for the wheatlands of Victoria and also exports the bulk of the wool clip.

The wharves are served by the State railway, and the 1000-mile (1600-km) Princes Highway joins the port by road to both Sydney and Adelaide. Geelong accommodates oil tankers of up to 34 feet (10 m) draught, and freighters of up to 30 feet (9 m); the latter discharge general cargoes and load bales of wool, or receive grain from the lofty silos or meat from the freezing plants.

A smaller industrial area has grown to the south, with light engineering works and carpet and paper felt factories, while to the east, on a

200-acre (81-ha) tidewater site at Port Henry, is the aluminium smelter of ALCOA of Australia. It draws its alumina from Kwinana (page 297).

Significant industrial developments are also taking place on the eastern side of Port Philip Bay at Western Port, about 45 miles (72 km) east of Geelong.[6] Here, at Crib Point, is Victoria's third oil refinery, established in 1966 with a capacity of 1·5 million tons, and since expanded to 2·2 million tons. It benefits from a greater depth of water than is available to the two refineries on Port Philip Bay, for here there is a minimum depth of 52 feet (16 m) of water at the jetty, sufficient to receive fully laden tankers of up to 100,000 tons d.w.

The refinery, built on a 425-acre (172-ha) site has been followed by a whole group of other plants. These include a second oil installation, on a 272-acre (110-ha) site at Long Island Point (see page 113) and a fertiliser and ammonia factory. Largest of all is a huge steel complex, to be built in four stages, and planned for an output of 4 million tons. The first stage alone, comprising a cold reduction mill, employs 1700 workers.

The Port Philip district, with its wide areas of level land available for large-scale factories and works, its proximity to the Melbourne market, its deep water and its accessibility to the oil and gas of Bass Strait, is becoming one of the greatest manufacturing regions of Australia.

For her size Victoria is the richest State in Australia. She produces one-quarter of the total meat of the Commonwealth, she grows one-quarter of the wheat, rears one-third of the cattle and raises nearly one-half of the hay crop. Yet at the same time Victoria is the most industrialised State. Her mineral development, formerly based on gold, is now more firmly founded upon the enormous deposits of brown coal. The population of Victoria is rapidly growing: it has doubled itself in fifty years, and today half the new immigrants and half the overseas investments into Australia are destined for this part of the continent. The future of Victoria is assured.

NOTES

1. D. C. Mercer, "Yallourn Digs Its Own Grave," *Geographical Magazine*, Vol. XLII (August 1970).

2. See the important chapter by J. Rutherford in *Studies in Australian Geography*, Ed. G. H. Dury and M. I. Logan, Melbourne, 1968.

3. R. J. Johnston, "An Outline of The Development of Melbourne's Street Pattern," *Australian Geographer*, Vol. X, No. 6 (1968).

4. Peter J. Rimmer, "The Altona Petrochemical Complex," *Australian Geographer*, Vol. X, No. 3 (1967).

5. L. J. Smail, "Postwar Urban Expansion in Geelong," *Australian Geographer*, Vol. X, No. 5 (1968).

6. D. C. Mercer, "Note on Westernport Bay, Australia," *Geography*, April 1972.

STUDY QUESTIONS

1. How do you explain the fact that Victoria is the most densely peopled State of Australia?

2. Examine critically the suggestion that Victoria has the ideal climate.

3. Estimate the value to Victoria of the brown coal of the Latrobe valley.

4. What are the distinctive features in the human geography of the Victorian Highlands?

5. Account for the distribution of: (*a*) wheat, and (*b*) sheep in Victoria.

6. Write an account of the irrigated lands of Victoria.

7. To what extent does the Victorian railway system reflect the relief?

8. How have physical features aided the development of Melbourne?

Chapter VII

NEW SOUTH WALES (INCLUDING
THE AUSTRALIAN CAPITAL TERRITORY)

NEW SOUTH WALES is the mother State of the Commonwealth. To the whole of the eastern seaboard which he discovered in 1770, Captain Cook gave the name "New Wales"; and when in 1778 the first English colony in Australia was founded it received the name New South Wales and extended, nominally at least, inland as far as longitude 135° E.— that is, it occupied roughly the eastern half of the continent.

As we have seen, Tasmania, South Australia, Victoria and Queensland were parted successively from the parent State, so that New South Wales is now the second smallest State on the mainland. It retains, however, near the centre of its coastline, the site of the first settlement in Australia, and on that spot has grown the largest city in the continent— Sydney.

Even so, New South Wales is more than three times as large as the United Kingdom. She contains nearly half the sheep of the continent and produces one-third of its wheat; and she leads all States, both in the value of her factory output and in the size of her population.

The boundaries of New South Wales are easily described. Her southern border with Victoria we have already met (p. 86). On the north the boundary follows latitude 29° S. until it meets the Dumaresq river; it follows that river upstream, then strikes across the highlands and along the summits of a prominent spur (Macpherson's Range) to reach the Pacific at Point Danger—very nearly the most easterly portion of the continent. The western boundary, marching with that of South Australia, follows longitude 141° E. (Fig. 39).

CLIMATE

Climatically New South Wales stands between monsoonal Queensland and Mediterranean Victoria. While theoretically this is the belt of the south-east trades, wind roses for typical stations such as Sydney, Canberra and Bourke show that winds blow almost equally frequently from all directions. The prevailing winds, in fact, seem to have been replaced by land and sea breezes on the grand scale. At Sydney the winds are predominantly westerly in the mornings, for then the land is cold and the air descends and presses outwards (and this is particularly true of the winter months); in the afternoons they are

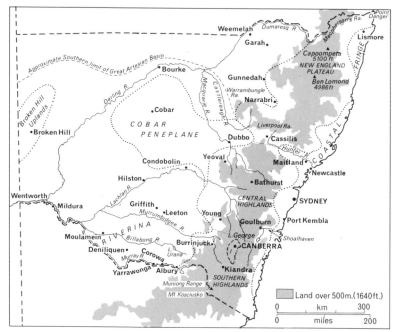

FIG. 39.—New South Wales: physical features, natural regions, towns.

predominantly easterly, for then the land is warm and air moves in to take the place of rising currents (and this is particularly true of the summer months). Sydney is thus a windy place, and if the year is an average one not a single day of calms can be expected.

In New South Wales the rainfall is more evenly distributed throughout the year than in any other State, and in this respect the transitional nature of its climate is well seen: in the highlands of the north-east the monsoonal summer maximum of rainfall is beginning to appear, while in parts of the southern border the winter maximum of the Mediterranean may be detected.

As we have seen (p. 32), the total rainfall diminishes westwards by fairly regular stages. In the far north of the coastal plain, Lismore, with 54 inches (1372 mm) per annum, has one of the heaviest falls in the State; and in general the total diminishes southwards and westwards, so that Sydney has 45 inches (1143 mm) and West Maitland, farther north but 18 miles (29 km) inland and somewhat sheltered has 33 inches (838 mm). The tablelands are well watered: Kiandra, at an altitude of 4578 feet (1396 m), in the north of the Muniong Range, receives a precipitation equivalent to 61 inches (1549 mm) of rain, though much of it is in the form of snow, and snowshoes are almost as common as the more prosaic form of footwear. Elsewhere on the plateaus the rainfall is more moderate, with 31 inches (787 mm) at Glen Innes (north of the

New England summit of Ben Lomond), 24 inches (635 mm) at Goulburn and 23 inches (584 mm) at Bathurst (respectively south-west and west of Sydney).

In the lee of the plateaus, the western slopes receive a rainfall which ranges from 28 inches (711 mm) at Albury (on the upper Murray river) through 25 inches (635 mm) at Young (150 miles (241 km) to the north-east) to 21 inches (533 mm) at Dubbo (175 miles (281 km) inland from Newcastle). Farther west the rainfall declines still further. Deniliquen in the south of the Riverina has 15 inches (381 mm) a year; Hay, farther north on the Murrumbidgee, receives 14 inches (356 mm); Wentworth, at the Murray–Darling junction, 11 inches (279 mm); and Broken Hill, centrally placed in the far west of the State, a mere 9 inches (229 mm).

Broadly speaking, then, we may describe the rainfall of the coastal tracts as being between 40 and 50 inches (1016 and 1270 mm); of the plateaus, between 30 and 40 inches (762 to 1016 mm); of the western slopes, between 20 and 30 inches (508 and 762 mm); and of the plains, between 10 and 20 inches (254 and 508 mm).

New South Wales benefits from a warm coastal current—the East Australian Current—which, sweeping southwards from the equatorial regions, so tempers the winter cold that the mean July temperatures fall below freezing point only in the highest parts of the plateaus. In winter the coast itself is 5–9° C (9–17° F) warmer than London, with Sydney experiencing an average (July) of 12° C (54° F), and a minimum (at about two o'clock in the morning) as high as 8° C (46° F). In the western plains the temperatures are about the same; the plateaus are about 4° C (8° F) cooler.

The summers are warm, but not excessively so. The mean January temperatures along the coast are usually between 18 and 21° C (65 and 70° F) but with 22° C (72° F) at Sydney (London has 18° C; 64° F). The plateaus again are about 4° C (8° F) cooler; but in the plains the range of temperature increases with distance from the sea, and summer temperatures at the Queensland border are about 27 to 31° C (80–89° F).

The whole of the State, excepting only the highland masses above 1000 feet (305 m), enjoys a frost-free period of at least 200 days, and from the point of view of temperatures is suitable for growing not only the temperate crops but also subtropical ones, such as cotton. In latitude, indeed, New South Wales corresponds with the American "South."

FARMING IN NEW SOUTH WALES

New South Wales has a balanced farming economy in which no single major element dominates; in addition it shows a great variety of output, which, as well as the familiar temperate products of wheat, wool and milk, includes such unexpected crops as cotton, sugar, rice and bananas. Table 28 indicates the values of the chief cultivated crops and of the pastoral and dairy products, and may be used as the basis for a general description of the farming of the State.

TABLE 28

New South Wales: value of the chief farm products, 1968–69, in million dollars

Crop	Value	Pastoral or dairy product	Value
Wheat	218·3	Wool	274·0
Hay	39·1	Cattle slaughtered . . .	106·1
Fruit other than citrus . .	28·9	Poultry	68·7
Oats	18·7	Milk and cream . . .	56·8
Vegetables other than potatoes	17·8	Sheep slaughtered . . .	50·7
Cotton	16·9	Pigs slaughtered . . .	24·2
Rice	14·3	Butter	18·7
Citrus fruit . . .	10·3	Cheese	2·1
Barley	10·0		
Green fodder . . .	9·9		
Sugar cane	7·1		
Grapes	6·9		
Potatoes	6·7		
All crops . . .	424·0	Total listed . . .	601·5

These figures vary considerably from year to year according to the climatic and economic conditions. Nevertheless, annual fluctuations in output do not mask the very real advances that are taking place in almost every branch of the agriculture of the State. In 1968–69, the latest year for which statistics are currently available, there were record outputs of wheat, wine, citrus fruits, cotton, rice, mutton and lamb and pig meat, and near records in several other products.

New South Wales is normally the greatest producer of wheat among the Australian States, though in two recent drought years (1965–66 and 1967–68) Western Australia achieved the first place. As Table 28 indicates, in 1968–69 the wheat crop more than equalled in value all the other crops combined. But wheat, perhaps more than any other product, is dependent on the vagaries of climate. In 1965–66 the northern half of the State suffered extreme drought and the wheat harvest amounted to only 39·1 million bushels. But a disastrous harvest is often followed by a bumper crop through the accumulation of unused moisture in the soil, and that of 1966–67 reached 202·5 million bushels.

An adverse climate shows itself in a poor yield per acre for that year; nevertheless there has been a general and significant improvement in yield per acre as a result of the use of fallowing, of improved strains of seed and of increased applications of fertiliser. At the beginning of the twentieth century the yield of wheat in New South Wales was below 10 bushels per acre; by the 1920s it had reached 12 bushels, by the early 1950s 15 bushels and by the middle 1960s 20 bushels. A record yield of 28·4 bushels per acre was attained in 1966–67, and the yield for 1968–69 was 21.6.

In a normal year about half the wheat output of the State is exported, and wheat accounts for about 10 per cent of the total exports of New South Wales. The ranking of the various customers for New South Wales wheat varies considerably from year to year: in 1968–69 38 per cent of the exports were shipped to the United Kingdom, 8 per cent to Peru, 6 per cent to China and 5 per cent each to Chile and the Netherlands.

After wheat, but a long way behind, comes hay; but as this is closely linked with pastoral and dairy farming it is more conveniently considered in that context.

Then follows non-citrus fruits. The climate of New South Wales ranges from the subtropical moisture and heat of the north coast to the comparatively cold plateaus of the Eastern Highlands, and so permits the growing of a wide variety of fruits. Bananas and pineapple flourish on the north coast; strawberries, peaches, plums and citrus fruits are seen in the Sydney district; apples, pears, citrus fruits and grapes are found in the west and south-west; and the tablelands grow the whole range of temperate fruits.

In 1968–69 the values of the main groups of fruits were as follows: orchard fruits, $A20 million; citrus fruits (chiefly oranges), $A10·3 million; bananas, $A8·8 million and grapes, $A6·9 million.

Of the orchard fruits, apples are by far the most important. In 1968–69 New South Wales produced 3·7 million bushels of apples, 1·1 million of peaches, over 0·5 million of pears and smaller quantities of apricots, prunes, plums and cherries. The apples and pears are grown around Bathurst and Orange in the central highlands, near Sydney and in the Murrumbidgee irrigation area. The apple orchards have shown a steady increase in area during the 1960s and the 1968–69 output was the greatest on record.

Almost half the area of the citrus orchards is found in the coastal districts north of Sydney and within about 50 miles (80 km) of the capital, such as in the neighbourhoods of Gosford, Wyong, Windsor and Hornsby. A further 25 per cent of the total area is concentrated in the Murrumbidgee irrigation district and the districts of Coomealla and Curlwaa on the lower Murray river, facing Mildura in Victoria.

Oranges form more than 80 per cent of the total citrus output, lemons nearly 10 per cent and mandarins about 2 per cent. The production of citrus fruit has shown a steady increase during the last 20 years or so. Just before the Second World War the output amounted to about 3·1 million bushels; by the early 1960s it had reached 5·3 million and in 1968–69 a record output was achieved of 6·6 million bushels; this corresponded with a record yield per acre (0·4 ha).

Valued at 8·8 million dollars in 1968–69, the banana crop of New South Wales ranked above sugar cane, grapes and potatoes. The plantations are found in the warmest parts of the State, and are confined mainly to the most northerly coastal districts, especially the Tweed valley and around Coff's Harbour. Output reached a peak by volume in 1963–64 and by value in 1965–66; since that time the problem of over-production has asserted itself: there has been a slight reduction in output and in 1970 a Banana Marketing Committee was inaugurated.

In 1968–69 the average value realised by an acre of grapes in New South Wales was $A351: this was higher than the yield from any other major crop excepting orchard fruits ($A515). It was higher than the return from sugar cane, cotton, potatoes or rice, and far higher than that from any of the temperate cereals. Grape cultivation thus forms a valuable addition to the farm economy of the State.

The area under grapes has shown a steady increase from about 17,000 acres (6800 ha) in 1960 to a record 22,700 acres (9080 ha) in 1969. The main object of grape cultivation in New South Wales is for wine-making (Table 29).

TABLE 29

New South Wales: output of grapes, by type, 1968–69, in tons

For the table	.	.	.	7,470
For drying	.	.	.	8,257
For wine	.	.	.	54,313
Total	.	.	.	70,040

While the output of table grapes and dried grapes (mainly sultanas) has remained fairly constant, the quantity of wine made has increased steadily and reached a record of 8·6 million gallons (39 million litres) in 1968–69. About 70 per cent of the area devoted to wine grapes is found in the Murrumbidgee irrigation district, and another 18 per cent or so in the central coastal area. Most of the table grapes are also grown in the Murrumbidgee area, while the sultana grapes are cultivated farther west,

TABLE 30

New South Wales: chief vegetable crops, by area, 1968–69

				Acres
Potatoes	.	.	.	29,236
Green peas	.	.	.	10,460
French beans	.	.	.	6,122
Tomatoes	.	.	.	4,965
Asparagus	.	.	.	3,462
Carrots	.	.	.	2,736
Cauliflowers	.	.	.	1,891
Lettuce	.	.	.	1,641
Cabbages	.	.	.	1,613
Onions	.	.	.	1,520

in the warm and sunny irrigated districts bordering the lower Murray, mainly in Wentworth Shire (facing Mildura) and to a lesser extent in Wakool Shire (opposite Swan Hill in Victoria).

New South Wales produces a wide range of vegetables, whose rank by area is indicated in Table 30.

It will be seen that potatoes are well in the lead. Their production is concentrated in the coastal and tableland areas. Output increased steadily during the 1960s, doubling in quantity to reach a record total in 1968–69 of 161,000 tons. But local potatoes satisfy only part of the State requirements, and need to be supplemented by imports: these are derived mainly from Tasmania and Victoria.

The leading subtropical crop of the State is cotton. This is of unusual interest since its rise has been so recent, and the area is quite specialised and confined. We consider here the economic background and refer to regional detail below (p. 135).

Until recently cotton growing in Australia was virtually confined to Queensland, which produced only a small proportion of the nation's needs. In 1960 New South Wales had only 97 acres (39 ha) planted with cotton; but since that time the rise has been rapid and consistent and it is convenient to study the details of the process in table form.

TABLE 31
New South Wales: the rise of cotton production

Year ending				No. of holdings (5 or more acres)	Area sown thou. acres	Output mil. lb	Yield per acre, 1000 lb per acre	Value mil. dollars
1962	.	.	.	10	2·0	0·6	0·3	0·1
1963	.	.	.	18	2·4	3·0	1·3	0·3
1964	.	.	.	41	10·9	8·2	0·7	1·0
1965	.	.	.	56	18·9	46·0	2·4	5·9
1966	.	.	.	58	33·2	103·3	3·1	11·1
1967	.	.	.	93	30·1	79·2	2·6	8·8
1968	.	.	.	98	53·5	170·1	3·2	15·7
1969	.	.	.	108	59·8	173·8	2·9	17·0
1970	.	.	.	93	56·7	138·8	2·4	14·9
1971	.	.	.	87	65·2	85·1	1·3	9.8

In New South Wales cotton is grown to a limited extent in the neighbourhood of Bourke (on the Darling River) and elsewhere, but 95 per cent of the total output of the State is grown in a small district along the Namoi River, near the western edge of the Northern Highlands (see Fig. 41, p. 136). The venture has been assisted by settlers of American origin with both knowledge and capital, and they have achieved yields well above those in Queensland, Western Australia and the Murrumbidgee irrigation district of New South Wales.

A major advantage of the Namoi district is the existence of a river dam whose water was not already committed for other purposes, and the whole of the cotton crop is irrigated. New South Wales now produces over 75 per cent of Australia's cotton and supplies more than three-quarters of the nation's requirements. Cotton growing in Australia is now judged to have reached "adult status": the Federal protective bounty has been gradually reduced and ceased to exist in 1972.

Not far below cotton in value are the returns from rice growing. The entire output is derived from the irrigated areas in the west of the State. During the 1960s the area, output and value of the crop doubled as rice growing was extended to additional irrigation districts, and in 1968–69 there was a record harvest by all three criteria. In addition there has been a steady improvement in the average yield per acre. The following figures illustrate the changes that have taken place during the decade.

	Holdings growing rice	Area sown acres	Output thou. bushels	Yield bushels per acre	Value thou. dollars
1960–61	783	46,117	6,001	130	5,376
1968–69	1,463	82,773	13,392	162	14,313
1970–71	1,821	95,332	15,140	159	11,097

Australia is now more than self-sufficient in rice and has a substantial surplus for export; in recent years the exports have approached 50 per cent of the total output. In 1968–69 30 per cent of the exports were shipped to Papua and New Guinea, 22 per cent to Okinawa, 12 per cent to India and 11 per cent to the United Kingdom.

New South Wales produces only about 5 per cent of the total sugar cane of Australia (the major producer is Queensland); but sugar is a valuable crop and in 1968–69 it ranked higher than the vines and potatoes of the State.

The sugar plantations are limited to the lowest portions of the three most northerly river valleys of the State—those of the Richmond, Tweed and Clarence. This is the subtropical portion of New South Wales, where the rainfall approaches 70 inches (1778 mm) annually and almost the whole year is free from frost. Soils do not form a critical element in the distribution of sugar plantations, for the plant grows equally well on peats, silts and prairie earths.

Each valley has its crushing mill and together the three mills employ about 360 people. The capacity of the mill sets a limit to the area of cane that can be handled, and a daily quota is allotted to each grower. The refining is done at Pyrmont (Sydney), which also treats raw sugar from Queensland.[1]

The production of cane increased rapidly in the 1960s from 600,000 tons in 1963–64 to a peak of 1,171,000 tons in 1966–67; since that time it has declined slightly to 998,000 tons in 1968–69.

As Table 28 indicates, the value of all the pastoral and dairy products in New South Wales is about 50 per cent greater than that of all the crops, and wool alone, even in its present depreciated state, still accounts for nearly half the total of the pastoral and dairy products.

Animal husbandry is dependent mainly on the state of the grasslands, and it is necessary first to consider the condition of the pasture and hay of the State. Pasture may be improved in various ways: the natural pasture may be treated to top dressings of fertiliser, or it may be ploughed up and replaced by sown pasture. This is then regarded as an arable crop and is so recorded in the statistics, though the position becomes complicated if the sown pasture remains for a number of years without reseeding. Nevertheless, certain broad conclusions can be drawn.

The area under sown pasture trebled during the 1950s and 1960s: from 3·7 million acres (1·5 million ha) in 1951 it reached a peak in 1966 of 10·9 million acres (4·4 million ha), though it then declined slightly to 10·3 million acres (4·1 million ha) in 1969. This expansion reflects a regional extension of the improved pastures: before the war they were confined mainly to the coastal districts, but since that time they have spread to the inland districts.

The process has been examined in detail for the northern tablelands,[2] where the 1950s and 1960s are seen as a new period in the stock-rearing industry in which the native pastures have been transformed into improved pastures. Basically the native pastures are deficient in three respects: their growth period is restricted mainly to the summer months; they are lacking in nutriment; and they have been made worse by selective overgrazing.

The soils can be improved through the application of fertilisers containing nitrogen, phosphorus and sulphur (and for some parts, potassium and molybdenum); then improved strains of pasture can be sown, such as the clovers, ryegrasses and fescues. Since 1950 traditional methods of reseeding have been augmented by the use of low-flying aircraft, pioneered in this area by a local pilot. Air seeding and fertilising is particularly efficient for hilly and remote areas.

It is calculated that between 1950 and 1965 in the northern tablelands the number of cattle increased by 40 per cent and the number of sheep by 90 per cent (Fig. 40). Moreover, a sheep fed on improved pasture carries a heavier fleece than one fed on the native pasture; and the quantity of wool produced in the period increased by 115 per cent. During the late 1950s and early 1960s there was a striking increase in both the quantities of fertilisers applied to the pastures of New South Wales and in the area treated. Between 1959 and 1965 the area fertilised almost trebled to reach 11 million acres (4·4 million ha), though it had shrunk by 1969 to 7·9 million acres (3·2 million ha). The quantity of fertiliser used followed a broadly similar trend; but the average intensity of application continued to rise, and reached a record of 132 lb (59·86 kg) to the acre (0·4 ha). Part of this expansion has been achieved through the use of low-flying aircraft, and the duration of

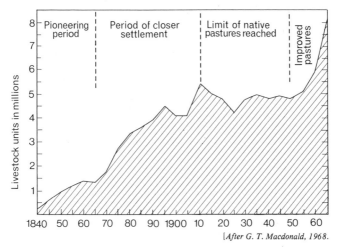

[After G. T. Macdonald, 1968.

FIG. 40.—New South Wales: the expansion in livestock numbers. The graph illustrates four stages in the development of the livestock industry on the northern tablelands of New South Wales. For calculating purposes, a "livestock unit" is reckoned as one cow or seven sheep.

flying time used in the service of agriculture actually multiplied between 7 and 8 times to reach 67,000 hours in 1964–65. It has since declined, however, to 43,000 hours in 1968–69.

Only a small proportion of this pasture is cut for hay, yet its value in 1968–69 exceeded that of all other crops excepting wheat (Table 28), and New South Wales is second only to Victoria in the value of its hay crop.

The pastures have thus greatly increased their carrying capacity, and this has been reflected in the steady increase in the number of cattle in the State (Table 32). The sheep flock has not shared in this expansion, but has remained fairly steady during the 1960s, no doubt owing to the adverse prices for wool.

TABLE 32
New South Wales: livestock numbers, in thousands

Year				Cattle	Sheep	Pigs
1941	.	.	.	2,769	55,568	508
1951	.	.	.	3,703	54,111	317
1961	.	.	.	4,242	68,087	455
1971	.	.	.	6,494	70,605	796

Dairying in New South Wales is mainly confined to the coastal areas, from which most of the demand for fresh milk originates, and 90 per cent of the dairy cattle are in those districts. Inland, dairy cattle are kept only to supply local needs, or in the irrigation districts where high quality pastures are available.

The trend during the 1960s has been a reduction in the amount of milk converted into butter and an increase in the proportion sold fresh; and in 1968–69 the quantity of milk distributed by the Milk Board reached a record figure of 95 million gallons (432 mil. litres).

The number of dairy cattle fell during the 1960s from 1,079,000 head in 1960 to 873,000 in 1969; this was more than offset, however, by the rise in the size of the beef herd, from 2,689,000 head in 1960 to 3,901,000 in 1969. New South Wales ranks well below Queensland in the production of beef and veal, but the general output has been increasing, though this is sometimes masked by adverse climatic conditions; thus the 5-year average output for the late 1940s was 160,000 tons, while that for the early 1960s was 250,000 tons. A record output of 303,000 tons was reached in 1964–65.

In 1968–69 about one-third of the beef and veal produced in New South Wales was exported; of this, 80 per cent went to the United States, 3 per cent to Japan and 2 per cent to the United Kingdom.

The size of the sheep flock in any given year is related to the state of the pastures and hence to the climatic circumstances (in particular the amount of rainfall). Thus in 1966 the number of sheep fell from a record 72 million in 1965 to 61 million; since that time it has gradually risen again, to stand at 70·6 million head in 1971.

Traditionally wool has been the staple export of New South Wales, and during the greater part of the 1950s it accounted for about 55 per cent of the total exports of the State. This dominance no longer obtains. Wool is still the leading export, twice as valuable as the wheat and nearly three times as valuable as the coal and the iron and steel; but in 1968–69 its share of the total exports had fallen to 21 per cent. About 40 per cent of the wool exports were shipped to Japan, 8 per cent to the United Kingdom, 6 per cent to France and 5 per cent to Belgium.

A record quantity of 731 million lb (332 million kg) was produced in 1963–64. The size of the wool output is related to the number of sheep, which as we have seen is linked with the condition of the pastures; but it also depends on the average size of the fleece (the "clip"). As a result of improvements in breeding and management there has been a gradual but consistent increase in the average clip from 8·2 lb (3·63 kg) in the early 1940s to a record 9·1 lb (4·87 kg) in 1968–69.

Unfortunately no simple technique can control the world price of wool; and in the 1960s the average price realised in New South Wales auctions fell from 58·6 cents per lb in 1964 to only 38·9 cents in 1970—the lowest price for twenty-two years. Not only does this result in a reduced return to the producer, but it raises the whole question of the profitability, and hence the very existence of the industry (*see* p. 167).

THE REGIONS OF NEW SOUTH WALES

In our description of the State we begin with the highland core (including Canberra), then discuss the coastal districts to the east (with Sydney) and the slopes and plains to the west, to finish at Broken Hill in the far west (Fig. 39).

THE EASTERN HIGHLANDS

The plateaus of New South Wales occupy nearly one-third of the area of the State and form its most striking physical feature. Everywhere they extend to within a few miles of the coast. Even at their narrowest, in the north, they are 80 miles (129 km) wide; at their widest, north of Newcastle, the main mass is 220 miles (354 km) broad and sends off a long spur beyond Cobar to the west.

Structurally they consist of folded Palaeozoic rocks together with granitic intrusions (especially in the northern and southern borders) and with extensive lava flows (particularly in the west). These masses have been subjected to long periods of erosion, and faulting on a large scale has produced many blocks of differing altitudes and with abrupt eastern slopes. Though we speak of the Australian Alps, these are similar to the Alps of Europe only in name. They are only half as high, as the folding took place much earlier; their contemporaries are the English Pennines, the Appalachians of the eastern United States and the plateaus of Bohemia, Spain and southern France.

The Eastern Highlands are remarkably compact, but they contain two transverse depressions which allow communication between the coast and the interior. The more obvious of these is the Cassilis Gate, which links the long, narrow valley occupied by the Hunter and its headstreams with the valleys of the upper Macquarie and Castlereagh, tributaries of the Darling. This is the only route across the highlands at less than 2000 feet (610 m) above sea-level (the summit of the saddle is at about 1500 feet; 457 m). Farther south, Lake George occupies a faulted trough between the headwaters of the Yass river (a tributary of the Murrumbidgee) and those of the Shoalhaven (which flows to the Pacific), and the highlands may be crossed there at a little over 2000 feet (610 m).

We may thus subdivide the highlands into a northern, a central and a southern section. The northern portion is the New England Plateau, whose average height is about 3000 feet (914 m), though its summits in Mount Capoompeta and Ben Lomond rise to 5000 feet (1524 m). Many so-called ranges are named here on the maps, such as the Hastings, Mount Royal and Liverpool Ranges; but these finger-like extensions from the main body of the plateau are merely remnants of a once much larger tableland, and the river systems are busily attacking them on all sides.

The central parts of the New England Plateau are composed largely of Silurian and Devonian sediments; these are flanked by masses of granite and similar rocks. Volcanoes burst into action during Tertiary times, and their lava outpourings are to be seen in the outlying westerly portions of the plateau (the Nandewar, Liverpool and Warrumbungle Ranges). In many parts of the plateau the surfaces are distinctly level: this suggests that they are in reality old peneplains, which, once near sea-level, have since been elevated between 3000 and 5000 feet (914 and 1524 m). The abrupt edges of these peneplains are being rapidly eroded, especially by the short eastward-flowing streams, which are fed by a high rainfall. It is this uplift which is responsible for the immense gorges and magnificent waterfalls which are to be seen in parts of the eastern slopes, as, for example, in the upper Macleay basin.

The plateau surface is largely clothed by various species of eucalypt. Where the rainfall is greater than 28 inches (610 mm) per annum we meet a remarkable variety: there is the ironbark—probably the world's strongest timber; the grey box—a tough timber; the red gum—resistant to the white ant; tallowwood—a durable and greasy timber; and the blackbutt or Australian mahogany—durable and strong. In value the forest products are at present small compared with farm products (they form only one-seventeenth of the total rural production of the State); but undoubtedly there is here a valuable reserve of timber for future generations. West of the 22-inch (560-mm) isohyet the trees begin to thin out, and by the time we reach the plains they are confined to the water-courses.

The New England Plateau is separated from the more southerly highlands by a structural basin, roughly rectangular in shape, whose rim is composed of Permo-Carboniferous coal measures and whose floor contains Triassic sediments. On the relief map this basin is obscured by the Tertiary lavas which form the Liverpool Ranges. The rivers have managed to excavate wide valleys in the softer strata, and in spite of the resistant volcanic rocks, a difficult railway route links the Hunter valley with that of the Mooki (a headstream of the Darling). Farther south the Liverpool Ranges can be by-passed and the easily excavated Permo-Carboniferous rocks allow the Hunter valley to link with that of the Macquarie. This route, the Cassilis Gate, was early utilised as a way to the interior, but in modern times, curiously enough, it has been almost completely neglected.

Structurally, the highland to the south forms a single region, built mainly of Silurian strata buttressed by granitic masses. To the west a long and broad extension of the Silurian rocks stretches beyond Cobar almost to the Darling, while to the east the dissected edge of the plateau forms the famous Blue Mountains behind Sydney. The highlands reach their greatest elevation in the Muniong and Snowy Ranges, where Mount Kosciusko rises to 7318 feet (2230 m). Within the plateau mass are several basins, elongated from north to south: these troughs are the result of subsidence along parallel fault lines: they are "rift basins" if not "rift valleys."

Economy. On the pastures of these tablelands both sheep and cattle are raised, and in the valleys maize, peas, oats, lucerne and the temperate fruits are cultivated. There is also an important tourist industry: there are spectacular waterfalls and 2000-foot (610-m) gorges in the Blue Mountains; Jenolan and Yarrangobilly possess remarkable limestone caverns; and Kosciusko offers winter sports: these districts together attract half a million visitors annually.

We have already referred to the rise of cotton growing in New South Wales (p. 128). It is almost completely concentrated in a narrow belt of land 7 to 8 miles wide (12 km) from north to south and about 30 miles (48 km) from east to west, lying astride the Namoi river near the north-western edge of the Eastern Highlands (Figs 41 and 42).

The project was launched following the completion in 1960 of the Keepit dam on the Namoi river, designed to supplement the water derived from boreholes for the stock-rearing industry. In the event, this proved unnecessary, so that the water was available for cotton growing.

The physical conditions are ideal: the local black soils are fertile and retentive of moisture; the high summer temperatures are accompanied by abundant sunshine; and the land is very flat but with a slight tilt down to the west, which facilitates irrigation and drainage. Many of the growers have had experience of cotton production in California.[3]

The cotton district centres on the small settlement of Wee Waa (population, 1966: 1492), which has a direct railway link with Sydney, and is the site of one of the seven ginneries. By 1968 the venture had proved itself and an oil processing mill was established at Narrabri, the nearest moderately-sized town (population, 1966: 5953). Its annual capacity of 50,000 tons is sufficient to absorb the whole output of cotton seed of the district.[4]

There are essentially three end-products of cotton seed milling: the oil, representing 63 per cent of the output by value, the meal (32 per cent) and the linters or fibre (5 per cent). The linters are used for upholstery in Sydney or Melbourne, or are exported for paper-making to Japan. The meal is used as a constituent element in the manufacture of poultry food, and assists that industry, especially in the Hunter valley. But the most important product is the oil, used as a domestic cooking oil, or in the canning of fish, or in the manufacture of margarine. It is marketed mainly in the three State capitals of south-eastern Australia, and in this respect Narrabri is conveniently situated, almost midway between Sydney and Melbourne, and served by good roads.

Not only is Australia thus approaching self-sufficiency in cotton fibre, but it also has the benefit of the valuable by-products. Future extension of cotton growing is likely to be in the Moree district, based on irrigation from the Gwydir river.

The older rocks of the plateaus contain a varied series of minerals. Gold has been found in widely scattered districts: in the middle of the Silurian masses such as Hillgrove (in the north) and at Cobar and

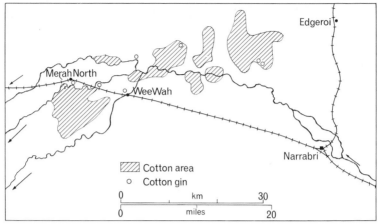

[After J. C. R. Camm and P. G. Irwin, 1971.

Fig. 41.—New South Wales: cotton growing in the Namoi Valley. The Namoi river flows westward and its water eventually reaches the Darling river. The cotton areas shown here are irrigated from the Keepit dam, about 50 miles (80 km) south-east of Narrabri. The district produces three-quarters of the Australian cotton crop and satisfies about half the nation's requirements of raw cotton.

[Courtesy the Agent-General for New South Wales.

FIG. 42.—New South Wales: unloading raw cotton in the Namoi Valley. Raw cotton is being unloaded from a mechanical harvester ready for transporting by truck to one of the ginneries. The district has several physical advantages for cotton growing, but the industry was sparked off by the unexpected supply of irrigation water from the Keepit dam.

Canbelego (in the Cobar plateau); and round their edges, such as at Peak Hill and Wellington (in the centre) and at Wyalong and Adelong (in the south). A century ago New South Wales was renowned for her production of gold; but output declined rapidly after the First World War, and in 1955 the State produced only 3 per cent of the total for Australia. Production was from an alluvial working of the gravels of the Macquarie river, where the precious metal has accumulated from parent veins in the Palaeozoic rocks.

Until 1963 lead and copper were being mined at Captain's Flat (close to Lake George in the south of the plateau); and lead is still being produced together with silver and zinc at several small places not to be found on atlas maps. As a producer of tin New South Wales ranks third, after Tasmania and Queensland; most of it is obtained by dredging and sluicing in the New England district, where Tingha (west of Ben Lomond) is a centre of the tin-bearing granites. Deposits of manganese, bismuth, wolfram and sapphires are also known to exist in the plateaus, together with useful building marbles, and the more prosaic industrial lime (Table 33).

TABLE 33

New South Wales: value of the chief minerals, 1970–71

Mineral	Value of output ($A million)
Coal	196·8
Silver–lead–zinc . . .	77·5
Mineral sands . . .	35·3
Roadstone etc. . . .	21·4
Sand and gravel . . .	17·5
Clay	3·0
Tin	5·3
Limestone	4·1
All minerals . . .	376·6

NOTE: In 1970–71 there were record outputs of coal, mineral sands, sand and gravel, roadstone and tin, and near records in clay and limestone.

The Snowy Mountains Scheme. In the southern part of the plateau interest centres on two major planning schemes, each outstanding in its own sphere: the first is the Snowy Mountains Scheme for hydro-electric power and irrigation; the second is the building of Canberra.

The principle behind the Snowy Mountains Scheme is simple. The Snowy river and its tributaries rise in an area of abundant rainfall and snow (more than 60 inches (1524 mm) per annum); but hitherto this water has run to waste in the Tasman Sea, while thirsty soils farther west lay barren through lack of water. Seven major dams impound the waters of the upper Snowy, its tributary the Eucumbene and the upper Murrumbidgee; and by means of three main tunnels the water so stored is conducted westwards below the continental divide to feed the head-waters of the Murray and the Tumut (which joins the Murrumbidgee).

There are considerable differences in level among these reservoirs and water-courses, and during its journey the water is used again and again to drive turbines and generate electricity. As Fig. 43 indicates, there are two main parts to the project.

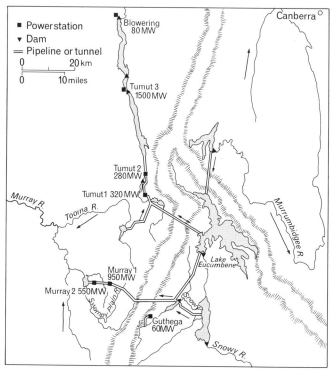

Fig. 43—The Snowy Mountains Scheme. This is a dual purpose project which combines irrigation with power production. Water from the Snowy headstreams and the upper Murrumbidgee is diverted westwards across the Great Dividing Range and used to supplement the irrigation water available from the Murray river. On the way it generates electricity in seven power stations with a combined capacity of 3740 MW.

In the northern section, water stored in the artificial Lake Eucumbene is diverted westwards across the divide into the Tumut river (a tributary of the Murrumbidgee). There it generates electricity in the three Tumut power stations and in the smaller Blowering plant; it also provides an additional 1·1 million acre/ft of water annually for irrigation from the Murrumbidgee lower downstream. The extensions in the irrigation area so permitted are indicated on Fig. 61 (p. 168).

In the southern section, water stored in the Jindabyne reservoir is fed westwards across the divide into the Murray via its tributary, the Swampy Plain river, and on the way generates power in the Murray stations. It provides an additional 800,000 acre/ft of water annually for use in the Murray irrigation areas.

Table 34 indicates the relative sizes of the power stations in this ambitious project, which will have taken twenty-five years to complete. It is expected that the total cost (which by mid-1970 had amounted to 732 million dollars) can be recovered from the sale of electricity, and no charge is being made for the irrigation water.

TABLE 34

Snowy Mountains Scheme: capacities of power stations

	Station					Capacity MW	Year of construction
Northern section	Tumut 1	.	.	.	.	320	1959
(Snowy–Tumut)	Tumut 2	.	.	.	.	280	1962
	Tumut 3	.	.	.	.	1500	1972–74
	Blowering	.	.	.	.	80	1969
Southern section	Murray 1	.	.	.	.	950	1966–67
(Snowy–Murray)	Murray 2	.	.	.	.	550	1969
	Guthega	.	.	.	.	60	1955
	Total capacity	.	.	.		3740	

Currently (July 1973) the Snowy Mountains Scheme is all but complete. Six of the seven generating stations are feeding their power into the grid, and construction of the final and largest plant, Tumut 3, is well advanced. Two aspects of the project are illustrated in Figs 44 and 45.

Canberra. The story of Canberra begins in 1900, when it was decreed that the Federal capital should be built in New South Wales and should be situated at least 100 miles (161 km) from Sydney. During the years 1902–8 eight other sites were considered, all west or south-west of Sydney, but Canberra was adopted in 1908, and three years later an area of 900 square miles (2331 km²) surrounding the site was constituted as Federal Territory.

Canberra lies near the northern slopes of the Australian Alps, only 35 miles (56 km) from the main Sydney–Melbourne railway. Here, in a broad "plain" at an altitude of 1900 feet (579 m), where a shallow river, the Molonglo, meanders lazily from south-east to north-west, the new capital is being built (still!). Overlooking the site are three conical hills whose summits rise 700–800 feet (213–243 m) above river-level. The city district is sheltered by spurs of the highlands, and receives a relatively low rainfall (24 inches (610 mm) average in the period 1928–55); but there will be no difficulty concerning the water supply, since the rainfall increases to 50 inches (1270 mm) per annum only 30 miles (48 km) to the south.

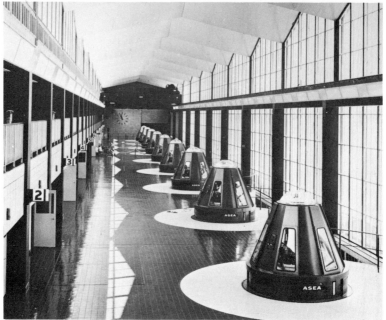

FIG. 44.—Murray No. 1 power station: the generating hall. The ten turbo-generators of Murray No. 1 reach a combined capacity of 950 MW. Completed in 1967, this power station will be exceeded in size only by Tumut No. 3.

FIG. 45.—Pipeline section for Tumut No. 3 power station. The photograph illustrates a section of one of the six huge pipelines that are being used to supply Tumut No. 3 power station—the largest and the last to be completed in the Snowy Mountains Scheme.

At 2000 feet (610 m) the air is clear and dry, and Canberra is a sunny place. Summer day temperatures soar to 38° C (100° F), but on the winter nights the air is generally below freezing point, so that chopping firewood becomes a ritual.

The plan of the city is based on that prepared by the Chicago architect, W. B. Griffin, who won the international competition organised in 1911. The street pattern combines the rectangular layout of most American cities with the circles, crescents and focal centres to

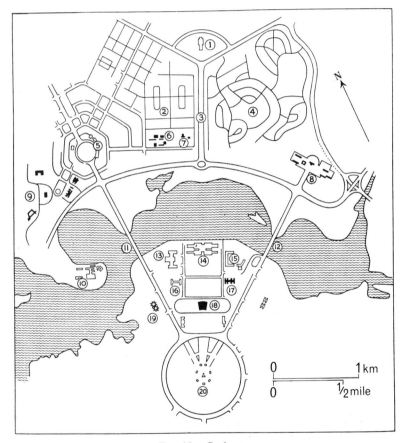

FIG. 46.—Canberra.

Key to numbering: 1, Australian war memorial; 2, Reid residential area; 3, Anzac Parade; 4, Campbell residential area; 5, Civic centre; 6, Technical college; 7, St John's Church; 8, Russell offices; 9, University; 10, Hospital; 11, Commonwealth Avenue Bridge; 12, King's Avenue Bridge; 13, National Library site; 14, Parliament House site; 15, High Court site; 16, Treasury building; 17, Administration building; 18, Parliament House; 19, Hotel Canberra; 20, National Centre, Capital Hill.

[*Courtesy Australian News & Information Bureau.*

FIG. 47.—Canberra: aerial view. The camera is pointing south-east. In the foreground
are the buildings of the civic centre, the commercial centre and the National
university. Lake Burley Griffin is crossed by the Commonwealth Avenue bridge;
beyond it is the parliamentary zone. With a 1971 population of 141,000,
Canberra is the largest inland city of Australia. Its population is planned to reach
250,000 in the next 20 years or so.

be seen in some English planned estates. A pleasing feature is the
damming of the river, so converting it into a series of lakes. The city lies
astride the flood plain. Its main axis (Commonwealth Avenue) runs
northwards from Capital Hill to the civic centre (with the university)
beyond the lakes (Figs 46 and 47). In this garden city 2 million trees
have been planted.

The plan provides for all the administrative buildings required in a
modern capital: the courts of justice, the mint, the government printer;
the residences for the Governor-General, the Prime Minister and the
Senators; the foreign embassies, the military barracks and the police
headquarters. In addition, there are the buildings required in any
large city: the cathedral, library, training and technical colleges, the
university, the schools, the power plant and so on. In 1927 the capital
was inaugurated, and a temporary but distinctive Parliament House
was opened and is still in use. An air view showing Parliament
House, together with its surrounding parks and gardens, appears in
Fig. 47.

Canberra differs from other capitals in that it has little industry. In
1928 the population numbered 7000–8000; in June 1966 there were
92,199 inhabitants and in 1971, 140,996; and they occupied an area as
large as Manchester.

THE COASTAL FRINGE, INCLUDING NEWCASTLE, PORT KEMBLA AND SYDNEY

There is no true coastal plain in New South Wales: rather is there a series of restricted and sometimes isolated lowlands, of which only the Hunter valley extends for more than about 40 miles (64 km) inland. While some of these lowlands have undoubtedly resulted from the accumulation of river sediments, not all of them are to be explained in this way. Thus, the lowland embayment around Sydney is composed of Triassic shales which by some chance escaped the remarkable earth movements which reared up the sandstones to form the Blue Mountains to the west; the Hunter valley has been carved out of the soft Permo-Triassic sediments which floor a basin between the more resistant formations of the Blue Mountains and the New England Plateau.

The lowlands differ widely in the uses to which they are put. The far north is favoured by an abundant rainfall: up to 80 inches (2032 mm) may fall in a year; and this, together with the high temperatures, has allowed remnants of Malayan flora to survive. But the level land suitable for cultivation has largely been cleared, and in this subtropical region sugar cane, pineapples and bananas are grown.

By contrast, the deep and sheltered valley of the Hunter river has an unusually low rainfall: here in fact some of the drier species representative of central Australia have found their way across the Great Divide. In the fertile lower portions of the valley there are market gardens, orchards and vineyards, together with fields of fodder crops intended for dairy cattle.

The Sydney embayment is largely devoted to growing market-garden crops for use in Sydney itself; but there is some specialisation here too: the Parramatta district is noted for its orange groves, and Campbelltown is a centre for dairy farming. Farther south the lowland becomes narrower or is entirely absent: a great scarp approaches to within a few miles of the steelworks at Port Kembla, and it has not been found practicable to extend the coastal railway beyond the Shoalhaven river.

South of Sydney the mountains are never far from the coast; this has discouraged the growth of market towns of any size, but the district has developed as an important recreational zone for the people of Sydney, Canberra and urban Victoria. North of Sydney, however, the highlands recede sufficiently to allow the development of several productive river basins between the Dividing Range and the coast: these have provided the setting for the establishment of some of the earliest towns in Australia.

The process is well documented and has been examined in detail.[5] The early settlers felt the need for centres of commerce and administration; this was recognised by the authorities, and sites were chosen and development plans drawn up, though in most cases insufficient attention was devoted to the possibilities of flooding.

Though the main highland belt is some 65 miles (104 km) inland it sends out broad spurs towards the coast, so that the belt is divided into a series of separate lowlands, each based on a river system. From south to north these are the basins of the Hunter, the Manning, the Macleay, the Clarence and the Richmond (Fig. 48).

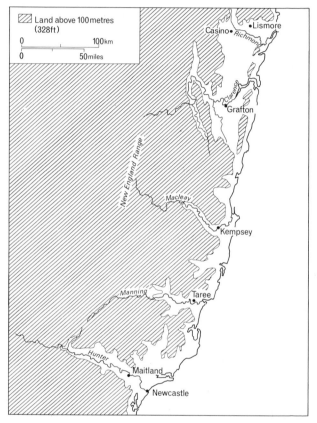

FIG. 48.—Early towns in coastal New South Wales. Each began as a port near the head of navigation of its river.

Broadly speaking, the tide of settlement flowed northwards. Usually the first to arrive was the timber cutter, anxious to exploit the stands of cedar that flourished on the foothills and in the mountains. He looked for a suitable centre for collecting the timber and floating it downstream. Later came the squatter-settler, who aimed to set up a sheep run. He was interested in the more level land of the river lowlands, but he too needed a port from which he could ship his bales of wool.

Thus the town site that emerged in each basin was a river port, situated at or very close to the head of navigation. Typically it was planned on a rectangular grid, in which one or more streets ran down to wharves on the river. An inn, a store and administrative offices formed the core of the new town, and the dwellings were on the outskirts. While an elevated site was sometimes chosen, often the town included quite extensive stretches of flood plain, and it is only in recent extensions of the residential areas that allowance has been made for the hazard of flood.

The earliest town to be laid out was Maitland, on the Hunter river; its grid was surveyed in 1829. Settlement in the district was attracted not only by timber and pastoral farming but by the presence of coal seams close to the surface. But for a dispute between the landowner and the authorities, the town might have been founded even earlier. The selected site was a compromise: it was not at the head of navigation, nor had it a river frontage, for it was set back nearly a mile from the river bank; but it did possess the real advantage of a flood-free location, on land mainly 50 feet (15 m) above sea-level, and with ample room for expansion. This is the present East Maitland.

It became clear, however, that the commerce of the district required a port, and two additional centres developed: West Maitland, at the head of navigation; and Morpeth, below a set of close meanders that reduced the advantage of navigation higher upstream. But their river frontages were gained at the expense of flood risk; and in 1955 134 homes in Maitland were washed away or demolished, and part of the business district was flooded to a depth of 9 or 10 feet (2·7 to 3 m).

Settlement in the Manning basin, a few miles farther north, had become well established by the 1840s, and the site of a village had been reserved on the north bank of the river at the head of navigation. This became the present town of Wingham. While it was sufficiently central for the large pastoral properties upstream, it was less adequate for the smaller farms that were becoming established in the more intensive occupation of the land to the east. Accordingly, in 1854 a "private" town was laid out on the same bank of the river but about 10 miles (16 km) lower downstream. This was Taree. It was a well chosen site, where the river was overlooked by firm, dry ground beyond the reach of flood. Its main street, Victoria Street, runs parallel to the river and the core of the settlement developed where this was joined by a street at right angles, running to the river. The six original rectangular urban blocks have become the commercial centre of the town.

The next important river basin to the north is that of the Macleay, whose headstreams rise high up in the heart of the New England Range. Here, there is a single large centre, Kempsey, which lies astride the river and has grown from four separate nuclei. The settlement began at the head of navigation on the south bank, for in the 1830s the river marked the northern boundary of the colony.

First to be built was a "private" town that originated from the sale of thirty-five allotments in 1836; they occupied a good flood-free site that

overlooked the deep water on a concave bend of the Macleay. This is
now East Kempsey. With the extension of settlement beyond the river
new farms were established and their wool required a new shipment
point. It was provided in 1855, when the new "Government Town of
West Kempsey" was laid out, mainly on the north bank, but including
also an orderly grid of streets south of the river. So to East Kempsey
there was added South Kempsey and West Kempsey. For the administrative focus of the Macleay, West Kempsey was selected, and today
large blocks in its centre and on its outskirts are devoted to health,
education and other public services. But the town still lacked any
important commercial centre, and this developed later in the 1960s on

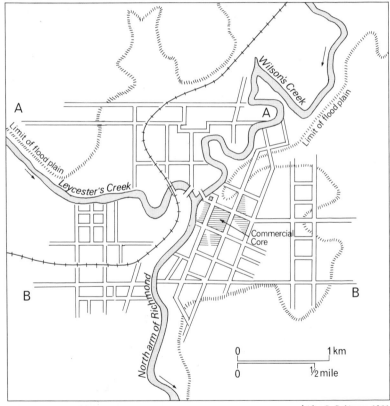

[After R. Robinson, 1966.

FIG. 49.—New South Wales: the site of Lismore. The settlement originated as a
collecting centre for cedar timber, at the effective head of navigation of the
Richmond river, marked by the junction of the two creeks. The plan, laid out in
1855, indicates the surveyor's preference for half-mile (1·30 km²) squares. The
roads indicated by AA and BB are exactly one mile (1·6 km) apart. In the choice
of the site, insufficient allowance was made for the risk of flooding.

vacant, low-lying land on the left bank within the loop of the river, and facing the original settlement of East Kempsey.

North of the Macleay basin a major spur of the New England range thrusts eastwards towards the coast to culminate in Round Mountain (5300 feet; 1590 m). Beyond it is the extensive basin of the Clarence river, and here the town of Grafton originated as a supply centre and collecting point for the cedar-cutters, at a point which gave access to the river. While the early settlement was on the south bank, it soon became clear that the north side provided a more extensive flood-free area, and a government town was laid out here in 1848; this was nominated as the official capital of the Clarence. The commercial life of the town clings to the broad and straight road that leads direct to the river, and the suburb on the south bank remains essentially residential.

The most northerly coastal basin in New South Wales is that of the Richmond. By the middle 1840s much of the accessible timber of the Clarence basin had been exploited and the cedar-cutters moved northwards into the Richmond; they set up a collecting station where the junction of two creeks marked the head of the navigation of the river. Here in 1855 the street plan of Lismore was laid out on a compact area on the east bank of the stream. At first it met some competition from the town of Casino: this had been established several years earlier as a commercial centre for the local sheep farmers, placed higher upstream at a fording point of the river. In 1871 Casino had a population of about 270, while Lismore had only 90 inhabitants; but as the level lands to the east became more closely settled the superior site of Lismore began to tell. By 1881 it had overtaken Casino and a decade later it was twice as large as its rival.

Lismore has now spread across both creeks; but the commercial centre remains inside the original rectangular grid, whose streets run right down to the river (Fig. 49). Extensive areas of the town, however, are liable to flood, and only in the later extensions of the residential area has the flood hazard been avoided by building on the higher ground on the outskirts.

TABLE 35

Population growth in five towns of coastal New South Wales north of Sydney

Year				Maitland	Lismore	Grafton	Taree	Kempsey
1954	.	.	.	25,676	18,312	14,964	9,068	7,600
1961	.	.	.	27,353	18,936	15,526	10,050	8,016
1966	.	.	.	28,428	19,734	15,951	10,560	8,181
1969 (est.)		.	.	29,650	20,140	16,230	11,050	8,340

Table 35 records the recent growth of the towns whose beginnings we have examined.

The coastal districts south of Sydney present striking contrasts to the quiet farming basins to the north. Kiama, 76 miles (122 km) south of the capital, lies on a geographical boundary that separates the urban and industrial area of metropolitan Sydney from a zone of resorts that stretches as far as the Victorian frontier. It contains no fewer than sixty-one holiday centres, all of them offering some form of beach and water activity. Among them they can accommodate more than 45,000 tourists.[6]

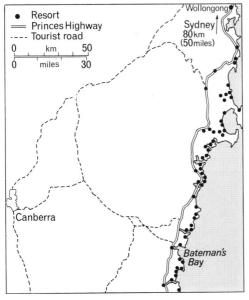

FIG. 50.—New South Wales: resorts. The map illustrates the close spacing of resorts along the northern half of the South Coast (the coast south of Sydney). Farther south the resorts are fewer and more widely spaced. All are served by the Princes Highway, which is joined at intervals by tourist roads from the interior. Six of the resorts indicated each accommodate over 2000 visitors, and twelve between 1000 and 2000.

The most active part is the northern portion of the zone, between Kiama and Bateman's Bay: here there are seventeen centres, each of which can cater for more than 1000 guests (Fig. 50). Their visitors originate mainly from Sydney. Bateman's Bay itself is linked with the western parts of the State by an easy road through the Clyde Mountain pass, and welcomes many visitors from Canberra. The quieter resorts

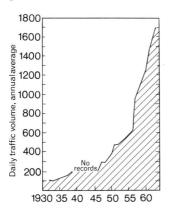

FIG. 51.—New South Wales: growth of the South Coast traffic. This graph illustrates the steep rate of growth of the tourist traffic of the South Coast. The census point was on the Princes Highway at Bateman's Bay and the graph indicates the average daily traffic (counting vehicles in both directions) for each year. Tourism has grown into a major industry along the South Coast.

[After B. Ryan, 1965.

farther south tend to be frequented mainly by visitors from inland New South Wales and from Victoria.

Climatically this holiday belt is attractive to people from Sydney and Canberra, who seek a cooler summer, and to those from Melbourne, who seek a warmer winter. Its rise has been relatively recent (Fig. 51), and is related to local improvements in transport. These include the sealing of the surface of the Princes Highway (1945–50), which links all the resorts together, and the replacement of the Bateman's Bay ferry by a bridge (1956). The industry is highly seasonal in intensity, and shows six peak periods in a typical year: they correspond with school and national holidays and the greatest surge is in the summer, between Christmas and early March (Fig. 52).

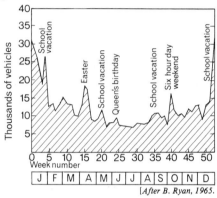

Fig. 52.—New South Wales: seasonal variations in the flow of tourist traffic, 1963. This graph indicates the typical nature of the traffic flow: the census point was at the northern end of the Bateman's Bay bridge. Peak traffic periods occur during the school holidays.

[After B. Ryan, 1965.

But the coastal fringe is chiefly significant as the setting for industry and towns, for this is the most closely settled belt of country in the whole of Australia. In describing it we have conveniently subdivided it into three: the Newcastle district; the Port Kembla area; and Sydney. All three are linked by the Newcastle coal basin, and this fuel is fundamental in their economic life.

COAL IN NEW SOUTH WALES

Coal is by far the most important mineral raised in New South Wales. During the early 1960s it represented more than half by value of all the mine and quarry products of the State, and although it had fallen a little below 50 per cent of the total by 1968 it was still twice as valuable as its nearest competitor (silver–lead–zinc) and four times as valuable as its second rival (building materials).

The Newcastle coal basin occupies an area of 16,500 square miles (58,275 km²), and is the largest in the southern hemisphere. It has fourteen workable seams, and there are outcrops at Lithgow (in the Blue Mountains, west of Sydney), at Newcastle (on the coast, 70 miles (113 km) north of Sydney) and in the cliffs at Bulli (nearly 40 miles (64 km) south of the capital). These districts have been named the western, northern and southern fields respectively. Sydney itself lies near the centre of the basin, and coal seams are present about 3000 feet (914 m) below the surface.

The development of the coalfield has followed the familiar pattern of small-scale workings at the outcrops of the seams, followed later by gradual expansion of the industry through the use of larger and deeper shaft mines.

The northern field (Fig. 53). In the northern district eight seams outcrop in succession following a series of elaborate sinuous curves

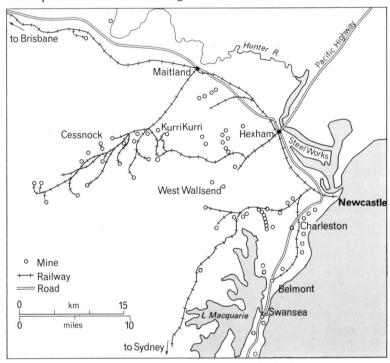

FIG. 53.—Coal mining in the Newcastle district.

with a general trend from north-west to south-east. The most valuable of these have been the Borehole and the Burwood seams, in the lowest part of the coal series.

Coal mining began soon after 1800, when shafts and tunnels were constructed at the mouth of the Hunter river and worked by convict labour. Until about 1875 the mines were still essentially outcrop workings, in which the seams were followed by tunnels up to about 2 miles (3·2 km) back from the outcrop. From this period date the early mines at Waratah and Lambton, about 5 miles (8 km) west of Newcastle.[7]

Between 1876 and 1900 there was a rapid expansion in mining. Close to the shore and within two miles (3·2 km) of Newcastle an outlier of the Borehole seam was found to underlie the estuary at a depth of 250 to 350 feet (75 to 105 m). Here it was up to 30 feet thick (9 m), and was tapped by pits at Hetton and Stockton and by the Sea Pit. In the 1890s shafts were opened farther south, at Burwood, Dudley and Redhead; but they had to penetrate 600 feet (183 m) or more of barren strata to find the seam. About the same time a group of pits was opened near the head of Lake Macquarie, including those at Rhondda, Killingworth and Seaham; and their output was gathered by a railway linking direct to Newcastle.

Few major extensions have since taken place in the Newcastle district, though one new mine was opened in 1927 at Belmont, about nine miles (14·5 km) south of Newcastle, to tap the Borehole seam at a depth of 878 feet (263 m). The main legacy of the period was the closure of many large pits during the depression years.

About 15 to 20 miles (24 to 32 km) west of Newcastle in the district between Maitland and Cessnock is another important coal producing area, developed mainly between 1890 and 1930. The seam worked is the Greta, whose outcrop runs south-west from Maitland to beyond Cessnock. Six mines were opened along the outcrop in the Kurri-Kurri area between 1889 and 1903. Later shafts were sunk 2 or 3 miles (about 3 to 5 km) back from the outcrop, and reached the seam at depths of 500 to 850 feet (150 to 255 m). By the 1920s pits were being sunk south and south-west of Cessnock to work the extremities of the coalfield, where at Kalingo the Greta seam was reached in 1927 at 1245 feet (374 m). The northern field now produces a little more than half of the total output of the coalfield (1968: 17·0 million tons, out of a total of 30·3 million tons).

But mining is a notoriously unstable occupation. During the 1920s three of the four main collieries in the West Wallsend area closed, and during the 1950s there was a drastic decline in mining employment in the Cessnock field. These settlements in fact have managed to survive only because their workers were able to commute to the expanding industries in Newcastle.[8]

The southern field. South of Sydney, between Helensburg and Port Kembla, the coast is backed by a cliff (the Bulli scarp) in which several coal seams are exposed, one above the other. This forms the core of the southern coal producing district.

The early pits, developed between the 1850s and 1880s, were strategically placed opposite convenient shipping points, where jetties could be constructed in the shelter of headlands or reefs. By the turn of the century the coastal railway had been constructed and the industry was no longer dependent on the local jetties, but could make use of the better facilities at Port Kembla. The establishment of a steel industry there in 1928 provided an assured market for the local coking coals. The southern districts account for about one-third of the total output (1968 production: 11·5 million tons).

The western field. West of the Bulli scarp the coal seams dip steeply so that mining would be difficult; but in any case, much of the land here is dedicated to water conservation. Development however has taken place west of the reservoirs, at Appin, where a shaft has been sunk to the exceptional depth of 1800 feet (540 m). In this area of newer exploitation there are no railways, and transport is by road.

Still farther west is the isolated district of Lithgow, about 65 miles (104 km) west of Sydney. The mining districts of the west produce mainly steam coals, and account for little more than 6 per cent of the total output (1968: 1·9 million tons).

Economic aspects. The coal industry of New South Wales is producing at a greater rate than ever before (Table 36).

TABLE 36
New South Wales: output of coal, in million tons

Year			Output
1958	.	.	15·9
1960	.	.	17·7
1962	.	.	19·0
1964	.	.	20·7
1966	.	.	25·5
1968	.	.	30·3
1970	.	.	35·0
1971	.	.	35·1

This increase in output has been in response to the needs of expanding industries at home and to a surge in the demand from Japan. Shipments to Japan rose from less than half a million tons in 1959 to 8·6 million tons in 1968, out of a total overseas shipment of coal in that year of 9·0 million tons (Table 37). The Australian coal industry is thus expanding at a time when those of other developed countries are running down.

TABLE 37
Exports of coal from New South Wales to Japan, in thousand tons

1958	.	.	361
1959	.	.	493
1960	.	.	1,373
1961	.	.	2,387
1962	.	.	2,521
1963	.	.	2,482
1964	.	.	3,314
1965	.	.	5,092
1966	.	.	6,440
1967	.	.	7,074
1968	.	.	8,607
1968–69	.	.	9,718
1969–70	.	.	10,755
1970–71	.	.	9,025

This surge in the coal export trade has brought significant improvements in the equipment of the coal ports. Newcastle is the outlet for the local steam and softer coking coals and those of the Cessnock field; its main shipping channel has been deepened, and conveyor belts have replaced the traditional cranes. Sydney and Port Kembla are busy supplying the long-term contracts with Japan for hard coking coal, and their wharves have been re-equipped in a similar fashion.[9]

At home, the chief consumer of coal is the steel industry, which during the 1960s steadily increased its requirements from 5·0 million tons in 1961 to 7·6 million in 1968. Only a little smaller are the needs of the State power stations, which rose during the same period from 4·4 to 6·5 million tons. No other industry uses coal in comparable quantities. The gasworks of the State are reducing their demands for coal as natural gas becomes more plentiful and oil forms an alternative source as raw material: during the 1960s their demands fell from 845 to 633 thousand tons. Cement works accounted for 463 thousand tons in 1968; brick and tile works and potteries a further 238 thousand.

Quite striking changes have taken place in the coal mining industry in recent years. During the 1950s and 1960s there was an important extension of mechanical cutting and loading. In 1949 only 37 per cent of the total output was mechanically cut and only 33 per cent mechanically loaded; yet by 1968 mechanical cutting and loading were virtually universal. As a result, the output per manshift worked at the coal face has steadily increased: during the 1960s it almost doubled, from 20·6 tons in 1960 to reach 39·5 tons in 1968.

The effect of these changes on the size of the work force has been rather complex. The number of employees in underground coal mines reached a peak in 1954, at 19,557 persons; with the increase in mechanisation the efficiency of the work force improved, and fewer workmen were required. During the later 1950s and early 1960s the labour force fell—sharply at first, and then more gradually, to reach a low point of 11,158 in 1964. Since that year, and contrary to the experience of most other developed countries, the trend has been reversed; the coal industry is buoyant, and employment rose during the later 1960s to reach 12,960 by 1968.

Newcastle and Port Kembla. It is fitting that at the mouth of the greatest coal-producing valley of Australia—the Hunter—there should be one of the greatest metal-manufacturing plants in the southern hemisphere—at Newcastle.

The steel industry of Newcastle dates from 1911, when the Broken Hill Proprietary Company chose a low-lying tract of alluvial land on the Hunter river, two or three miles (3 or 5 km) above the town, as the site for its steel works. In the words of the company, it was "black slimy mud and mangrove swamp, awash at high water and alive with mosquitoes." The engineers dredged out sand from the harbour and used it to raise the level of the land; they drove in 25,000 piles to provide a firm foundation for the plant, and in January 1913 the first blast furnace was blown in.

A completely integrated steel works has been built up at Newcastle: it includes blast furnaces, batteries of coke ovens which match the world's largest, by-products plant, steel furnaces, rolling mills, foundries and machine shops. An important development programme has been completed: it includes the construction of a fourth blast furnace and a new rod mill, and the raising of the steel-making capacity to 2 million tons per annum. Steel-using industries have been attracted to the neighbourhood: among them are the manufacture of wire products, corrugated iron and railway locomotives and rolling stock.

All the fuel required in the works is supplied from the local coal mines; the iron ore arrives by sea from Iron Knob (South Australia) and Yampi Sound (Western Australia); and the fluxing limestone is brought from Devonport (Tasmania).

We have referred above to the mangrove swamps that formerly occupied the site of the Newcastle steel works. Further reclamation of the Hunter estuary lands has taken place from time to time to provide more space for industry. In 1950 the Broken Hill Company was given permission to fill in one of the river channels and now a rod mill and an oxygen plant are operating on its site. Elsewhere, on the main islands, the State Department of Public Works is dredging silt from the river and building up the land above flood level. In this way more than 1000 acres (400 ha) have been reclaimed and are supporting new factories, linked by road and rail, and served by a new deep-water wharf designed to handle bulk cargoes.[10]

Newcastle is the outlet for this important coal and steel district; but it has a considerable farming hinterland too, yielding grain, meat, wool and cotton. Important extensions have recently taken place in the cultivation of wheat (*see* p. 164) and the harbour, which till recently offered only 25·5 feet (7·5 m) at low water, has been dredged to accommodate vessels drawing up to 30 feet (9 m). The four staple exports of the port are coal, wool, wheat and iron and steel, in that order by value.

The most southerly outpost of industry in the coastal fringe is Port Kembla, which lies on the exposed coast about 50 miles (80 km) south of Sydney. This is the district of the southern coalfield, and Port Kembla began life as a coal-shipping port. In 1907 copper-smelting works were set up, largely owing to the abundance of fuel; but since large quantities of sulphuric acid are needed in the smelting of copper, chemical and fertiliser works were next added. Then in 1928 a steel plant was established, and this has been expanded to reach a capacity of 1850 thousand tons per annum.

The four blast furnaces at Port Kembla include the largest in the southern hemisphere (Fig. 54). A £30 million hot strip mill was opened in 1955, and this feeds a tin-plating plant, which began operating in

1957. Australia uses a great deal of tin-plate in the canning of fruit and vegetables, jam, milk and meat; and for the first time she is producing her own. In 1962 the capacity of the tin-plating plant was increased to 150,000 tons a year, so that the whole of Australia's domestic needs can now be met, with a surplus for export.

[*Courtesy Australian News & Information Bureau.*

FIG. 54.—New South Wales: Port Kembla. This is the fourth blast furnace plant at the Port Kembla iron and steel works, and is the largest in Australia. It has cost $A20 million.

The harbour which serves these works has become the third port of New South Wales. It receives iron ore from Iron Knob in South Australia and from Cockatoo Island, off the north-western coast, and it ships coal and steel. In addition, there are imports of phosphates from Nauru, sulphur from Texas and copper from South Australia and Queensland. The harbour of Port Kembla is quite artificial and is enclosed by two long breakwaters. A major dredging scheme has achieved 50 feet (15 m) of water at low tide at the harbour entrance and up to 42 feet (12·6 m) at the berths.

The progressive expansion in the steel plants at Newcastle and Port Kembla is reflected in the steady growth in the output of steel (Table 38).

TABLE 38

New South Wales: output of pig iron and steel ingots, in thousand tons

Year				Output of pig iron	Output of steel ingots
1939	.	.	.	1105	1168
1959	.	.	.	2049	3190
1969	.	.	.	4201	5565
1970	.	.	.	4299	5698
1971	.	.	.	4521	5618
1972	.	.	.	4503	5726

New South Wales is now more than self-sufficient in iron and steel. Her overseas exports of pig iron and steel ingots are increasing, and she has a net surplus of exports in most types of manufactured steel.

Sydney. The heart of industrial New South Wales, however, is the Sydney district. It stretches 40 miles (64 km) along the coast and forms a lowland embayment about 40 miles (64 km) wide, overlooked from the west by the steep edges of the Blue Mountains. This area, together with its outliers in Newcastle and Port Kembla, contains nearly a quarter of the total population of Australia.

As the site for the first settlement in Australia, Captain Philip chose in 1788 a small inlet (Sydney Cove) in the south shore of the sheltered, deep-water harbour of Port Jackson. Around this small bay has grown the metropolis of Sydney. What are the physical advantages of the site?

First, the drowning of this portion of the Australian coastline, which has converted the lower portions of the valleys of the Hawkesbury, Parramatta and George's rivers into sheltered arms of the sea (Fig. 55). Second, the capture of the headstreams of the Parramatta river by the more vigorous Hawkesbury, so that silting in Sydney Harbour is virtually absent. Thirdly, the presence to the west of a circular level area with relatively fertile soils (derived from Triassic shales), into which Port Jackson extends. The northern shore of the harbour is much steeper than the southern, for in this direction one first encounters the uplifted plateaus which hem in the capital on all sides. These slopes were too steep for the early roads, so that Sydney has developed almost entirely on the south side of the harbour.

Forty miles (64 km) to the west lie the Blue Mountains, composed of sediments which in Tertiary times were raised 3000 feet (900 m) above sea-level; yet in the Sydney area the surface layers (composed mainly of the sterile and unattractive Hawkesbury Sandstone) escaped that uplift and remain for the most part at an altitude of less than 500 feet (150 m). The rivers of the region have been rejuvenated as a result of the uplift, and, maintaining their former courses, have cut immensely deep gorges through the sandstones of the Blue Mountains, so that the valleys are now barriers rather than aids to communication.

Sydney, then, has neither the long Hunter valley of Newcastle nor the

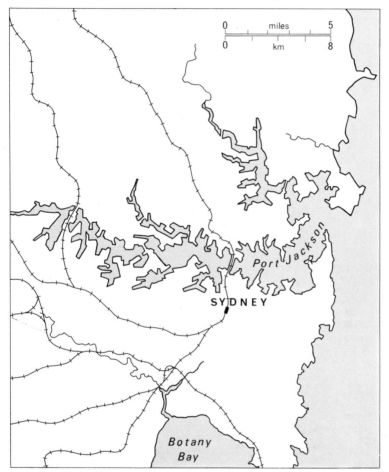

FIG. 55.—The site of Sydney. Virtually the whole of this land has now become a built-up area. Note the bridge connecting the north and south shores of the Bay.

Kilmore Gap of Melbourne; and the city has grown in spite of its girdle of mountains. But it benefits from the momentum of an early start; there is coal not far away and it possesses a fine, land-locked, deep-water harbour.

The core of the city consists of four main streets of shops, offices and theatres. These streets lie on a northward-pointing peninsula between Woolloomooloo Bay on the east and Darling Harbour on the west. The

158   AUSTRALASIA

central area is bordered on the east by a row of three pleasant parks
which contain the Parliament House, the Law Courts and other administrative buildings; to the west are the commercial streets which serve the
seventy or eighty berths on the east side of Darling Harbour. The city
area has for long been served by an efficient underground railway
system (Figs 56, 57).

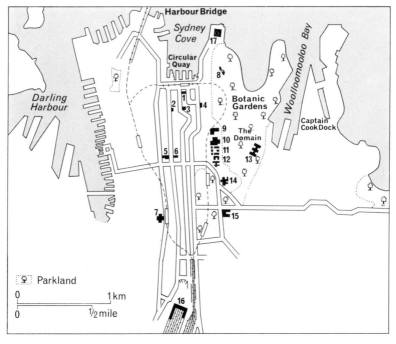

FIG. 56.—Central Sydney.

Key to public buildings: 1, Customs House; 2, Royal Exchange; 3, Education,
Agriculture; 4, Public Works; 5, General Post Office; 6, Commonwealth Bank; 7,
Town Hall; 8, Government House; 9, Libraries; 10, Parliament House; 11,
Hospital; 12, Law Courts; 13, National Gallery; 14, St Mary's Cathedral; 15,
Australian Museum; 16, Central Station; 17, Opera House.

Sydney is the chief port of Australia. In 1968–69 Sydney handled 93
per cent of the overseas imports of New South Wales by value and 75
per cent of the exports. The harbour entrance is 80 feet (24 m) deep: the
shipping channels have a minimum depth of 40 feet (12 m); and the
principal wharves provide 4–5 miles (6 to 8 km) of berthing length.
Since the mean tidal range is only 3·5 feet (1·05 m), vessels load and
discharge at open jetties which reach out into the harbour at right angles
to the shore, New York fashion.

A whole range of commodities is handled in the port, including many
primary products such as wool, wheat, meat, butter and fruit. Wool is

[*Courtesy the Agent-General for New South Wales.*

FIG. 57.—Sydney: aerial view, looking west. In the foreground is Sydney Cove, with Circular Quay at its head, and beyond, some of the high-rise office blocks of the business district. The commercial quays of Darling Harbour are seen in the background and to the right of the centre, close to the southern end of the Sydney Harbour Bridge. The striking building at bottom, centre, is the Opera House, partly financed by a state lottery, and opened by H.M. the Queen in October 1973.

perhaps the most typical cargo, for Sydney is the largest market for that commodity in Australia. Woolloomooloo Bay is the principal part of the harbour for the overseas traffic; Glebe Island handles grain, wool and timber; the graving docks are situated on the north shore and on the nearby Cockatoo Island (not to be confused with the larger island of the same name mentioned on p. 155).

Until recently heavy industry was not well represented in the Sydney district; but in 1961 an important lead–zinc smelter commenced operations at Cockle Creek, about ten miles (16 km) west of the capital. It receives lead–zinc concentrates from Broken Hill, in the far west of the State and from Cobar, in the centre; from them it produces the two refined metals, together with cadmium and sulphuric acid.

Among the many other industries of Sydney are the manufacture of clothing, metals and machinery and the preparation of foods and drinks. The industrial areas are chiefly on the southern outskirts, while the residential areas are to the west or on the north shore. The chief link between the north and south shores is the famous Harbour Bridge—one of the world's greatest single-span steel arch bridges. Two and three-quarters of a mile (4·426 km) long (including its approaches), it carries two footways, four railways and six traffic lanes.

Sydney has not the wide boulevards of Melbourne nor the mountain grandeur of Hobart; but its harbour is one of the deepest and safest in the world; it has fine parks where palms impart a subtropical flavour (Sydney is in the same latitude as the southern Mediterranean Sea); and it enjoys a sea frontage where a host of sandy beaches alternate with bold cliffs of reddish sandstone. As the metropolis of Australia, Sydney houses the national art collection, the Australian Museum, two cathedrals, two dozen theatres and a brand new opera house. Its population in 1966 was 2,539,627 and in 1971, 2,717,069.

THE WESTERN PLAINS

The Western Plains form the largest of the major regions of New South Wales. They include all the land to the west of the foothills of the Eastern Highlands, which may perhaps be demarcated by the 1500-foot (457-m) contour. Several physical sub-regions may be distinguished, which differ greatly among themselves. Extending westwards from the

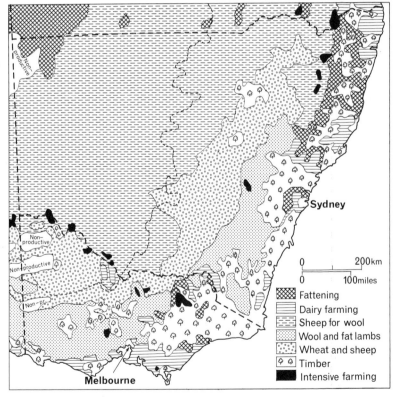

FIG. 58.—New South Wales and Victoria: land use. The curving dotted line that runs through the middle of the States represents the mean annual rainfall line of 15 in (375 mm). This may be regarded as the effective limit for wheat cultivation: farther inland, crops can be grown only by irrigation.

centre of the highlands like a broad, flattened spur is the Cobar Peneplain, which reaches as far as the Darling river: a low plateau, it consists largely of Silurian sediments. In the far north-west of the State are the Broken Hill Uplands, which, with their continuations, are formed of ancient folded sediments. The rest of New South Wales is composed of much younger sediments: north of the Cobar Peneplain and the Broken Hill Uplands the rocks are of Cretaceous age, and this region forms part of the Great Artesian Basin; to the south are Tertiary sediments, and within this sub-region is the important Murrumbidgee Irrigation Area.

Almost the whole of the Western Plains receives an annual average rainfall of between 20 inches (508 m) (in the east) and 10 inches (254 mm) (in the west). A relatively small portion—chiefly the land which lies west of the Paroo river and the lower Darling—receives less than 10 inches (254 mm) of rain; moreover, the rainfall is most unreliable, and this district, together with some of the adjoining land to the east, must be classed as semi-desert.

For the rest, this is extremely productive farmland: it constitutes the heart of agricultural New South Wales. The wetter eastern strip forms the main wheat belt of the continent; the drier western portion includes the principal sheep-grazing lands of Australia. (See the land use map, Fig. 58.) Both these belts cut across the geological divisions: their boundaries are climatic and have little connection with the underlying rocks.

TABLE 39

New South Wales: area under the principal crops, in thousand acres

Crop				Area, 1965–66	Area, 1968–69
Wheat	.	.	.	4,577	9,962
Green fodder	.	.	.	1,951	2,428
Oats	.	.	.	1,033	1,185
Hay	.	.	.	490	536
Barley	.	.	.	236	487
All crops	.	.	.	8,790	15,259

Wheat cultivation. Wheat occupies more than half the total crop land of New South Wales: both in the quantity produced and in the area cultivated, wheat is the one outstanding crop of the State (Table 39). As in the Canadian Prairies the wheat belt may be recognised by the density of its railway network, for most of the land was settled well before 1925, when the car or lorry was not yet an important factor in transport. The peak of railway construction occurred during the seventies and eighties of last century; today most farmers have less than twelve miles (19 km) to haul their wheat to the nearest railway station (it is estimated that 18 of the 20 million acres (8 million ha) which are suited to wheat growing are within a dozen miles of the railway).

Of the potential wheat-growing land, little more than one-third is actually under cultivation, and of this area, little more than one-half is growing wheat in any given year. The rest of the land is growing other crops, such as barley or oats; or it is fallow or under temporary pasture. Nearly all the wheat land is, in addition, suitable for sheep; and nearly two-fifths of the farmers also rear pigs. In this belt, then, there is a balanced system of farming, in which wheat is the chief but not the only product. It is a system which should maintain the fertility of the soil, and in which there should be little danger of soil erosion.

The sheep–wheat belt may be illustrated by a farm next to the small town of Yeoval, 32 miles (51 km) south of Dubbo.[11] It lies mainly in rolling country at about 1300 feet (396 m) above sea-level, drained northwards by headstreams of the Macquarie river. Almost the whole of the farm land has been ploughed at one time or another. The soils, derived from igneous rocks, are reddish-brown loams, rather coarse in texture but with a good crumb-structure, naturally rich and responding well to superphosphates.

The average rainfall for the period 1947–56 was 32·2 inches (818 mm) per annum; but the fall varies greatly from month to month and from year to year. In 1950, for example, the farm gauge registered 58·6 inches (1488 mm); yet three years later there was a fall of only 18·9 inches (480 mm). Wise farmers therefore supplement the surface-water supply by wells or bores, of which five are indicated on Fig. 59.

With 2300 acres (931 ha) this is by Australian standards a small farm. It contains twenty-two main paddocks together with some smaller ones near the homestead. The latter are important in that here, on alluvial flats, the farmer has installed an irrigation spray system by pumping from Buckinbah Creek (which also supplies the homestead with water). The irrigation has proved highly successful: lucerne in particular responded extremely well, for it yielded six cuts during the summer and the lambs pastured on it fetched an excellent price.

Figure 59, which indicates the cropping in October 1971, shows a quarter of the land under wheat. It is grown both for grain and for seed, and its unusually high quality is probably related to the system of rotation which the farmer practises (rotation of crops is rather unusual in Australia). He grows oats for two years, for pasture and hay as well as for grain; this has a cleaning effect on the land and provides a nutritious fodder. In the third year he grows wheat, and finally sows a grass and clover ley.

There are about 3500 sheep on this farm, including young animals; they are divided into about ten mobs, which are moved round from paddock to paddock, with the best pastures reserved to fatten the lambs. The farmer also maintains a herd of about sixty-five cattle, with the object of fattening calves for veal; and he has a few pigs. On the farm there are 80 miles (129 km) of fencing and 54 gates; and its boundary fence is rabbit-proof—that is, the netting runs right to the top of the posts, 3 feet 6 inches (1 m) from the ground. The whole enterprise depends on the labour of the farmer, his two sons, and only one other permanent hired worker.

In the past the main products of this farm, in order of value, have been wheat, wool and fatstock. In the early 1960s the farmer doubled his wheat acreage and achieved a completely merino flock of sheep for the sake of their high quality wool. More recently, however, he has found it increasingly difficult to find the labour for the cultivation and

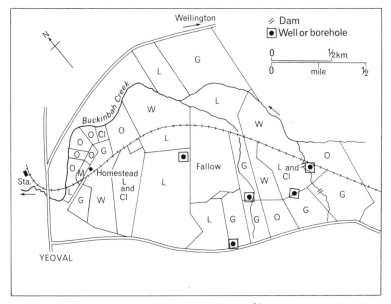

[*Courtesy Association of Agriculture.*

FIG. 59.—A sheep–wheat farm in New South Wales. The cropping relates to 1971.

O = Oats; W = Wheat; Cl = Clover; M = Millet; G = Grass; L = Lucerne.

harvesting of cereals, so he is reducing his wheat acreage in favour of fodder oats (Fig. 59). In addition the price of wool has been disheartening, so he is now concentrating on the fattening of lambs and calves, and fatstock are becoming the leading source of farm income.

The New South Wales wheatlands typically have a rainfall of about 20 inches (508 mm) per annum. In the warmer north, however, 20 inches is not enough, and Narrabri has an average of nearly 26 inches (660 mm); in the cooler south the crop can manage with a smaller rainfall, and wheat is grown as far west as Hillston—50 miles (80 km) beyond the 15-inch (380-mm) isohyet.

This is a region chiefly of winter and early spring rainfall, and the grain matures quickly. In the warmer parts the harvest is in November (which in the northern hemisphere corresponds to May)—four months earlier than that in East Anglia. The summers are hot and almost rainless, for the wheat belt lies in the same latitudes as the Mediterranean Sea. But the actual rainfall is liable to vary greatly from year to year. Wheat growers must be prepared for the occasional drought, and the quantity harvested in any given year may be three or four times as great as in the previous year.

Mechanisation has been brought to a fine pitch, and distinctive machinery has been evolved to meet the special requirements of Australia. Such is the plough whose share rises automatically to clear the stumps left behind the hurried clearing of the land of trees. Implements are exceptionally wide to economise in labour: the harrows are up to 24 feet (7 m) in width, drills up to 12 feet (4 m) and harvesters up to 10 feet (3 m). With such machinery the farmer with the help of only one labourer can sow and harvest as much as 300 acres (121 ha) of land. While the tractor is becoming increasingly common, one still sees the teams of six, eight or ten horses dragging multi-furrow ploughs in the New South Wales wheat belt.

More than one-third of all the Australian wheat is raised here. Its outlets are the ports of Sydney and Newcastle: at Newcastle there is storage for nearly a million bushels of wheat, at at Sydney for $7\frac{1}{2}$ million bushels, with the facilities for loading three grain ships simultaneously.

The recent extensions of wheat cultivation have taken place mainly in the north-west of the wheat belt, where there are stiff black soils. Formerly considered too difficult to cultivate, they have now yielded to improved techniques and more powerful machinery. During the 1950s wheat spread to Narrabri and Gunnedah, and in the early 1960s farther north and north-west to Garah and Weemelah (Fig. 39, p. 123). In these westerly regions the rainfall is unreliable; but wheat may be snatched in a good year, and even if it does not mature for grain, once it is a foot high the farmer benefits in that he can use it for fodder.[12]

The expansion in wheat cultivation is having notable consequences: more vehicles are in use for transport; new storage silos have been built in the areas recently brought into cultivation; and the Port of Newcastle is coping with larger freighters and more frequent sailings.

Sheep rearing. Of the total sheep in Australia, nearly 45 per cent are to be found in New South Wales. As we have seen, sheep are kept on most farms in the wheat belt; but the real sheep-grazing lands lie farther west. To English eyes these farms are large. We may take as an illustration a property in the southern Riverina, close to Lake Urana, where the mean annual rainfall is about 15 or 16 inches (381 to 406 mm). There are about 30,000 sheep in the flock, and they range over an area of 47,000 acres (19,020 ha)—about half the size of Rutlandshire. The nearest town of any size, Corowa, is 64 miles (103 km) away. Around the whole property is a rabbit-proof fence which costs £100 a mile. In all there are 140 miles (225 km) of fencing, and this divides the farm into 37 "paddocks": a single paddock may comprise six square miles (15·5 km²), and its clusters of bushes probably shelter dozens of kangaroos and perhaps a pair of emus (both creatures when chased can run at 35 miles (56 km) an hour). There are creeks to be seen, but they run only intermittently, and the regular water supply is from two wells (100 feet (30 m) deep) and fourteen bore-holes (90–200 feet (27–61 m) deep).

Three hundred miles (531 km) to the north-west, where the normally dry Paroo Creek meets the Darling, is another large sheep property— Mount Murchison, named after an isolated rocky peak that rises to 661 feet (198 m) above sea-level. On the National Geographic map of Australia of 1962 Mount Murchison is elevated to town status; yet it is normally worked by only three people: the farmer and two permanent helpers! Here the average annual rainfall has dwindled to about 9·2 inches (230 mm), and drought may be expected one year in four.

Most of the subsoil consists of a reddish-brown ancient alluvial sand, and on this the meagre rainfall supports bluebush—a low shrub with small semi-succulent leaves. Sheep feed on it when they can find nothing better; but it grows only slowly and is easily damaged by over-grazing. Summer temperatures are high, and the thermometer reaches 35° C (95° F) by day in January; but the winter nights are cold, and the mean minimum on a July night, at 4·4° C (38° F), is only a little above freezing point.

In these conditions one of the first requirements is a reliable water supply to supplement the low and erratic rainfall and to counter the extremely high rate of evaporation (an open tank will lose by evaporation $6\frac{1}{2}$ feet (2 m) of water in a year).

The farm taps subterranean water through a deep borehole; it also uses several shallow wells and tanks which trap surface or near-surface water; but fortunately the property fronts the Darling river and draws on its water through two pipelines, $3\frac{3}{4}$ and 7 miles (6 and 11 km) long. Pumped to towers, the water gravitates from there to tanks and troughs in the paddocks (Fig.60(a)).

So scanty a pasture will support only a low density of sheep. Mount Murchison, extending over 124,000 acres (49,600 ha), is two and a half times as large as the Lake Urana property, yet its sheep flock, numbering about 10,000, is only one-third as large. The farm stretches across 17 miles (27 km) from east to west and 15 miles (24 km) from north to south. In the absence of any road network, the proprietor uses a light aircraft to reach all parts of his estate and to make social calls on his neighbours. Assisted by kelpie dogs he rounds up his sheep on a motor-bicycle.

The nearest town is Wilcannia, with a population of just over one thousand. Here the farmer meets his friends in clubs and can transact any business connected with the property. The Royal Mail provides the

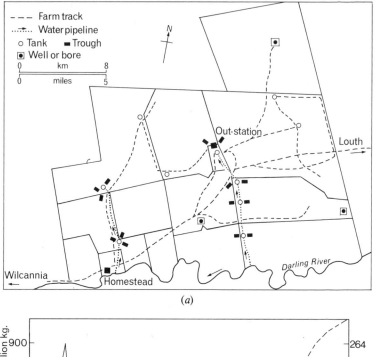

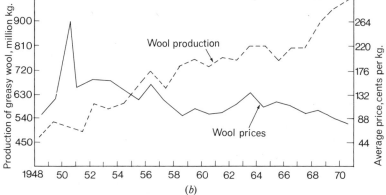

FIG. 60.—Australia: the wool industry.

(a) Mount Murchison. This large property extends over 124,000 acres (49,600 ha)
and rears about 10,000 sheep.

(b) The graphs show that the output of wool in Australia is rising, in spite of a continued decline in prices.

only public transport link with the outside world. For medical and dental treatment, for a choice of clothing or furniture he has to travel to Sydney.[13]

The vital product of his farm is merino wool. In July a hired gang of fourteen sheep-shearers arrive at the farm and work their way through the flock at the rate of over 100 sheep per shearer per day. It takes them three or four weeks to complete the task. Thus the price of wool is all-important. In 1950–51 wool prices reached a peak of about 260 cents per kg; they fell rapidly in the following year to 140 cents, and afterwards in general they declined, reaching their lowest point at about 66 cents per kg in 1970–71 (Fig. 60(b)).

The wool producers, who for generations had been a mainstay of the Australian economy, were at last forced to ask for government support in order to survive. This they received in the form of a guaranteed minimum price for the season 1971–72. The sheep farmers of semi-arid Australia have no real defence against economic adversity for they have no alternative product to offer the market. If wool prices had remained at the 1970–71 low level the prospects of the industry would indeed have been bleak. Fortunately by March 1973 a dramatic recovery had taken place, to an average price of over 180 cents per kg.

The Riverina. The south-central portion of the State, including parts of both the wheat and sheep belts, is known as the Riverina. Broadly speaking, this district comprises the land between the Lachlan and the Murray rivers, extending eastwards roughly as far as a line joining Condobolin and Albury (the term has been restricted, however, to designate the land between the Murrumbidgee and Murray): it includes, then, the foothills of the Eastern Highlands. If we neglect these foothills the most obvious physical characteristic of the district is its extreme flatness. The rivers fall less than 1 foot in each mile; in the western portions the fall is as small as 4 to 5 inches (100–125 mm) per mile. In consequence, the rivers meander slowly through vast spreads of alluvium, branching out into distributaries, only to receive them back lower downstream; it is a region of swamps, lagoons and water-courses which are often dry but occasionally in flood. This is the home of the billabong and the anabranch.

The word "billabong" is derived from the two native words, "billa," meaning a river, and "bung," meaning dead; it implies, then, a watercourse which contains water only rarely. The more specific Billabong is a creek which rises north-east of Albury and meanders for 450 miles (724 km) before joining the Edwards river at Moulamein. Left to itself, the lower half of the creek would be dry in summer; but its flow is maintained by diverting water from the Murrumbidgee into some connecting creeks.

The term "anabranch" was coined in 1834 by the Secretary of the Royal Geographical Society as a shortened form of the phrase, "anastomosing-branch"—which means a branch which, after separation, reunites with its parent; the so-called "Ana Branch of the Darling," which enters the *Murray* west of Wentworth (near the extreme southwest corner of the State) is therefore a misnomer and is apparently due to the perpetuation of a misprint.

The Riverina includes much good wheatland (near Hillston, for example) and good natural fodder for sheep (such as saltbush); but

perhaps its most interesting district is that of the Murrumbidgee
Irrigation Area. This is the largest single irrigation area in the State, but
even so, amounts to only one-sixth of the total irrigated land of New
South Wales.

Its water stems from the high concrete dam at Burrinjuck (40 miles

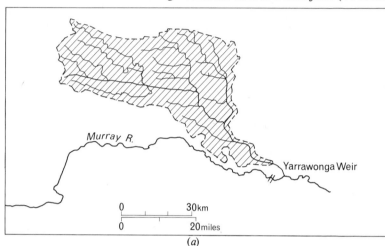

(a)

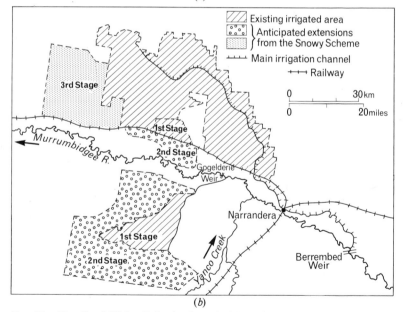

(b)

Fig. 61.—New South Wales: Irrigation from the Murray and Murrumbidgee.
(a) The map shows the extensive canal system based on Yarrawonga Weir.
(b) The map shows the important extensions in the irrigated area that have been permitted by the additional water from the Snowy Mountains Scheme.

(64 km) north-west of Canberra), which regulates the flow in the river channel below. At Berrembed Weir, 240 miles (386 km) lower down, the water is diverted into the main supply canal, and after a journey of 40 miles (64 km) it enters the distribution system of irrigation ditches (*see* Fig. 61).

The Murrumbidgee scheme is technically an "Irrigation Area," that is, a scheme designed for intensive irrigation and closer settlement. The land is divided into new farms which are leased from the Crown. The Murrumbidgee is the largest by far of the eight Irrigation Areas of New South Wales and accounts for more than two-thirds of the whole. More than half its irrigated land is under crops.

The characteristic crop of the Murrumbidgee scheme is rice, and half of the irrigation water is used for this purpose. Cultivation of rice began in 1925; there are now 83,000 acres (33,589 ha) planted, and Australia is not only self-sufficient in this crop, but exports nearly 50 per cent of the output. It is shipped to New Zealand, New Guinea, the Pacific Islands, Canada and the United Kingdom. The farming is highly mechanised: Australian engineering firms have devised machines which cut, thresh, winnow and clean the paddy in a single operation; they are fitted with platforms on which the grain is bagged while the machine is moving through the fields. The bags are then sent to the miller by lorry, the largest of which carry 425 bags at a time, totalling 27 tons.

This fertile land produces in addition, 76,000 acres (30,756 ha) of cultivated pastures, 18,000 acres (7284 ha) of orchards and 7000 acres (2832 ha) of grapes. Among the fruits are pears, plums, peaches, apricots, nectarines, citrus fruits, figs and olives; the grapes are grown for the table, for drying and for wine. Originally a district of large sheep stations, with a sparse population, the area doubled its population after 1923, to reach 24,000 in 1954. The commercial centres are Griffith and Leeton: they have industries such as the milling of rice, the canning and drying of fruit and the production of wine.

Broken Hill. In the far west of the State, and less than 30 miles (48 km) from the border of South Australia, lies the fourth city of New South Wales—Broken Hill. It is separated by 250 miles (402 km) of semi-desert or poor pasture from Hillston, the most westerly outpost of wheat cultivation.

Broken Hill is one of the world's major mining centres. It has been claimed as the biggest ore deposit in Australia. Taking into account its grade, it is probably the largest lead–zinc body in the world.

How did all this begin? In 1880 this district, primarily a cattle-rearing region, had already become known for its deposits of silver ore. In 1883 some of the ranchers at Mount Gipps agreed to try their fortune by mining in the long, low, serrated ridge of brownish rock which extended to the south-west of the homestead; and the next year they struck the famous lode of Broken Hill.

Both physically and economically the links of Broken Hill are with

South Australia rather than with the rest of New South Wales. The Barrier or Stanley Range on which it is situated forms part of a zone of ancient sediments which are joined to those of the Flinders Range in South Australia. These sediments consist of crumpled and contorted slates, quartzites, sandstones, limestones and conglomerates, intruded by bosses and dykes of coarse granite and other igneous material; they show no traces of life, and are believed to be of Precambrian age.

The lode itself is shaped rather like a huge sword blade, buried on edge, arranged from north-east to south-west, and dipping steeply to the north-west. The length of its outcrop is about $3\frac{1}{2}$ miles (5·6 km); its width ranges from a few feet to 200 feet (about 1–61 m), and its greatest depth is more than 3000 feet (914 m). As a result of the dip most of the mining has taken place on the north-west side of the outcrop, and here we find the commercial area of the town and its main street (Argent Street), which follows the course of an old stock route.

The town has been laid out with long, wide, parallel streets running the whole length of the lode, and arranged on both sides of it, so that the mining properties lie in the middle—a clear example of the way in which the geology has influenced the layout of a town. The mean annual rainfall is only about 9 inches (230 mm) and the local water supply has been supplemented by a pipeline from the Darling. Formerly bearing the marks of a frontier town, Broken Hill is now a city of 30,000 people, with parks and gardens and swimming pools.[14] The Broken Hill Proprietary Company, however, one of the world's greatest mining and manufacturing concerns, no longer operates within the city.

The central area of the lode is now largely worked out, and here the remains of old workings are to be seen in the shape of derelict machinery, sheds and spoil heaps. Mining is now most active at the ends of the lode, and is expected to continue on an important scale for several decades.

A visit to the mines of the Zinc Corporation Ltd., at the south-west end of the lode, shows us something of the activities in this important strip of land. The main shaft descends to 3000 feet (914 m) below the surface, and the ore is worked at fourteen or more levels. The crude ore here averages 14 per cent lead, 11 per cent zinc and 4 ounces of silver per ton. It is crushed to powder, and then mixed with water to form a thin mud, which flows into a trough with one low side. A few drops of a mixture of eucalyptus oil with sodium ethyl xanthate are allowed to fall into the mud; this causes the lead and silver to rise to the surface in the form of a silvery scum, and wipers then sweep it into a gutter; it is dried, and the result is lead concentrate. This is the flotation process, first developed at Broken Hill, and now used throughout the world. In a similar way, but with the use of different chemicals, the zinc is next made to rise to the surface, and is skimmed off and recovered. The sand is returned to the mine to fill the cavities and the water is used again: nothing is wasted.

Broken Hill is now connected by rail with both Adelaide and Sydney:

Adelaide is 335 miles (539 km) away; Sydney, 703 miles (1131 km). But for long the only rail connection was to the south-west, and today the concentrates still move in that direction. The lead is smelted at Port Pirie (where is the largest lead-smelting plant in the world) or at Port Kembla in New South Wales; the zinc concentrates are shipped to Risdon in Tasmania, or to Cockle Creek (Sydney) or are exported to the United Kingdom.

So the minerals of Broken Hill, together with the raisins of the Murrumbidgee and the grain and wool of the Riverina, find their way half across the world to the United Kingdom.

NOTES

1. B. W. Higman, "Sugar Plantations and Yeoman Farming in New South Wales," *Annals of the Assoc. of American Geographers*, Vol. 58 (1968).

2. G. T. Macdonald, "Recent Pasture Development on the Northern Tablelands of New South Wales," *Australian Geographer*, Vol. X, No. 5 (1968).

3. J. Brown, "Cotton Growing on the Namoi (New South Wales)," *Australian Geographer*, Vol. IX, No. 6 (1965).

4. J. C. R. Camm and P. G. Irwin, "Cotton Seed Processing at Narrabri, New South Wales: Locational Considerations," *Australian Geographer*, Vol. XI, No. 6 (1971).

5. R. Robinson, "Site and Form in the Valley Centres of the New South Wales coast North of the Hunter," *Australian Geographer*, Vol. X, No. 1 (1966).

6. B. Ryan, "The Dynamics of Recreational Development on the South Coast of New South Wales," *Australian Geographer*, Vol. IX, No. 6 (1965).

7. M. G. A. Wilson, "Changing Patterns of Pit Location on the New South Wales Coalfields," *Annals of the Assoc. of American Geographers*, Vol. 58 (1968).

8. J. H. Holmes, "External Commuting as a prelude to Suburbanization (Newcastle, New South Wales)," *Annals of the Assoc. of American Geographers*, Vol. 61 (1971).

9. M. G. A. Wilson, "The New South Wales Export Coal Trade," *Australian Geographer*, Vol. IX, No. 3 (1964).

10. P. G. Irwin, "Reclamation of the Hunter River Islands," *Australian Geographer*, Vol. X, No. 5 (1968).

11. Association of Agriculture, *A Sheep–Wheat Farm in New South Wales, 1958 onwards*.

12. J. Brown, "Wheat Growing in the North-West of New South Wales," *Australian Geographer*, Vol. IX, No. 6 (1965).

13. K. L. Bardsley, "Australian Wool Joins the Assistance Queue," *Geographical Magazine*, Vol. XLIV, No. 2 (November 1971).

14. L. St. Clare Grondona, "The Romance of Broken Hill," *Geographical Magazine*, Vol. 38, No. 1 (May 1965).

STUDY QUESTIONS

1. "New South Wales has a transitional climate." Discuss this dictum.

2. Compare and contrast the Australian Alps with the Alps of Europe.

3. Explain the principles behind the Snowy Mountains Scheme.

4. Examine critically the choice of site and the layout of Canberra.

5. Describe the economic geography of the Newcastle coalfield.

6. Make a comparative study of the ports of Sydney and Melbourne considering (*a*) site; (*b*) hinterland and (*c*) commodities handled.

7. What advantages does New South Wales offer for: (*a*) the cultivation of wheat and (*b*) the production of wool?

8. What are the characteristics of the Riverina?

9. Describe the site and functions of Broken Hill.

Chapter VIII

QUEENSLAND

QUEENSLAND has many contrasts. The Atherton Tableland near the north-east coast receives the highest rainfall in Australia, yet in the Channel Country of the far south-west pastures spring up only after occasional rainstorms. In the east are lofty mountain ranges with stupendous waterfalls; in the west are plains almost at sea-level. Lying astride the Tropic of Capricorn, Queensland offers a variety of products: tobacco, maize, peanuts and tropical fruits thrive in the north; cotton, peanuts, citrus fruits, wheat and sorghum are grown in the centre; and wheat, barley and oats, pineapples and deciduous fruits are cultivated in the south-east. Sugar flourishes along almost the whole of the east coast, and sheep and cattle are pastured on the vast western plains. Queensland has probably more land suitable for settlement than any other State in Australia; it covers a vast area—667,000 square miles (1,727,519 km²), or more than the combined areas of the British Isles, France, Germany and Italy. Brisbane, the capital, tucked away in the south-east corner of the State, is less metropolitan than other state capitals in Australia; and Queensland has a greater proportion of its population than other States in small towns of about 10,000 people.

THE PHYSICAL BACKGROUND

The so-called "Great Dividing Range," which is named on the maps, is difficult to find on the ground. Rarely does the water-parting correspond with a prominent mountain rampart: instead there are a series of flat-topped highland masses which the rivers are rapidly eroding. Those rivers which flow eastwards have by far the shorter journey to the sea, and therefore the steeper gradients. They are active rivers, cutting deep valleys, tumbling down in waterfalls and forcing the water-parting ever westwards.

The original watershed must have been much nearer the coast, but all that now remains of it is a line of detached granite masses and volcanic peaks. Subsidence has produced a complicated coastline with numerous inlets and rocky islands; and the Great Barrier Reef, which runs parallel with the present coastline but in places 150 miles (241 km) east of it, probably marks the position of the earlier edge of the continent.

173

From Cape York to Innisfail ($17\frac{1}{2}°$ S. lat.) the watershed lies near the coast and there is virtually no coastal plain. Southwards from Innisfail, however, it makes a wide sweep away from the shore, to reach a maximum distance of 250 miles (402 km) from the sea, and then returns close to the sea near the New South Wales border. Between the "Divide" and the coast are the extensive and well-watered river basins of the Burdekin and the Fitzroy, and the Eastern Highlands are here at their greatest width in the continent—they occupy, in fact, as much as two-thirds of Queensland.

Like their counterpart in New South Wales and Victoria, the Eastern Highlands consist of uplifted blocks rather than simple folds, and the coastal plains, where they exist, represent "stillstands"—that is, portions of the surface which have taken no part in the general uplift. The Eastern Highlands are formed largely of Palaeozoic rocks, particularly of Carboniferous age in the north and south, and here, in the basin of the Fitzroy river, is the scene of the recent important developments in coal mining (p. 200). Lying astride the border with New South Wales, however, is a prominent basin floored with Triassic material. This basin, extending from Grafton on the New South Wales coast to Roma (between Brisbane and Charleville), contains further coal deposits, in the Ipswich and Maryborough districts. In the heart of the mountain masses occur granite and ancient rocks; and associated with these are important mineral deposits, such as those of the Atherton Tableland (tin), Mount Morgan (copper) and Charters Towers (formerly a gold-producing district).

Volcanic outflows have left their mark on the landscape. In addition to the coastal peaks there are lava plateaus in the Darling Downs (p. 204), and there is an interesting collection of Recent (Quaternary) small volcanoes, lava flows and crater lakes in the Atherton Plateau, near Mount Bartle Frere (5287 feet; 1611 m)—the highest peak in Queensland.

West of the Eastern Highlands extends a wide area of monotonous, level or gently rolling land, formed of horizontal sediments which were formerly regarded as of Cretaceous age, but are now classed as Jurassic. These are the lonely "sunlit plains." Usually clad in only a scanty vegetation, they bloom like a garden after rain; but this forms part of the Great Artesian Basin: there is water from wells, and stock may be fed on irrigated pastures.

Finally, in the region of the Selwyn Range in the north-west of the State lies a broad area of extremely old rocks, largely Cambrian and Precambrian in age, and this is probably the most easterly portion of the ancient massif of central and western Australia. Here is the most productive mineral field of Queensland—that of Cloncurry, Mount Isa and Mary Kathleen.

CLIMATE

Throughout the greater part of Queensland the most frequent winds are from the east (including north-east and south-east). These are the so-called South-East Trades, though, being strongest in summer, they have much of the character of a monsoon. They vary in direction more between day and night than they do from month to month. Consequently, as in New South Wales, the heaviest falls of rain are experienced on the coast, and precipitation diminishes with distance from the Pacific. The rainiest portion of the whole continent, as we have seen (Chapter III), is the eastern slope of the Atherton Tableland, where two small areas respectively north and south of Innisfail receive more than 160 inches (4064 mm) per annum; and the record is held by Tully, south of Innisfail, with a mean annual rainfall of 179·26 inches (4553·2 mm).

The Innisfail district is exceptional for two reasons: here the edge of the Eastern Highlands is unusually close to the coast, and overlooks the Pacific in a mountain wall; moreover, this particular stretch of coast runs nearly north and south, and more than most districts faces the dominant winds. Throughout the Queensland coast, indeed, one can detect a close relationship between aspect and rainfall, for the north–south stretches receive a decidedly larger amount than the north-east to south-west stretches. The coast north of Brisbane experiences 70 inches (1778 mm) per annum, north of Rockhampton more than 60 inches (1524 mm) and at Proserpine 70 inches (1778 mm). All these face the prevailing winds. Intervening stretches of coast receive only 40 inches (1016 mm), such as the districts south-east of Rockhampton and Townsville.

Westwards everywhere the rainfall diminishes. Even where rainfall is heaviest on the coast there is a rapid decline westwards, so that behind Tully in the space of only about 50 miles (80 km) the average rainfall has diminished to a mere 30 inches (762 mm). If we follow the railway from Rockhampton to Longreach (which runs almost along the Tropic) we cross the 25-inch (635-mm) isohyet west of Dingo, the 20-inch (500-mm) line between Alpha and Jericho and do not quite reach the 15-inch (375-mm) line at the terminus at Longreach. Places farther west, such as Boulia, Windorah and Thargomindah, have barely 10 inches (254 mm) as their average, and a small area in the far south-west receives only 5 inches (127 mm) per annum.

But the annual rainfall map is an imperfect guide to what can be expected in any given year, for it tells us nothing about either the seasonal distribution of the rainfall or its reliability. In the coastal districts the rainfall is both heavy and reliable; but as one moves inland the rainfall becomes more uncertain. The farmer in the Darling Downs must be prepared for one dry year in four; farther west, at Charleville or Longreach, he must be prepared for three dry years (of about 10 inches

(254 mm) per annum) and only one wet year (of about 15 inches; 381 mm).

Everywhere in Queensland the bulk of the rain falls in the summer months; and the summer maximum becomes more and more marked as one moves farther north. What is the cause of this?

In July (the Australian winter) a belt of high pressure stretches east and west across Australia; virtually the whole of the tropical part of the continent has steady outward-blowing winds and cloudless skies. By November the high-pressure belt has weakened and has moved farther south. Its place has been taken by a low-pressure system whose centre lies over the north-west of Australia: the winds now blow inwards, and in November rain begins to fall in the far north in Arnhem Land. The rainy season is at its height in December and then covers the whole of the Queensland coast.

Turning now to temperatures, we notice first that Queensland extends over about 18 degrees of latitude. In terms of the Americas she stretches from the latitude of Florida to that of the Panama Canal. Thursday Island, close to Cape York, has an equatorial flavour, with the thermometer registering an average of 27° C (80° F) for each month and a mean monthly range of only $2\frac{1}{2}$° C ($4\frac{1}{2}$° F). At Brisbane, however, the monthly range is 11° C (19° F)—only 2·8° C or 5° F less than that of London; with maximum temperatures at 29° C (85° F), her summers are decidedly warm, though her winters (averaging about 16° C; 60° F) are pleasantly cool. Cloncurry, in tropical latitudes and 200 miles (322 km) from the sea, lacks the moderating influence of a large body of water; there the *mean* summer temperature is as high as 31° C (88° F) while the mean winter temperature (18° C; 64° F) is almost as low as that of Brisbane.

To summarise: only the coastal belt has a really adequate rainfall (though, as we see later, there are underground supplies of water to compensate for lack of surface supplies); the rainfall comes mainly in summer, when it is most needed; and where water supplies are sufficient the temperatures are such as to allow a wide range of temperate and tropical cultivated products.

FARMING IN QUEENSLAND

Queensland farming is distinguished by two characteristics: these are the prominent status of the beef cattle industry and the significance among the cultivated crops of tropical and subtropical products.

Table 40 provides a general view of the different types of farming in Queensland according to the value of their output. It will be seen that the returns from cultivation are approximately equal to those from pastoral farming in the narrow sense; if, however, we include with the latter the products of dairy, poultry and pig farming, then we find that in

TABLE 40
Queensland: value of farm output in $A million

Crop Farming	1964–65	1968–69
Sugar cane	127·2	151·7
Grain crops	55·9	90·3
Fruit	19·6	26·1
Tobacco	11·0	16·7
Fodder other than hay	7·3	9·5
All crops	270·6	363·7

Pastoral Farming		
Cattle slaughtered	131·2	185·4
Wool	110·4	101·7
Live cattle exported	13·3	30·5
Sheep slaughtered	14·3	13·9
Live sheep exported	1·4	8·1
All pastoral products	270·9	340·0

Dairy, Poultry and Pig Farming		
Milk	25·4	28·7
Pigs slaughtered	16·5	19·0
Butter	27·4	15·1
Eggs	7·9	13·2
Poultry	6·6	10·6
Total dairy products, etc.	85·7	87·9

1968–69 stock raising accounted for about 54 per cent of the total value of the farm output, and crop raising about 46 per cent.

LIVESTOCK

Queensland is by far the foremost State of Australia in the number of cattle, and in 1969 possessed 37 per cent of the total. Cattle are more suited than sheep to the generally warm and damp conditions that prevail over large areas of the State, and most of them are found in the broad zone that runs parallel with the coast and receives between 20 and 40 inches (500 and 1000 mm) of rain annually (Fig. 63). The cattle thin out south and west of the 20-inch (510-mm) isohyet, and very few are found where the mean annual rainfall is below 10 inches (254 mm)—that is to say, west and south of Boulia, Windorah and Thargomindah.

In the drier parts cattle rearing is on an extensive scale and requires great skill in management. Some owners hold several stations, some of which are in the better watered districts, and move their stock around to catch the pastures.

The rainfall is unreliable, and in recent years there have been severe droughts in 1945–6, 1951, 1957, 1965 and 1968–70; these help to explain the fluctuations in the number of cattle through time (Fig. 62).

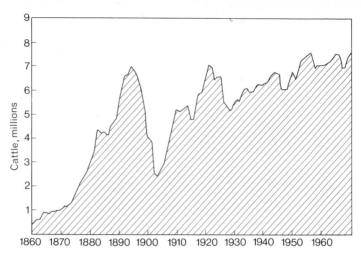

FIG. 62.—Queensland: changes in the number of cattle since 1860. The general trend is one of steady increase; this is interrupted by variations in climate, especially rainfall. Note the effect of the disastrous drought of 1900–1902.

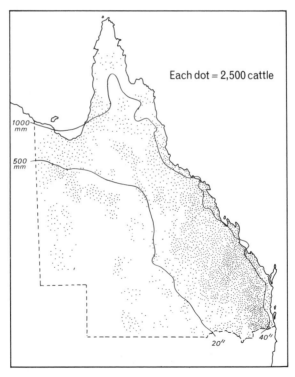

Each dot = 2,500 cattle

1000 mm

500 mm

20″   40″

FIG. 63.—Queensland: distribution of beef cattle, 1968. Beef cattle are widespread: they thrive in warm, moist conditions but do not tolerate drought.

The worst drought on record occurred from 1900 to 1902, and is eloquently reflected in the graph of numbers. Nevertheless, the general trend is upward, and the total number of cattle in 1968—nearly 7·7 million head—was the highest ever.

Fewer than 10 per cent of the number are dairy cattle, for these thrive better in cooler conditions, and most of the dairy herds are concentrated on the plains and plateaus within a radius of about 140 miles (224 km) of Brisbane, which forms the chief market for fresh milk (Fig. 64).

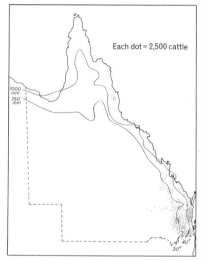

FIG. 64.—Queensland: distribution of dairy cattle, 1968. The pattern is closely related to local markets for milk and other dairy produce.

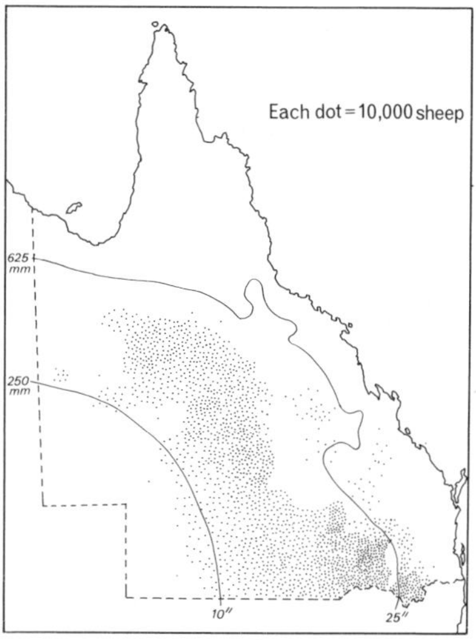

FIG. 65.—Queensland: distribution of sheep, 1968. Sheep are less tolerant of heat than cattle but more tolerant of drought.

British breeds form the basis of the Queensland cattle herds. About 50 per cent of the beef cattle are Herefords and a further 40 per cent Shorthorns; the remaining 10 per cent are of Brahman stock, which are more suited to the damp heat of the Cape York peninsula and the east coast northward of Mackay. The dairy breeds consist of Illawarra Shorthorns (about 50 per cent), Jerseys (40 per cent) together with Friesians, Guernseys and Ayrshires.

In 1968–69 the exports of beef and veal from Queensland were worth $A127 million. The United States took nearly the whole supply, her share being valued at $A95 million. Other Australian States received $A8·2 million worth of Queensland beef and veal; shipments to Japan were valued at $A7·5 million, to the United Kingdom at $A5·7 million and to Canada $A5·4 million dollars.

While cattle are very widely distributed in Queensland the sheep are

more closely confined to the relatively dry parts of the State, though as
with cattle, very few are found south or west of the 10-inch (254-mm)
isohyet (Fig. 65). The precise limits of the main sheep area have been set
in practice by the location of the great dingo-proof fence (*see* Fig. 17, p.
52).

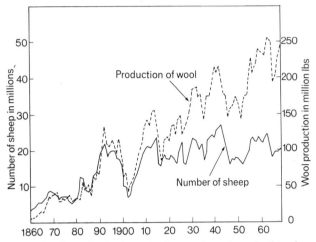

FIG. 66.—Queensland: sheep numbers and wool production since
1860. Notice the effect of the drought of 1900–1902. Since that
time the expansion in wool production is related to the increased
weight of the fleeces.

The fluctuations in the number of sheep, like those of cattle, reflect
the condition of the pastures; but since about 1910 the size of the total
flock has oscillated around the 20 million mark (Fig. 66 and Table 41).
While the number of sheep shows no clear general increase, selective
breeding and careful management has resulted in a considerable
increase in the weight of the average fleece. In 1968 the flocks were still

TABLE 41

Queensland: numbers of cattle, sheep and pigs in thousands

Year	Beef cattle	Dairy cattle	Sheep	Pigs
1940	4,764	1,447	23,936	436
1945	5,100	1,443	18,944	415
1950	5,373	1,361	17,478	375
1955	6,001	1,329	22,116	373
1960	5,847	1,157	22,135	448
1965	5,930	958	18,384	417
1966	6,020	899	19,305	468
1967	6,526	835	19,948	520
1968	6,910	758	20,324	535
1969	6,808	707	16,446	480
1970	7,278	667	14,774	491
1971	8,375	646	14,604	535

recovering from the drought of 1965, yet the total wool clip of that year was surpassed only narrowly by that of 1964 (Table 42).

About 95 per cent of the total sheep in the State are pure-bred merinos. Many of the sheep properties are very large, and shear 50,000 sheep or more. Holdings of about 20,000 acres (8000 ha) are run by individual families; larger properties are often managed by pastoral companies. There is no need for further comment on the price of wool, which determines the value of the fleece (*see* p. 167).

TABLE 42

Queensland: quantity and value of the wool clip

Year	Quantity mil. lb	Value mil. dollars
1940	214·7	23·5
1945	173·2	21·7
1950	154·7	177·6
1955	194·0	106·3
1960	235·6	101·7
1961	230·3	101·3
1962	233·6	115·5
1963	255·4	141·5
1964	251·4	117·2
1965	192·8	91·0
1966	203·7	93·2
1967	226·8	94·9
1968	247·0	108·1
1969	196·0	69·8
1970	168·5	44·9
1971	183·0	61.7

Significant changes are taking place in the direction of the wool exports from Queensland. As in other spheres, Japan is increasing her share of the market. During the 1960s the United Kingdom share fell from 23 per cent to 10 per cent of the total wool exports, while that of Japan rose from 23 per cent to 35 per cent. Other customers for Queensland wool during 1968–69 were Italy (10 per cent), Germany (7 per cent), France (6 per cent), Belgium (5 per cent) and the United States (4 per cent).

AGRICULTURE

Queensland agriculture is interesting in that so large a proportion of the total consists of tropical crops; moreover here is the only important example of the cultivation of these crops by people of European stock. If we are to judge by the growth in output, value and yield, this practice has been most successful. In 1968–69 there were record outputs of wheat, sugar and pineapple and a near record of cotton; within a generation improved techniques and the selection of new varieties have resulted in remarkable increases in yield (Table 43).

The outstanding crop of the State by value is sugar cane, which is

TABLE 43
Queensland: crop yields per acre

Crop	Unit				Yield, 1939–40	Yield, 1968–69
Sugar cane	tons	.	.	.	23·0	31·9
Barley	bushels	.	.	.	20·4	30·1
Maize	bushels	.	.	.	18·9	30·5
Sorghum	bushels	.	.	.	14·1	27·0
Wheat	bushels	.	.	.	18·8	23·5
Hay	tons	.	.	.	1·7	2·4
Cotton	lb	.	.	.	152·0	687·0
Potatoes	tons	.	.	.	2·3	6·6
Tobacco	lb	.	.	.	573·0	1411·0
Apples	bushels	.	.	.	72·0	193·0
Bananas	bushels	.	.	.	133·0	207·0
Pineapples	dozens	.	.	.	437·0	561·0

nearly three times as valuable as its nearest competitor, wheat (Table 44), in spite of the fact that it occupies little more than one-third of the area.

Australia's sugar-cane industry is unique in that cultivation is entirely by white (largely Italian) labour. But the change from coloured to white labour is fairly recent. Labourers from the Pacific islands (Kanakas) were introduced into Queensland in 1863 and during the following twenty years they were recruited on a large scale. A notorious traffic developed in which kidnapping was frequent; but one of the first decisions of the Federal Government (in 1901) was not only to prohibit the importing of Kanakas, but to return 8000–9000 islanders still in the sugar plantations to their homes. Since that time the Commonwealth

TABLE 44
Queensland: gross value of main crops, 1968–69, in $A million

Crop					Value
Sugar cane	.	.	.	.	151·7
Wheat	.	.	.	.	55·8
Tobacco	.	.	.	.	21·8
Fodder other than hay	.	.	.	16·7
Sorghum	.	.	.	.	13·1
Barley	.	.	.	.	12·8
Potatoes	.	.	.	.	11·7
Hay	.	.	.	.	9·5
Pineapples	.	.	.	.	7·4
Tomatoes	.	.	.	.	6·1
Maize	.	.	.	.	4·8
Citrus fruits	.	.	.	.	3·7
Bananas	.	.	.	.	3·4
Peanuts	.	.	.	.	3·1
Pumpkins	.	.	.	.	2·5
Cotton	.	.	.	.	2·1
Onions	.	.	.	.	2·0
Grapes	.	.	.	.	1·6
All crops		.	.	.	363·7

and Queensland Governments have exercised a firm but beneficent control over the industry. By agreement between the two governments the wholesale price of sugar is fixed from time to time (the last agreement was made in 1967). This makes for stability in the industry. The Queensland Sugar Board buys the whole of the crop and sells it to the mills: there are thirty-one of these, and fourteen of them are controlled co-operatively by the growers. Each mill crushes the cane grown over a particular area. Both the area cultivated and the number of people employed have expanded steadily, and in the last few years Australia has been able not only to satisfy her home requirements for sugar but also to export about three-quarters of her output of raw sugar. Next to wheat, sugar is Australia's second most valuable export crop. Australia is currently the fourth producer of sugar in the world, and the second largest exporter. In 1971 her chief customers were Japan, the United Kingdom, Canada, the United States and New Zealand, in that order. Of all this sugar, 95 per cent is produced in Queensland.

TABLE 45

Queensland: sugar cane: area cut and sugar made

Year	Area cut thou. acres	Sugar made thou. tons
1940–41	263·3	759
1945–46	229·7	645
1950–51	263·7	880
1955–56	365·3	1136
1960–61	327·2	1320
1965–66	487·4	1883
1966–67	535·0	2203
1967–68	530·8	2214
1968–69	546·3	2604
1969–70	506·0	2081
1970–71	522·7	2338
1971–72	554·5	2627

TABLE 46

Australia: exports of raw sugar, year ending 30th June 1971

Country	Thou. tons
Japan	473
United Kingdom	433
Canada	347
U.S.A.	206
New Zealand	49
Singapore	25
Total exports	1557

Queensland has only a relatively small area that is climatically suited to wheat, and produces less wheat than any other mainland State of Australia. With an output of 42 million bushels out of the Australian

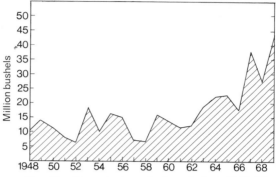

Fɪɢ. 67.—Queensland: production of wheat, 1948–69.

total of 544 million in 1968–69, Queensland accounted for 6·7 per cent of the total crop. Nevertheless, there has been a general increase in the output of wheat in Queensland, interrupted only by the poor harvests consequent on drought years (Fig. 67); and in 1968–69 both the area and the output constituted records.

Most of the wheat crop is grown on the Darling Downs, and it is appropriate that the headquarters of the State Wheat Board should be located at Toowoomba, the regional commercial centre. Bulk handling

TABLE 47

Utilisation of Queensland wheat, 1969, in thousand bushels

Consumed in Australia

Flour	5,969
Stock feed . . .	736
Seed	173
Cereal foods . . .	190

Overseas exports

Grain	21,276
Wheat products . . .	1,843
Total	30,187

TABLE 48

Queensland: directions   of   wheat   exports,   1968–69,   by   value,
in $A million

To Japan	28·4
United Kingdom . . .	1·4
E.E.C.	0·7
Total overseas . . .	34·4
To other Australian States . .	0·7
Total exports . . .	35·1

was pioneered in 1951–52 and has become general. The State produces considerably more wheat than it needs, and in 1969 it exported more than two-thirds of the total output, mainly to Japan. The chief exporting ports are Brisbane and Gladstone, and the capacity of both terminals has been recently increased. Brisbane can now store 2·1 million bushels and Gladstone 1·1 million.

After sugar cane and wheat the third most valuable crop in Queensland is tobacco. Its high value is illustrated by the fact that it occupies only a little more land than the cotton crop, yet cotton ranks sixteenth by value. Tobacco needs skill and care in cultivation, and grows best on light soils. The crop is grown also in Victoria and New South Wales, but Queensland is the largest producer, with 57 per cent of the total in 1968–69. Nearly all of this was grown in the Mareeba district of the Atherton Tableland, and almost entirely under irrigation.

The 1968–69 output, at 19·5 million lb (9 million kg) of dried leaf, was one of the highest on record. Queensland however is not self-sufficient in tobacco, and needs to import roughly half of her requirements.

Queensland grows such a variety of crops that we can mention only briefly some others. Queensland produces about 9 per cent of the apples of Australia, 20 per cent of the bananas, 10 per cent of the citrus fruits, only 1 per cent of the grapes, but virtually all the peanuts and pineapples. In addition Queensland is the only producer of such tropical products as arrowroot and ginger.

We have seen that in most essentials the picture of farming in Queensland is one of expansion—in area, output, yield and value. As in most developed countries, there is a drift from the land; but in Queensland this is of only modest proportions; and as elsewhere, it is matched by increases in the use of machinery (Table 49). It is clear that Queensland farming is in a healthy condition.

TABLE 49

Queensland: farm employees and farm machinery

	1964–65	1968–69
Full-time male employees	66,125	64,250
Fertiliser distributors	12,758	15,906
Combine grain drills	12,468	14,066
Grain harvesters	7,220	7,586
Forage harvesters	961	1,352
Tractors	64,440	70,238

THE REGIONS OF QUEENSLAND

The natural regions of Queensland bear a certain resemblance to those of New South Wales. Each has a coastal region, and behind it a plateau region; each has a mineral district in the far west together with a region of low rainfall. But Queensland has only the northern fringes of the wheat and sheep belts and there is nothing to compare with the Murrumbidgee irrigation area. On the other hand, it possesses a tropical coastal fringe important for sugar and already valuable for bauxite; and off the east coast is the fascinating Great Barrier Reef, with which our

FIG. 68.—Queensland: physical and towns.

description begins (Fig. 68). We discuss next the coastal fringe: its farm economy depends on sugar; its beaches produce mineral sands, and remote outposts are developing their bauxite deposits. Since the interior regions are firmly linked by road and rail to the coast, it is natural to find here the State capital, Brisbane.

The second main region comprises the plateaus that border the coast. Here temperate cereals are grown and beef cattle are fattened. This is the scene of the Brigalow development scheme and the expanding coal industry. To conclude, we examine the Great Artesian Basin of the interior, with its isolated mining centres and its ever-present problem of drought—a problem which is being attacked by the construction of "beef roads."

THE GREAT BARRIER REEF

The Great Barrier Reef is the largest coral structure in the world. It extends from Fraser Island in the south (lat. 25° S.) to New Guinea in the north—a total length of 1250 miles (2012 km). In the north its front lies close to the mainland: at Cape Melville it is only ten miles (16 km) distant; but farther south the edges of the Reef lie far from the land, and reach their maximum distance of about 175 miles (282 km) in the neighbourhood of Rockhampton.

Beyond the seaward edge of the Reef the floor of the ocean drops rapidly to a depth of 14,000 feet (4,200 m); but within the barrier the sheltered sea is shallow—usually between 100 and 400 feet (30 and 120 m) deep, and the surface of the water is broken by scores of low coral islands.

Coral is formed by minute marine creatures known as polyps; these are closely related to the sea-anemones, but differ in that they build up external limy skeletons. Several theories have been advanced to account for the formation of barrier reefs; but that proposed by Darwin in 1838–42 still remains largely unassailed. He regarded a barrier reef as the result of the upward growth of coral on a shallow but gradually subsiding sea floor. The island-fringed coast of Queensland, with its numerous rocky inlets, shows evidence of submergence; and the shallowness of the sea within the barrier suggests that we have here a continental shelf whose floor in the past may have been dry land and whose seaward border represents the real edge of the continent.

The coral polyp flourishes only in water which is warm, saline and free from sediment. The termination of the Reef southwards at lat. 25° S. reflects the gradual fall of temperature to the critical level of 20° C (68° F). Major gaps in the reef appear to be related to important influxes of fresh water: Capricorn Channel lies opposite the mouth of the Fitzroy system; Flinders Passage faces the outlet of the Burdekin; and the Barrier Reef peters out in the Gulf of Papua, where the wide Fly river and numerous neighbouring muddy creeks provide conditions which are unacceptable to the coral.

Coral grows most actively from depths of about 150 feet (45 m) to just below the level of low tide; and since it is a marine animal, it follows that the islands themselves have been built up of dead coral: this has been pounded into fragments by the waves and reared up into banks whose shapes are dictated by the prevailing winds. Soon the islands become colonised by various salt-tolerant plants, such as mangroves, pandanus palms and casuarinas.

The coral polyp, however, has its enemies. A hurricane will bring in its wake muddy flood waters which destroy the coral in its path. Pollution from oil prospecting and by effluents containing pesticides from the sugar and tobacco plantations takes its toll. A natural predator is *acanthaster planci*, "the crown of thorns starfish," which eats the polyps; the female is believed to lay between 12 and 24 million eggs each summer. Since the reef is 1,250 miles (2000 km) long it is difficult to know precisely how great is the damage, but on Green Island, a national park in the Cairns district, 80 per cent of the coral has been destroyed; and it takes twenty years for new coral to establish itself.[1]

From the economic point of view the Great Barrier Reef is already an important asset to Queensland, and it may become more so. It forms a sheltered waterway for craft trading coastwise and with New Guinea, though the tidal range is high, currents are swift, and care is needed to navigate reefs and rocks. Fish are plentiful, and some of them are commercially exploitable. Oysters are fished for the sake of the pearls which they may contain, and trochus shells are collected—conical objects up to 8 inches (203 mm) in diameter which are cut to provide the raw material for "pearl" buttons. Huge shoals of a small herring-like fish, the Murray Island sardine, are to be found throughout the year in the neighbourhood of the island group of that name in the northern part of the Reef, north-east of Cape York: these are suitable for drying or canning. Sharks abound in the waters of the Reef generally and could be a source of oil, meal and leather; there are large quantities of the edible green turtle in the Capricorn Group of islands, east of Rockhampton, and in the far north, and there is undoubtedly a large potential overseas market for turtle soup.

In spite of all this, perhaps the chief value of the Great Barrier Reef lies in its tourist attraction. Near the coast there are mountainous islands which some say are more beautiful than those of Greece. Over 80,000 square miles (207,200 km²) the angler can "hunt" big game, such as swordfish, tiger sharks or leaping tuna, in reefs, islands and sheltered channels. Corals abound in every conceivable shape and colour: corals fluted and corrugated, many-pointed antler corals, flat tables, immense hemispheres, corals as delicate as fine lace—all of exceeding beauty (Fig. 69), yet sharp and hard as rock, as Captain Cook found to his cost (p. 4). Only 20 of the 744 named islands off the Queensland coast are in use as resorts, but among them they attract more than 250,000 tourists annually. Most of these are from New South Wales and Victoria, but they are coming too in growing numbers from New Zealand and California.

Resort development is not haphazard but is supervised by the Queensland Tourist Bureau, which also handles the tourist bookings. The State assists by providing a 75 per cent grant towards the building of jetties. The mainland towns derive definite economic advantages: thus

[*Courtesy Australian News & Information Bureau.*

Fig. 69.—The Great Barrier Reef. An underwater scene illustrating the fantastic variety of form attained by coral "growths." The picture does not do justice to the brilliant colours.

the commercial centre for the seven resorts of the Cumberland and Whitsunday Island groups is Mackay; it benefits from a new airport, jetty and access road; it supplies the food and other equipment needed by the resorts, and in its shops most of the wages of the 375 or so employees are spent.[2]

THE COASTAL FRINGE AND BRISBANE

The Great Barrier Reef ends at Great Sandy Island, in lat. 25° S. Beyond that point portions of the Queensland coast have become important tourist areas, especially the districts immediately north and south of Brisbane. South of the capital is the so-called "Gold Coast" with its 20 miles (32 km) of broad sandy beaches ideal for surfing, and its modern hotels, motels and villas. Its resident population of 65,000 is swollen by visitors to reach at peak times 200,000. North of the capital is the "Sunshine Coast," which stretches 40 miles (64 km) between Bribie Island and Noosa Head.

The beaches themselves are of value, for the sands contain rutile, zircon, ilmenite and monazite—rare minerals which among other things are used for the production of titanium. Titanium is the tough, lightweight and heat-resistant metal used in the manufacture of jet engines. These sands form one of the world's chief sources of rutile, but production began on an important scale only in 1955. The industry is of recent growth and shows a steady expansion (Tables 50 and 51).

TABLE 50

Queensland: output of mineral sands concentrates, in thousand tons

Year				Output
1950	.	.	.	14·7
1955	.	.	.	42·2
1960	.	.	.	73·3
1965	.	.	.	104·6
1966	.	.	.	131·1
1967	.	.	.	159·4
1968–69	.	.	.	190·3
1969–70	.	.	.	309·4
1970–71	.	.	.	284·2
1971–72	.	.	.	197·2

TABLE 51

Australia: output of rutile, zircon and ilmenite concentrates, in thousand tons

				New South Wales		Queensland	
				1968	1969–70	1968	1969–70
Rutile	.	.	.	184·4	226·4	80·7	130·2
Zircon	.	.	.	176·3	218·0	75·2	90·7
Ilmenite	.	.	.	11·4	11·1	2·9	88·1

At the opposite end of the Queensland coast, in the Cape York peninsula, a major mining venture is in operation. Here, around the shores of Albatross Bay, on the west coast of the peninsula in lat. 13° S., a red band up to 20 feet (6 m) wide shows itself along 15 miles (24 km) of cliffs. This is the mineral bauxite, the chief ore of aluminium, and its presence is known over 220 square miles (570 km²) of land—forming the world's largest known deposit. In 1958 the Queensland Government authorised the Commonwealth Aluminium Corporation to work these bauxite deposits. A 10-mile (16-km) long shipping channel was dredged, and by the end of 1962 the first shipments of ore had been made—to Japan.

The nearest settlement was at Weipa, a mission station of only 150 people, and the Corporation has turned this into a port and town of 5000. In 1967 the rate of extraction of Weipa bauxite was raised to $2\frac{1}{2}$ million tons annually and by 1971 it had risen to 7·5 million tons (Fig. 70).

Bauxite mining and processing is an important growth point in the economy of Queensland. Mining is being extended north of Weipa to Andoom. This involves the building of 15 miles (25 km) of railway, spanning the Mission river by a bridge nearly a mile long, the construction of new housing and railway rolling stock, and the provision of water and power. As a result the output of bauxite will be raised to 10·5

FIG. 70.—Bauxite mining at Weipa. Bauxite mining and processing is one of the major growth industries of Queensland, where Gladstone already has the world's largest alumina plant. At present Australia is second only to Jamaica among the world's bauxite producers; it may soon become the leading producer.

million tons annually. Australia has already moved into second place among the bauxite producers of the world and may soon surpass Jamaica to become the leading producer of this important mineral.

The increased output of the Weipa district makes it necessary to improve the port facilities and the State is financing the construction of a second export wharf and a new heavy equipment wharf at Weipa. About 45 miles (72 km) farther south, at Aurukum, is a further deposit of 300 million tons of bauxite, and plans have been prepared to begin mining here. The project includes an alumina refinery of 1 million tons capacity.

At present, however, the bauxite intended for refining in Australia is shipped to Gladstone, about 60 miles (96 km) south-east of Rockhampton. Here a new alumina plant was opened in 1967 with an initial output of 600,000 tons annually. Its capacity was raised in 1968 and again in 1971 to reach 1·2 million tons. Already the largest in the world, it has been enlarged once more, to reach a capacity of 2 million tons annually. The plant now provides permanent employment for about 950 people.

The sugar industry. The leading farm product by far in the coastal belt is sugar cane, which forms the distinctive crop of Queensland. Only wheat and fodder crops exceed sugar cane in area. According to the botanist, sugar cane is a member of the grasses; but it grows very tall (6–12 feet (1·8–3·6 m) high) and its purply-red, shiny stems are woody and jointed, rather like bamboo, and grow to about $1\frac{1}{2}$ inches (40 mm) thick. About 85 or 90 per cent of the cane consists of a sweet juice (children love to chew it), and from a ton of cane it is possible to extract nearly 3 cwt (152 kg) of sugar.

Sugar cane flourishes on rainy tropical coastal lowlands. Rainfalls of up to 180 inches (4600 mm) per annum, which would be excessive for almost any other crop, do no harm to sugar cane unless the fields are actually inundated. Where the rainfall is less than about 40 inches (1000 mm) irrigation is successfully practised; and there is an interesting correlation between rainfall and sugar cultivation. We have already noticed two stretches of north-to-south shore where high mountains face the prevailing winds and the rainfall is accordingly high. Here between Cairns and Ingham and between Proserpine and Saint Lawrence are the most important areas of sugar cane.

Mackay, in the more southerly stretch, with seven crushing mills, is the headquarters of the Queensland sugar industry. By contrast, sugar cultivation is virtually absent from the Rockhampton district, where the rainfall is less than 40 inches (1000 mm) per annum, though it again becomes important farther south, between Bundaberg and Brisbane.

In addition to abundant rainfall, sugar cane requires warm sunshine, freedom from frost, and a deep, well-drained soil. The reliable rainfall and sunny weather of the Queensland coast north of the Tropic of Capricorn makes for a dependable crop of cane.

Sugar cane is grown from cuttings of mature stalks. Like all the other processes in the industry, the planting is now completely mechanised. The plant is allowed to grow for 12 to 16 months (in the cooler southern parts, 18 to 24 months) before harvesting.

The high temperatures and abundant rainfall brought by the summer monsoon promote the growth of the cane; but with the falling temperatures and reduced rainfall in winter, the growth is arrested and the plant now produces sugar, which it stores in the stalks. This is the time for harvesting, which takes place between June and December. Figure 71 illustrates the monthly temperature and rainfall conditions of Innisfail, which may be regarded as typical of the sugar areas.

After the first harvest, the stubble puts out new shoots, and grows into what is known as a "ratoon" crop. Usually two successive ratoon crops can be grown before the stubble is ploughed in; then the farmer grows a leguminous crop in rotation before growing new sugar.

Sugar cane was carried in the first fleet to Australia; but it is not until 1823 that there is any record of production. In that year 70 tons of sugar were manufactured at Port Macquarie in New South Wales (lat. $31\frac{1}{2}°$ S.). Commercial production in Queensland is barely a century old (it began in 1863); but the tropical coast now depends on this harvest, which has led to an important influx of population. In 1918 there were

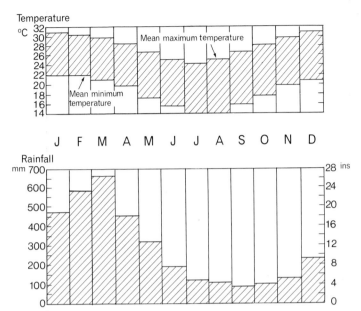

FIG. 71.—Mean monthly temperature and rainfall at Innisfail. The monsoonal rainfall regime is favourable for sugar: the cane grows fast during the summer rainy season; with falling temperatures and reduced rainfall the growth slackens and the plant makes and stores sugar. The harvest season is from June to December.

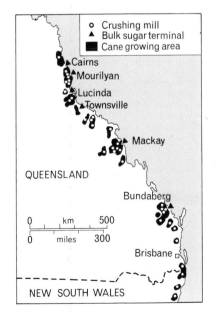

FIG. 72.—The sugar districts of Australia. Sugar cane is grown in a discontinuous coastal strip about 1300 miles (2100 km) in length, stretching from Grafton in New South Wales to Mossman in North Queensland. Within this belt 8000 farmers grow sugar cane and the cities and towns are dependent on the industry. The 1971 production of raw sugar, 2,749,000 tons, formed a record output.

fewer than 15,000 people in the coastal strip between Cairns and Innisfail, and Australia imported the bulk of her sugar. Two years later the Federal Government subsidised local production. There was an immediate increase in sugar planting: by 1923 the population had grown to 26,000; by 1933, 53,000; and by 1938, 60,000.

In fertile pockets of land along 1300 miles (2000 km) of coast, extending from Mossman in north Queensland to Grafton in New South Wales, about 8000 farmers are growing sugar cane (Fig. 72). They own and work their farms, which average about 90 acres (36 ha) in size.

The Mackay district, with a rainfall of about 60 inches (1524 mm) soon became the leading producer. With the aid of government grants central crushing mills were established, whose object was to encourage cutting by white labour only. The first of them was built at Mackay, where there are more sugar mills than in any other area in Australia. In this district about one-quarter of the entire Australian sugar crop is harvested from 1800 farms.

Mackay itself is a thriving town of 27,000 people, with modern hotels, shops and public buildings—a town of verandahs, shady arcades and palm-bordered boulevards. In 1939 a new artificial deep-water harbour was opened. With 54 feet (16 m) of water at the wharves at high-water spring tides, this is Queensland's deepest harbour. Bulk

[*Courtesy the Agent-General for Queensland.*

Fig. 73.—A bulk sugar train at Innisfail. Two thousand miles (3200 km) of narrow-gauge railway track link the farms with the mills, and the mills with the loading terminals. Here sugar is being hauled by diesel locomotives to Mourilyan Harbour, near Innisfail. Each waggon holds 22 tons (22·3 t) of raw sugar, in four bins. Ripe cane is in the background.

loading, introduced at Mackay in 1957, has enormously speeded up the handling of sugar. Formerly to load 9000 tons of sugar required the services of 300 men spread over three weeks; now the task is done by seventeen men in a single day.

There are now bulk-loading facilities at all the sugar ports: from south to north these are Bundaberg, Mackay, Townsville, Lucinda, Mourilyan and Cairns. Their total capacity, of 1,450,000 tons (1,473,000 t) in 1973, constitutes the largest bulk storage facility for sugar in the world. The Mackay terminal, in the central part of the coast, fed by eight mills, can store 420,000 tons (427,000 t) and is the world's largest single sugar terminal.

The Pioneer Valley, behind Mackay, is intersected by a maze of light railways and cane tramlines. Diesel locomotives speed through the fields and haul long trains stacked high with purple rods of succulent cane (Fig. 73). In the crushing season the mills work incessantly, grinding ton after ton of cane, and the air is full of the scent of molasses. The Mackay district, with an output of 740,000 tons (752,000 t) of raw sugar, was the leading producer in 1971.

Second was the Cairns–Innisfail–Mourilyan district, with an output of 634,000 tons (644,000 t). The town of Innisfail has a population of 7500, and in the surrounding area are a further 10,000 or so people. Most of these depend on the sugar industry (Fig. 74).

Research for the industry is carried out in several institutions, including the universities of Townsville and Brisbane. Improved farming techniques, more effective pest control and the development of new varieties have resulted in greatly increased yields per unit of area. Sixty years ago the yields of cane and raw sugar were respectively about 16 tons and 2 tons per acre (40 t and 5 t per ha); today the yields are more than double, at about 33 tons and 4·8 tons per acre (84 and 12 t per ha).

Cooktown and its district. Sugar plantations extend north of Cairns into the Mossman district, where the Cook Highway threads its way between jungle-clad mountains and the Coral Sea. Here is the most northerly sugar mill in Australia—in the summer months a hive of industry—and nearby, at Daintree, is its most northerly butter factory. Here the Highway ends; and the outpost of the coastal railway system is at Rumula, 20 miles (32 km) south. There is a short, isolated stretch of railway serving Cooktown, but for the most part this region north of Cairns is virgin land whose wealth is as yet untapped.

Cooktown was named in honour of Captain James Cook, who made fast the *Endeavour* to a tree on the river bank. In 1873 gold was discovered on the Palmer river to the west. Cooktown was established to serve the gold miners, and after twelve months boasted a population of 2000. During the next three years 15,000 Europeans and 20,000 Chinese passed through the port. A railway to the goldfields, 100 miles (161 km) distant, was planned; and by 1888 it had reached Laura. But by that time gold was on the decline, and there the railway stopped.

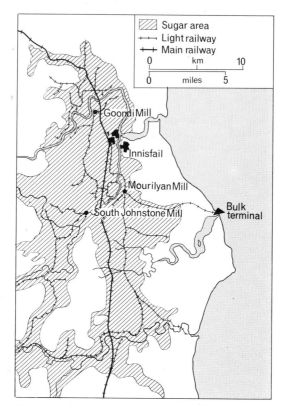

Fig. 74.—The Innisfail sugar district. About 700 farmers
grow cane in this district on 64,000 acres (26,000
ha) of land. The cane is planted and harvested
mechanically, crushed in one of the three local mills
and loaded at Mourilyan Harbour, where the storage
capacity was increased during 1973 from 140,000
to 175,000 tons (142,240 to 177,800 t). Bulk loading is at the rate of 1000 tons (1016 t) or more an
hour; a ship which during the 1950s would have
taken three weeks to load by hand is now loaded in
less than a day. Some of the sugar is transported by
road, but in this map the roads have been omitted for
the sake of clarity.

Cooktown has declined to about 500 people, and there are deserted
hotels and banks in the town; yet this is a potentially rich area; a State
government survey has been carried out, and the future may see new life
in this now remote township.

Brisbane and Ipswich. In September 1824 a party of convicts and a
detachment of the 40th Regiment landed at Redcliffe (a few miles north
of what is now Brisbane) from the brig, *Amity.* In the following

February they moved up the Brisbane river, and so the future State capital was born. As in many another Australian town, we know the precise stages by which the town developed. *Amity* had been sent out by the then Governor of New South Wales, Sir Thomas M. Brisbane—a soldier-scientist who charted the southern skies, and introduced the cultivation of grapes, sugar cane and tobacco into the new colony. The settlement named after him became a free town in 1842 and the capital of Queensland in 1859, when this State was proclaimed.

The founders had chosen wisely. The semicircular lowland behind Brisbane is one of the largest in the whole of the eastern coast. With a radius of about 60 miles (100 km), its area is roughly equal to the combined English counties of Kent, Surrey and Sussex. From the encircling hills drain several rivers; these flow into a sheltered bay (Moreton Bay), whose entrance is protected by two islands from the easterly swell. The largest of the rivers is navigable, and is named the Brisbane; 12 miles (19 km) from its mouth stands the capital of Queensland.

How does Brisbane differ from the other State capitals? Set in a warm climate, Brisbane has a subtropical appearance, with a profusion of palms, bamboos and ferns in its many parks. There are important commercial wharves in the centre of the city, though the largest liners perforce now berth at Hamilton. Compared with other cities, there is a notable absence of pure manufacture in Brisbane, for the Queensland Government aims at dispersal of industry; but Brisbane remains the administrative, financial and commercial capital of the State.

The life of Brisbane springs from its rich hinterland, productive of cattle and sheep; wheat, barley and oats; pineapples and other tropical fruits; citrus and deciduous fruits, and tobacco and minerals. It forms an important focus of railways, though it cannot claim to rival the network of Victoria; northwards runs the coastal railway (the "Sunshine Route"), threading the sugar lands a thousand miles (1600 km) to Cairns; westwards runs the line to Charleville and Quilpie, in the heart of southern Queensland; southwards are the two parallel routes linking with Sydney—the older line running mainly west of the Great Divide, the more modern line following the coast.

By rail and by road come raw materials for the industries of the capital. Busy works along the river-front process beef and mutton or refine the raw sugar from the coastal crushing mills; and freighters at the wharves load butter, meat and wool for the United Kingdom and many other Commonwealth and foreign lands. Brisbane is the third port of Australia as measured by the value of her overseas trade; she is favoured by a low tidal range (never more than 7 feet; 2·1 m) and is reached by a dredged channel 400 feet (120 m) wide and with a minimum depth of 24 feet (7·2 m) of water.

Brisbane boasts a magnificent City Hall, two cathedrals and the University of Queensland. During the last forty years her population has increased consistently, almost at the rate of 10,000 people a year. It reached the half-million mark in 1954, and in 1971 amounted to 866,200.

Brisbane is fortunate in her proximity to an old-established coal-producing district, whose centre is at Ipswich, only 25 miles (40 km) upstream. The coal is of Triassic age; it is worked in nine seams up to 6 feet (1·8 m) in thickness, and there are fifty-three mines in the district, though they are small compared with those of the Newcastle field. Much of the coal of the Ipswich district is conveyed downstream by river craft for use in Brisbane.

An important expansion in coal mining is taking place, for a new field has been opened up at Callide, about 65 miles (100 km) south of Rockhampton. The proved reserves amount to 1000 million tons, and the mining concern is aiming at an output of 2 million tons a year: it is to build a 100-mile (160 km) electric railway to the port of Gladstone. The coal is of coking quality, and the intention is to supply the steel industry of Japan; but some of the coal will be used locally, in a large new power station at Callide (*see* Fig. 68, p. 186).

THE PLATEAU BELT

The most northerly of the plateaus which form the Eastern Highlands is the Atherton Tableland. It has its own distinct character. Its eastern edge rises steeply from the Coral Sea, and the plateau stretches westwards at an average height of about 2500 feet (750 m). At this elevation the climate is sufficiently cool to allow the growth of temperate crops, though it is only 17 degrees from the Equator. The land is well watered and the soils are formed from volcanic material. In a state of nature this was clothed in rain-forest, which contained, and still contains in parts, many valuable cabinet woods: there are kauri pines, silver ash, rose mahogany, tulip oak, white and red cedar, rosewood, maple and many others. One giant walnut log was 26 feet (7·8 m) across, and too large to pass through the railway tunnels to Cairns. The early pioneers cut down the forests ruthlessly, building their huts, sheds and fences of magnificent cabinet timber. Today the trees are highly prized for use as veneers, and a single log may give rise to £250 worth of veneers.

A mill in Cairns specialises in veneers. The tree-trunk is cut into 12-foot (about 3·7 m) sections, each of which may weigh up to two tons; the bark is removed and the logs are soaked in boiling water for two days. They are then quartered, and each piece is passed backwards and forwards through the slicing machine, whose blade is three yards (3 m) long. A single veneer is usually only one-twenty-eighth of an inch (about 0·9 mm) thick, but the blade can be adjusted to produce a shaving as thin as one-sixty-fourth of an inch (0·4 mm).

But most of the land has now been cleared for agriculture. The farmers grow wheat, and more particularly, maize; they cultivate peanuts and tobacco; they rear dairy cattle and send the milk to co-operative butter and cheese factories, and they raise pigs for the bacon factories; there are citrus groves and apricot orchards, vineyards, straw-berry beds and coffee plantations in this fruitful country. An irrigation project in the Mareeba–Dimbulah district (west of Cairns) is expected to increase greatly the area under tobacco.

Atherton itself is a centre for the storage of maize; Herberton is a focus for the farms of the south-western part of the plateau. The latter town grew to supply the needs of tin miners, for it stands at the north-eastern end of the Queensland tin belt, running from Herberton through Mount Garnet to Koorboora (40 miles; 64 km to the west). The output of tin has declined since the early years of the century; nevertheless, the dredgers of this district produce nearly two-thirds of Australia's tin.

We have seen that there are volcanic outflows in the Atherton Tableland: Lakes Barrine and Eacham, near the water-parting, are crater lakes. The short, eastward-flowing rivers have been rejuvenated, and are cutting deep gorges. Here are two outstanding waterfalls (among the hundreds to be found in Queensland). The magnificent Barron Falls, where the river tumbles 770 feet (230 m) in a tangle of tropical forest, have been harnessed for electricity: the generating station, which is underground, supplies the coastal areas around Cairns and Innisfail together with most of the Atherton Tableland. In 1957 power from the Barron was supplemented by that from the Tully river, which drops 962 feet (289 m) to the south-west of Innisfail. These majestic falls rival those of the Barron river; they are set in a district of palms, ferns and creeping plants, where that large but elusive flightless bird, the cassowary, makes her nest. A head of nearly 6000 feet (1800 m) has been contrived on the Tully river, and power is supplied as far south at Townsville; it is expected to reach Bowen eventually and even Mackay.

The coastal portion of the Tableland receives the heaviest rainfall in Australia, and here are the finest examples of Malayan type of flora—the "vine-scrubs"—dense forests with vines and epiphytes on their branches, but with little grass below. Cairns is the chief town of the coastal strip, and is of late growth. In 1876 gold was discovered to the west, and Cairns, named after the then Governor, was established on a bay to serve the goldfield. Today the town depends on timber and sugar, though the neighbouring farmers produce pigs and poultry, maize, peanuts, tobacco and vegetables. We have already mentioned the veneer works: there are also sawmills and cabinet and joinery works. More important is the sugar industry: there are three local crushing mills, and the district is noted for the Badila variety, an exceptionally sweet cane. Here is the chief sugar experimental station in Queensland, where scientists test young canes, combat pests and diseases and supply cane to the other sugar-producing districts farther south.

West of the volcanic area on the Atherton Plateau—with its cones, craters and lava flows—is an area of granite. The rainfall is lower, and the forests thin out. It is a region of scattered gum trees where anthills are the most prominent features of the landscape. Farther west still, the granite gives place to limestone, which has weathered into crags and columns of fantastic shapes; below the surface are labyrinths of caves, few of which have been explored, and a great variety of minerals which may have their importance in the future.

Nickel mining. Large though the developments are in bauxite mining and processing, they are surpassed in terms of resources employed by a completely new project that is under way in the plateau that backs the coast midway between Cairns and Townsville.

Here, at Greenvale, 114 miles (182 km) north-west of Townsville, a productive deposit of nickel has been discovered and is being developed for open-cast mining by a joint American–Australian concern. The mine is designed for an output of 2·7 million tons of ore annually, from which will be derived 2500 tons of nickel oxides and 1500 tons of cobalt oxides. A new township at the mine will house 120 employees and their families; the treatment plant near Townsville will employ over 600 people and a new railway, 140 miles (224 km) long, is under construction to link Greenvale with Townsville.

Involving a total investment of 223 million dollars, this is the largest single project under way in the whole of Queensland. Production is due to begin in 1974.

The expansion in coal mining. In addition to its growing traffic in bauxite and alumina, Gladstone is handling increasing quantities of coal for export, and has become the chief port of Queensland in terms of cargo tonnage. The expansion that has taken place in the production of coal in Queensland is indicated in the following table:

TABLE 52

Queensland: production of coal in million tons

1950	.	.	. 2·3
1955	.	.	. 2·7
1960	.	.	. 2·7
1965	.	.	. 4·2
1966	.	.	. 4·7
1967	.	.	. 4·7
1968	.	.	. 6·6
1968–69	.	.	. 7·4
1969–70	.	.	. 9·4
1970–71	.	.	. 10·9
1971–72	.	.	. 13.8

But this is only the beginning: five important projects are under development in the extensive basin of the Fitzroy river, for which Gladstone and Hay are the shipping ports. Three of them are in the neighbourhood of Blackwater, on the Rockhampton to Longreach railway; the fourth is near Goonyella, about 40 miles (64 km) east of Blair Athol; and the fifth is at Moura, on the Dawson river.

They may be summarised as follows:

Location	Investment, million dollars	Company & contracts in million tons	Output in mil. tons		Employment
			Present	Planned	
Blackwater	50·0	Utah Development 21·4 to Japan over 10 years	3·0	4·0	—
South Blackwater	22·5	Thiess Holdings 21 to Japan over 15 years	—	c. 1·3	500
Leichhardt, nr. Blackwater	19·0	Broken Hill Proprietary	0·8	—	—
Moura	62·0	Thiess–Peabody–Mitsui	4·0	5·0	700
Peak Downs, nr. Goonyella	70·0	Utah Development 34 to Japan over 12 years 24·5 elsewhere	—	5·0	350

More than half of the coal being won in these new projects is from open-cast workings, and the costs are exceptionally low: Queensland coal can be sold at prices that are about 25 per cent below those prevailing in Europe. It will be seen that this burst of activity is largely related to contracts for sales to Japan, and it is arguable that there is an unwise dependence on the economy of a single country.

The Moura project has several features of interest. Here the development is controlled jointly by the American Peabody Coal company (58 per cent), the Australian Thiess Holdings (22 per cent) and the Japanese Mitsui company (20 per cent). Three underground mines are operating, together with an open-cast working; and the latter makes use of the world's largest dragline to remove the over-burden—a monster that digs out 200 tons at a single bite.

A significant rise in coal output took place in 1968 (Table 52) following the completion of important railway projects. In that year a new and more direct line 112 miles (179 km), in length, was opened to link the expanding Moura coalfield with its shipping port of Gladstone. In the same year a 12-mile (20-km) spur was constructed from the Central railway (Rockhampton to Longreach) to serve the Blackwater mine, and at the same time the line between Blackwater and Gladstone was upgraded to accommodate the heavy coal traffic (Fig. 75).

By 1969 the Queensland railways had completed their conversion from steam locomotives to diesel-electric units: these are more powerful, faster and more economical both to fuel and to maintain.

In 1959 a trainload of coal from the Kianga field to Gladstone comprised 400 tons. The trains from Moura now carry 3000 tons of coal in sixty steel wagons; those from Blackwater and South Blackwater carry 2400 tons in fifty aluminium wagons. All these are loaded mechanically from overhead chutes at the mines, and discharged at Gladstone through bottom doors.

The latest development has been the construction of a completely new railway 124 miles (198 km) long to link the coal deposits at Goonyella

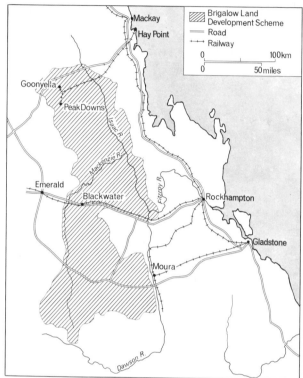

Fig. 75.—Queensland: the new coal industry and the Brigalow Scheme. Two main developments are taking place in this central portion of the plateaus. A vast area is being cleared of brigalow mainly for pastoral farming; and important new coal-mines are being developed, mainly for export to Japan. The area of the Brigalow Scheme is shaded, and the new mines are indicated, together with their rail connections.

with a shipping port established at Hay Point, 12 miles (20 km) south-east of Mackay. This railway, built within two years, and equipped with new locomotives and rolling stock, embodies the heaviest rails in Queensland, the stoutest sleepers and the strongest bridges.

The locomotives in use are the most powerful in the State: they weigh 96 tons and develop 2200 horse-power. Each train is hauled by three locomotives; it transports 4000 tons of coal in seventy-two wagons and is more than half a mile (1 km) long (Fig. 76).

At Hay Point the wagons are automatically tipped over, two at a time, into a hopper which is linked to an extensive system of conveyor belts. The actual loading point is at the end of a jetty more than a mile long stretching into the deep water offshore. The new mine at Peak Downs is being connected to the Goonyella railway by a short spur 30 miles (48 km) long.

[*Courtesy the Agent-General for Queensland.*

FIG. 76.—Transporting coal from Goonyella. A triple-engined diesel-electric train is conveying coal from the Goonyella mine to the shipping terminal at Hay Point. These engines are the most powerful in Queensland; they weigh 96 tons (97·5 t) and develop 2200 horse-power. The train carries over 4000 tons (4064 t) of coal in 72 aluminium wagons and is more than half a mile (804 m) long. The 124-mile (198-km) Goonyella line was opened in 1971. A 30-mile (48-km) spur is under construction to open up the coalfield at Peak Downs.

At full production the Goonyella mine will yield four million tons of coal annually and the Peak Downs mine five million tons. The new Goonyella railway will then be the busiest coal line in Australia. These will form only part of the total shipments from Queensland. Under contracts already made (mainly with Japan) the shipments will rise from the 10 million tons or so of 1971–72 to 20 million tons during the next few years, and could reach 30 million tons in the foreseeable future.[3]

But it is not only mineral wealth that is contributing to the growth of this district, for within the region is one of Australias greatest projects of land improvement—the Brigalow Scheme.

The Brigalow Scheme. We have already referred briefly to brigalow (p. 42). This is a native acacia which ranges in height from a low shrub up to 60 feet (18 m), according to the rainfall. In its tree form it provides useful timber which has been utilised for a variety of purposes, including boomerangs and roofing material. It is of limited grazing value, but the soil in which it grows is capable of yielding an improved pasture, if it can be cleared. This, however, is difficult owing to the rapidity with which the plant re-establishes itself through the vertical shoots that it sends up from the remaining roots.

The usual method of clearing brigalow is by dragging across the land a steel chain attached at each end to a tractor. The uprooted trees are then burnt, and the land is sown with recommended grasses that can compete with new brigalow. Reclaimed brigalow country will support up to four times the number of cattle compared with native brigalow, or it can grow wheat, sorghum or cotton.

The brigalow zone is very extensive, stretching from the Isaac river in east-central Queensland southwards across the Great Divide and into New South Wales as far as Narrabri. A restricted portion of this zone has been selected for systematic improvement: this is the Brigalow Scheme of Queensland (Fig. 75).

The area contains 11·2 million acres (4·5 million ha) and is roughly bisected by the Rockhampton to Longreach railway. The reclaiming of this vast area began in 1962: the 5 million acres (2 million ha) south of the railway are already cleared and improved, and have been divided into 139 pastoral properties. Development of the northern portion is under way, and the land here is being divided into 110 blocks. The total cost is estimated at $A23 million, and the entire scheme is expected to be complete by 1975.

Three generations ago the plateau belt was renowned for its minerals; Charters Towers and Mount Morgan have become famous names in the story of gold mining.

Charters Towers, on the railway between Townsville and Cloncurry, was proclaimed a goldfield in 1872; at its peak there were 100 mines in the district with 2000 prospectors at work, and several hundred distinct gold-bearing reefs had been discovered. Little gold is now found here, and the town is noted now more for its schools, its pleasant climate, and its glorious blossom. Mount Morgan lies in a similar position but farther south, on the railway between Rockhampton and Longreach. It has been described as the most famous gold mine in Australia. The "mount" had a cap of white quartz which for years yielded fantastic quantities of pure gold; at lower levels there were valuable deposits of copper, and Mount Morgan still produces that metal, though as a gold-field it is extinct.

The Darling Downs. The limits of this important region are somewhat vague. *The Times Atlas* includes all the land between the Balonne river and the Great Divide; but official publications prefer a more restricted area, roughly triangular in shape and bounded in the east by the Great Dividing Range and in the west by a line passing through Cooyar and Bell (in the north), Dalby and Tara (in the west) and Warwick and Killarney (in the south): this, broadly speaking, is the basin of the Condamine river.

The Darling Downs form one of the most closely settled regions in Queensland. They produce almost the whole of the wheat of the State, two-thirds of its cheese, much of its barley, oats and rye, its maize, sorghum and millet, its lucerne, its fat lambs, its butter and its bacon (Fig. 77).

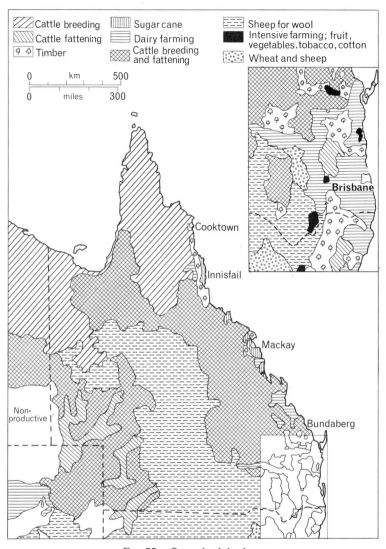

Cattle breeding
Cattle fattening
Timber
Sugar cane
Dairy farming
Cattle breeding and fattening
Sheep for wool
Intensive farming; fruit, vegetables, tobacco, cotton
Wheat and sheep

0 km 500
0 miles 300

Cooktown

Innisfail

Mackay

Brisbane

Non-productive

Bundaberg

FIG. 77.—Queensland: land use.

How can we explain so fruitful a region? An altitude of 1500–2000 feet (450–600 m) tempers the subtropical heat of summer and allows the growth of temperate crops; the region possesses an adequate rainfall, nowhere less than 25 inches (635 mm) on the average; and the soils are rich, deep and fertile, and have benefited from the presence of volcanic material.

It is to the explorer Alan Cunningham that we owe our first description of the Darling Downs. The date was 5th June 1827. "A hollow in the forest ridge, immediately before us," he wrote, "allowed me distinctly to perceive that at a distance of 8 or 9 miles, open plains or downs of great extent appeared to extend easterly to the base of a lofty range of mountains, lying south and north, distant by estimation about 30 miles." A gap in the mountain wall promised to provide a gateway to the downs from the coast; but it was not easily found, and only at the second attempt was Cunningham's Gap discovered—to take its place as an important road to the west.'So was the young settlement at Moreton Bay enabled to overflow to the west—first by road, after 1863 by rail.

Most of the larger towns of the region lie on its eastern border; they thus benefit from a cooler climate (at 1000–2000 feet; 304–608 m) and can easily transport to the coast the products from the surrounding farms. The first towns were established about 1840, when the Darling Downs were occupied as large sheep runs. Warwick, north-west of Killarney on the Condamine river amid wooded ridges, was founded in 1847 on the site of a sheep station belonging to the pioneer Patrick Leslie. Today Warwick is an important centre of the wheat belt, though production is even greater to the north-west, around Dalby, Pittsworth and Milmerran. In all, the Darling Downs harvest a million bushels annually and raise about one-quarter of the total Queensland crop. Maize flourishes too and gives a heavy yield with little need for fertiliser. The farm products are varied: dairy farming has been practised for two generations, and 7000 bales of wool are clipped from 300,000 sheep.

Stanthorpe to the south, beyond the strict limits of the Darling Downs, is the centre of an area whose granite soils are unfavourable both to grain and pasture. But deciduous fruits flourish, and here are the finest gum trees in Queensland. As in the granites of Cornwall, tin ores are present, though little metal is now produced.

Sixty miles (96 km) to the north is Toowoomba, the largest city and market for the Darling Downs. A network of roads and railways brings grain, wool, sheep, fat lambs, fruit and cream to this busy city—the products of the fertile volcanic soils to the west. Toowoomba collects this produce and forwards it eastwards to Brisbane: 85 miles (137 km) by road, or 100 miles (161 km) by rail. Toowoomba seems to realise its dependence on past volcanoes, and the City Council has preserved a section of columnar basalt as a geological monument.

It was at Moonie, in the western portion of this region, that oil was struck in 1961 (the Moonie river is a northern tributary of the Darling). Two years later the first commercial oilfield of Australia was opened here, and in 1964 a 200-mile (322-km) pipeline was laid from Moonie to Brisbane. By the end of 1965 two new refineries were open in Brisbane to process the crude oil, and a new source of energy was available for the farmer, the manufacturer and the home.

The search for oil brought to light a field of natural gas in the north of the region at Roma, and these successes stimulated the search for oil and gas in other parts of the State.

By the end of 1971, 801 oil or gas wells had been drilled in Queensland—nearly one-third of all those in Australia. Although the Moonie field was the first Australian oilfield to be developed, its output was soon overtaken by the fields in other States following the discovery of oil in Victoria and Western Australia (Table 53); and the output of the Moonie field has declined to a modest figure. Nevertheless, the oil provides a welcome addition to the energy supply of Queensland.

The gasfields of the Roma district are increasing their output; a 280-mile (450-km) gas pipeline has been constructed to Brisbane, and the new form of energy has stimulated the construction of a large fertiliser plant. Until 1969 Queensland was the largest producer of natural gas in Australia, though in later years she was overtaken by Victoria and South Australia (Table 54).

TABLE 53

Australia: production of petroleum, in million barrels

Year				Queensland	Victoria	Western Australia	Total
1968	.	.	.	3·1	—	10·7	13·9
1969	.	.	.	1·9	0·5	13·4	15·8
1970	.	.	.	1·4	47·1	16·7	65·1
1971	.	.	.	1·0	95·7	16·2	112·9

TABLE 54

Australia: production of natural gas, in thousand million cubic feet

Year				Queensland	Victoria	South Australia	Western Australia	Total
1968	.	.	.	0·1	—	—	—	0·1
1969	.	.	.	3·9	3·5	0·6	—	8·0
1970	.	.	.	7·6	16·0	22·2	—	45·7
1971	.	.	.	8·2	26·1	32·0	1·2	67·5

THE GREAT ARTESIAN BASIN

Below the Darling Downs, and stretching far to the west and north-west, lies the Great Artesian Basin—the largest in the world. It is 1270 miles (2032 km) from north to south and 900 miles (1440 km) from east to west; it covers an area of about 600,000 square miles (1,560,000 km²) or more than six times that of the United Kingdom. The greater part of this region lies in Queensland, but it extends southwards into New South Wales and westwards into the Northern Territory and South Australia.

It is appropriate to examine first the structure of this region, for it is the underground water supply which has turned a semi-desert land into the home of flocks and herds.

The floor of the Great Artesian Basin is composed of Upper Jurassic

[*Courtesy Australian News & Information Bureau.*

FIG. 78.—Artesian water. This deep borehole is in New South Wales, east of the Darling river. In the background are stacks of surplus tubing.

sediments, which reach a thickness of 5000 feet (1524 m). Their lower layers are of porous sandstone, and the upturned edges of these beds outcrop at the surface in the eastern highlands of Queensland. These, it is generally thought, receive and store the rainfall, and supply the wells hundreds of miles to the west. Above the sandy strata are thick deposits of shale, which seal off the water and prevent it from rising to its natural level, so that almost everywhere in the basin the water is truly artesian—that is, it rises without any need for pumping (*see* Figs 78 and 79).

The water is freshest near the intake zone, and saltiest—with more than 20 grains of sodium carbonate to the gallon (28·5 mg/dm^3)—in the west, around Lake Eyre. It is frequently warm, and in places is from such depths that it is actually boiling when it emerges. There are 3060 artesian bores in the Great Artesian Basin of Queensland (of these 2022 were actually flowing in 1968). These wells are estimated to have doubled the stock-carrying capacity of the land in many parts: they supply ditches which run for miles through the paddocks to water the thirsty animals. But wells are expensive to drill—costing about £2000 apiece (depending on the depth and size of the bore and labour costs)—and the yield of water has been gradually declining, so that its use is now carefully regulated.

The stores of artesian water are particularly valuable in that they lie in a region of low and erratic rainfall, for it is precisely this marginal land which stands to benefit most from an additional source of water.

[*Courtesy Australian News & Information Bureau.*

FIG. 79.—A shallow sub-artesian well in New South Wales—*i.e.* one in which pumping is required. The wind provides the power.

The *average* rainfall declines westwards from 20 inches (500 mm) in the intake areas to below 5 inches (127 mm) in the Lake Eyre region; and the low rainfall is accompanied by high rates of evaporation. Boulia, 150 miles (240 km) south of Cloncurry, holds the record for all Australia, with an evaporation rate of 124 inches (3150 mm) a year.

The surface of the Great Artesian Basin is monotonously undulating. It falls gently westwards from an altitude of more than 1000 feet (300 m) above sea-level east of Longreach and Roma to the flats of Lake Eyre, which are 35 feet (10·5 m) *below* sea-level. In the north a broad belt of higher land (the Selwyn Range) runs east and west and forms the divide between the rivers which flow north to the Gulf of Carpentaria (the Flinders, Leichhardt and Gregory and their tributaries) and from those "flowing" to Lake Eyre (the Thomson, Diamantina and Hamilton). The latter are hopefully indicated with double lines on the atlas maps; and indeed, in times of flood they may be many miles wide. The lower Diamantina has an average rainfall of 6 inches (150 mm) per annum—yet 12 inches (305 mm) of rain fell in a single day in February 1906! But most of the time these "rivers" are dry, or at best only chains of muddy pools, fringed with acacias. In the northern districts there are two useful fodder grasses: Mitchell grass and Flinders grass; these are natural, and they support important concentrations of sheep and cattle.

This vast area had the beginnings of settlement, however, before the advent of the artesian well. Most centres originated as halting places on the stock routes, which in general followed the main water-courses. Their origins and later development have been studied in interesting detail.[4]

Among the early foundations were Aramac (named in 1859), Cloncurry (founded about 1867), Charleville (surveyed and named in 1868), Winton and Thargomindah (established about 1875), Boulia and Bedourie (about 1879) and Birdsville (1880).

Aramac, on the western slope of the Great Divide, grew as a supply centre for pastoralists who were settling in the surrounding districts of Mitchell grass. Cloncurry was exceptional in that its rise stemmed from the discovery of copper ores. Winton began with a single store at a water hole; Thargomindah was at the intersection of two stock routes. Bedourie and Birdsville were both stages on the Georgina stock route, and there is a local account of the foundation of the latter place: "Burt arrived from Adelaide (in 1880) with a dray loaded with supplies and started a store. He was accompanied by a man called French Charley, who started a grog shanty." The Georgina stock route centres were nourished by camel trains from South Australia, and mobs of cattle passed through them southwards on their way to Adelaide.

To the south-east, Thargomindah, Cunnamulla and other centres were supplied from Bourke, about 130 miles (210 km) within New South Wales. This had the great advantage that it was linked by water transport with the populated country to the south by way of the Darling and the Murray. Wheat brought by this route indeed cost £22 per ton; but it could not be supplied from the east for anything like that price.

During the 1880s the fortunes of the frontier towns were improved by the forging of new links with the eastern coastal districts. First came the inauguration of mail services. They were operated by aboriginal runners, or by packhorses, or by bicyclists; and later these were augmented or superseded by mail coaches. The aboriginal mailman would swim a swollen creek holding his letter above the water in a cleft stick; the packhorse postman would turn back only if the water reached his saddle flaps; the cyclist postman would be prepared to cover 100 miles (160 km) in a day.

By 1887 a complete network of postal services had been organised, and for the first time many of the remote settlements had connections with the eastern towns. In the later 1880s this link was further strengthened by the construction of the railways, which stretched westwards in long lines from the coast.

From Brisbane the railway reached Charleville in 1888 and
Cunnamulla to the south in 1898. At last Bourke lost its position as the
supply centre for the settlements of south-western Queensland, and from
now on they looked towards Brisbane. Farther north, the railway from
Rockhampton stretched out westwards to Longreach, and was connected to Winton in 1899. The line from Townsville reached
Hughenden in 1888, Cloncurry in 1908 and Duchess and Dajarra in
1915–16. Remote settlements like Thargomindah and Boulia looked
eastwards to the railheads, though the distance involved was around 100
miles (161 km). Only Bedourie and Birdsville were so far west as to be
beyond the influence of the railway; and they retained their traditional
links with Adelaide (Fig. 80).

It was in the late 1880s and in the 1890s that the fortunate discovery
of artesian water had its strengthening effect on the economies of the
inland settlements. The first well was sunk near Blackall (about 150
miles (240 km) north of Charleville) and within the next 20 years nearly
a thousand had been drilled. A further impetus to settlement was
brought by the discovery of opals in the 1890s: this brought a shortlived

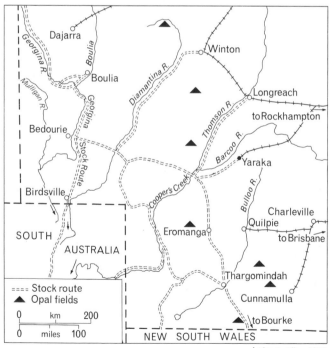

[*After A. Allen, 1969.*

FIG. 80.—Western Queensland: early settlements. Many of the small
settlements of western Queensland have a social and economic
significance which bears no relation to their physical size.

prosperity to Eromanga, Duck Creek and the appropriately named Opalton (near Winton).

A series of drought years at the turn of the century played havoc with the pastoral industry and was reflected in the dwindling fortunes of the settlements. During the twentieth century the only real surge in urban development took place in the 1930s at Mount Isa, following the discovery and successful working of copper, lead and zinc. Every other town declined in population during the 1960s, in spite of the improvement in communications and the provision of medical services based on the Flying Doctor.

Yet in spite of their tiny populations these centres perform vital services for the surrounding pastoral properties. Thus Birdsville in 1961 had only fifty-two residents; yet it possessed the only store for 250 miles (400 km). Thargomindah in 1967 had a hotel, a stock agent, three stores and 298 residents. The railhead settlements are rather larger: Winton in 1966 had a population of 1653 and Cunnamulla 1992; both had declined by more than 7 per cent in five years. Yet the spheres of influence of these centres for such items as banking, groceries, clothing and medical supplies extend to distances of more than 150 miles (240 km).

The most hopeful sign for the future stability of these towns is perhaps the establishment of an improved road system: this is the "beef roads" project. It stems from legislation in 1961 which paved the way for the expenditure of $A16 million from Federal funds and further expenditure from the State funds of Western Australia and Queensland.[5]

In Queensland the scheme has involved the upgrading of a thousand

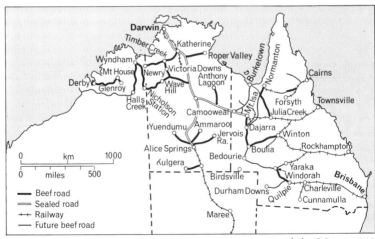

[After C. Duncan, 1964.

FIG. 81.—The "beef roads" of northern Australia. Sheep and cattle losses through drought are greatly reduced by the existence of an efficient transport system. The slow and uneconomic drove roads are now almost extinct.

miles (1609 km) of roads, of which the chief are from Windorah to Quilpie, from Boulia to Winton and from Normanton to Julia Creek (on the Townsville–Mount Isa railway) (Fig. 81). They are thus essentially feeders to the railways, and so they continue the process of strengthening the eastward links of the frontier towns.

"Beef roads" are sealed highways intended to speed the passage of "road trains." A road train consists of a prime mover, a semi-trailer and two trailers; it is a quick and efficient method of transporting stock. It has clear advantages over the stock route: cattle that are driven along the stock routes lose up to 150 lb (68 kg) apiece and must be at least 5 to 7 years old to withstand the journey; cattle that are transported by road arrive in prime condition even if they are young. Moreover, with speedy transport the animals can be moved out of drought areas quickly and into better watered country: losses are reduced and the pastures are more efficiently used.

It has been officially estimated that the number of cattle in western Queensland is capable of being raised from about 250,000 to about 730,000. The improved prospects of the pastoral industry will undoubtedly result in a greater stability in the fortunes of the frontier settlement.

THE CLONCURRY REGION

Like an island, extremely old Cambrian sediments rise in the north-west of Queensland from beneath the Jurassic deposits which floor the Great Artesian Basin; they form a low, undulating plateau whose summits in the Selwyn Range reach 650 feet (495 m). The rainfall in this region is brought by the summer monsoon, which sweeps in from the Gulf of Carpentaria, and it decreases southwards. The northern slopes of the plateau rejoice in an adequate rainfall (Burketown, near the coast, has a mean annual rainfall of 26·9 inches (680 mm)), and many long and permanent streams flow northwards to the Gulf. Farther inland, as always in Australia, the rainfall is deficient. Cloncurry, on the northern edge of the plateau, receives only 16·9 inches (425 mm)—hardly adequate in the tropical summer heat, where December temperatures regularly reach 38° C (100° F). Moreover, the rainfall is markedly seasonal in character, with about 95 per cent falling in the summer months, and variable in quantity: in 1950 Cloncurry received 37·1 inches (940 mm); two years later only 12·3 inches (310 mm). Mount Isa, Duchess and Selwyn lie on the water-parting, and receive about 15 inches (375 mm) annually; Urandangi and Boulia, 80 miles (128 km) to the south-west, have barely 10 inches (250 mm), and their southward-pointing water-courses flow only in summer.

The land is pastoral in character. There are the Flinders and Mitchell fodder grasses, though other edible plants, such as mulga, wilga and myall, are absent. Cloncurry began as a cattle market and still acts as a centre for pastoral products. It is the natural outlet for most of the cattle of the Gulf of Carpentaria region, and there are large tracts of grazing land to the east, south and north. These are tapped by railways running north to Dobbyn, west to Dajarra and south to Selwyn. Built to carry minerals, the railways now bring in wool to Cloncurry to be forwarded to the coast.

There is great scope for a more intensive development of the pastoral industries in central and western Queensland, and the State and Federal governments are combining to this end. $40 million are being spent on road construction, so that the traditional droving will give place to the road train, which can transport 80 head of cattle at 30 or 40 miles (50 to 65 km) per hour. A further $A32 million are being spent on clearing the land, constructing fences, providing water and sowing new pastures over 6 million acres (2·4 million ha) of central Queensland.

The fame of the region, however, springs from its minerals. Cloncurry has been claimed as the centre of the largest copper belt in the world. Here ancient slates and quartzites have been raised almost vertically, and the copper deposits run in fissures parallel with the grain of the land: they have apparently been concentrated here by water percolating through strata which have since been removed.

Cloncurry dates only from 1880. The railway link with the coast—still only a single track—was achieved in 1910. Only valuable minerals could justify such a purposeful line, 481 miles (770 km) long, through sparsely peopled country. For seven years (1910–17) Cloncurry boomed; but the price of copper fell; mining declined and at present plays only a small part in the life of the town. Nevertheless, there are deposits of low-grade ore of very great extent and almost untouched in a region 250 miles (400 km) long and 40 miles (64 km) wide, and given favourable conditions, Cloncurry may yet regain its position as a significant mining centre of Australia. Today the town ranks as an important market centre for the north-west of Queensland. Until 1965 Cloncurry was the headquarters of the Royal Flying Doctor Service (*see* p. 344); but in that year the base was transferred to the more populous and fast-growing city of Mount Isa.

Mining now centres on two other towns of the region, Mount Isa and Mary Kathleen, and so important are they that the Queensland Government has reconstructed the long railway to the coast at an estimated cost of $A58 million.

Mount Isa lies due west of Cloncurry, 63 miles (101 km) as the crow flies but 122 miles (193 km) by rail, and is situated on the Leichhardt river. It is one of the newest and one of the fastest-growing towns in Australia. During 1923 bodies of silver–lead ore were discovered here, ranking with the world's largest. Present too are ores of zinc and copper, so that Mount Isa has become one of the most important producers of the base metals in the continent.

Production began in 1932, with the separation and concentration at the local mills of silver, lead and zinc; the lead was exported in the form of bullion, and the zinc in the form of a powdery concentrate. By the outbreak of the Second World War Mount Isa was already a comfortable and well-planned town with a population of 4000—double that of Cloncurry. Copper was then considered more essential to the war effort, and the Mount Isa mills were directed to that end. In 1946 they reverted once more to the production of silver, lead and zinc, and this district is now by far the leading producer in Queensland of all three metals. Meanwhile, in 1953 a new copper-smelting plant was opened; copper mining was resumed, and within two years Queensland quadrupled her production of copper; and today Mount Isa produces over half the entire output of copper in Australia. Copper, indeed, valued at almost $A120 million in 1968–69, is by far the most important mineral produced in Queensland.

Mount Isa has a bright future: the mining company is in the middle of an expansion programme costing $A370 million, planned for completion by 1978; by that time it will have become the largest silver–lead–zinc mine in the world. The known reserves of copper at Mount Isa have more than doubled: placed in 1968 at 46·5 million tons of ore, they were known in 1971 to be 120 million tons. Table 55 indicates the growing output of these metals in Queensland, virtually all of which are derived from Mount Isa.

TABLE 55

Queensland, production of copper, zinc, lead and silver, in terms of metallic content

Year				Copper thou. tons	Zinc thou. tons	Lead thou. tons	Silver thou. oz
1950	.	.	.	5·2	25·8	39·2	2,941
1955	.	.	.	31·9	17·1	48·8	4,396
1960	.	.	.	82·8	24·4	57·5	5,122
1965	.	.	.	60·4	31·0	49·7	4,636
1966	.	.	.	72·6	43·6	65·5	6,192
1967	.	.	.	51·5	51·0	76·4	6,832
1968	.	.	.	69·4	84·1	116·7	9,624
1968–69	.	.	.	81·0	96·8	135·9	10,692
1969–70	.	.	.	93·8	109·4	150·3	12,584
1970–71	.	.	.	120·7	106·7	146·2	11,805
1971–72	.	.	.	119·9	108·8	122·0	9,263

The copper plant near Townsville, which came into operation in June 1959, handles all the copper concentrates from Mount Isa, and a major railway reconstruction was completed in 1965 to carry the increased output over the 600 miles (966 km) to Townsville.

The story of Mount Isa shows clearly that while geology presents the possibilities of a mineral area, only economics and politics will decide the nature of the actual product.

Since 1940 the town has grown rapidly—from 4000 to 12,000 inhabitants by 1960, 17,000 by 1966 and 22,000 by 1971. One-quarter of the present population are in the employ of the mining company.

Newer even than Mount Isa was the mining community of Mary Kathleen, where, half-way between Mount Isa and Cloncurry, a local taxi-driver found in 1954 the black ore of uranium. The rush which followed attracted people from all over Australia and from many countries of Europe. A modern township was laid out, designed in the first instance for a thousand people, with shops and school, cinema, swimming-pool and a beer garden. Three or four miles away was the uranium mine—an open quarry on the hill face, to be worked at six levels. From this remote spot in the heart of Australia came raw material to feed the nuclear power stations of the United Kingdom. It flourished from 1958 to 1963, when the market became saturated; it is now a modern "ghost town."

Such, then, is the Queen State—a land of sunshine and a land of contrasts. It includes the rainiest place in the continent and also that with the driest atmosphere; it includes in the south-east, land at 4500 feet (1372 m), and in the south-west, land at or near sea-level. It is rich in coal, copper, lead, zinc, bauxite and uranium; and it is the chief producing State of sugar, maize, beef and pineapples. The people of Queensland look with confidence to the future.

NOTES

1. *The Times*, 23rd April 1970.

2. B. S. Marsden, "Recent Developments on Queensland's Resort Islands," *Australian Geographer*, Vol. X, No. 4 (1967).

3. Queensland Railways, *Opening of the Goonyella Line*, Commemorative brochure: 1971.

4. A. Allen, "Frontier Towns in Western Queensland," *Australian Geographer*, Vol. XI, No. 2 (1969).

5. C. Duncan, "Beef Roads of Northern Australia," *Australian Geographer*, Vol. IX, No. 4 (1964).

STUDY QUESTIONS

1. "The annual rainfall map of Queensland is an imperfect guide." Discuss this statement.

2. Discuss the origin and economic value of the Great Barrier Reef.

3. Examine the mineral wealth of Queensland.

4. Write an account of the sugar industry of Queensland.

5. What are the distinctive features of: (*a*) the Atherton Tableland, and (*b*) the Darling Downs?

6. With the aid of a sketch map describe the site and functions of Brisbane.

7. How far is it legitimate to regard the Great Artesian Basin as a distinct natural region?

8. Describe briefly the pastoral industries of Queensland.

Chapter IX

SOUTH AUSTRALIA

THE settled portions of South Australia consist of a relatively small but fertile farming area bordering the Gulf of St Vincent. They are bounded to the north, west and east by desert or semi-desert and to the south by sea. The limits of the State are straight lines which have evidently been drawn on a map in an office rather than on the ground: to the east the boundary follows long. 141° E., to the west long. 129° and to the north, lat. 26° S. The land so demarcated has a maximum width from east to west of nearly 750 miles (1200 km) and a length from north to south of nearly 850 miles (1360 km). It is exceeded in size by Western Australia, Queensland and Northern Territory; even so, its area (380,000 square miles; 988,000 km²) is four times as great as that of the United Kingdom.

STRUCTURE AND RELIEF

Physically South Australia has a distinct personality: it includes the largest lakes, the most prominent inlets, the best examples of rift valleys, and the driest portion of the continent. To the east is an almost isolated ancient plateau system; to the north-west is a portion of the ancient block of western Australia; elsewhere there are level or gently undulating plains, for the most part too dry for habitation.

The Mount Lofty and Flinders ranges are composed of ancient sediments (Cambrian or Precambrian) which were folded in early times. After erosion through hundreds of millions of years they were thrust upwards in geologically recent (Pliocene) times. Faulting took place, and earthquakes are an indication that movement has not entirely ceased. A trough was formed to the west, and its deepest portions were filled with water.

The gulfs of Spencer and St Vincent are twin rift valleys, floored with Tertiary material, bounded by faults and flanked by Cambrian or Precambrian sediments. The Yorke Peninsula, which separates them, remained apart from the foundering movement and now forms an elevated block or horst. Lake Torrens is accepted as forming part of the floor of the trough, and Lake Eyre is so clearly in line with the gulfs and Lake Torrens as to suggest that faulting has played some part here too (Fig. 82).

The Flinders and Mount Lofty ranges rise to just over 3000 feet (900

Fig. 82.—South Australia: the core of the State, physical and towns. Outlying tracts, not shown here, are virtually uninhabited. Goyder's Line still encloses almost all the crop land and close settlement in the State.

m): Freeling Heights in the far north attain 3120 feet (936 m). Mount Remarkable, north of Port Pirie, reaches 3100 feet (930 m). Both their eastern and western faces exhibit step faulting, and three levels have been discerned, at about 1500 feet (450 m), 1000 feet (300 m) and 400 feet (120 m); there are believed to be two more steps below the sea, at depths of about 220 feet (66 m) and 2000 feet (600 m). The ranges form an important element in the human geography of the State: their northern and north-eastern portions are too dry for permanent settlement, but elsewhere they form attractive, cool and well-watered lands, well served by roads and railways, with many fertile valleys whose pastures, orchards and vineyards send their produce to a host of market towns. Kangaroo Island is a detached portion of the ranges.

The structure of the rest of the State is relatively simple. To the north-east, an area of level Jurassic sediments forms part of the floor of the Great Artesian Basin, which we have already noticed in Queensland (p. 207); to the east in the basin of the lower Murray are Tertiary sands and limestones which mark the site of a former wide bay, and in the extreme south-east are volcanic cones together with the sheets of lava which emanated from them. Both the Tertiary and the volcanic rocks have already been described in connection with Victoria.

In the west there are young sedimentary rocks, which, however, mask the ancient shield of western Australia. Finally, the Great Australian Bight is fringed by a belt of Tertiary limestones, formed originally upon the sea-bed, but now elevated and converted into the barren and waterless Nullarbor Plain.

CLIMATE

Of all the Australian States South Australia is the driest. In one small district of the Mount Lofty Ranges south-east of Adelaide the rainfall reaches 40 inches (1000 mm) per annum; at Mount Gambier and in the higher tracts of the ranges it is above 30 inches (750 mm). But these form an exceedingly small portion of the whole, and it is a startling fact that 83 per cent of the area of the State receives a mean annual rainfall of below 10 inches (250 mm).

The driest part of the continent is a roughly circular tract lying around and to the north of Lake Eyre, with a diameter of about 350 miles (560 km). Marree (on the Alice Springs railway) lies near its southern edge; Oodnadatta (on the same railway) and Finke (just within Northern Territory) are near its western border and Birdsville (just within Queensland) is on its north-eastern boundary. This extensive region receives less than 5 inches (125 mm) of rainfall on the average, and almost the whole of it lies in South Australia. The driest known place on the continent is actually Mulka, about 50 miles (80 km) east of the edge of Lake Eyre. Its mean annual rainfall is 4·05 inches (102·9 mm).

As usual, where the rainfall is lowest it is also the least reliable. The Lake Eyre district has an average deviation of 50 per cent from the mean: in other words, while the theoretical rainfall is more than 5 inches (125 mm) one must be prepared for as little as $2\frac{1}{2}$ inches (62 mm) and yet not surprised at $7\frac{1}{2}$ inches (188 mm). Adelaide has both a greater and a more reliable rainfall. Its average annual total is 21·1 inches (536 mm) and its deviation between 15 and 20 per cent: its actual rainfall in any given year may therefore be expected to lie between about $17\frac{1}{2}$ and $24\frac{1}{2}$ inches (444 and 622 mm). Nevertheless, Adelaide is the driest of the eight capitals.

To the farmer the distribution of the rainfall throughout the year is as vital as its annual total. The Adelaide region lies along a west-facing sea-board and in about lat. 35° S.: theory would lead us to expect here a "Mediterranean" type of climate, with the dry south-east trade winds blowing in summer, to be replaced by the damp north-west anti-trades in winter.

As usual, the actual records are less simple. Protected by the scarp of the Flinders and Mount Lofty Ranges, the Adelaide Plains rarely experience east winds, except on winter mornings, when land breezes occur. The dominant winds in winter blow from the north-west, west and north: these are the "north-west anti-trades," and it is they which bring the reliable winter rains to Adelaide and its district. The summer winds, theoretically the "south-east trades," blow in fact chiefly from the south-west, south or west. Yet they bring less rain than the winter winds even when they blow from the sea; for they are moving from cooler to warmer regions (they are moving towards the Equator, and in any case, the land is warmer than the sea); they therefore tend to hold their moisture, and summer is the dry season.

This winter maximum of rainfall is accepted as natural by South Australians. It is found in Eyre's Peninsula and Yorke Peninsula, in the Mount Gambier district, in the plateaus east of Port Pirie and in the Murray valley. Only in the interior is the rainfall (small as it is) well distributed throughout the year, for here we are half-way between the "Mediterranean" south and the monsoonal north.

Adelaide enjoys abundant sunshine throughout the year, and averages seven hours of sun a day; she expects only four foggy days in the year, and she has the lowest humidity (52 per cent) of all the capitals. With mean January temperatures of 23° C (73° F) and maxima of 29° C (85° F) her summers are decidedly warm—nearly 10° F higher than those of London. Her winters, on the other hand, are pleasantly mild, with mean June temperatures of 12° C (53° F) and maxima of 16° C (60° F)—8° C (14° F) above those of London.

The climate of the State, then, has much to commend it. Much of South Australia, it is true, is too dry for successful farming. But where rainfall is adequate or irrigation water is available the climate favours a wide range of crops. The moist springs encourage the growth of grain, and the dry and sunny summers ripen the crop and facilitate harvesting. The brilliant summer sunshine allows the growth of most of the temperate fruits—in particular, the grape—and permits the open-air drying of plums, peaches and apricots, and raisins, currants and sultanas. South Australia possesses more than one-third of the acreage of vineyards in the continent, and she is the wine State *par excellence*, accounting for two-thirds of the nation's output.

SETTLEMENT

The possible limits of close settlement were early recognised by an able Surveyor-General, G. W. Goyder, who in 1865 journeyed into the dry lands of the interior with the object of delimiting the habitable lands of the colony. Goyder discovered a sufficiently clear response in the vegetation to enable him to plot a line of the map. On the desert side the ground was bare of herbage and contained only scattered saltbush, mulga and dwarf mallee, closely cropped by stock; on the seaward side the bushes were fresher and more healthy and the ground cover gradually increased until there was a fair cover of grass.

"Goyder's Line" still encloses the closely settled portion of South Australia—the region within which it is reasonably safe to grow wheat. It runs from near Swan Reach to Mount Remarkable, to Broughton and so on to the Gawler Ranges; though drawn at a time when rainfall records were non-existent, it has since been found to correspond quite closely with the 12-inch (300-mm) isohyet. The test of experience has shown it to be remarkably accurate. After 1872, in a time of farming expansion, good rainfall and public works, the farmers advanced eastwards to Clare and beyond to Burra Creek; they rashly overstepped Goyder's Line, penetrating to the Minburra district in the north-east and into the far west. Hopefully they planted grain in the middle of large sheep runs. But the wet years of the seventies were followed by dry years in the eighties. The farmers were forced to retreat, and Goyder's ghost must have grinned.

These desert and semi-desert areas are of little value to South Australia; but the portions which remain are sufficiently varied to require a division into separate regions. We may distinguish: (1) the fruit and dairy lands of the Adelaide Hills; (2) the pastoral lands of the far north and far west; (3) the grain lands, including the Murray mallees; and (4) the Murray irrigated lands.

First, however, it may be helpful to put the farming of South Australia into perspective by discussing it briefly in general terms.

FARMING IN SOUTH AUSTRALIA

We have already seen that South Australia is the driest of all the States. As much as 83 per cent of its area has a mean annual rainfall of less than 10 inches (250 mm) and is too dry for normal agriculture. Only 3 per cent of its area has more than 20 inches (500 mm) of rain annually, which, given the high summer temperatures, may be considered adequate without irrigation. There is only one substantial river in the State—the Murray—and even here the salinity level of the river is giving rise to concern.[1]

This is the background against which the farming of the State should be viewed: it flourishes not because of but in spite of its climatic conditions. Yet the season 1969–70 was one of the most productive in the history of the State. There were larger areas under orchards and vineyards than ever before; there were record numbers of sheep and cattle on the land and the highest ever outputs of milk and wool. The wheat and barley harvests were almost records; there were more tractors in use than ever before.

Table 56 summarises the main characteristics of farming in South Australia. It will be seen that in the year reviewed almost exactly half of the proceeds from farming were derived from crops: this is unusual for Australia, where normally the main producers of farming wealth are cattle and sheep. Unlike Queensland, it is the temperate cereals that predominate in the agriculture of South Australia, where they account for between a quarter and a third of all the farm output by value.

TABLE 56

South Australia: value of farm output, 1969–70, in $A million

Agricultural output

Cereals	111·9
Orchard and berry fruits	24·3
Grapes	18·9
Vegetables	17·1
All crops	186·6

Pastoral and dairy products

Wool	91·2
Other pastoral products	57·9
Dairy products	45·4
Total pastoral and dairy products . . .	194·3
Value of total farm output	380·9

AGRICULTURE

In South Australia the crops are normally sown after the first rainfall of the year, which is expected in April or May (that is, autumn), and they are growing until November (early summer). During this period an adequate rainfall is vital to the success of the harvest, and there is usually a fairly close correlation between the amount of rainfall and the size of the harvest (Table 57).

TABLE 57

South Australia: outputs of wheat, barley and hay in relation to rainfall in the growing season

Average rainfall April–November over the main crop area				*Wheat delivered mil.*	*Barley delivered mil.*	*Output of hay thou.*
		Rainfall	*Farming*			
Year	*mm*	*inches*	*year*	*bush.*	*bush.*	*tons*
1965	. .	268	10·51	1965–66	32·6	13·3	368
1966	. .	282	11·09	1966–67	50·0	18·7	729
1967	. .	162	6·37	1967–68	22·1	7·1	418
1968	. .	430	16·63	1968–69	79·4	21·4	985
1969	. .	281	11·07	1969–70	55·7	—	608
1970	. .	312	12·32	—	—	—	—

Wheat is by far the leading cereal in South Australia, but its success has depended on the development of suitable varieties to match the rather special climatic conditions: the quite sudden end to the rainy season in spring, accompanied by rather strong winds. The wheat strains, the chief of which is known as Heron, have therefore been selected for early maturing and a short, strong straw.

South Australia grows far more wheat than she needs to feed her own population, though owing to fluctuations in the size of the harvest, the amount available for export varies greatly from year to year. In 1969–70 about two-thirds of the total crop were exported. For several years China has been the chief customer, and in that year she took 63 per cent of the total exports; the Middle East countries of Iraq, Saudi Arabia and South Yemen also took appreciable quantities.

Bulk handling of wheat began in 1952—this was later than in other States, perhaps owing to the dispersed character of the wheat areas in South Australia, and hence the need for many shipping ports and the consequent duplication of facilities. But the economies of bulk handling were clear. Bulk wheat commands better prices in overseas markets; it allows easier grading and safer storage; above all it is handled far more quickly at the terminals. When wheat was bagged it took two to three weeks to load a cargo of 10,000 tons; the same quantity handled in bulk is loaded in less than three days, with a consequent saving of nearly £1 per ton.[2]

Soon bulk handling silos were built in all the wheat districts, with major terminals at six ports (Fig. 83 and Table 58).

TABLE 58

South Australia: capacities of grain terminals, 1970, in million bushels

Port				*Wheat*	*Barley*	*Oats*
Port Adelaide	.	.	.	23·4	4·9	0·5
Port Lincoln	.	.	.	21·2	4·1	0·1
Wallaroo	.	.	.	12·5	2·4	—
Port Pirie	.	.	.	11·1	0·8	—
Thevenard	.	.	.	9·0	0·4	0·1
Ardrossan	.	.	.	6·7	4·3	—

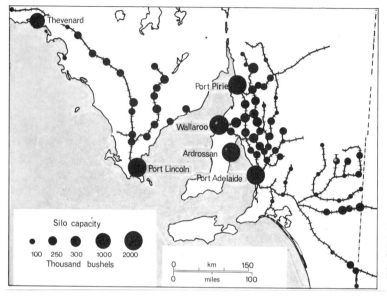

Silo capacity

100   250   300   1000   2000
Thousand bushels

[After M. Williams, 1964.

Fig. 83.—South Australia: grain silos. There are bulk silos in all the wheat districts
and major terminals at six ports. The dispersed character of the wheat areas has
necessitated the duplication of facilities.

Virtually all these silos forward or receive their grain by rail. Their
capacities reflect the productivity of the districts that they serve: in the
main wheat belt they hold 400,000 or 500,000 bushels; in the areas
with lower or variable rainfall they are of 100,000 bushels capacity.
The tall concrete grain silo has become the symbol of wheat-growing.

Following wheat, the next most valuable crop in South Australia is
barley (Table 59).

TABLE 59

*South Australia: chief cultivated crops, 1969–70, in order of value, in
$A million*

	Crop				Value
Wheat	.	.	.	.	84·8
Barley	.	.	.	.	23·6
Grapes	.	.	.	.	18·9
Citrus	.	.	.	.	8·4
Hay	.	.	.	.	7·4
Apples	.	.	.	.	4·4
Apricots	.	.	.	.	3·7
Oats	.	.	.	.	3·3
Peaches	.	.	.	.	2·9
Potatoes	.	.	.	.	2·6
All crops	.	.	.		186·6

South Australia is by far the leading State in Australia in the production of barley, and in 1968–69 produced 41 per cent of the total output. Most of it is grown for grain, and in that year 37 per cent of the crop was used for milling, 26 per cent for malting and the remainder for feed. The best malting barley requires a prolonged ripening period without high temperatures or drying winds. These conditions are met in the Yorke peninsula, where cool and moist breezes move in from the gulfs to the east and west: this district is reputed to grow the best barley in Australia. Australia exports barley to Europe, the Middle East and Japan.

Grapes rank highly in the farming economy of South Australia. In 1969–70 they were more valuable than all the vegetables put together, and were not far short of the combined value of all the other fruits. The State contains about 42 per cent of all the Australian vineyards by area, and produces 70 per cent of the nation's wine. Grape-growing is an expanding industry, and the area under grapes in 1971 was the highest ever (Tables 60 and 61).

TABLE 60
Australia: vineyards, 1970–71

State	Vineyard area thou. acres	Table grapes thou. tons	Wine made mil. gals	Currants thou. tons	Sultanas and raisins thou. tons
South Australia .	68·3	1·0	37·2	3·2	1·3
Victoria . .	50·9	10·8	6·6	3·0	40·6
New South Wales	27·8	6·9	10·4	0·6	9·2
Western Australia	6·7	1·9	1·0	1·5	—
Queensland . .	3·8	4·2	—	—	—
Australia . .	157·6	24·9	55·3	8·3	51·2

TABLE 61
South Australia: vineyards, 1961–71

Year ending		Area thou. acres	Output of grapes thou. tons	Production of wine mil. gals
1961 . . .		56·9	178·3	25·1
1966 . . .		58·7	183·8	23·9
1967 . . .		57·1	225·4	29·3
1968 . . .		58·1	201·2	30·1
1969 . . .		60·6	217·3	36·1
1970 . . .		64·8	268·0	43·3
1971 . . .		68·3	221·1	37·2

Grapes are grown in a variety of conditions in the State. The so-called "Upper Murray" belt receives less than 10 inches (250 mm) of rain annually, and grape-growing is completely dependent on irrigation. More than half the acreage under grapes lies within 60 miles (96 km) of the capital, and receives between 19 and 26 inches (475 and 650 mm) of rain; but even here some irrigation is practised, for this can treble the yield to reach 7 or 8 tons of grapes per acre. With only a little greater area than the Mount Lofty vineyard district, the Murray vineyards produce 70 per cent of the total quantity of wine grapes in the State.

After grapes the next crop in order of value is citrus fruit. In South Australia this is virtually synonymous with the orange, and almost the entire output is produced under irrigation from the Murray. During the 1960s there was an important increase in production. Output first exceeded 2·5 million bushels in 1962–63, and reached a record total of 4 million in 1968–69. This increase was largely a result of newly developed irrigation districts near Waikerie. More than one-fifth of the oranges are exported, and these represent about 60 per cent of the total exports of oranges from Australia.

Next in order of value comes hay; but this is more appropriately noticed in connection with stock rearing. Most of the apricots and peaches are grown in the Murray district, and as with oranges, there has been a significant expansion in recent years. During the 1950s and 1960s the area under peaches more than doubled and the output multiplied sixfold. The increase in apricots was less spectacular but the output almost doubled. South Australia is the leading State for this fruit: most of the crop is dried, and the remainder canned.

The apple orchards, on the other hand, are mainly in the Adelaide and Mount Lofty districts; and although their area has declined by about 50 per cent since the early 1930s, better management has brought about an improvement in yield. During the 1960s alone the average yield per acre rose by about 70 per cent and in 1969–70 there was a record crop of 1561 thousand bushels. About 20 to 25 per cent of the crop is exported.

PASTORAL AND DAIRY FARMING

We have seen that in 1970 there were record numbers of both sheep and cattle. The growth of the flocks and herds since 1940 is indicated in Table 62.

In large measure these increases have been due to the progressive

TABLE 62

South Australia: numbers of sheep and cattle since 1940

Farming year ending			No. of sheep million head	No. of cattle thousand head
1940	.	.	.	9·9	351
1945	.	.	.	8·5	391
1950	.	.	.	9·5	464
1955	.	.	.	12·8	524
1960	.	.	.	14·0	500
1965	.	.	.	17·3	697
1966	.	.	.	18·0	690
1967	.	.	.	17·9	687
1968	.	.	.	16·4	695
1969	.	.	.	18·4	865
1970	.	.	.	19·7	1026
1971	.	.		19·2	1196

improvements in the pastures, which have enabled them to carry greater densities of stock. The production of hay in any year, however, is very dependent on the climatic conditions; nevertheless, allowing for these fluctuations, there has been an upward trend in the hay crop, with a record output in 1968–69 of 985,000 tons. In part this is due to the increased application of fertilisers: during the 1960s the area of pasture treated increased from 3·3 to almost 5 million acres (1·3 to almost 2 million ha).

Over wide areas the character of the pasture has been upgraded. In the cereal districts new varieties of nitrogen-building clovers have raised the status of the soil and increased the crop yields, as well as providing nutritional pastures. In the drier parts lucerne has been introduced: it is salt-resistant and drought-resistant and it also thrives under irrigation. In Kangaroo Island and in parts of the south-east (as we see below) the application of trace elements to deficient soils has doubled or trebled the sheep-carrying capacity of the land.

Over 80 per cent of the sheep are of merino stock; but the South Australian merino has been bred especially for a robust constitution and a heavy frame: it withstands heat and drought and can travel long distances to water. Yet it bears an exceptionally heavy fleece: in 1969–70 a record average clip was achieved of 13·8 lb (4·4 kg) per head—well above that of any other State.

During the 1950s and 1960s the average size of the fleece more than doubled, and the output of wool has increased at a greater rate than that of the sheep population (Table 63). About 85 per cent of the wool clip of South Australia is sold by auction in the Adelaide Wool Exchange; about 9 per cent is marketed outside the auction system, and the rest is sold in Victoria. In 1969–70 the leading customer was Japan, which took $A21·7 million worth of South Australian wool; next in order were the U.S.S.R. ($A9·4), the United Kingdom ($A6·4), France ($A6·2), Western Germany ($A5·8) and Italy ($A4·8 million).

TABLE 63

South Australia: wool, dairy cattle and milk since 1940

Farming year ending	Output of wool mil. lb	Number of dairy cattle thou. head	Output of milk mil. galls.
1940 . . .	105	173	77·3
1945 . . .	107	187	72·2
1950 . . .	121	203	89·4
1955 . . .	156	199	90·7
1960 . . .	198	170	78·6
1965 . . .	216	182	102·3
1966 . . .	230	176	98·4
1967 . . .	237	170	98·7
1968 . . .	223	157	88·8
1969 . . .	238	163	102·8
1970 . . .	275	149	106·2
1971 . . .	259	—	103·6

With so small a proportion of its land well watered, South Australia is less important than other States for cattle rearing: it has a smaller number of cattle than any other mainland State; it contains only 4 per cent of the beef cattle of Australia and only 5 per cent of its dairy cattle. With the improvement of the pastures, however, the total number of cattle has increased substantially, having almost trebled since 1940. The cattle herd of the State surpassed one million for the first time in 1970.

During that time there has been a striking change in the relative strengths of the beef and the dairy numbers. In 1940 there were two beef cattle for each dairy cow; but while the number of beef animals has steadily increased, the dairy herd has declined, so that by 1970 there were almost seven beef cattle to each dairy cow.

The explanation is probably twofold. The demand for milk in the State increases only slowly, with the expanding population and rising standards of living. At the same time improvements in breeding, pastures and dairy techniques have brought about considerable increases in the average yield of milk per cow, so that in spite of the smaller size of the dairy herd there has been an expansion in milk production, and the output of 106·2 million gallons (483 Ml) in 1969–70 formed a record (Tables 63 and 64).

TABLE 64

South Australia: average milk production per cow, 1957–71

Year	Annual milk output per cow, gallons
Average, 1957–61 . . .	523
Average, 1962–66 . . .	600
1967	624
1968	590
1969	708
1970	724
1971	707

Until the 1950s more than half the beef cattle were reared in the dry pastures of the north of the State. With the recent improvements in the pastures most of them are now in the southern districts, and those that remain in the north are moved out for fattening. As in other States, the dairy herds tend to be concentrated in the neighbourhood of the main centres of population; and in South Australia most of the dairy cattle are within an 80-mile (130-km) radius of Adelaide. Especially important are the Mount Lofty ranges, where there are sown pastures of clover and ryegrass; but there are dairy herds too on the reclaimed swamps of the lower Murray and on the borders of the lakes at its mouth. Barrages across the mouth of the river have greatly improved these pastures, for they prevent the inflow of saline water and allow complete control over the water level in the field drains.

THE REGIONS OF SOUTH AUSTRALIA

THE ADELAIDE HILLS

The most southerly portion of the highlands of South Australia is known as the Mount Lofty Range. Mount Lofty itself (2334 feet; 707 m) is only 7 miles (11 km) from the centre of Adelaide, and sufficiently close to give at night a distant view of the twinkling lights of the city, while the range extends in a gentle curve from Cape Jervis in the south to Kapunda in the north—a distance of more than 100 miles (160 km). Lying between latitudes 34 and 36 degrees South, these districts correspond in Europe to Gibraltar, Crete and Cyprus; but altitudes of generally more than 1000 feet (300 m) temper the heat, so that orchards of apples, cherries, pears and plums, apricots and peaches flourish, while in addition here is one of the chief vineyard districts of the State. Adelaide provides a regular demand for foodstuffs, and with the abundant rainfall (more than 25 inches (635 mm) per annum) which favours the growth of natural and cultivated grasses, we find the farmers rearing dairy cattle, raising poultry and growing market-garden crops.

Many prosperous market towns in the hills handle this varied produce. Woodside and Gumeracha, east of Adelaide, are dairying centres, set amid rich pastures of fodder grasses and possessing factories for the processing of bacon, butter and cheese; Willunga and McLaren Vale, south of Adelaide, are wine-making towns in the midst of orderly vineyards with their rows of staked vines. The fruitful Barossa valley, north-east of the capital, is another wine-making district, with Nuriootpa (south of Kapunda) and Angaston as centres of the industry; here too are orange groves and orchards of apricots, peaches and plums. Farther north still, 75 miles (125 km) from Adelaide, around the town of Clare, is an outpost of the grape, orchard and dairy land (Fig. 82, p. 218).

A second and more distant outpost of this productive country lies in the Mount Gambier district in the far south-east of the State. The name is applied both to a town and a hill.

The "mount" itself is a prominent volcanic cone which rises steeply from the plains, and its crater contains a lake—Blue Lake—which forms a convenient high-level reservoir for the district. The town of Mount Gambier is one of the largest provincial centres of South Australia. The surrounding land was formerly clothed in eucalyptus forest; but the trees have long been cleared for farming, and this is high-quality dairy country, with modern and efficient farms and factories. The district is noted too for its potatoes, which grow well in these volcanic soils. Mount Gambier (the town) has two butter factories and four or five cheese factories. Plantations of pinewoods (chiefly *Pinus radiata*) have been established to provide a local supply of building timber, and at sawmills such as those of Mount Burr the logs are cut into planks or into strips for fruit boxes. The Mount Gambier district is only just within the South Australian border, and is actually nearer to Melbourne than to Adelaide.

The last of the dairy districts is Kangaroo Island. As we have seen, it forms a detached portion of the South Australian Highlands. Its rather poor soils are being improved by scientific methods: clover is being introduced and appropriate trace elements supplied to repair deficiencies. From the point of view of the stock farmer Kangaroo Island has the great advantage that rabbits and foxes are unknown there.

THE PASTORAL AREAS

We have seen that Goyder's Line still marks the approximate boundary of the possible crop lands of South Australia. Farther north, where

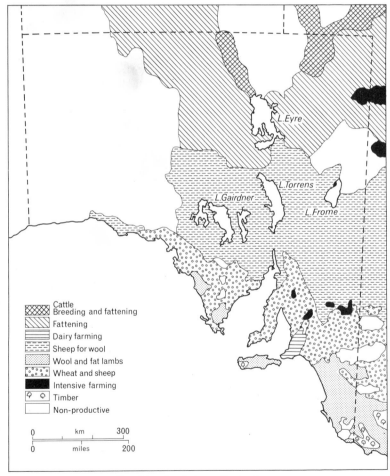

Cattle
Breeding and fattening
Fattening
Dairy farming
Sheep for wool
Wool and fat lambs
Wheat and sheep
Intensive farming
Timber
Non-productive

0   km   300
0   miles   200

Fig. 84.—South Australia: land use.

the rainfall is below about 12 inches (300 mm) annually there are only widely spaced sheep and cattle stations. Over wide areas the land is quite unoccupied: this is true of almost the whole western third of the State, where there are sheep stations only along the shores of the Great Australian Bight. There are deserted tracts too north of Lake Eyre and north-east of Lake Blanche, where the rainfall is less than 5 inches (125 mm); northwards, however, right as far as the state boundary, the land supports sheep and cattle.

Roughly speaking the boundary between the sheep and cattle lands follows lat. 30° S. which passes between lakes Eyre and Torrens (Fig. 84). With their woollen coats, sheep are unsuited to the tropical heat, and they are found to the south, while the cattle are to the north. The precise boundary exists on the ground in the shape of a dingo-proof fence. This is one of the less-publicised triumphs of South Australian farmers. It is about 1500 miles (2400 km) long—more than twice the length of the United Kingdom—and runs right across the State from the Great Australian Bight to the New South Wales border. The object of the fence is to keep the dingo to the north of it, that is, out of the sheep lands to the south, for a dingo can play havoc with young lambs. Cattle, however, can better resist the dingo, and fencing to the north is less essential.

The scanty herbage will support but not fatten cattle, and they must travel long distances on the hoof towards fattening pastures and the port. The railway from Port Augusta northwards towards the centre of the continent was built partly to bring stock from these northern districts to Adelaide for fattening and then slaughter. In 1927 it was extended from Oodnadatta to Alice Springs; and though it is exceedingly expensive to run, the railway is of vital concern to the sheep and cattle farmers. Even with its aid there is still the necessity of slow herding along hundreds of miles of stock route to reach the nearest point on the line. The longest of the South Australian stock routes runs for 400 miles (644 km) from Birdsville, just over the Queensland border, to Marree on the railway. The State Government has drilled artesian bores at strategic points and the cattle are driven from well to well. Some have names which, like Helen's Well and Sullivan's Well, echo people of the past; others bear aboriginal names, like Kintalamanko or the more formidable Piamooguaninnia. More descriptive and simple is Blazes Well. The thirsty cattle after their long trek reach Marree, south of Lake Eyre. A crowded rail journey follows, with a short break at Quorn, about half-way. When the animals reach Adelaide they are fattened in the stockyards; finally, they are slaughtered and the carcasses are frozen in readiness for the long journey to the United States or Britain.

THE GRAIN AREAS

The grain lands are regions of moderate rainfall, where the annual average is usually between 15 and 20 inches (381 and 508 mm). This is a low rainfall in view of the high temperatures—Adelaide is in about the latitude of Gibraltar and Tunis—but it is the more valuable in that it is predominantly a winter and spring rainfall. This particularly suits the temperate grains, which require a bright and sunny harvest. Naturally it is not possible to produce wheat on the same land year after year, and it is grown in rotation with root crops and fodder grasses. The grain lands are therefore in fact districts of mixed farms, where the emphasis is upon wheat for export. Sheep are grazed for wool; cattle are reared for milk, and the milk is sent to butter factories at inland market towns such as Laura (east of Port Pirie) and Gawler (north of Adelaide). Among the grains barley and sometimes oats are rivals to wheat, and in parts flax is grown for fibre. To serve the needs of Adelaide there are local concentrations upon poultry and eggs, peas and other vegetables.

As in the Canadian prairies, the railway map is a fair guide of the location of the grain lands. The core of the region is the coastal plain north of Adelaide, where thriving market towns such as Gawler and Balaklava have their flour mills and workshops for the manufacture of farm machinery.

The farms extend eastwards across the lower portions of the Flinders Range, above the 1000-foot (300-m) contour into the districts of Kooringa, Eudunda and Kapunda. Northwards the limit of successful cultivation of wheat may be put at about Quorn; southwards the area includes the Yorke Peninsula, excepting only its south-western promontory. From this main core grain farming has extended both westwards into Eyre's Peninsula and eastwards into the Murray lands; both these extensions are known as mallee lands. Here there are large tracts of light, sandy soils underlain by limestones. The porous soils together with a low rainfall prohibit the growth of trees of normal height, and in nature the mallee lands were covered with twisted and stunted gums. Both the stems and the roots are cut for fuel, and when cleared the land is suitable for wheat growing, provided always that the danger of soil erosion is recognised.

The rescue for farming of these two regions, for long considered to be unproductive, forms a testimony to the perseverence of the State agricultural advisers and to the determination of the farmers concerned.

Eyre's Peninsula. E. J. Eyre, exploring the northern parts of the peninsula that bears his name, wrote in September 1839,

... our route today was through a perfect desert, very scrubby and stony with much prickly grass growing upon the sand ridges, which alternated with the hard limestone flats.

Soon after the turn of the century, however, there were those who felt that Eyre's description might prove to have been unduly pessimistic; and in 1906 the Surveyor-General's Department commissioned E. B. Jones to investigate the possibilities of farming in Eyre's Peninsula.[3]
He reported the existence of low granite domes that interrupted the

mass of sand dune: on their borders, where water was available, he estimated that there were about 200,000 acres (80,000 ha) of potentially arable land; and in patches on the inter-dune flats and elsewhere there were a further 100,000 acres (40,000 ha). In this first estimate Mr Jones appears to have failed to allow for any use of fertiliser, for a few years later he raised his estimate to the surprising figure of 2 million acres (800,000 ha), on three assumptions: first, that phosphate fertilisers would be available; second, that a railway would be built and third, that the potential water supplies would be developed.

In the event, a Royal Commission, reviewing Jones's report and

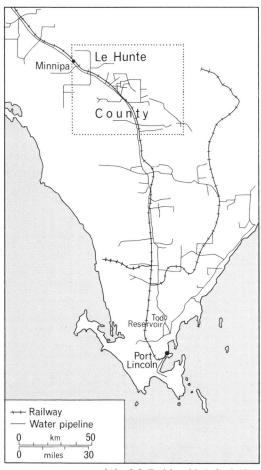

[After C. R. Twidale and D. L. Smith, 1971.

FIG. 85.—South Australia: Eyre's Peninsula. The map indicates the railway and the water pipelines, essential for the development of this area.

earlier estimate, and investigating in the field, had already recommended action. The railway reached Minnipa in 1913, aligned along the granite outcrops, with their water supply and better soils, and crossing the belt of sand ridges at one of its narrowest points. The following year an experimental farm was established at Minnipa.

Crops and stock would meet a harsh climate. The summers were hot, and five or six heatwaves could be expected annually, with temperatures exceeding 38° C (100° F) for three or more days. The winters were generally mild, allowing continuous though slow plant growth; but night temperatures were likely to fall below freezing point throughout the three winter months.

These temperature conditions combined with a rainfall that totalled only 12 to 14 inches (300 to 350 mm) annually, most of it falling in winter. In the extreme south of the area, however, a small district was better watered, and received over 20 inches (500 mm) of rain. Here was the only river of the region, the Tod; in 1922 the river was dammed and by 1926 its water was piped to Minnipa. This pipeline, with its extensive system of branches has been a vital element in the development of the peninsula.

By 1928 the State Government had organised eight other water supply schemes to conserve the run-off from the granite outcrops and the way was clear for farmers to move in (Figs 85 and 86). The land was cleared, first by man or animal power, then in the later 1940s with the help of tractors as in the Brigalow Scheme in Queensland (p. 203).

Statistics are available for Le Hunte County, which straddles the railway and occupies part of the centre of the peninsula (Fig. 85) (after 1935 the population figures relate to a slightly different area, the local government area). From only 3 people in 1911, the population of the

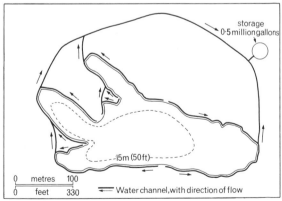

[*After C. R. Twidale and D. L. Smith, 1971.*

Fig. 86.—Pildappa Hill, Eyre's Peninsula. This is one of the granite outcrops; the diagram illustrates the method of water conservation. The contour line indicates the height from the base of the hill.

county grew to 724 in 1921, 1,914 in 1933, and an estimated 2,215 in 1935. The Great Depression that followed took its toll, a number of holdings were combined, and there was some emigration. But during the 1950s and 1960s the population began to rise again, and in 1968 was estimated at 1,950.

Table 65 suggests the type of farming that is being practised and indicates the expansion that is taking place. Between 1945 and 1967 the area under wheat multiplied by 3 while its yield multiplied by 7; sown pastures have become significant and the number of sheep has reached a record total.

TABLE 65
Le Hunte County, Eyre's Peninsula, farming growth

Farming year ending	Wheat area thou. ac.	Wheat yield bush/ac.	Barley thou. ac.	Sown pasture thou. ac.	Sheep thou. head
1945 . . .	50	3·0	3	—	124
1950 . . .	74	8·3	4	—	98
1955 . . .	66	6·5	13	21	106
1960 . . .	75	4·4	20	51	152
1965 . . .	129	14·9	15	101	171
1966 . . .	136	12·9	15	87	181
1967 . . .	159	22·9	15	98	190

The legumes that are being sown as pasture are playing an important part in the improvement of the soil: they will grow in a rainfall as low as 11 or 12 inches (275 or 300 mm) annually; they add nitrogen to the soil and improve its structure; and they nourish sheep and so make animal manure available. In areas of sand dune there is a risk of wind erosion, and the Government makes it a requirement that the larger dunes be left with their native cover of eucalypt scrub. Soil erosion is thus prevented.

This is a balanced farming system, in which wheat brings in up to three-quarters of the total farm income, and wool most of the remainder, but with a small proportion from fat lambs, beef cattle and pigs. The farmer is therefore in a fairly good position to weather economic storms by modifying the farming policy. He sends his bales of wool to the Adelaide auctions and his wheat to the new terminal at Thevenard or Port Lincoln (Fig. 83). Eyre's "perfect desert" has been transformed into a stable farming region.

The Murray mallee. About 1930, when the development of Eyre's Peninsula was well under way, the State agricultural authorities turned their attention to the Murray mallee country.

This area had a strange problem: stunted and twisted, often spiny bushes grew from loose white sand amid a jumble of dunes and flats, with never a watercourse. This was the so-called "Ninety Mile Desert" which appeared on the maps for a century, lying across the main route between Adelaide and Melbourne. Yet the mean annual rainfall here is about 17 inches (425 mm) annually, which elsewhere would be considered quite adequate for wheat growing.[4]

In 1886 the railway link between Adelaide and Melbourne was completed; the town of Keith was established and very limited areas of wheat cultivated around it. Some huge sheep runs were established: a 12,000-acre (4800-ha) property would support only 500 sheep—and some of these died from an unknown disease. Neither cereals nor introduced pastures would grow, and it was clear that there was something wrong with the soil.

During the late 1930s a Federal scientific committee investigated the problem and concluded that there were deficiencies of copper and cobalt in the soils over a wide area south-east of Adelaide and beyond the border into Victoria. Appropriate fertilisers were distributed to the farmers and the results were soon evident. One farmer about 1940 had planted wheat in newly cleared land, but the yield was only 3 or 4 bushels per acre; he then applied the new fertilisers, and by 1945 his yield had increased to 30 to 40 bushels to the acre.

Soon the Murray mallee land was being cleared using tractors and chains; the scrub was being burnt, fertilisers applied, seeds sown and wells dug to provide irrigation water. Farmhouses, roads, schools and hospitals were built on hitherto almost uninhabited country. Much of this development was undertaken as an investment by the Australian Mutual Provident Society, which has settled 150 farmers on 250,000 acres (101,171 ha), essentially for sheep rearing, based mainly on lucerne pasture. The "Ninety Mile Desert" has become "Coonalpyn Downs" (Fig. 87).

Most of the grain crop is exported; not only to the United Kingdom

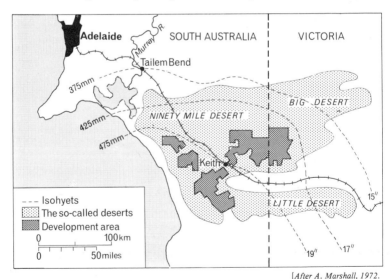

[After A. Marshall, 1972.

FIG. 87.—The Murray mallee. Formerly known as the Ninety Mile Desert, this area has now been developed for wheat and sheep.

but also to South Africa, Japan and Indonesia. Railways and roads focus on the seaports, and some grain is also brought in by coastal craft to be transhipped into ocean liners. Adelaide is the port for the grain lands east of the Gulf of St Vincent: from the Murray mallees six railways converge upon Tailem Bend and send on their produce to Adelaide. The lands east of Spencer Gulf are served by Port Pirie and Walleroo, while Port Lincoln and Thevenard (Ceduna) handle the grain of the mallees of Eyre's Peninsula. The small port of Ardrossan on the east side of the Yorke Peninsula has the distinction of being the first to introduce bulk loading of grain.

THE IRRIGATED LANDS OF THE MURRAY

There is only one river of value for irrigation in South Australia: the Murray. Nor was the Murray ideal in a state of nature: it was an unpredictable river in which periods of drought alternated with floods 25 feet (7·5 m) high. Like the Tennessee, the Murray has now been tamed by a series of dams and weirs, which have converted the river into a stairway of reservoirs. The Murray waters reach the sea by way of the shallow fresh-water Lake Alexandrina, and its mouth is all but blocked by a remarkable sandspit, nearly 100 miles (160 km) long, the Younghusband Peninsula; this is backed by an equally long lagoon. In terms of the United Kingdom it is as if a sandspit stretched across southern England from Dover to Yarmouth.

Before the regulation of the Murray, in time of drought lakes Alexandrina and Albert were invaded by sea-water and were rendered useless as sources of water supply. To prevent this, four islands at the river mouth have been joined by means of a series of five barrages. A small lock allows fishing-boats to enter. The Murray thus forms a great store of precious water; and with its aid the rainfall, which in the upper half of the river's course through South Australia amounts to only 10 inches (250 mm) per annum, can now be "increased" to the equivalent of 30 inches (750 mm).

In the upper irrigation areas water is raised by pumping from the river; and in places it is lifted as much as 135 feet (40 m). The water first enters the main irrigation canals, which are cement-lined trenches about 6 yards (5·4 m) wide. From these, smaller branches conduct the water to the orchards and vineyards. The fruit grower prepares furrows to lead the water between his rows of trees and controls the supply by sluice gates; or he pumps it once more through pipes to spray the fruit from above. Irrigation began here 80 years ago under the direction of the Chaffey brothers, who were invited to come from California by the Government of Victoria. In 1887 they made an agreement with the South Australian Government, and it was as a result of this that the first irrigation settlement, that of Renmark, was established. Today there are about 5000 people at Renmark, and an irrigated area of 9,870 acres

(3994 ha), of which about 55 per cent is under vines and 38 per cent under orchards.

Many other irrigation settlements have been founded on the riverbanks lower downstream: they include Loxton, Kingston and Waikerie. In the 1850s and 1860s the river was busy, with paddle-steamers carrying manufactures and supplies upstream for the fruit growers and the stockmen, and returning laden with bales of wool, bags of grain and boxes of dried fruits. Today these towns are served by the railway; the occasional pleasure steamer is the sole survivor of the river traffic, and the once crowded wharves of Morgan are deserted.

Between Morgan and Renmark the irrigated lands total 32,000 acres (12,800 ha). They include orange groves and vineyards, together with orchards of apricot trees, peaches, pears and plums in a land which nature clothed only in sand and scrub and stunted gums. The harvesting is spread out over several months. The grapes are ripe in February and March (which correspond to August and September in Europe). First to be picked are the currant grapes; then come the sultanas, and lastly the raisins. During the same period the peaches and apricots are ready; but the oranges ripen more slowly and are not picked until the winter.

Irrigation along the lower Murray is rather different. Here there are extensive tracts of land below normal flood level. In a state of nature these were reedy marshes inhabited only by wildfowl. But they possessed black soils rich in organic matter; and with the aid of a controlled water supply they have been converted into productive fodder-growing lands for dairy cattle. Pumping here is unnecessary except to return the water to the river; but the banks must be maintained in good order and equipped with sluice gates. There are about 12,400 acres (4,960 ha) of reclaimed swamp land irrigated in this way. They include the district of Wellington (the earliest of all the irrigated settlements in the State, established in 1881), the lands around Murray Bridge and other settlements extending as far north as Mannum (Fig. 82, p. 218).

Irrigation by its nature fosters the growth of a community spirit. Each man co-operates with his neighbour in the use of water and is dependent on the maintenance by the State of dams, barrages and sluices. There are co-operative packing stations, wineries, and distilleries, co-operative stores and even community-owned hotels.

From Morgan to Lake Alexandrina the Murray is flowing from north to south, so that the irrigated settlements of the upper portion are isolated from the populated lands of the Adelaide district. There are bridges at only two points: Renmark and Murray Bridge. The rest of the cross-river traffic is handled by a dozen or so vehicular ferries: these are operated by leisurely moving punts which can carry about six cars at a time. The river presents quite an obstacle to land transport, for it is bordered by a wide belt of marshland. At Murray Bridge the road and rail bridges, including their approaches, are half a mile (0·8 km) long.

The dried fruits of Renmark have a rail journey of 200 miles (320 km) before even beginning their sea journey. Morgan sends its produce direct to Adelaide, by a 100-mile (160-km) line which crosses the Mount Lofty Range. Murray Bridge is nearer than either: half a dozen railway lines focus on the town from north, east and south, collecting fruit, wine and dairy produce from the irrigated settlements and bringing grain from the mallee lands. Murray Bridge forwards most of this produce to Adelaide, only 50 miles (80 km) distant; but the town processes some of it on the spot, in its lofty flour mills, butter factories, cheese factory and milk depot.

ADELAIDE AND GAWLER

The Capital. With a population of 809,466 (1971) Adelaide contains nearly 70 per cent of the inhabitants of the entire State; it must therefore be regarded as an important region in itself. When South Australia was settled, in 1836, the Surveyor-General, Colonel William Light, was entrusted with the task of choosing a suitable site for a capital and of planning its layout.

The Colonel visited in turn the mouth of the Murray, Kangaroo Island and Port Lincoln. These he wisely rejected choosing instead the well-watered and roomy site at the foot of the Mount Lofty Range. A winding stream, the Torrens, promised fresh water; 5 miles (8 km) away it reached the sea in a sheltered estuary offering the site of a port. Both north and south of the stream the land was sufficiently high to be beyond the reach of floods either from the river or the sea. Here on a low plateau, 140 feet (42 m) above sea-level, William Light planned the capital city, and at the King's request named it after Adelaide, the queen of William IV.

The plan of 1837 in all essentials survives today (Figs 88 and 89). The major portion of the city is south of the river—a rectangle whose streets cross at right angles and follow the cardinal points of the compass. At the centre is an open space, and each quadrant too has its garden. Reminiscent of the plan of the Roman town, the chief public buildings adjoin the central park: at or near its four corners are the Town Hall, the General Post Office, the Court of Justice and the police headquarters. Farther north is the "west end": grouped together here in three or four streets are the larger shops, seven or eight hotels and a dozen or so theatres (Fig. 90).

The whole is surrounded by a "green belt" of parkland, through part of which flows the Torrens, dammed to form a pleasant long and narrow lake. North Terrace fronts this parkland—a fine, broad, leafy boulevard—and on its north side, with views over the lake and to the Mount Lofty Range beyond, are the government and cultural zones. Here are the stately Government House, the monumental Parliament building, the libraries, art gallery, museum and exhibition hall, together with the university buildings.

North of the river Colonel Light planned a smaller portion of the

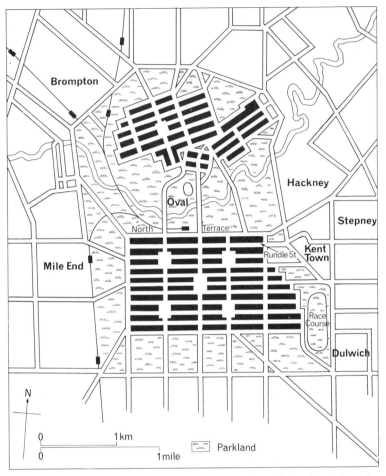

Fig. 88.—Central Adelaide: Adelaide is a spacious planned city, threaded by the river Torrens and encircled by parklands.

city—North Adelaide. It has a single central park, and its streets, too, cross at right angles, but the alignment is modified to conform with that of the river. North Adelaide, too, is surrounded by parklands.

We cannot but admire the generous scale on which the Surveyor-General planned for the future. Adelaide has grown well beyond the planned area, but the ring of green remains to form the boundary of government, finance, commerce, amusement and culture. The factories are situated chiefly in the suburbs, especially on the north-west side, between the city and the port. The Londoner feels quite at home in Adelaide, for many of the suburban names suggest the origin of the newcomers. To the north are Croydon, Enfield and Islington; to the east Hackney and Stepney jostle with Kensington; to the west are

[*Courtesy Australian News & Information Bureau.*

Fig. 89.—Central Adelaide from the air, showing the rectangular pattern of the business area and the central square. The Torrens and the belt of parkland may be glimpsed in the distance.

[*Courtesy the Agent-General for South Australia.*

Fig. 90.—Adelaide: King William Street. This is the main north-to-south thoroughfare established by Colonel Light, looking south towards the central open space. It represents an impressive piece of town-planning: it dates from 1837 yet is adequate for the transport requirements of a modern metropolis.

Mile End and Richmond; and to the south are Highgate, Clapham and Mitcham.

The industries of the city are varied and comprise many that are to be found in any capital city: clothing and textiles, electrical goods and metal manufactures, food processing and canning. Of more than local importance, however, are the large railway workshops at Islington and the motor-body plant at Woodville, half-way between the city and the port: this is the largest factory in South Australia.

The sheltered estuary which Colonel Light noticed at the mouth of the Torrens has developed into one of the major ports of the continent. Port Adelaide, with a population of 40,000, is the chief single inlet for the needs of the State and the outlet for its products. Among the imports are coal and petroleum for fuel, jute for binder twine, phosphates for fertilisers, together with iron and steel and timber. The primary products of wool, wheat, barley and oats figure prominently in the exports, together with frozen meat, locally refined salt, dried fruits and motor bodies. The traffic in the port is a comment on the life of the State. With 3 miles (5 km) of wharves and minimum depths of up to 33 feet (10 m), Port Adelaide can accept all but the very largest cargo liners.

For statistical purposes the Adelaide metropolitan region extends 30 miles (48 km) south of the city centre, beyond Port Noarlunga, and 25 miles (40 km) north of the centre, to include Elizabeth, Virginia and Gawler. The development of Gawler forms an interesting study in itself; but the whole of this northern district is important as the main source of supply of vegetables for the capital. If it is to continue as such, a serious problem of shortage of water will need to be solved, as we shall see below.

The Development of Gawler. After the foundation of Adelaide in 1837 no time was lost in the establishment of country towns. Two years later, a group of twelve landholders with a block of 4000 acres (1600 ha) about 25 miles (40 km) north of Adelaide saw the need for a commercial centre in their area. It was close enough to the newly planned capital to share in its port and metropolitan services, yet a day's ride away, and at that time sufficiently remote to develop its own social and economic functions.

Appropriately enough the landholders approached the Surveyor-General, Colonel Light, fresh from the planning of Adelaide, to plan a town for them: this became Gawler. Colonel Light selected a high but flat 240-acre (96-ha) site in the angle between the junction of the North and South Para rivers (Fig. 91), and incorporated in his plan the principles he had adopted for Adelaide. The plateau top he reserved for administrative and residential purposes: here he placed three successive and connected squares, each to be centred on a church, together with the sites for schools, a courthouse, police station and other public buildings. The surrounding slopes and flood plains he reserved as parklands.

The main north–south highway (Murray Street) joined several parallel secondary roads and led directly southwards to Adelaide. Murray

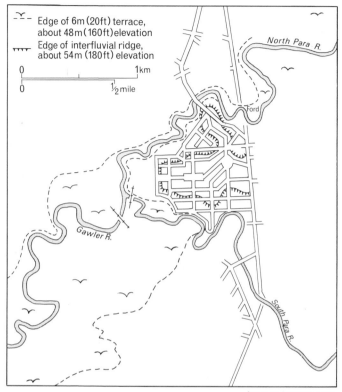

Edge of 6m (20ft) terrace,
about 48m (160ft) elevation

Edge of interfluvial ridge,
about 54m (180ft) elevation

0   1km

0   ½ mile

North Para R.

Ford

Gawler R.

South Para R.

[*After M. Williams, 1964.*

Fig. 91.—The physical setting of Gawler. Colonel Light selected a platform at about 160 feet (48 m) in the angle between the junction of the
North and South Para rivers. The town centre was higher still, at
about 180 feet (54 m).

Street soon became the commercial focus of the new town. Here
Colonel Light made his only error of judgment. The straight line of
Murray Street when extended to the north and south needed to cross the
two rivers, and these crossings began as fords. Unfortunately they
remain so, for when they were replaced by bridges the flood waters
descending the Para rivers washed the bridges away. More suitable
bridging sites had to be found lower downstream, so that the highway
from Adelaide through Gawler now has to make awkward diversions
from the direct line to negotiate the streams.[6]

This however was a mere detail. The site was well chosen and within
twenty years seven named suburbs had grown up, three of them following the arrival of the railway in 1857. For about a century Gawler
maintained an independent existence. From the 1840s it was a resting
place for the teams of bullock drays that brought copper concentrates

from the mines at Kapunda and Burra, and returned with supplies. It was also on the supply route for German immigrants who were opening up for intensive cultivation the valuable lands of the Barossa valley, and later, in the 1870s, for the farmers pioneering the northern wheatlands.

The town developed characteristic industries, which included flour milling and the manufacture of farm implements, railway locomotives and rolling stock, and mining and smelting equipment. With the expansion of Adelaide these industries declined, and Gawler has been transformed into an annexe of the capital. What was formerly a day's ride by horse has become a 45-minute journey by car, and now about half of the work-force of the town commutes daily to and from Adelaide.

Since about 1960 the district has gained a new significance, for the fertile plains south-south-west of the town have developed into the largest and most rapidly growing source of tomatoes and vegetables for Adelaide. The area with its problems has been the subject of a careful study by Mr D. L. Smith.[7]

Twenty years ago the city was supplied by growers who cultivated plots on the western, and more particularly, the eastern outskirts of the built-up area. In 1951 more than 1500 acres (600 ha) of vegetables were cultivated on land close to the lower Torrens below the city, while

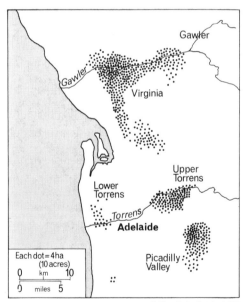

[After D. L. Smith, 1972.

FIG. 92.—Adelaide: horticulture on the urban fringe. The two districts closest to the city are both declining; that to the south-east remains fairly steady; the Virginia–Gawler district is rapidly expanding.

to the east and south-east the Torrens valley above the city and the Piccadilly valley each contributed a similar area.

Since then the Piccadilly valley has managed to retain its area under vegetables, but the market gardeners closer to the urban fringe have been unable to compete with the demands for building land. The upper Torrens district declined to about 1000 acres (400 ha) while the lower Torrens district became almost extinct.

Many of the displaced growers moved to sites well to the north of the city, and a new market gardening district arose in a triangle with corners at Gawler, Two Wells and Salisbury, and with a concentration at Virginia (Fig. 92). From a mere 150 acres (60 ha) or so in 1950 the vegetable area grew to 1000 acres (400 ha) in 1959, to 2000 acres (800 ha) in 1962 and to more than 4000 acres (1600 ha) in 1969 (Fig. 93).

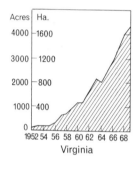
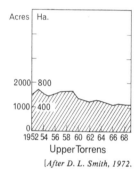

[*After D. L. Smith, 1972.*

Fig. 93.—Horticulture on the urban fringe: changes in two Adelaide districts.

These growers rely extensively on irrigation, and the tomato crop, which is grown under glass, depends on it completely. Consequently the vegetables and tomatoes can be marketed out of season, to command high prices. Thus, the potatoes, which represent 42 per cent of the total quantity, are on sale in June, when those from the cooler Adelaide Hills are over, and they span the whole gap in supplies until the following February. The lettuces, cabbages and cauliflowers are sold mainly in winter, while those from the Piccadilly valley arrive in summer.

Virtually every plot in this northern triangle has its own water borehole; but the different crops range widely in their water requirements. It is estimated that each acre of lettuces requires 230,000 gallons (1 Ml) of water to mature: this is relatively low on account of their speed of growth. Onions need about 540,000 gallons (2·5 Ml) per acre, cabbages and cauliflowers 800,000 (3·6 Ml) and potatoes 870,000 (3·9 Ml). Glasshouse tomatoes need 1,630,000 gallons (7·4 Ml) per acre; thirstiest of all is celery, which uses more than 2,000,000 gallons (9 Ml) for each acre!

The life-giving water that nourishes this industry is contained in a bed

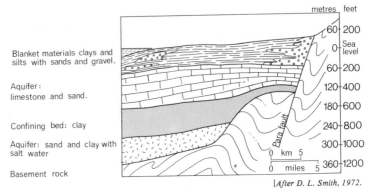

Blanket materials clays and
silts with sands and gravel.

Aquifer:
limestone and sand.

Confining bed: clay

Aquifer: sand and clay with
salt water

Basement rock

[*After D. L. Smith, 1972.*

FIG. 94.—The Gawler district: geological section. The water is contained in
limestones and sands about 300 feet (90 m) from the surface; but it is being
extracted faster than the rainfall can replenish it.

of Tertiary sands and limestones which attains a maximum thickness of
about 400 feet (120 m) and is usually within about 300 feet (90 m) from
the surface (Fig. 94). But it is becoming clear that the rate of pumping
has now outstripped the rate of replenishment and the water-level in the
wells is falling fast. In one monitored borehole near Virginia, until the
middle 1950s the summer water-level had been higher than 20 feet (6 m)
above sea-level. In the summer of 1957–58 it fell to −10 feet (−3 m); in
1962–63 to −22 feet (−6·6 m); in 1965–66 to −28 feet (−8·4 m) and
in 1967–68 to −54 feet (−16·2 m).

At last the authorities acted. From February 1967 a permit was
made necessary for the sinking of a new bore or the repair of an existing
one. Control was strict, and during the ensuing four years two-thirds of
the applications were refused. In November 1970 all irrigation bores
were required to be fitted with meters, and an annual quota of water was
allocated to each user. These quotas appear to be reasonably adequate,
except that celery will probably be found too water-demanding to be
cultivated on any scale; and the main effect at present will be to avoid
the wastage of water which must have been taking place on a considerable scale owing to a lack of knowledge of the water requirements of the
various crops. The South Australia Department of Mines is at present
aiming at a 17 per cent reduction in the removal of water from the
aquifers. But it is the firm conclusion of Mr D. L. Smith that this will
not suffice.

INDUSTRY AND ENERGY

MINING

Mining in South Australia is limited chiefly to iron and brown coal;
but the mines of Broken Hill are only just over the border of New South
Wales, and these ores are partly processed at Port Pirie.

The deposits of iron are among the richest known in the continent, and it was these which led to the establishment of the Australian steel industry. They occur in the Middleback Ranges, 35 miles (56 km) north-westwards of the head of Spencer Gulf. Here a hill known as Iron Monarch rises 600 feet (180 m) above the plains: it consists of a mass of high-grade iron ore, with an average content of 62 per cent. Gradually the mechanical shovels are eating it away. Until 1941 the ore was railed from the mining town of Iron Knob to the small port of Whyalla, on the shore of the Gulf, and then shipped for smelting at the furnaces of Newcastle and Port Kembla in New South Wales. These date from 1916. But the Second World War stimulated the Australian steel industry: the Broken Hill Proprietary Company built a large blast furnace at Whyalla itself and established a shipbuilding yard on the adjoining site. To assist in these developments the State Government promised to provide an adequate and reliable water supply.

Whyalla now has a population of 32,085 (1971) and has become the second city in the State. The promised water supply was inaugurated in 1944, when water pumped from the river Murray at Morgan began to flow through a 223-mile (359-km) long pipeline to reach Whyalla, benefiting all the towns on the way. Water has ceased to be a scarce commodity, and the way is now open for further expansion.

The iron works and the shipyard are arranged round three sides of a rectangular dredged basin (Fig. 95). At its base are the building slips with their hammer-head cranes; to the right are the fitting-out berths, to the left are the towering blast furnaces with their attendant air heaters, together with the wharf, the travelling cranes and the coal and ore stockpiles.

The Whyalla shipyard is the largest in Australia: it has built naval vessels and coastal freighters, in particular the large ore carriers which themselves form a vital link in the iron and steel industry. In 1972 it launched the *Clutha Capricorn*, an 83,000 dwt. ore carrier, and the largest vessel yet to be built in Australia.

Until 1965 the steel needed at Whyalla had to be brought from New South Wales; but in that year a $A100 million steelworks was opened and a second blast furnace installed, so that for the first time the shipyard and other steel-using industries of the State had their own supplies of steel. More recently a pellet plant has been established in this growing complex.

Far more iron than is needed at Whyalla is being mined from the Middleback Ranges and these deposits in fact for many years have formed the main supply for the iron and steel industries at Newcastle and Port Kembla. The reserves of high-grade ore are estimated at about 170 million tons, but there are also much larger reserves of leaner ore, the future use of which is already being planned.

The iron of South Australia represents by far its most valuable mineral, and in 1970 it accounted for 60 per cent by value of the entire

[*Courtesy the Australian News & Information Bureau.*

FIG. 95.—South Australia: Whyalla. The town began as a shipping port for ore from the Broken Hill Proprietary Company but with the establishment of shipbuilding yards the whole outlook changed. Note in the background the steel plant (left), shipyard (centre) and blast furnace.

mineral production of the State (including natural gas). The output of iron has expanded steadily, and in 1970 reached the record figure of 7·6 million tons (Tables 66 and 67).

On the eastern shore of Spencer Gulf, facing Whyalla, is Port Pirie. This is the terminus of the 300-mile (480-km) narrow gauge railway

TABLE 66

South Australia: production of iron ore, 1930–70, in million tons

Year	Output
1930 . . .	0·9
1935 . . .	1·9
1940 . . .	2·3
1945 . . .	1·5
1950 . . .	2·4
1955 . . .	3·0
1960 . . .	3·4
1965 . . .	4·4
1966 . . .	4·8
1967 . . .	4·6
1968 . . .	5·5
1969 . . .	6·9
1970 . . .	7·6

TABLE 67
South Australia: chief minerals produced, by value, 1970, in $A million

Iron ore	66·7
Limestone . . .	7·9
Opal	7·7
Natural gas . . .	6·3
Quartzite . . .	3·5
Coal	3·1
All minerals . . .	110·6

from Broken Hill in New South Wales (*see* p. 171). The famous galena ores are concentrated on the spot and then sent by rail to Port Pirie; there, at one of the largest lead smelters in the world, the lead is extracted, and from the same ore, gold, silver and antimony are refined, while the zinc concentrates are shipped to Risdon in Tasmania (p. 83). Port Pirie has grown into an important commercial and industrial centre, and has a population of 15,506 (1971).

Energy. The indigenous energy sources of South Australia comprise coal and natural gas, with petroleum as a future possibility.

Coal. Until 1941 the State relied for all her energy on bituminous coal imported from New South Wales. It was expensive, and the required

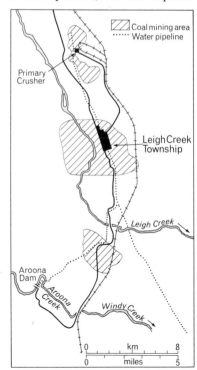

Fig. 96.—The Leigh Creek Coalfield. The sub-bituminous coal at Leigh Creek is suitable for the generation of electricity, and is the source of about two-thirds of the electric power used in South Australia.

[*After F. D. Wallace van Zyl, 1968.*

quantities were not always available. In that year, however, the first small quantities of sub-bituminous coal were raised at Leigh Creek—a remote and uninhabited area, 350 miles (563 km) from Adelaide, yet by good fortune adjoining the Port Augusta to Alice Springs railway.

The calorific value of Leigh Creek coal is a little more than half that of normal bituminous coal; most of it occurs in a single seam 40 feet (12 m) thick, with an overburden that ranges between 15 and 1500 feet (4·5 and 450 m). In 1971 the reserves were estimated at 52 million tons recoverable by opencast methods, and a further 370 million tons by shaft mining (Fig. 96).

The relatively low grade of the fuel makes it necessary to minimise transport costs; but the nearest point with adequate cooling water for the siting of a generating station was at Port Augusta, 150 miles (240 km) away. Virtually the whole of the output is conveyed to this power station, and is used to supply about two-thirds of the electricity used in the State. The venture has succeeded in reducing the cost of power by 20 to 30 per cent below that formerly produced from imported fuel.[5]

The output of coal from Leigh Creek is expanding, and reached a record quantity in 1969 (Table 68).

TABLE 68
South Australia: production of coal 1945–69, in thousand tons

Year	Output
1945 . . .	41
1950 . . .	261
1955 . . .	455
1960 . . .	885
1965 . . .	2016
1966 . . .	2021
1967 . . .	2045
1968 . . .	2078
1969 . . .	2210

Natural gas. In December 1963 the first significant supplies of natural gas were encountered in South Australia at Gidgealpa, in an uninhabited area on the western edge of Sturt Desert, east of Lake Eyre and north of Lake Frome. Subsequent discoveries have revealed seven gas fields in the area, and it is clear that this is one of the major Australian resources of natural gas, comparable to the fields in Bass Strait.

By November 1969 a pipeline 487 miles (780 km) long had been completed to Adelaide, and early in 1971 the capital had been converted to natural gas. The new fuel is already transforming the energy supply of the State. All the metropolitan coal gas plants have been closed down, and natural gas is driving the generators of the Torrens Island power station. It is clear that the gas resources are more than sufficient to supply the needs of the State, and in 1971 agreement was reached to

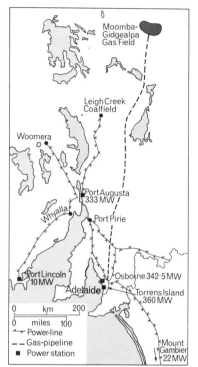

FIG. 97.—South Australia: sources of energy. In addition to the Leigh Creek coalfield, South Australia is fortunate in the possession of one of the two major known gasfields of Australia. The gas is piped to Sydney as well as Adelaide. The map indicates the electricity generating stations with their capacities. There is an oil refinery in Adelaide.

[After F. D. Wallace van Zyl, 1968.

supply natural gas to Sydney. So, after a generation, the energy roles of the two States have been reversed.

Figure 97 indicates the location of the Leigh Creek coalfield, the gas deposits, the generating stations and their connecting links.

The story, however, may not yet be complete, for in June 1970, the first important oil strike was made in the State, at Tirrawarra, close to the gasfields. It is too early at present to evaluate this discovery. Table 69 compares the outputs of the Gidgealpa and Bass Strait gasfields and indicates the high value of the gas produced.

TABLE 69

Australia: natural gas, output and value

					Gas output, million cubic feet	
					1970	1971
Moomba–Gidgealpa	(South Australia)	.	.	.	23,001	33,328
Bass Strait	(Victoria) .	.	.	.	22,089	35,757
Roma	(Queensland)	.	.	.	7,564	8,155
Barrow Island	(Western Australia)	.	.	.	406	1,801
South Australia:	Value of coal output	.	.	.	$A3,097,275	
	Value of natural gas output	.	.	$A6,250,000	

MANUFACTURE

South Australia is relatively poor in raw materials, and yet has built up a thriving manufacturing industry with its own distinct character.[8]

Its most important group is that connected with transport: shipbuilding, automobile manufacture and the production of railway and tramway materials. In 1969 these industries employed almost 26,000 people, or 22 per cent of the work-force of the State. This proportion is nearly twice as great as the Australian average, and the fact is not easily explainable.

The shipyard at Whyalla alone employed about 1400 people in 1969, and this total will be swollen by the recently established steelworks. The location of heavy industry at Whyalla dates from 1940, and was carried out by the Broken Hill Company in return for long-term leases on the iron ore of the Middleback Ranges.

More important from the point of view of employment are the automobile industries. The Adelaide district contains seven large plants; and of these, the General Motors–Holdens group alone employs more than 7000 people, while a further 7400 are occupied in motor repair workshops. The ancestors of the industry may be detected in the saddlers, coach-builders and dray manufacturers of the middle nineteenth century.

About 3800 people are employed in the manufacture of railway and tramway rolling stock. This is virtually a government monopoly: the workshops are established in a northern suburb of the capital.

The second main group of industries includes those concerned with machinery. In 1968 they employed 18,800 people, or 19 per cent of the total labour force, and in no other State does this group occupy so high a rank. It traces its origin back to the nineteenth-century manufacture of farm machinery, including such innovations as the stump-jump plough. These industries again are located almost entirely within the metropolitan area.

In contrast are the factories concerned with food processing: they include wine making, fruit and meat packing, dairying, baking, flour milling and brewing. Over half of the 700 factories lie outside the confines of the metropolitan area.

These three groups, transport, machinery and food industries, together employ more than half of the labour force of the State and help to impart a distinct character to its industrial structure.

South Australia is an expanding economy, well balanced as between farming and industry. Her habitable area and natural resources are smaller than those of her neighbours to the east; but she is devoting her energies to the task of making the best possible use of her land and of endowing her people with the highest standard of life.

In the field of farming expansion has taken place in almost every branch of production—wheat, wool, wine, orchard fruits, meat and milk. Mineral output shows a similar growth. The quarrying of brown coal at Leigh Creek is a post-war operation undertaken by the State Government: output doubled during the 1960s to reach 2·2 million tons by 1969. During the same decade the production of iron ore more than doubled and an integrated steelworks was established at Whyalla.

Manufacture too is expanding. During the 1960s the number of factories increased from about 5000 to 6255, and the people they employed from 100,000 to 121,000. Indigenous natural gas is injecting new life into the economy, and there is the hope of oil in the same area. The population of the State is growing rapidly, and in 1966 surpassed the million mark. In South Australia the stage is set for steady progress.

NOTES

1. J. F. Livermore, "Some Aspects of Salinity in the South Australian Upper Murray," *Australian Geographer*, Vol. X, No. 6 (1968).

2. M. Williams, "The Bulk Handling of Grain in South Australia," *Australian Geographer*, Vol. IX, No. 3 (1964).

3. C. R. Twidale and D. L. Smith, "A 'Perfect Desert' Transformed: the Agricultural Development of North-western Eyre Peninsula, South Australia," *Australian Geographer*, Vol. XI, No. 5 (1971).

4. A. Marshall, " 'Desert' becomes 'Downs': the Impact of a Scientific Discovery," *Australian Geographer*, Vol. XII, No. 1 (1972).

5. F. D. Wallace van Zyl, "Power Supply and Industry in South Australia," *Australian Geographer*, Vol. X, No. 6 (1968).

6. M. Williams, "Gawler: The Changing Geography of a South Australian Country Town," *Australian Geographer*, Vol. IX, No. 4 (1964).

7. D. L. Smith, "The Growth and Stagnation of an Urban Fringe Market Gardening Region—Virginia, South Australia," *Australian Geographer*, Vol. XII, No. 1 (1972).

8. Tom McNight, "The Anatomy of Manufacturing in South Australia," *Australian Geographer*, Vol. X, No. 5 (1968).

STUDY QUESTIONS

1. What are the special characteristics of the climate of South Australia?

2. Explain the significance of "Goyder's Line."

3. Examine the distribution of (*a*) sheep, (*b*) cattle and (*c*) wheat in South Australia.

4. Describe the methods of irrigation in use along the Murray river.

5. Outline the industrial developments which have taken place near the head of Spencer's Gulf.

6. In what ways does the layout of Adelaide differ from that of other Australian cities?

Chapter X

WESTERN AUSTRALIA

WESTERN AUSTRALIA has much in common with her neighbour, South Australia. Both contain small areas of relatively dense settlement near the coast, backed by large tracts of desert or semi-desert. In both those areas of close settlement enjoy the sunny, subtropical climate of winter rainfall which has its counterpart in the Mediterranean coastlands of Europe, so that fruit and wheat, cattle and sheep are typical products of both States.

Yet Western Australia has its own distinct personality. It has both the largest area and the lowest density of population. With an area of 975,920 square miles (2,527,633 km²), Western Australia contains almost one-third of the entire continent. Within her borders we might fit New South Wales, South Australia, Victoria and Tasmania—and there would still be room for the United Kingdom. This vast area in 1971 had a population of 1,027,372—smaller than that of every other State except Tasmania. The density of population was 1·05 persons to the square mile (2·59 km²)—a sparsity exceeded only by Northern Territory. The settlement of the State was greatly hastened by the gold rush of 1893. Western Australia is still by far the chief producer of gold in the Australian Commonwealth; and the State still exhibits some of the marks of a pioneer region: here is the highest masculinity, with 105·41 males for every 100 females.

CLIMATE

While South Australia is notorious for possessing the driest portion of the continent, Western Australia can claim the hottest part: this is a narrow belt running parallel with the north-west coast of the State, a few miles inland from Onslow and Port Hedland. Here the normal daily maximum temperature is greater than 41° C (105° F) in the shade. At times the thermometer registers 49° C (120° F), and for weeks on end it may pass 38° C (100° F) each day. In 1924 this happened through the whole of November, December, January, February and March— twenty-three weeks without a break. These places are almost on the Tropic of Capricorn, and the overhead sun beats fiercely down upon them. In summer even the lowest night temperatures are between 24 and 27° C (75 and 80° F).

Close by is the sea; yet it has little cooling effect, since the winds are predominantly offshore. The winds, indeed, provide the clues to the climate of Western Australia.

The Bureau of Meteorology publishes wind roses for ten stations in the State, and these give us a fair picture of the conditions. It is by no means simple, but we may perhaps recognise three divisions: the north-eastern coastal strip, with its monsoonal summer rains; the south-western corner, with its winter rains; and the large area between, in the trade-wind belt at all seasons.

The monsoonal area may be illustrated from Wyndham, the beef-exporting port near the border of Northern Territory. Here there are pronounced northerly (onshore) winds in summer, particularly in the afternoons, when land temperatures are at their peak; in winter, southerly and south-easterly (offshore) winds are experienced, particularly in the mornings, when the land is at its coolest. The monsoons are thus modified slightly by the effects of land and sea breezes; but the rainfall is very clearly confined to the period of onshore winds, and almost the whole of it falls in the four summer months, December to March, with January as the wettest month. In this region we find a combination of tropical heat with a short rainy season: and on the whole it is not favourable to economic development.

The climate of Perth well illustrates the winter-rainfall region. In the winter months west and north-westerly winds predominate: this is what we should theoretically expect—they are the north-west anti-trades, and it is they that bring the welcome rainfall of this south-western corner of the State. The summer winds are less easily explained: in the mornings they tend to be easterly or north-easterly, in the afternoons, southerly or south-westerly—in fact almost any direction except that which we have been led to expect, namely south-easterly (the south-east trades).

The summer winds of Perth can be explained only as land and sea breezes. At night and in the early morning the land is relatively cool and a local high-pressure area develops; consequently the wind blows from land to sea. Conversely, by the afternoon a low-pressure area has replaced the high pressure, and the wind reverses its direction. The winter rainfall of the Perth region is far more attractive for settlement than the summer rainfall of Wyndham: it is greater in amount and it is better distributed throughout the year; moreover, the average temperature is lower, and here we have an ideal climate for timber, crops and grazing animals. Unfortunately, it covers only a small proportion of the State.

The third region, which experiences the trade wind at all seasons, may be illustrated from the inland stations of Muniwindi (south-east of Onslow) and Hall's Creek (in the Kimberley goldfield). Temperatures are high, and the dominating winds—day and night, summer and winter alike—are easterly, south-easterly or north-easterly. They bring little or no rain, and these are regions of poor pasture or actual desert.

The heaviest rainfall in Western Australia occurs in two districts in the south-west corner of the State. One is a narrow coastal fringe west of Albany, only 15 miles (24 km) wide, extending between Denmark and Augusta; the other is a similarly small area 60 miles (96 km) south-south-east of Perth. Both are hilly, wooded areas, and the latter forms the heart of the immensely tall Jarrah forest land. These two districts receive more than 50 inches (1250 mm) of rainfall per annum, with a concentration in the winter months, May to October.

As usual in Australia, the total diminishes rapidly inland, though the winter maximum remains. A journey along the railway from Perth towards the Kalgoorlie goldfields soon makes the traveller aware of the effects of reduced rainfall. Perth itself has a mean annual total of 36 inches (920 mm): here are good dairy lands and market gardens, but the land is rather damp for wheat. Thirty miles (48 km) from Perth (as the crow flies) we are at Wundowie, and the mean annual rainfall has dropped to 30 inches (750 mm). Soon we are in the midst of the grain and sheep lands. Twenty miles (32 km) on, at Northam, the rainfall has dropped to 20 inches (500 mm); and a further 20 miles (32 km), at Meckering, it has dropped to 15 inches (375 mm). Dry farming methods with selected seeds are necessary here. We cross the 13-inch (325-mm) isohyet near Merredin, about 140 miles (224 km) from Perth as the crow flies. This is the virtual limit of cultivation, and it encloses almost the whole of the railway network of the State. Beyond lie the rabbit-proof fence, the desert and the goldfields; and man can live and cultivate his gardens only by virtue of the goldfields' water-supply pipeline.

STRUCTURE AND RELIEF

We have already sketched the geology and physical features of Western Australia, and need add little here. Structurally Western Australia is the simplest of the States: she lacks the folded ranges and sedimentary plains of the eastern States, and she lacks the horsts and rift valleys of South Australia. Essentially Western Australia consists of the Precambrian shield, which, together with those of southern India, Arabia, Brazil, most of Africa and Antarctica, is held to have constituted in Palaeozoic times the ancestral continent of Gondwanaland.

Most of the State comprises an undulating plateau whose average height is about 1500 feet (450 m) but from which isolated summits rise to over 3000 feet (900 m). The highest point, Mt Bruce (4024 feet; 1219 m) is one of several summits in the Hamersley Range in the north-west of the State.

A coastal plain exists; but it is one of the misfortunes of Western Australia that where the coastal plain is widest it is too dry for agriculture. The plain is 250 miles (400 km) wide in the north—but here is the Great Sandy Desert; it is 200 miles (320 km) wide in the south—but here is also desert, the Nullarbor Plain. In the climatically favoured south-west the coastal plain is only 25–50 miles (40–80 km) wide; yet here are most of the dairy cattle of the State, and here are grown the greater part of the fruit and vegetables.

From about lat. 27° southwards the western edge of the plateau is a fault scarp—the Darling Fault—and on the plateau about 40 miles (64 km) to the east of the scarp have occurred the two most severe earthquakes known in the recorded history of Australia, with epicentres at Meeberrie in the north (April 1941) and Meckering in the south (October 1968).

Meckering is about 65 miles (104 km) east of Perth, on the railway to the Golden Mile. The track was cut, the goldfield's water-supply pipes were burst and almost the whole of the small town was destroyed. There was structural damage as far afield as Kalgoorlie and Albany. Perth narrowly escaped disaster, and it is clear that the earthquake hazard cannot be dismissed by the city planners.[1]

FARMING IN WESTERN AUSTRALIA

We have seen that Western Australia is larger than the combined areas of New South Wales, South Australia, Victoria and Tasmania. How does this vast area compare in farm outputs with the other States of the Commonwealth?

In the production of wheat Western Australia ranks above Queensland and South Australia, but well below New South Wales, which produces more than twice as much as Western Australia. Western Australia is low in the output of hay: of the mainland States only Queensland produces less. She also produces a smaller output of potatoes than any other mainland State. Both these crops do well in damp conditions, which are in general absent from Western Australia. That State is a significant producer of apples and grapes, ranking fourth in each case.

On the pastoral side Western Australia is more prominent: in the number of sheep she is second to Queensland, though she is the third in wool production, after New South Wales and Victoria. Dry conditions are less suitable for cattle than for sheep, and Western Australia ranks fourth among the cattle-rearing States. Her dairying industry is the smallest of all the States, and she produces little more than half as much milk as tiny Tasmania.

Comparing the relative importance of the various types of farming in Western Australia we see that agriculture and pastoral farming rank virtually equally by value of output (Table 70) and together account for 85 per cent of the total primary product (excluding minerals). Dairy farming ranks low on the list, and is below fishing and forestry. Farming, however, in Western Australia is prosperous and expanding, and during the five years ending in 1970 there were record outputs of barley, hay, bananas and tomatoes; there was a record number of

TABLE 70

Western Australia: net value of primary production, average, 1965–70

	$A million	%
Agriculture	138·3	43·1
Pastoral farming	135·3	42·2
Fishing, pearling, whaling	18·0	5·6
Forestry	12·6	3·9
Dairying	11·7	3·7
Poultry farming	3·7	1·1
Hunting	0·8	0·2
Bee keeping	0·5	0·2
Total	320·9	100·0

animals killed for food, and record production of eggs and of poultry for the table. In addition there were near records in the output of milk, apples, oranges and grapes.

The one outstanding crop in the State is wheat: in 1969–70 it accounted for 63 per cent of the entire output of crops by value (Table 71). Wheat is normally grown on mixed farms, whose other main

TABLE 71

Western Australia: gross value of principal farm products, 1969–70

Agriculture	$A million	Pastoral farming	$A million
Wheat	94·4	Wool	120·6
Hay	13·5	Livestock slaughtered	55·6
Barley	8·9		
Apples	8·1	*Dairying*	
Oats	5·9	Milk	16·3
Potatoes	5·4	Livestock slaughtered	16·3
Bananas	2·1		
Pasture seed	2·0	*Poultry farming*	
Tomatoes	2·0	Eggs	6·3
Cotton	1·6	Poultry slaughtered	6·7
Oranges	1·3		
Nursery products	1·3		
Vines	1·3		
All crops	147·8		

product is wool (*see* p. 269). A glance at the changes that have taken place in the cultivation of wheat during the present century reveals the expansion in area, output and yield.

The area sown to wheat first exceeded a million acres (404,690 ha) in 1913, 2 million (809,380 ha) in 1924 and 3 million (1·2 million ha) in 1928. It fluctuated for thirty years, and then passed 4 million acres (1·6 million ha) in 1960, 5 million (2 million ha) in 1964, 6 million (2·4 million ha) in the following year and 7 million (2·8 million ha) in 1968 (Table 72). Owing to variations in weather conditions the fluctuations in output are greater than those of area; but the general trend is similar. A

TABLE 72

Western Australia: area and output of wheat, hay and barley

Year	Wheat Area mil. ac.	Wheat Output mil. bush.	Hay Area thou. ac.	Hay Output thou. tons	Barley Area thou. ac.	Barley Output mil. bush.
1940 .	2·6	21·1	418	375	66	0·7
1945 .	1·8	20·9	218	287	66	0·7
1950 .	3·2	49·9	177	227	59	0·9
1955 .	2·9	53·3	269	384	337	4·7
1960 .	4·0	63·9	284	381	541	8·5
1965 .	6·2	102·2	291	414	413	6·5
1966 .	6·3	103·2	295	417	373	6·7
1967 .	6·6	107·0	318	421	416	7·0
1968 .	7·3	112·5	341	500	553	9·2
1969 .	6·8	66·7	500	508	900	12·1
1970 .	5·8	108·9	469	662	1562	53·9
1971 .	5·0	79·6	—	—	2246	44·0

record of 53·5 million bushels in 1930 stood until 1958 (57·6 million bushels); but in the late 1950s and in the 1960s new records were soon set and as quickly broken. The 100 million bushels mark was surpassed in 1965 and the current record of 112 million bushels was achieved in 1968. Yields, too, have shown a general rise, from an average of about 10 bushels to the acre in the 1930s to 11 or 12 in the 1940s, about 14 in the 1950s and 15 in the 1960s.

Second to wheat by value, but a long way behind, is hay: in 1969–70 it accounted for 9 per cent of the total value of the crops. Like other crops, hay is very dependent on the weather, and in particular, the amount of rainfall. A record output of 492,000 tons stood unassailed from 1930 till as recently as 1968; but new records were set in 1969 and 1970. About half the hay crop in recent years has been produced from meadow grasses and clovers, and most of the remainder has been cut from oats.

For long, barley and oats were relatively unimportant compared with wheat. In 1941, for example, the output of wheat was 37·5 million bushels, while that of oats was 5·3 and barley 1·0 million bushels: six times as much wheat was grown as oats and barley combined. In 1951 the proportion had fallen to 5 : 1; in 1961 it was less than 3 : 1. In 1971 the output of wheat was 79·6 million bushels; of oats, 22·8 and of barley, 44·0 million bushels: that is, the combined output of barley and oats was not far short of the output of wheat.

Barley and oats are both largely grown for feeding to stock, and the expansion in their cultivation is in part related to the increased numbers of sheep and cattle. In addition barley is grown on the lighter soils, which are less suited to wheat. Since the introduction of wheat quotas, many farmers have turned to barley as it offers an alternative crop whose output at present is not restricted. More is produced of both crops than is required for local use and there are substantial quantities exported.

A great variety of other crops is grown in Western Australia—too many for individual discussion. The production of cotton is confined to the Ord irrigation area (p. 277). Bananas form an interesting specialisation in a narrow strip of land following the course of the Gascoyne river close to Carnarvon in the north-west of the State. The river-bed, however, is usually dry and the plantations are nourished with water pumped from below the bed. There has been a steady increase in the acreage and output in recent years and the 1969–70 harvest of 255,000 bushels, valued at $A2·1 million, forms a record. The bananas have a road journey of 600 miles (960 km) to reach the market in Perth. The same district grows oranges, pineapples and such exotic fruits as mangoes, pawpaws, avocados and passion fruits.

We have mentioned the growth in the numbers of sheep and cattle in the State. If we ignore temporary fluctuations in the size of the sheep flocks we find a steady expansion in numbers since the first thousand head were recorded in 1829. There were a million sheep by 1880, 5 million by 1910, 10 million by 1931, 15 million by 1957 and 20 million by 1963. The 30 million mark was passed in 1967 and in 1970 there were a record 34·7 million head of sheep (Table 73).

TABLE 73

Western Australia: numbers of stock since 1940

Year	Sheep mil. head	Cattle thou. head	Pigs thou. head
1940 . . .	9·5	840	218
1945 . . .	9·8	834	138
1950 . . .	11·4	841	90
1955 . . .	14·1	897	99
1960 . . .	17·2	1100	176
1965 . . .	24·4	1271	144
1966 . . .	27·4	1357	161
1967 . . .	30·2	1427	183
1968 . . .	32·9	1546	220
1969 . . .	33·6	1681	250
1970 . . .	34·7	1781	278
1971 . . .	34·4	1975	427

The statistical tables distinguish between sheep in the pastoral areas and those in the agricultural districts. The latter comprise essentially the south-western corner of the State together with a coastal strip stretching almost to Shark Bay. It is at first sight surprising to find that 89 per cent of the sheep in 1970 were not in the vast pastoral areas but in the agricultural districts, largely on farms which also produced grain crops. With the extension in the agricultural area and the increased production of fodder crops this proportion has been growing.

The sheep are reared essentially for wool, and in 1968 merino breeds accounted for 91 per cent of the total number of sheep. Most of the wool is sold by auction at Fremantle or Albany; the chief buyers are Japan,

Western Germany, France, the United Kingdom, Italy and the U.S.S.R.

The number of cattle in Western Australia has remained stable for a longer time than the number of sheep, and real expansion has taken place only during the last two decades. As early as 1910 there were 800,000 head of cattle in the State, and a record of 944,000 head in 1918 stood unchallenged until as late as 1956. The subsequent growth, however, was rapid; the million mark was passed in 1958, 1·2 million in 1961, 1·4 million in 1967 and 1·6 million in 1969. By 1971 the number was very nearly 2 million.

Only a small proportion of these cattle are for milk production. In 1970 the dairy herd of the State numbered 182,075, forming just over 10 per cent of the total. The beef cattle are almost equally divided between the agricultural and pastoral lands, and as with sheep flocks, the trend is for an increase in the proportion reared in the agricultural areas. Very large tracts of country in Western Australia carry virtually no stock at all, and most of the beef cattle in the pastoral areas are in the Kimberleys (p. 276). The outlets for this important region are the abattoirs and freezing works at the ports of Wyndham, Broome and Derby. The expansion in cattle numbers here has been made possible by more efficient transport, and the use of large trucks on the new beef roads had also made droving almost obsolete.

The overseas exports of beef and veal are twice as valuable as those of mutton and lamb, though only one-quarter as great as those of wheat and one-sixth as great as the wool exports. More than half of the total exports of beef and veal are shipped to the United States; there follow Japan, the United Kingdom and Canada, in that order.

THE REGIONS OF WESTERN AUSTRALIA

THE GOLDFIELDS OF THE INTERIOR

Victoria was the pre-eminent gold producer of the 1850s and 1860s and until 1882 Western Australia produced little or nothing of the precious metal. In that year the Government Geologist reported traces of gold in the Kimberley region of the north-east; and in the following years gold was discovered 200 miles (322 km) east of Perth in the Yilgarn area and in the Pilbarra district of the north-west. In 1887 came the discovery of Fraser's Reef at Southern Cross (about 220 miles (354 km) east of Perth), and by that time prospecting had become general throughout the State.

Then in 1892 Bayley and Ford, working eastwards from Southern Cross, stopped at Coolgardie and gathered 500 ounces of gold in a few hours. A full-scale gold rush began, and diggers flocked in from the eastern States. Within ten years the population of the State quadrupled (1890: 46,290; 1901: 194,889) and the interior, hitherto almost unknown, became thoroughly explored. Goldfields were proclaimed covering

400,000 square miles (1,036,000 km²)—about two-fifths of the area of the State. By the turn of the century Western Australia had become the leading gold-producing colony. She has maintained her lead ever since, and now produces between 70 and 80 per cent of all the gold mined in the continent.

TABLE 74

Australia: output of gold, 1969–70

				Fine oz
Western Australia	.	.	.	542,139
Northern Territory	.	.	.	87,784
Queensland	.	.	.	54,156
Victoria	.	.	.	10,167
Australia	.	.	.	694,583

There are twenty or so distinct goldfields in Western Australia. Of these, the East Coolgardie field is by far the most productive, containing as it does the "Golden Mile" of Kalgoorlie. Gold is still produced in many other areas, the chief of them being Leonora and Laverton in the Mount Margaret field (the railheads of the line which runs north from Kalgoorlie), Cue and Meekatharra in the Murchison field and Sandstone in the East Murchison field (three mining camps served by the railway which runs inland from Geraldton) and Norseman in the Dundas field (on the line which runs southwards from Coolgardie). Coolgardie itself, the scene of the sensational discovery of 1892, has now been eclipsed by Kalgoorlie (Fig. 98).

During the last fifty years the output of gold has declined, for deeper mining has entailed increasing overhead expenses. Some of the Kalgoorlie mines now reach down more than 3000 feet (914 m). Yet from time to time spectacular discoveries are still made, matching the excitement of the old pioneer days. Such was the discovery of the Comet Lode at Marble Bar (west of the Great Sandy Desert), proving to be one of the richest reefs in the State. The largest nugget so far found in Western Australia was discovered in 1931 at Larkinville in the Coolgardie field: it contained 947 ounces of pure gold, and it capped the discovery of a dozen other nuggets in the space of a few weeks.

The rainfall at Kalgoorlie averages only 9 inches (229 mm) a year, and even then is erratic. For the first few years the prospectors and diggers were forced to rely on tanks to catch the rain, on wells and borings, or on the slow process of distillation of salt water. In 1896 the engineer-in-chief reported in favour of constructing a long water pipeline from the west; within two years construction had begun, and after five years of difficult work the spectacular goldfields' water-supply scheme was complete.

At Mundaring, on the Helena river, 26 miles (42 km) east of Perth, a reservoir was built where the rainfall is almost 40 inches (1000 mm) per annum. As originally constructed, the dam was 100 feet (30 m) high; it

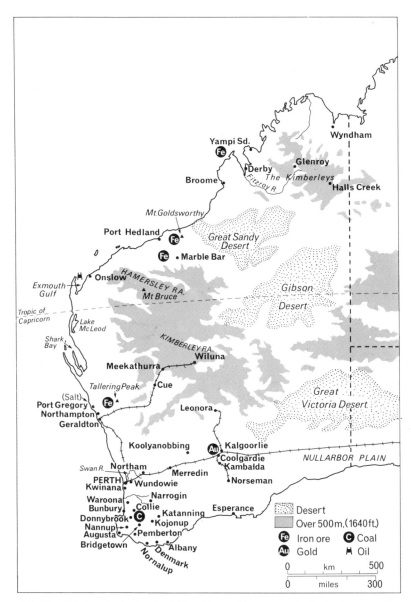

FIG. 98.—Western Australia: physical and towns. Western Australia, the largest by far of all the Australian States and Territories, occupies almost one-third of the total area of Australia. Its relatively small population (1,027,372 in 1971) is confined mainly to the south-western corner of the State. Details of the Pilbara district are indicated on Fig. 104.

[*Courtesy the Agent-General for Western Australia.*

FIG. 99.—Western Australia: the Goldfields' water supply. This is the main conduit of the Goldfields' water supply, about two miles from Mundaring Weir: the water has a journey of more than 340 miles (544 km) before reaching Kalgoorlie. In general, its diameter is 30 inches (76 mm) but close to the weir there are sections of up to 48 inches (122 mm). This is now far more than a goldfields project: it serves 112 towns and a farming area of 5·8 million acres (2·3 million ha).

was raised an additional 32 feet (9·6 m) in 1951, and as a result the capacity of the reservoir has been trebled. From Mundaring 346 miles (554 km) of pipeline were laid to reach Kalgoorlie, and pumping stations were built to give the water the necessary lift (Fig. 99).

It was an amazing feat of engineering and faith carried out in land where water is scarce, and at a time when the population of the whole State was less than 200,000—about equal to the present town of Sunderland or Plymouth. In terms of the United Kingdom it is as if a pipeline beginning in Perth, Scotland, brought water into the heart of London.

The water scheme has developed into something much bigger than a private supply for Kalgoorlie. All the towns along the railway receive or supplement their water from the main. Extensions have been made to supply wide areas of the grain and sheep lands between Northam and Merredin. From Southern Cross a 25-mile (40-km) extension to the north serves the mining town of Bullfinch; and from Coolgardie 100 miles (160 km) of pipeline stretch southwards to serve the gold centre of Norseman. In all, fifty-four towns and 1·8 million acres (0·72 million ha) of farm land are supplied from Mundaring Weir.

About half the gold produced in Western Australia is mined in the "Golden Mile"—acclaimed the richest square mile in the world: it has yielded 830 tons of pure gold from 50 million tons of ore, worth $A54 million at current prices. The Golden Mile lies between the twin towns of Kalgoorlie and Boulder, within a lens-shaped exposure of quartz. Here the rocks have been sheared as a result of earth movements, and in the shear planes are the gold-bearing lodes. In this district there are thirteen mines, formerly worked by many different companies, but now, owing to amalgamation, by four groups. The deepest of them is the

[*Courtesy Australian News & Information Bureau.*

FIG. 100.—Western Australia: the Golden Mile. A general view of Great Boulder mine. One of the earliest mines, it continues to be one of the most productive.

Chaffers mine, whose shaft has been sunk to more than 4100 feet (1230 m). Still one of the most productive is the Great Boulder, which has been under the same ownership since it began in 1893 (Fig. 100). The most productive mine in the whole of Australia is the Lake View and Star.

Gold mines the world over look much the same, with their pithead gear, tall chimneys, crushing mills and great whitish slag heaps. The Golden Mile is different in that here the mines are crowded close together, and in that they operate in a semi-desert made tolerable only by the stream of fresh water from Mundaring.

Kalgoorlie is a thriving town with substantial public buildings, comfortable hotels, smart shops, parks and gardens, and a huge Olympic Pool built for championship swimming events. Yet here in 1893 thirsty prospectors paid two shillings a gallon for drinking-water. Coolgardie, in contrast, is a shadow of its former self. At its prime, 30,000 people lived here; today the land is littered by a mass of untidy abandoned workings, buildings are closed and the population has shrunk to a mere 622 (1971).

An unexpected rise in the price of gold brings a spurt of energy into gold-mining towns. The stores do a brisk business in windlasses and buckets, picks and shovels, cooking and camping gear. They sell the ingenious dry blower, in which the ore is concentrated by means of wind instead of water. But the solid foundation of the Australian gold-mining industry lies not in the small prospector but in the large company, with its modern equipment, its continuous research and planned development.

The State Government plays its part in the mineral industry. It prepares geological maps and maintains collections of typical minerals; it provides free assays and gives advice concerning likely markets; and it maintains batteries at a number of mining centres to enable small concerns to crush their ore.

During the 1960s there was a gradual decline in the output of gold, which reflects the exhaustion of the more accessible lodes (Table 75).

TABLE 75

Western Australia: production of gold since 1940

Year	Output thou. fine oz	Value $A millions
1940	1191	25·4
1945	469	10·0
1950	610	18·9
1955	842	26·7
1960	856	28·1
1965	659	22·4
1966	629	23·3
1967	576	21·7
1968	512	19·4
1969	465	18·6
1970	342	14·4
1971	348	14·1
1972	349	14·9

The role of gold as a driving force has now been usurped by the humble base metal, nickel. Nickel has many vital functions in the modern world, mainly as an alloy in producing steels of special character and in great variety.

Exciting discoveries of nickel were made early in 1966 at Kambalda, 30 miles (48 km) south of Kalgoorlie; they were described as the richest and most extensive bodies of high-grade nickel sulphide yet to be found in Australia.[2] While ore with a nickel content of 1 per cent is considered profitable, tests at Kambalda showed nickel contents with an average of about 4 per cent but reaching up to 8·3 per cent. "It is already clear" maintained *The Economist* "that Australia has more nickel than Canada," and went on to forecast that by 1980 or sooner Australia would be the chief nickel producer in the world.

Mining began at Kambalda in 1967. By 1971 additional mines were operating at Scotia and Nepean and preparations were in progress at six other sites. Table 76 indicates the surge that has taken place in the production of nickel concentrates since its beginning in 1967.

TABLE 76

Western Australia: output of nickel concentrates

Year				Output thou. tons
1967	.	.	.	15·8
1968	.	.	.	36·9
1968–69	.	.	.	51·1
1969–70	.	.	.	157·6
1970–71	.	.	.	299·2

A new township is under construction at Kambalda, and its population approaches 3000: it obtains its water through an extension of the Goldfields Water Supply from Coolgardie. Esperance, on the south coast, has gained a new lease of life as an exporter of nickel concentrates, and a new sealed highway replaces the old road from Kalgoorlie. A smelter to convert nickel concentrate into nickel matte is under construction at Kalgoorlie. The Golden Mile has awakened to the existence of a nickel boom and is gripped once more by mineral fever.

THE FOREST DISTRICTS OF THE SOUTH-WEST

With nearly 42,000 square miles (108,780 km²) of forest land Western Australia is the leading State in respect of timber reserves. This is the more remarkable in that so large a proportion of the State has a deficient rainfall; and her forests in fact occupy only 4 per cent of the total area of the State.

The forest district is situated in the extreme south-west, and the whole of it receives more than 25 inches (625 mm) of rain per annum. The forests begin in the latitude of Perth and extend southwards in a long and narrow belt about 20 miles (32 km) from the coast. The plateau which they clothe receives in most parts more than 30 inches (750 mm) of rain; the karri lands in the far south have between 40 and 50 inches (1000 and 1270 mm); and the heart of the jarrah forests, as we have seen, form one of the wettest portions of the State, with more than 50 inches (1270 mm) in the middle Murray river basin. The Murray river of Western Australia reaches the sea at Pinjarra, 50 miles (80 km) south of Perth.

As far south as Donnybrook the forest belt is only about 30 miles (48 km) wide. Beyond, it widens considerably, spreading both to the south-east and south-west to reach a maximum width of about 100 miles (161 km). Almost the whole of this is classed as jarrah forest; but in the extreme south is a relatively small area extending in a narrow strip from Nornalup on the south coast through Pemberton almost to Nannup (south of Bunbury). This is karri forest. A much smaller district of mallet forest lies in the drier country to the east, north-west of Narrogin, where the rainfall is barely 20 inches (508 mm) per annum. Mallet (technically *Eucalyptus astringens*) is valued on account of its bark, which yields a tanning extract; the species was becoming scarce, and to safeguard future supplies 20,000 acres (8000 ha) of new mallet seedlings have been planted.

Jarrah and karri are broadly similar trees. Both are eucalypts (jarrah, *Eucalypt marginata*; karri, *E. diversicolor*); both are hardwoods which grow exceedingly tall and straight and are renowned for their strength and durability.

Jarrah covers by far the greater area. Its timber, mahogany red in colour, resists the attacks of both the white ant on land and borer pests in sea-water (particularly the notorious teredo). Jarrah is thus of great value in shipbuilding and harbour works, for railway sleepers, piles and telegraph poles. It has also a remarkable resistance to heat, and locally in the home the chimney and much of the fireplace is frequently constructed of jarrah.

Karri is stronger and taller than jarrah. It is noted for its long, clean and straight trunk, which may rise 120 feet (36 m) before the first branch. A large specimen may have a girth of 30 feet (9 m). In one fine tree the trunk below the first branch was 160 feet (48 m) long and contained 230 tons of timber. The tallest measured specimen which is still growing has a height of 281 feet (84·3 m). Karri may be used in preference to jarrah where extremely large beams are required. In 1950 twenty-six loads of these timbers were shipped from Fremantle for use in the building of the bombed Antwerp cathedral.

More than half the forest lands are in private hands, but 4 million acres (1·6 million ha) have been dedicated as State forests, and here a sound policy of management is pursued. Felling is regulated so as to maintain a permanent timber industry. Fire precautions include a telephone network linking thirty-one lookout towers with headquarters, and each felling gang is provided with its own fire-fighting apparatus.

There are nearly 300 sawmills in the forest areas. About 260 of these are "spot-mills," which are moved from place to place as the timber is cut out; but the total includes five very large mills, where the bulk of the timber is handled. Seven thousand people are directly employed in the industry, and whole towns depend entirely on timber cutting, sawmilling and furniture making. Here the ring of the logger's axe and the crash of the forest giant are familiar sounds. A great truck carries the trees in chains to the sawmill, where they are converted into huge beams for bridge-building, or perhaps into tiny staves for apple boxes.

Such a town is Pemberton, in the heart of the karri country. It lies in the secluded valley of the Lefroy Brook, where trout abound. Hills clothed in towering trees surround the hollow which contains the town. The older houses are roofed with the local raw, grey timber. But the growing number of new houses with their red-tiled roofs are a sign of a prosperous, developing township, which now has a population of about one thousand. Its heart consists of a single sawmill—the largest in Australia.

Nothing is wasted in the timber industry, and the by-products are valued collectively at $A4 million a year. They include 800,000 tons of firewood, 70,000 tons of bark for the extraction of tanning agents, 10,000 tons of charcoal and thousands of piles, poles and posts. Even the sawdust—113,000 tons of it a year—is collected and used as fuel.

THE GRAIN AND SHEEP LANDS

North and east of the forest lands are the grain and sheep lands (Fig. 101), extending in a narrow belt south-eastwards from Northampton (on the west coast, a few miles north of Geraldton); they broaden southwards to reach a maximum width in the latitude of Perth, then shrink farther south and terminate close to the sea, near Albany. Apart from the coastal strips in the north and south, this is an inland belt, rarely within 50 miles (80 km) of the sea; it is characterised by a close network of roads and railways.

The boundaries of the wheat and sheep belt correspond closely with rainfall lines—the 10-inch (250-mm) isohyet marks the north-eastern limit and the 20-inch (500-mm) the western limit. Southern Cross lies on the former line, and Narrogin on the latter; and the wheat acreages are at a maximum midway between the two boundaries. To the south-east wheat growing tails off, though the climate remains quite favourable, for here the soils are saline and there are certain poisonous plants in the herbage which would injure stock. So the railway network ceases and farming stops short.

The sheep and wheat belt produces not only almost the whole grain crop of Western Australia but also nearly three-quarters of her sheep. Most of the land was occupied between 1905 and 1930. First the farmer fenced his land and cleared it of timber or scrub. He broke down small trees by dragging across them steel rollers drawn by a tractor; he then burnt the timber. Next he ploughed the soil and dressed it with superphosphate. Meanwhile the Government was building roads and railways, constructing schools, contriving water supplies, arranging credit facilities for the farmers and developing drought-resisting varieties of seed for the eastern fringe of the region.

Sheep were first introduced as an accessory to wheat farming, for they were easily managed. They find nourishment in the weeds of the fallow paddocks and they eat the stubble after the grain harvest. Quick-growing fodder crops are fitted into the crop rotation and provide green feed during the leaner time of the year (late summer and autumn). Sheep have proved a boon to the farmer, and on the average farm they provide

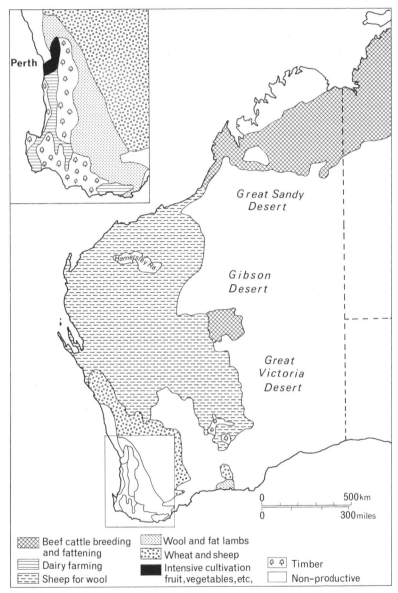

Fig. 101.—Western Australia: land use. It must be remembered that maps of this type give little indication of the intensity of the utilisation. In this case the density of sheep in the wheat and sheep belt is far greater than in the sheep for wool region and the density of cattle in the beef cattle belt is less than in similar regions in Queensland and New South Wales.

more revenue than grain. All the aspects of sheep farming are important here, including the production of fat lambs and the rearing of stud rams.

The wheat growing is highly mechanised. Three eight-furrow tractor-drawn ploughs make light work of a large field. Planting takes place in May and superphosphate is applied at the same time; in the wetter parts the wheat follows a grass ley, in the drier parts a bare fallow. The grain is ready for the harvesting team in November or December. It is handled in bulk, not bagged, and trucks convey it to the railway station, which is usually less than 12 miles (20 km) away. A feature of the Western Australia system is that it is stored in simply constructed corrugated-iron sheds while awaiting transport to the coast. Three-quarters of the grain crop is exported, from Fremantle, Geraldton, Albany or Bunbury. Most of this is in the form of grain; but flour milling has developed at the ports in excess of local needs, for the by-products are valuable as feed to dairymen and poultry keepers; about one-tenth of the wheat is therefore shipped in the form of flour, chiefly to the countries of South-East Asia and to Africa.

The outlet for the northern part of the wheat/sheep belt is Geraldton, the fourth city of the State (population, 1971: 15,330). The town and its region derived their early importance from the nearby mining of copper, lead and gold. These have declined, but talc and manganese are mined at present and rutile and coal have been discovered. Currently, however, the most valuable minerals are iron ore and natural gas.

The iron mines are at Koolanooka, about 85 miles (136 km) east-south-east of Geraldton. These were the first deposits to be worked during the mineral boom of the 1960s. A short stretch of railway, 13 miles (21 km) long, was needed to link the mine to the State railway to Geraldton; this was opened early in 1966, and the first shipments of Australian ore to Japan were on their way. Iron ore is now the leading export from Geraldton, though wheat is close behind (Table 77). The commerce of the port is expanding, and the tonnage of shipping using it doubled between 1964 and 1970.

TABLE 77
Port of Geraldton, exports, 1970–71

				Thousand tons
Iron ore	.	.	.	691·2
Wheat	.	.	.	591·5
Barley	.	.	.	100·9
Oats	.	.	.	26·4
Total exports	.	.	.	1413·4

The discoveries of natural gas have formed the culmination of long and costly explorations during the 1960s by the West Australian Petroleum Company (WAPET). In 1970 the company was able to delimit a commercial field of gas in the Dongara area, about 60 miles

(96 km) south-east of Geraldton. In August 1971 a 255-mile (408-km) pipeline was completed to Perth, Kwinana and Pinjarra, and during 1972 the metropolitan consumers were converted to natural gas. Table 78 shows only the initial stages of production, before the completion of the pipeline.

TABLE 78

Western Australia: production of natural gas

Million cu. feet

1967	.	.	.	25·6
1968	.	.	.	92·9
1968–69	.	.	.	143·6
1969–70	.	.	.	301·6
1970–71	.	.	.	544·0

Sufficient reserves have been proved to supply the market with 70 to 80 million cubic feet ($2·0$–$2·3$ million m^3) daily for fifteen years, and the new source of energy is especially welcome in Western Australia, which hitherto has faced a shortage of local fuel.

The farming district that is tributary to Albany—the land south of Kojonup and Katanning—has witnessed important developments during recent years. The area under wheat almost doubled during the 1960s, and as a result of the quota restrictions, many farmers are turning to oats, the output of which now equals the wheat harvest. The area is noted for its apple orchards, and it produces nearly 9000 tons of seed and ware potatoes annually, together with 1000 tons of green peas and a variety of other vegetables.

New crops are being introduced: there are demands for linseed and rape seed from South-East Asia and Japan, and a beginning is being made in their cultivation. During the 1960s the numbers of both sheep and cattle in the district more than doubled.

Solid and prosperous towns are to be seen in the wheat and sheep belt. Kojonup is set in a hollow among pastures, orchards and patches of forest; Katanning, a railway junction in the midst of fine grain lands, was formerly noted for its vineyards; but this town of 3600 inhabitants is now renowned for its wool. In some parts water supply is a factor which limits growth. Narrogin (population about 4800) is approaching this stage, and at Pingelly, 25 miles (40 km) north of Narrogin (population about 1500), the ground water has become saline. But the grain and sheep lands are vital to the farming of Western Australia; and the State which conceived and carried out the goldfields' water supply will not find it difficult to bring water to towns close at hand.

A prosperous agriculture has assisted in the development of flourishing industries. The Albany woollen mills are the largest in the State and employ up to 250 people in the manufacture of worsteds, blankets, furnishing fabrics and carpet yarns. There are butter and cheese factories at Albany and Mount Barker. Albany is an important centre for wool sales, it is expanding its meat industry and it operates the largest super-phosphate works outside the Perth area. At Frenchman Bay, near Albany, is the only whaling station in Australia. Equipped with radar and echo-sounding equipment and assisted by spotter aircraft the whale-catchers took 799 sperm whales during 1970: these yielded over 5000 tons of oil, 2000 tons of solubles and 1500 tons of meal; the last two form valuable ingredients in animal foods.

The port of Albany in 1969–70 ranked second in Western Australia (after Fremantle) in terms of import tonnage handled, though having no minerals for export in its hinterland it ranked tenth in the export trade. Its commerce is expanding: its grain terminal has been enlarged to accommodate 5·8 million bushels, and new berths and cargo handling facilities have been installed. With the sheltered, branching inlet of King George Sound Albany possesses one of the finest natural harbours in the southern hemisphere. Its 1971 population was 13,055.

THE FRUIT AND DAIRY LANDS OF THE SOUTH-WESTERN COASTAL STRIP

During 1969–70 the following items appeared in the list of products of the farms of Western Australia:

			Gross value, $A thou.
Milk	.	. .	16,255
Apples	.	. .	8,072
Potatoes	.	. .	5,390
Tomatoes		. .	2,024
Oranges	.	. .	1,344
Grapes	.	. .	1,282

These products originated chiefly from the narrow coastal lowland 165 miles (264 km) long and about 20 miles (32 km) wide, extending from Perth in the north to Augusta in the south, and sandwiched between the forest belt and the sea. This is a well-watered district, receiving on the average about 40 inches (1000 mm) of rain per annum, with a winter maximum. Grain crops do not ripen well in such con-ditions, but the relatively heavy rainfall encourages the growth of lush pasture and swells the fruit. Abundant sunshine ripens the fruit and allows their open-air drying.

There is no large nearby market for these products (as we have seen, the population of the whole State in 1971 amounted to only one million persons), so the emphasis is on butter, and to a less extent on dried or condensed milk and cream, together with cheese.

The dairy industry is of recent growth in Western Australia: it is only since 1932 that the State has changed from being an importer to an exporter of dairy produce. Dairy herds have been established and have multiplied though they form only about one-tenth of the cattle of the

State. Of the milk they yield, about 25 per cent is sufficient for local needs, and is consumed fresh; roughly 60 per cent is churned at the many butter factories; about 5 per cent reaches the market as cheese, and an equal quantity is sent to the condensed milk factory at Waroona, on the main road and railway 45 miles (72 km) north of Bunbury.

Orchards and orchard crops. This region contains in addition the chief orchard lands of Western Australia, most of her vineyards, her orange groves and her potato fields. Apples are by far the chief of the fruits, and there is a large surplus for export (Western Australian apples may be recognised from the red wood of their boxes). They are grown in the cooler parts of the belt: in the extreme south-west corner of the State, on the hillsides around Bridgetown (in the forest region) and around Mount Barker.

Of the citrus fruits oranges are by far the chief fruit grown, representing about four-fifths of the total—the rest being lemons. The groves may be seen among the hills to the east of Perth and scattered throughout 100 miles (160 km) of the coastal belt to the south. The vineyards are concentrated in the basin of the upper Swan river, east of the capital. They yield about 2000 tons of table grapes and 3000 tons of dried fruit (chiefly currants). Potatoes are grown in the coastal belt, south of Perth, in particular around Harvey. The yield is the highest in Australia, and there is a considerable export to other States of the Commonwealth.

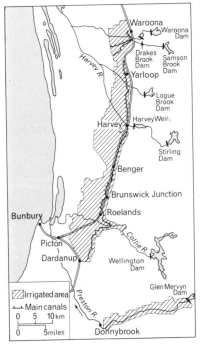

FIG. 102.—Western Australia: irrigation in the south-west. About 800 farms are irrigated from water stored in reservoirs on the plateau to the east. Their main object is dairy farming.

This south-western corner of the continent is climatically suited to a wide range of other fruits. Figs, olives and mulberries grow well, but cannot compete commercially with the established sources of these commodities. Peaches, plums, apricots and nectarines are grown for local consumption. Lemons are produced on a small scale, and these too, together with most of the oranges, are sold within the State.

Irrigation. The most productive portion of the region is a narrow zone at the foot of the plateau scarp about 43 miles (71 km) long and with a maximum width of about 6 miles (10 km). It is irrigated from water stored behind a series of dams on the plateau to the east. During the course of three decades seven dams have been constructed (including an outlying work to the south-east, on the Preston river), and the formerly separate irrigation areas have now merged to form a continuous belt of cultivation from Dardanup in the south to Warooma in the north (Fig. 102). The progress of dam construction and the quantities of water impounded are indicated in the following table:

TABLE 79

Western Australia: water conservation in the south-western irrigation district

Dam	Year constructed	Water impounded million gallons
Harvey Weir . . .	1916	520
	enlarged 1931	2,275
Drakes Brook . . .	1931 ⎫	
Samson Brook . . .	1941 ⎭	2,281
	enlarged 1960	2,525
Wellington . . .	1933	8,000
	enlarged 1960	40,790
Stirling	1948	12,060
	enlarged 1958	12,552
Logue Brook . . .	1963	5,358
Waroona . . .	1966	3,290
Glen Mervyn . . .	1969	—

In all these irrigation districts excepting the Preston valley the main object of the irrigation is the promotion of the dairy industry, and pastures account for about 95 per cent of the total of 35,000 acres (14,000 ha) of irrigated land. Of the remainder, fodder crops, orchards and vegetables (especially potatoes) occupy approximately equal shares.

On the 800 or so farms in the belt the black and white Friesian cattle graze on the lush plots of irrigated clover, and most of their milk is forwarded to the Perth area. The rest is converted into butter or cheese or condensed milk in the local towns such as Harvey and Bunbury. The farms are not completely specialised, however: they grow fruit, potatoes and vegetables, and they rear fat lambs, young cattle and pigs.

The Collie coalfield. About 30 miles (48 km) inland from the coast is the only source of coal in Western Australia—the Collie coalfield. It yields a soft bituminous coal which is not of coking quality but is suitable for steam raising (and hence for conversion into electricity). There are three basins, at Collie itself, at Muja to the east and at Wilga to the south-east (the last is as yet undeveloped).

The coalfield was opened up in the early years of the twentieth century to fuel the expanding railway net in the wheat belt and in the goldfields. In 1927 the output reached 500,000 tons; it surpassed 700,000 tons in 1947 and attained a peak of over a million tons in 1954. The introduction of diesel locomotives has set free Collie coal for the production of electricity, and it fires the 240 MW power station at Muja, the largest coal-fired station in the State. During the late 1960s the output continued at over a million tons, and reached a record in 1970 of 1,198,000 tons, valued at $A5·8 million. About 700 people are employed in the coal mining industry.

Bunbury. The port and commercial centre for the south-west is Bunbury, which with a 1971 population of 17,762 ranks after Perth and Kalgoorlie–Boulder as the third urban centre of the State. Bunbury processes the mineral sands that are quarried in the coastal belt; it ships grain, fruit and timber (for example, for use as sleepers in the new railways of the north-west); it manufactures super-phosphate fertilisers and produces woollen textiles. Its new 120 MW generating station is conveniently placed to use Collie coal.

Its chief export consists of mineral sands, and in 1968–69 a record 609,000 tons of this commodity were shipped. In the same year there was a record shipment of 497,000 cases of apples. Bunbury is also the shipping port for alumina from the new refinery completed at Pinjarra: this commodity is likely to increase in importance, for an additional alumina refinery is projected for the town itself. The port is thus growing in status, and a substantial development programme is under way. The mouth of the Preston river is being diverted, extensive dredging is taking place, and a completely new port is being constructed north of the existing harbour, with a minimum depth of 40 feet (12 m)—sufficient to accommodate vessels of up to 40,000 tons.

THE BEEF-CATTLE LANDS

There are nearly 2 million beef cattle in Western Australia, and about half of them are concentrated in the Kimberleys. This is a well-watered plateau region extending east of Broome and south of Wyndham, isolated from the rest of the State by the Great Sandy Desert, yet itself receiving an adequate rainfall of 20 inches (508 mm) or more per annum, brought by the summer monsoon.

The Kimberleys form very attractive country, traversed by many rivers, such as the Fitzroy and the Drysdale, which flow throughout the year and contain water throughout their courses. Yet the land is largely unfenced and unimproved—in fact there are extensive areas not yet taken up.

The main economic product of this large region is beef. The cattle stations are vast, some of them exceeding a million acres (400,000 ha) in extent—that is, about equal to the county of Kent or Sussex in the United Kingdom—yet even these are dwarfed by some of those in the adjoining Northern Territory. Undoubtedly a more intensive occupation of the land could be made were there more capital available. Without internal fencing it is impossible to guard against the overgrazing of favoured pastures. In the absence of roads and railways long overland treks are necessary to herd the animals towards the coastal slaughterhouses; and the going is rough, so that the animals arrive in poor condition and their meat cannot command the best prices. Drought may bring disaster, as it did in 1952, when a million cattle died in the north of Australia.

The ports for this large region are Wyndham and Broome, and on these the stock routes focus. At Wyndham 30,000–35,000 cattle are slaughtered annually during the four months' season, May to August, giving rise to about 6000 tons of frozen beef. There is no local labour supply, and the 300 or so employees of the meat factory are engaged in Perth and transported to and from the works each season. Six to nine meat vessels are used in shipping the beef abroad; they can safely use the quay at Wyndham, which has a depth of 26–33 feet (8–10 m) of water.

Work at the cattle stations is largely carried on by aborigines, who make excellent stockmen; they are supervised by a handful of Europeans. Future development of the region seems to lie in the increasing use of air transport in these remote areas. Almost every station has its own airstrip, where a regular weekly or fortnightly plane lands with supplies and mail. The Flying Doctor service (p. 344) brings help in case of sickness, and in one instance, at Glenroy, stock until recently were slaughtered locally and the carcasses flown to the port.

The Glenroy abattoir and chilling plant were constructed in 1948, and they have a capacity of 5000 head of cattle each season. All the parts of the building and the equipment were flown in. The carcasses were flown out to the freezing plant at Derby, about 150 miles (240 km) away, and a much longer annual drove through the mountain passes was avoided. "Air beef," however, is now obsolete. A new motor road has been built from Derby across the King Leopold Ranges and reached the Glenroy area by mid-1963. This is part of a larger scheme of road improvements in the northern cattle lands (Fig. 81, p. 212), where the beef industry has for long been hampered by inadequate transport. The Derby to Glenroy road alone has opened up 5 million acres (2 million ha) of potential cattle country.

Irrigation is rare in tropical Australia, but a major development is under way in the basin of the Ord river.

The Ord irrigation project. The Ord river rises near Mount Wells in plateau country in the north-eastern corner of the State. Its headstreams flow through the Antrim plateau, so named on account of the volcanic rocks, which were reminiscent of those found on the plateau of the same name in Northern Ireland. Volcanic debris carried northwards has an improving influence on the soils and helps to explain the choice of the region for the growing of cotton and other tropical crops. The river receives many tributaries from the west, but its water is augmented only slightly from the east; the boundary between the Northern Territory and Western Australia passes in such a way that almost the whole of the Ord basin is in Western Australia, though the irrigation project does extend into a small portion of Northern Territory.

The commercial centre for the Ord basin is Wyndham (1971 population: 1496)—a port situated on a sheltered tidal channel, 50 miles (80 km) from the open sea. Wyndham has had a varied career: it was founded to serve the Kimberley goldfield. On the decline of gold, the settlement was saved from extinction by the establishment of a State meat works; this has reverted to private hands, and has had a moderate success. The animals are slaughtered in winter by seasonal workers from Perth, and the beef and by-products are shipped from the port. The beef roads scheme may react adversely on Wyndham by drawing off the trade to other ports, but the town now has a new interest as the port and commercial centre for the Ord irrigation scheme.

From the point of view of water supply this is a marginal area. The southern half receives a mean annual rainfall of about 20 inches (500 mm), and this increases to about 30 inches (750 mm) near the coast. Wyndham itself receives an average of 27·2 inches (691 mm), which is markedly seasonal in character, with a peak in January and slightly less in February: these two months account for half the annual total, and on the average there are only eight wet days between April and October. Tremendously heavy falls of rain have occurred: in one day during April a record 17·3 inches (433 mm) fell—more than half the mean annual total!

While the mean total of rainfall is sufficient, it needs to be regulated, and this is the purpose of the Ord scheme. It was preceded by twelve years of painstaking trials between 1945 and 1957 at the Kimberley Research Station established on Ivanhoe Plain (Fig. 103), which later was to become the first irrigated area. These experiments showed that given adequate irrigation water cotton, safflower, linseed and sugar cane would flourish in the district.

The scheme is planned in two main stages, which involve first the construction of a diversion dam, and later a major storage dam.

The diversion dam has proved to be a major engineering project. It is located at Bandicoot Bar, where the river cuts through a reef of quartzite that provides a solid rock foundation. The erratic flow of the river made a long and high barrage essential: the dam with its levees is 3 miles (4·8 km) long and it ponds back the water for 25 miles (40 km) upstream. It was completed in 1963. With a full reservoir, the water will feed by gravity into the irrigation channels; but until Stage Two is completed pumping is necessary to fill the channels.

Following the completion of the diversion dam thirty-one farms were allocated to it, each containing an average of 660 acres (264 ha). The total area of land involved in the First Stage of the project is 30,000 acres (12,000 ha); of this, the irrigated area in 1969–70

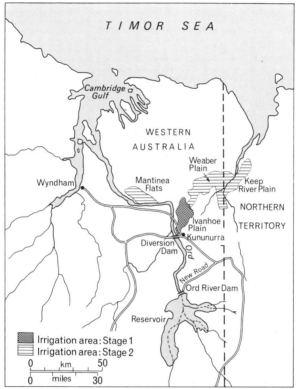

FIG. 103.—Western Australia: the Ord irrigation project. The scheme is planned in two stages. Stage one (now complete) has involved the building of a diversion dam at Kununurra, and the irrigation of the Ivanhoe Plain. Stage two involves the construction of a major dam and power station higher upstream, and will multiply the irrigation area by six. The storage reservoir shown will be the largest in Australia (its shape is diagrammatic).

amounted to 9500 acres (3800 ha). Cotton forms the major crop and two gineries have been established in the district: this is the only cotton-producing area in Western Australia. In addition, small quantities of sorghum, oats and fodder are produced.

A new settlement at Kununurra, close to the dam, forms the hub of the irrigation district. In its planning a new principle has been adopted: the farmhouses are not on the individual irrigated plots but are grouped together to form a "new town" complete with all modern amenities.

This, the first new settlement to be built in the Kimberleys during the twentieth century, had in 1971 a population of 1182.

The construction of the main storage dam began in 1969 and was spread over three years. The reservoir covers 286 square miles (744 km²) and forms the largest artificial lake in Australia: it allows an expansion in the area of the project to 178,000 acres (71,000 ha)— multiplying the area of Stage One by almost 6.

It is too early to evaluate Stage Two; but already cotton is an established product of the Ord basin, in land which hitherto has been purely cattle range country, with widely spaced homesteads.

A political decision, however, on the part of the Federal Government is likely to affect adversely the cotton growers of the Ord. We have already seen (p. 129) that the cotton bounty has been progressively reduced and ceased in 1972. This will undoubtedly add to the burden of the growers, who already face severe difficulties of isolation and marketing. It remains to be seen whether a greater diversification of production can ensure the success of the scheme.

The details relating to cotton production are indicated in Table 80.

TABLE 80

Western Australia: production of cotton

Farming year ending			Area thou. acres	Output thou. cwt	Value $A mil.
1966	.	.	8·3	182	1·9
1967	.	.	11·9	263	2·4
1968	.	.	11·8	232	1·9
1969	.	.	8·3	193	1·7
1970	.	.	7·2	186	1·6
1971	.	.	8·5	247	2·3

It seems likely that the Kimberley area possesses rich stores of minerals: promising concentrations of copper, lead, zinc and nickel have been found together with showings of oil and gas. At present, however, developments are limited to two coastal areas, the first at Yampi Sound and the second close to Admiralty Gulf.

Yampi Sound is about 100 miles (160 km) north of Derby. Here the Precambrian rocks that form Koolan Island (25 square miles; 65 km²) and the smaller Cockatoo Island (2 square miles; 5·2 km²) contain at least 68 million tons of high-grade iron ore, most of it on Koolan Island. It is being mined by the Broken Hill Company to feed its blast furnaces in New South Wales.

First to be worked were the Cockatoo Island deposits, from which shipments began in 1951. Here the ore body lies along more than a mile of cliffs, 260 feet (78 m) high. It is worked by open-cast methods in great terraces. The undertaking is serviced by a village of about 300 people in this remote and hot corner of Australia. Shipments from Koolan Island began in 1965. A useful two-way traffic has developed, for the ore vessels return with steel billets for fabricating at Kwinana and water to replenish the supplies on the islands. Shipments from Yampi in 1969–70 amounted to 2·6 million tons.

At Admiralty Gulf an important regional project is under way. It is based on the mining of the extensive deposits of bauxite discovered in 1965 by the Amax Bauxite Corporation, the subsidiary of an American firm. The company will develop its mine, build a 12-mile (19-km) railway, construct a port capable of receiving 50,000 ton ore carriers, and a town for 3000 people at Port Warrender. Shipments of bauxite are expected to begin towards the end of 1974; and after fifteen years it is expected that an aluminium smelter will be planned.

But the Amax operations are more comprehensive than mining and shipping: it has acquired the lease of the 795,000 acre (318,000 ha) Mitchell River Station, on which it proposes to spend half a million dollars on the development of the beef, agriculture, fishing and tourist industries. Here is an example of regional development by a private company which forms a model for use elsewhere.

The Pilbara. The Pilbara statistical division runs eastward towards the centre of the continent from a coastal stretch that extends from a point south of Barrow Island to Cape Kerandren in the east. Conveniently enough, within its boundaries are to be found all the major iron discoveries of recent years, together with the associated economic developments. Even these, however, are confined to the western two-thirds of the division. To the east lie the deserts—Gibson's Desert and the Great Sandy Desert—apart from one or two outlying cattle stations and possibly a few wandering aboriginal groups it is uninhabited.

The western third had a limited value even before the revolution wrought by iron. In 1960 the region contained about 500,000 sheep and 25,000 cattle scattered among some sixty properties, and had a population of about 6150 (including 2900 aborigines).

Theoretically the region experiences between 10 and 15 inches (255 and 375 mm) of rainfall during the year. Port Hedland reports 11·6 inches (295 mm), Marble Bar, 13·2 inches (335 mm). But owing to the erratic nature of the rainfall, the averages mean little, and one station has experienced a minimum of 0·5 inch (12·7 mm) and a maximum of 28 inches (700 mm) in a year. The summer rainfall is associated with tropical cyclones—the "Willy Willies" that we have mentioned above (p. 26). About two a year may be expected, and they bring violent winds with gusts of up to 120 miles (192 km) an hour. The dry watercourses are suddenly flooded, but the water quickly runs to waste over the baked ground.

Summer temperatures are everywhere high. On the coast even the winter temperatures reach 26° C (79° F). Port Hedland has a mean July maximum of 26° C (79° F) and a mean January maximum of 34·5° C (94° F). Marble Bar is notorious as the hottest recorded place in Australia, where the temperature exceeds 38° C (100° F) on 145 successive days in the average year. Its mean maximum temperature in December is 42° C (107·5° F).

The coast is low-lying and fringed with mangroves, and subject to a tidal range of 25 feet (7·5 m). Until recently there were only a few small ports and service centres. The scattered and rough roads were traversed by great ruts when dry, and after rain were impassable.

The year 1960 marked a turning-point for the Pilbara. In that year the Federal Government revoked its ban on the export of iron ore from Australia. Hitherto it had subscribed to the view that Australia was short of iron ore. The ban itself had removed most of the incentive to prospect for ore; nevertheless, by 1960 it was already clear that there was sufficient ore in the north-west to make the ban unnecessary. Its removal sparked off a wave of new discoveries, and a mineral boom was soon in full swing.

The iron deposits of Pilbara are linked with its geological structure. Almost the whole of Australia west of long. 122° is composed of Precambrian material. From an undulating plateau of crystalline Archaean rocks, ranging between 1000 and 2000 feet (300 and 600 m) in altitude, there rises a ridge formed of the slightly less ancient Proterozoic sediments, consisting mainly of sandstones. This is the Hamersley Range, famous for its wealth of iron ore. Mainly between 2000 and 3000 feet (600 and 900 m) above sea-level, it rises to a summit of 4056 feet (1237 m) in Mount Meharry, the highest point in the State.

Uplift has given added height to these mountains, which overlook the plateau to the south in a striking fault scarp. In most of the Hamersley Range the strata are more or less horizontal; in the south, however, is an area of complex folding and erosion, and here solution has helped in concentrating the iron minerals into almost pure hematite, with an iron content of 60 to 70 per cent. The ore bodies form huge masses which may be several miles long and 990 feet (300 m) deep.

North-west of the Hamersley Range in the Robe river district is iron ore of a different character. This is limonite, formed from the decomposition of the older iron-bearing rocks and their re-deposition in old drainage channels. The deposits now appear as flat-topped ridges in which the beds of limonite may be as much as 200 feet (60 m) thick. Limonite is leaner than hematite, though it may range in iron content up to 58 per cent; but it is easy to mine, and it can usually be upgraded to meet the requirements of the iron and steel industry.

North-east of the Hamersley Range, within the Archaean rocks but close to their border, are the lenses of rich hematite of Mount Goldsworthy: these were the first of the Pilbara iron deposits to be worked.

When in 1960 the ban on the export of iron ore was lifted there was an immediate incentive to explore. As early as the turn of the century iron had been known to exist in the region; but only now did an appraisal of the size of the deposits begin. They were soon found to be immense. The estimates of the size of the high-grade deposits rose from 400 to 2000 million tons, then to 4000 and to 8000, and by the end of 1962 the known reserves stood at 15,000 million tons.

By 1963 several companies had concluded agreements with the State Government on the manner of development; and by 1965 they had signed long-term contracts with Japan.[3] A mineral boom was under way. In 1966 the Melbourne Stock Exchange listed 92 mining companies; by 1969 the number had grown to 195. Between 1967 and 1969 mining shares trebled their value. Expenditure on mineral exploration grew from $A12 million in 1964 to $A40 million in 1968.

First in the field was the Goldsworthy Mining Company. Their known reserves of high-quality ore (with an iron content of 64 per cent) were estimated at 45 million tons, and the company contracted to supply Japanese mills with $16\frac{1}{2}$ million tons of ore, spread over seven years. The nearest shipping point was at Port Hedland, and a completely new

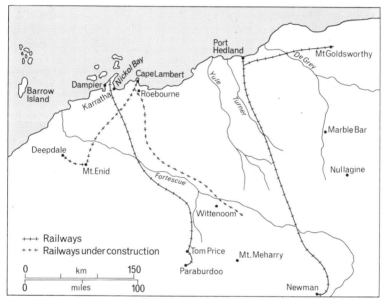

Fig. 104.—Western Australia: the Pilbara. The map indicates the new mining centres and the railways that link them to the shipping ports.

70-mile (112-km) railway was constructed to link the mine to the port (Fig. 104). At the same time the harbour was deepened sufficiently to accommodate 40,000 ton ore carriers, and an approach channel $4\frac{1}{2}$ miles (7·2 km) long was dredged out. In May 1966 the preparations were complete and 2·4 million tons of ore were shipped from the Pilbara to Japan during the next twelve months—the first instalment of what was to become an immense traffic.

The pattern was established, and it was soon being repeated elsewhere. Massive equipment at the mines rapidly converts a mountain of ore into a cargo ready for shipment. Mechanical shovels scoop up 24

FIG. 105.—Mount Newman: loading a truck. At the quarry face huge power shovels scoop out the ore in 24-ton "bites" to fill the 100-ton capacity trucks.

FIG. 106.—Port Hedland: ore vessels. Two Japanese bulk carriers, the *Eisho Maru* and the *Fukukawa Maru*, each of over 100,000 tons, are loading iron ore at Port Hedland. The outlet for Mount Goldsworthy and Mount Newman, it handles more cargo than any other port in Australia.

tons in a single "bite" and load it into lorries, each of 100 tons capacity (Fig. 105). The lorries convey the ore to a primary crusher, which can convert boulders weighing 20 tons into lumps with a diameter of $7\frac{1}{2}$ inches (190 mm). From the crusher the ore is loaded on to enormously long trains, each drawn by three diesel locomotives. With 240 wagons, each containing 100 tons, the train conveys 24,000 tons of ore speedily to the coast. The ore ports are already accepting 100,000 ton ore carriers (Fig. 106), and there are plans to receive vessels of 150,000 tons or more.

At the mines new towns are constructed. They include hospitals, schools and shops whose prices are the same as those ruling in Perth. The houses are built of brick and are air-conditioned, with lawns and flower gardens. Newman boasts an Olympic-size swimming pool.

The years 1966–69 saw great activity in opening up the Pilbara. While the Goldsworthy Company was building its railway parallel to the coast, Hamersley Holdings, operating about 400 miles (640 km) to the south-west, was building a railway 182 miles (205 km) long to link its mine at Tom Price to the coast at Dampier. Tom Price is the name of a former President of the Kaiser Steel Corporation of America and is a reminder of the part that American technology is playing in the development of the Pilbara. The Hamersley group controls an estimated 1624 million tons of high-grade hematite, and its reserves are among the largest yet known in the region. By 1967 the group had negotiated contracts to supply $65\frac{1}{2}$ million tons of ore to Japan, spread over sixteen years; and in 1969 a further contract added 112 million tons, spread over fifteen years.

Tom Price in 1969 was yielding ore at the rate of about 14 million tons annually, and the company had deepened the port of Dampier to take 65,000 ton ore carriers. It had also built at Dampier the first pellet plant of the region, with an annual capacity of 2 million tons. In view of its new contract it prepared to open up a new mine at Paraburdoo, together with a sister port to Dampier on East Intercourse Island, where 150,000 ton carriers could be received.

About 150 miles (240 km) south-east of Tom Price, and near the eastern limit of the Precambrian rocks is the mine of the Mount Newman consortium. Its reserves in Mount Whaleback are estimated at 2000 million tons, and form the largest single deposit known in the Pilbara (Fig. 107). By 1967 the group had secured contracts to supply Japan with 100 million tons of iron ore, spread over fifteen years, and the Broken Hill Company with a further 70 million tons. The mines are farther inland than those of any other goup, and they have entailed the building of a railway 265 miles (424 km) long, which was completed in 1969. Like the Mount Goldsworthy railway, it connects with Port Hedland. Mount Newman is named after a member of the party led by Edward Giles, who explored the Gibson desert in 1876. In its first stage the mine is producing at the rate of about 11 million tons annually, and

[*Courtesy the Agent-General for Western Australia.*

FIG. 107.—Mount Newman: aerial view. This mountain of iron ore is being carved into terraces and gradually quarried away by the Mount Newman Consortium. It is the largest of the Pilbara deposits. The loading terminal with its stockpile is to the right; from here the ore trains leave for their 265-mile (424-km) journey to Port Hedland.

the company plans to increase this to more than 30 million tons by 1975.

A fourth iron project is under way: this is the exploitation of the limonite deposits of the Robe river valley, on the north-western flank of the Hamersley Range. In April 1969 the Cleveland Cliffs consortium negotiated with Japan the largest contract ever made so far: it involves the supply of 123 million tons of pellets and fine ore, worth $A1071 million. The company has built a railway from its mine at Deepdale through Mount Enid to Cape Lambert, near Roebourne. Here it is developing a new port sufficiently large to accommodate ore carriers of 250,000 tons capacity. It shipped its first cargo of 76,000 tons to Japan in October 1972. It is building a new town a short distance north-east of Dampier, at Wickham; and this will contain the largest pellet plant of its kind in the world. The output of the mine, initially at 10 million tons annually, is planned to expand to 20 million and perhaps 30 million tons per annum. The capital expenditure involved on this project, at $A280 million, is the highest in the Pilbara.

These developments do not exhaust the possibilities of the region. Extensive iron deposits are known to exist near Wittenoom, where the asbestos mine closed down in 1966. A railway route has been surveyed, to join that from the Robe river near Cape Lambert. Wittenoom township could be revived to form the nucleus of a new mining community; but this project may have to wait for an extension in the markets for iron.

Pilbara has its problems.[4] It is clear that the region is almost completely dependent on a single commodity—iron—and on a single market—Japan. This product is bringing great material wealth to the State. The royalties on sales, rentals and company taxes are in the region of $A8 million annually. The companies are building railways, towns and ports, and are achieving standards of comfort quite unlike anything before in such a climate.

As the former Minister of Industrial Development for Western Australia has put it, "In five years Australians have literally jumped off the sheep's back on to an ore train."[5] In 1959 minerals represented 6 per cent of the nation's exports; in 1969 they represented 24 per cent and in 1970 about 30 per cent, supplanting wool as the leading export. In five years Pilbara has become the nation's leading producer of minerals, and has risen to the fourth place in the world. In terms of tonnage Port Hedland has become the chief port of Australia and the fifth in the world.

A region which in 1960 had only a scatter of cattle stations is now served by a growing net of communications. The railways are already operating, sealed highways are under construction, jet air services have been organised and there are dial telephone links between Port Hedland and Perth. From a sleepy port of 1000 inhabitants in 1960 Hedland has grown to over 7000 in 1971 (Fig. 108). Dampier and Tom Price have reached their planned targets of 3000 each. Newest of the towns is Newman: its first inhabitants arrived in 1968 and in three years it had grown to 3000: its planned target is 5000 inhabitants.

But experience shows that mining is a precarious basis on which to build an economy. Are there any other resources for permanent occupation that the region can offer? There are indeed, but at present they are limited.

The hot climate and dry atmosphere combine to produce a very high evaporation rate, of 90 to 100 inches (2250 to 2500 mm) per annum. While this heightens the problem of water supply, it does facilitate the production of salt by the evaporation of sea-water, and there are coastal shallows which can readily be used for the construction of evaporating basins. Here is an industry with an inexhaustible supply of raw material and a free source of heat, yielding a product which finds a ready market in the chemical industries. Salt industries have been established close to Dampier and Port Hedland, and shipments from each port are at the rate of about 1 million tons annually, destined for the Japanese chemical industry.

FIG. 108.—South Hedland township. This self-contained township of about 250 dwellings illustrates the layout of the new towns that are growing in the Pilbara. All the houses are air-conditioned. The population of Port Hedland has reached 7000.

Other salt deposits are being developed in three areas farther south, beyond the confines of the Pilbara: they are in the lagoons and gulfs in the neighbourhood of Carnarvon. From north to south these are Exmouth Gulf, Lake Macleod and Shark Bay.

At Exmouth Gulf a company plans to develop a saltworks with an eventual capacity of $1\frac{1}{4}$ million tons annually. In Shark Bay part of the inlet at Useless Loop has been closed to form evaporating ponds: it now belies its name, for the Shark Bay company has contracted to supply 1·6 million tons of salt to Japan over seven years, and has developed a plant with a capacity of 0·5 million tons annually for the purpose. Shipments began in 1968.

Lake Macleod is interesting in that here in addition to common salt are valuable deposits of potash—a mineral which hitherto has not been commercially exploited in Australia. Potash is the last of the series of salts to crystallise out during the process of evaporation of sea-water. The developing company is Texada Mines, of British Columbia; they began to ship salt to Japan in 1969, from a new deep-water jetty at Cape Cuvier, and they are developing the potash deposits with a view to an annual output of 200,000 tons. This is the equivalent of the entire annual requirements of potash in Australia.

In 1969–70 the exports of salt from Western Australia were valued at $A4,002,000. These industries are transforming hitherto uninhabited areas into productive districts with thriving communities enjoying the benefits of modern amenities. A new energy source is now being tapped in the oilfield at Barrow Island, about 50 miles (80 km) south-west of Dampier. After twelve years of patient search, the West Australian Petroleum Company struck oil in 1964, and two years later this was

[*Courtesy the Agent-General for Western Australia.*

FIG. 109.—The oil industry. These "roughnecks" engaged in the drilling of Onslow No.1 well, between Barrow Island and Exmouth Gulf in the north-western corner of Western Australia, typify the vigour of Australia's newest industry.

declared to be a commercial field (Fig. 109). Production began in 1967, and the oil is currently flowing at the rate of about 50,000 barrels a day from reserves estimated at 200 million barrels: thus at present rates of flow the oilfield has a life of about eleven years. Unless there are significant new discoveries some other source of energy will be needed, and it seems that the ultimate answer lies in electricity based on nuclear power.

Water too will be required in considerable quantities. The immediate answer is desalination, and the first of such plants is in operation at Dampier, which yields a town water supply of 200,000 gallons (900,000 l) a day. The region possesses only one important river, the Fortescue; a regional plan has been prepared, which envisages the construction of seven dams and the growing under irrigation of crops sufficient to meet local needs. Underground supplies of water are known to exist.

The railways have been built as private ventures with the simple object of linking the mines to the ports; but with suitable interconnections they could form the basis of a regional system; and in the meantime work proceeds to complete the sealing of the North-West Coastal Highway, which provides a direct route between Perth and Port Hedland. Construction of the major regional centre is in progress at Karratha, which is being planned for a population of 25,000.

In 1971–72 80 per cent of the output of iron ore in Australia was shipped to Japan, and this represented 42 per cent of the Japanese requirements of iron ore. As the flow reaches the maximum envisaged in the contracts so the economic ties between the two countries become stronger still; and it is anticipated that by 1975 Japan will be drawing 60 per cent of her supplies from the Pilbara.

Doubts have been expressed concerning the wisdom of maintaining so restricted a pattern of trade. Wise or not, however, there was no other way available that promised the rapid development of the ore supplies. It is certainly clear that any important change in the economic fortunes of Japan will be felt at once in the Pilbara.

Early in 1971 the economic progress of Japan suffered a setback, and the Nippon Steel Corporation, representing seven Japanese mills, informed the Australian producers that it was exercising its option in the contracts to take 10 per cent less than the basic rate of flow. This economy, however, was insufficient to meet the recession, and in March the Hamersley company agreed to a new contract which reduced its sales by a further 6 per cent. These changes followed closely upon a monetary crisis which left the companies with unexpected reductions in earnings. At the end of the year the Hamersley company announced that it was delaying the start of its new Paraburdoo mine, which had been scheduled to begin in 1972.

Industry must learn to live with changes in the pace of economic development, and though the rapidity of the advance may not satisfy all the earlier hopes, solid and swift progress has indeed been made and the Pilbara has awakened from its slumbers. The following tables summarise some of the aspects of the development of the Pilbara.

TABLE 81

The ore railways of Western Australia

Railway				Length, miles	Date opened
Westmine–Tilley (Geraldton)	.	.	.	13	January 1966
Goldsworthy–Port Hedland	.	.	.	71	May 1966
Tom Price–Dampier	.	.	.	182	July 1966
Koolyanobbing–Kwinana	.	.	.	306	April 1967
Newman–Port Hedland	.	.	.	265	January 1969
Deepdale–Cape Lambert	.	.	.	—	October 1972

Ore carried on these railways:

Year				Million tons
1967	.	.	.	9·7
1968	.	.	.	15·5
1969	.	.	.	26·0
1970	.	.	.	36·6
1971	.	.	.	44·7
1972	.	.	.	49·8

TABLE 82

Western Australia: production of iron ore

Year				Quantity mil. tons	Iron content mil. tons	Value $A million
1966	.	.	.	6·1	4·0	29·9
1967	.	.	.	12·2	7·9	70·3
1968	.	.	.	18·8	12·2	110·9
1968–69	.	.	.	23·3	14·9	140·1
1969–70	.	.	.	34·1	21·5	195·1
1970–71	.	.	.	45·7	28·9	279·5

TABLE 83

Western Australia: exports of iron ore and concentrates

Year				Quantity mil. tons	Value $A mil.
1961	.	.	.	1·0	2·1
1966	.	.	.	2·6	7·0
1967	.	.	.	8·4	50·9
1968	.	.	.	14·3	104·5
1969	.	.	.	19·6	151·8
1970	.	.	.	31·4	233·6
1971	.	.	.	45·5	341·7
1972	.	.	.	47·9	347·5

TABLE 84

Western Australia: changes in the direction of exports, by value, expressed as a percentage of the total exports

Receiving country				1967–68	1968–69	1969–70
				%	%	%
Japan	.	.	.	34·1	41·5	45·8
United States	.	.	.	10·4	12·1	10·2
United Kingdom	.	.	.	7·3	6·9	5·7

TABLE 85

Western Australia: exports to Japan, by value, in $A millions

Year				Value of exports
1967–68	.	.	.	162·0
1968–69	.	.	.	226·6
1969–70	.	.	.	309·3
1970–71	.	.	.	428·6

PERTH, FREMANTLE AND KWINANA

In 1829 a small band of settlers led by Captain Stirling (later the first Governor of Western Australia) cast anchor off the site of Fremantle. Stirling had seen the mouth of the Swan river two years previously, and had been greatly impressed with it. From the first he decided that the capital of the new colony should be separate from its port. The port of Fremantle was established on the south shore of the river mouth, while a site for the capital city was chosen on the north bank, 12 miles (19 km) upstream, where rising ground provided security from flood.

Between the two the river widens to form a broad lake (Melville Water), and Perth has now expanded as far as its northern shore. With creditable foresight the city fathers preserved a broad strip of the river frontage here as a natural park (King's Park), where the original woodland together with many species of colourful primitive wild flowers may be seen (Fig. 110). Melville Water is bounded upstream by the

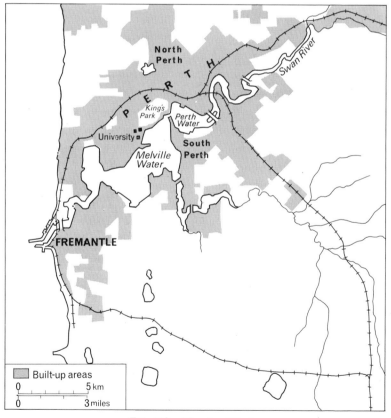

FIG. 110.—The site of Perth.

Narrows, where the river shrinks to only 300 yards (270 m) in width; here a modern bridge has been built, and has relieved the congestion formerly felt on the neighbouring ferries. Above the Narrows is a smaller broadening of the stream (Perth Water), and it is on the north bank here that the original city was established. Farther upstream the river meanders lazily through a flood plain whose flats have provided suitable ground for an airport and three race-courses, while an island allowed the construction of the Causeway—formerly the only road spanning the Swan river.

Perhaps the most remarkable feature of Perth has been its extremely rapid growth following the discovery of gold in the Kalgoorlie district (1892–93)—a growth which has continued into modern times. It is best seen in table form:

Year			Population, with suburbs
1890	.	. .	9,617
1901	.	. .	36,274
1921	.	. .	64,166
1933	.	. .	207,440
1961	.	. .	420,133
1966	.	. .	500,246
1971	.	. .	639,622

Within this century the city has thus multiplied seventeenfold, and it now includes more than half the population of the entire State.

The administrative and business centre of the city is contained within five long streets which run parallel to the shore of Perth Water. Here are the Town Hall, Government House and Parliament House, and the monumental columned and arcaded Commonwealth Bank and Post Office buildings (Fig. 111). Beyond lie the residential areas, and at the south end of King's Park, overlooking their own bay (Matilda Bay), are the university buildings, with their cheerful red-tiled roofs, tall Italian-style clock tower and arcaded halls—a unique university in that it charges no fees.

Perth itself is fortunate in that its major industries are situated away in the port area. Here are the soap works, the flour mills and tanneries, the breweries and biscuit works, the sawmills and furniture factories, and the miscellaneous industries which one expects to find in any capital city. In 1929 Fremantle became a city in its own right, though it is now considered to form part of Urban Perth. The port benefits from a low tidal range—only 4 feet (about 1·2 m)—and it has not been difficult to secure a minimum depth of 36 feet (11 m) of water in the harbour at low tide—sufficient to float the largest liners.

Perth is linked by rail with the goldfields to the east, with the grain and sheep lands to the south-east, with the timber lands to the south, and with the fruit, market-garden and dairy lands to the north and south along the coast. Only the cattle lands of the far north lack railway connection with the capital, and these are served by regular airways.

Fig. 111.—Perth: the central commercial district. Perth is growing faster than any other State capital: its population increased by over 50 per cent between 1961 and 1971. Much of this expansion may be attributed to the development of the Pilbara. This view shows the new multi-storey office blocks that have become a feature of the commercial quarter. The building to the right of centre is the Council house.

The industrial heart of Western Australia lies about 10 miles (16 km) south of Fremantle, at Kwinana; the seaborne traffic associated with it falls within the port of Fremantle.

Until the early 1950s this was a barren sandy coast useless for farming and virtually uninhabited. But it backed a broad and deep bay—Cockburn Sound—sheltered from the west by Garden Island, and it offered almost unlimited flat and cheap land suitable for the development of heavy industry; it was also within easy reach of the main railway to the "Golden Mile."

In 1954 the British Petroleum Company opened Australia's largest oil refinery at Kwinana, and by this single operation doubled the capital investment in industrial plant and buildings within the State. Since that time the refinery has grown in size and complexity and its capacity has been increased from 3·0 to 5·2 million tons annually; it now ranks jointly with the refinery at Geelong as the largest in Australia. At its jetties three tankers each of 80,000 tons d.w. can berth simultaneously.

In its turn the refinery provides energy and raw materials for other activities. To the north is an expanding power station, fired by oil from the refinery. The initial 240 MW plant was doubled in 1972–73, and the increasing demands from industry have made further expansion necessary. An additional capacity of 400 MW is scheduled for completion in 1976, so that the total capacity will then be 880 MW, and provision has been made for an eventual 1600 MW.

A pipeline from the refinery supplies fuel to the Cockburn cement company a mile or two north of the oil installation; here too there has been rapid expansion. From a single kiln in 1955, the works had grown to a complex of four kilns in 1968 with a total capacity of 560,000 tons of cement annually, and further extensions are planned to raise the capacity to nearly a million tons annually.

Not only does the refinery supply energy to neighbouring industries, but its by-products form raw materials for chemical works. Immediately south of the refinery are a nitrogen plant and a fertiliser works: between them they produce annually up to 500,000 tons of super-phosphates, 100,000 tons of ammonia, 110,000 tons of ammonium nitrate and 90,000 tons of nitric acid. These plants have made Western Australia self-sufficient in nitrogenous fertilisers.

The oil refinery was only the first of several major works established at Kwinana (Figs 112 and 113). A vital element in the industrial pattern is the gradual establishment of an iron and steel industry by the Broken

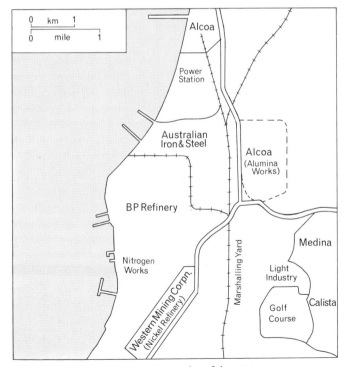

FIG. 112.—Kwinana: plan of the estate.

FIG. 113.—Kwinana: aerial view. This photograph illustrates the extensive level tracts of land with shipping facilities that are available for heavy industry at Kwinana. The jetty nearest to the camera serves the alumina refinery of ALCOA; just beyond it is the generating station. The vessel beyond is at the pier of the iron and steel works. Farther south, opposite the headland, is the BP oil refinery, one of the two largest in Australia; beyond it, and a little to the left is the only nickel refinery in Australia: it treats the ores from Kambalda. Kwinana forms the industrial heart of Western Australia.

Hill Proprietary Company on a site immediately north of the oil refinery. This process is linked with agreements between the company, the State Government and the Federal Government. The State Government granted the company leases of high-grade iron ore deposits at Koolyanobbing and Bungalbin (about 150 miles (240 km)—west of Kalgoorlie) and undertook to build a standard gauge railway to link the mines with Kwinana. This railway, 310 miles (496 km) long, was built with the help of Federal funds and opened in 1967. The company for its part undertook to establish an integrated iron and steel industry at Kwinana, and it is this process that we must now notice.

A steel fence post plant was opened at Kwinana in 1954 and a steel rolling mill in 1956. In 1965 the company began to construct a blast furnace plant, and by the time it was completed in 1968 the Koolyanobbing mine was in operation and its railway link open. The new blast furnace has an annual capacity of 600,000 tons of basic pig iron or 48,000 tons of foundry iron, and marks an important stage in the development plan.[6] The output of ore at Koolyanobbing is about 1·1 million tons annually: about half of this is used to supply the blast furnace and the rest is shipped to the company's plants in New South Wales. It is anticipated that the industry will be completed by the establishment of steel-making plant by 1978. This will result in important economies in transport, for at present, in addition to receiving coke from Newcastle and manganese from the Gulf of Carpentaria, Kwinana ships its pig iron 2000 miles (3200 km) to Port Kembla in New South Wales for conversion into steel, and receives steel from Whyalla and Port Kembla for re-rolling. This is not all, for about three-quarters of the output of the rolling mill and fence post plant is shipped to markets in the east.

Immediately east of the iron and steel site is an alumina refinery opened by Alcoa of Australia Ltd. This is fed with bauxite mined in the Darling Range, east of Perth, at Jarrahdale, 32 miles (51 km) by rail from Kwinana. The bauxite, which has an alumina content of 30 to 45 per cent, occurs in pockets close to the surface and is covered by a mantle of overburden only $2\frac{1}{2}$ feet (0·75 m) thick. The crushing plant at the mine has a capacity of 1000 tons an hour. After the complex processes in the refinery the pure alumina emerges in the form of a white powder and is shipped for smelting to Geelong or overseas to Japan, the United States or the Middle East.

Since it was opened in 1964 the refinery has expanded rapidly: from an initial capacity of 210,000 tons a year it has grown in six stages to reach 1,250,000 tons by the end of 1970. On the recommendation of the State Government the Kwinana refinery has been limited to this size, and the company has accordingly opened a new plant at Pinjarra. Both are supplied with natural gas from Dongara, near Geraldton. The production of bauxite in Western Australia is indicated in the following table.

TABLE 86
Western Australia: production of bauxite

Year				Output thou. tons
1968	.	.	.	1608
1968–69	.	.	.	2075
1969–70	.	.	.	2861
1970–71	.	.	.	4140

We have already referred to the discovery and exploitation of the extensive deposits of nickel close to the "Golden Mile" of Kalgoorlie. At first, in 1967, the concentrates were shipped from the south coast for smelting in Japan; but the possibility of smelting in Western Australia was not overlooked, and Kwinana, on the direct rail route from Kalgoorlie, was selected as the site. Here was built the first nickel refinery in Australia; production began in 1970, and the designed capacity of 15,000 tons of metal annually is being increased to 20,000 tons. The 200-acre (80-ha) site is south of the oil refinery, and the works employ about 300 men. Their by-products include 2000 tons of copper sulphide concentrates, 1000 tons of mixed nickel and cobalt sulphides and 150,000 tons of ammonium sulphate.

We have noticed the major industrial plants at Kwinana; but by 1971 two dozen other concerns had been attracted. Among them was the first stage of a $A40 million integrated grain terminal whose ultimate capacity will be over 50 million bushels.

Two other projects remain to be noticed. For over a century there have been proposals to construct a Federal naval base at Cockburn Sound. After many vicissitudes the Commonwealth Government announced in 1969 that it would develop a base there as soon as possible, and in 1971 work began on the first stage of the project—the construction of a $2\frac{1}{2}$-mile (4-km) causeway costing $A9 million to link Garden Island with the mainland.

In addition, the State Government has accepted in principle a long-term development plan for the port of Fremantle. It includes the construction of container and general cargo berths both on the mainland and on Garden Island. It is clear that Kwinana, with its wide spectrum of industry and commerce, has an assured future.

Two miles (3 km) east of the industrial area a new town is approaching completion, separated from the industry by a broad belt of parkland. In 1971 Kwinana New Town had a population of 10,096, while Rockingham, to the south, had 11,990 inhabitants. Both had grown by about 140 per cent since 1966.

THE FUTURE

It is clear from our brief survey that Western Australia is making tremendous strides in its economy. Its farming is prosperous and expanding; new industries are developing; the road and railway systems are being extended; new towns are taking shape. Above all, a surge has taken place in the development of minerals. Bauxite, nickel and oil are new to Western Australia, but it is in iron that the greatest advances are under way. Gold, formerly all-important, has been quite outstripped by the base metal, whose output is now considerably more valuable than all the crops put together and very nearly equal to all the pastoral and dairy products combined.

In 1969–70 Western Australia produced 35 per cent of Australia's bauxite, 51 per cent of her crude oil, 77 per cent of her iron ore and 78 per cent of her gold. In 1970–71 51 per cent of all the nation's tonnage of overseas cargo shipments originated from Western Australia.

With so great a variety and abundance of resources Western Australia should have no fears for the future. Yet it has been argued powerfully that the Federal Government, by devaluing the Australian dollar has put the iron industry of the State at a serious disadvantage and that other actions have shown a similar disregard for the economy of the State.[7] The change in the Federal government that took place following the 1973 elections, it is hoped, will provide an opportunity to restore understanding between Canberra and the industrial leaders of Western Australia.

NOTES

1. A. J. Conacher and I. D. Murray, "The Meckering Earthquake, Western Australia, 14th October 1968," *Australian Geographer*, Vol. XI, No. 2 (1969).

2. *The Times*, 11th April 1966.

3. M. G. A. Wilson, "Australia's Built-in Prosperity," *Geographical Magazine*, December, 1971.

4. A. Marshall, "Iron Age in the Pilbara," *Australian Geographer*, Vol. X, No. 5 (1968).

5. C. Court, *The Times*, 25th October 1971.

6. J. M. Allen, "Kwinana's Blast Furnace," *Australian Geographer*, Vol. X, No. 6 (1968).

7. Lang Hancock, "Is Western Australia Ripe for U.D.I.?" *The Times*, 1st March 1973.

STUDY QUESTIONS

1. Divide Western Australia into its climatic regions and describe briefly the characteristics of each.

2. Describe the physical and economic background of the gold mining industry of Western Australia.

3. What is meant by the "goldfields' water-supply scheme"?

4. Assess the contribution made by the forests of Western Australia to the economic life of the State.

5. How do you explain the remarkable differences in the density of population throughout Western Australia?

6. Is there any justification for the suggestion that Western Australia might profitably secede from the Australian Commonwealth?

Chapter XI

NORTHERN TERRITORY

Since 1911 the Northern Territory has been the responsibility of the Federal Government. This in itself is an acknowledgement that its problems lie beyond the powers of any individual State. It is a land of vast distances, of inadequate transport and far from markets; a land of deserts in the south and grassland or woodland in the north, where there is drought throughout the winter, searing heat in early summer, followed by torrential rain, flood and swamp.

Its population, though increasing, is far below that of each of the six States. Tasmania, the smallest of all, had in 1971 a population of 389,874; Northern Territory had only 85,519 people. This figure includes about 21,000 aborigines, so that here the natives form a more significant element in the population than anywhere else in the continent.

Northern Territory has an effective history of barely 100 years; and throughout that time its lifeline or backbone has been a narrow corridor of land where water is available at or near the surface. It passes north and south for more than a thousand miles from Darwin through Tennant Creek and Alice Springs to Charlotte Waters and so on into South Australia (Fig. 114). Almost all the economic development of the Territory is linked with this zone, and again and again it recurs in its story: first as the path of Stuart's epic journeys, then as the route of the Overland Telegraph, later as the track of the projected Transcontinental Railway and finally as "The Bitumen" or modern motor road—the Stuart Highway.

STUART'S JOURNEYS

John McDouall Stuart had accompanied Sturt in the 1840s during his seventeen months' quest for the "inland sea" of Australia, and was determined to find for himself what lay in the centre of the continent, and to discover a route to the northern shore. He did so; but it took him four years, it involved him in 10,000 miles (16,000 km) of travelling, and he was forced to turn back five times before his final triumph.

Stuart set out from the Flinders Ranges on his first journey in May 1858 with only two men and six horses. One of his companions was an aborigine, who ran away when the country became unfamiliar. Mile after mile of bare stones crippled his horses, and he was forced to strike south-westwards to Streaky Bay, where was the nearest habitation,

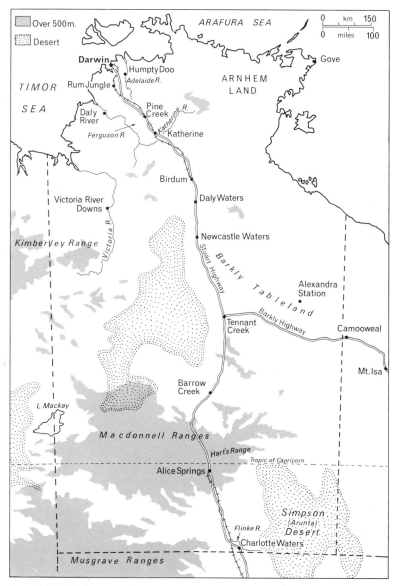

Fig. 114.—Northern Territory. The trail blazed by J. M. Stuart in 1861–62 was followed closely by the Overland Telegraph (opened 1872), omitted from this map for the sake of legibility. The railways date from 1886 onwards, the highways from the Second World War. The Northern Territory is more than five times as large as the United Kingdom but its population is smaller than that of an English country town such as Winchester. The shaded areas are higher than 1640 feet (500 m); the stippled areas represent deserts.

1000 miles (1600 km) away. On his second journey he made the vital discovery that artesian water escaped in a chain of springs to the south and south-west of Lake Eyre. Some were cold, some hot; some were salty, some fresh; but here was good drinking-water in the driest part of the continent. Thirty to fifty miles apart, the springs led him forward for 500 miles (800 km) to the Neales river, where now is the railway town of Oodnadatta. But his stock of horseshoes was fast running out, and again he turned back.

On his third journey he was unfortunate in his choice of companions, and made no progress beyond the Neales river: 1400 miles (2240 km) riding to little effect. He returned to find that the Government of South Australia had offered a reward of £2000 to the first man to cross the continent.

On his fourth journey Stuart blazed a trail into the heart of what is now Northern Territory. It had been a year of good rainfall, and the salty lagoons had become vast fresh-water lakes. A broad river he named the Finke, after one of his patrons, and Finke appears as a station on the present-day railway. A residual monolith 150 feet (45 m) high he named Chambers' Pillar after his other supporter: this landmark can be seen 80 miles (128 km) south of Alice Springs. Stuart came to the Macdonnell Ranges, naming them after the Governor of South Australia, and found a way through them. Beyond them he computed that he was in the very centre of the continent, and named a peak after his old leader, Sturt. An appreciative government later amended the name by adding a single letter, and so it remains, "Central Mount Stuart," 40 miles (64 km) south-west of Barrow Creek. Stuart discovered Tennant Creek, in the middle of the Territory, and noted signs of gold there. Tennant Creek is still the most constant producer of gold in the Territory. Forty miles north hostile aborigines barred his way; and here, at Attack Creek, for the fourth time Stuart turned back.

Three months later Stuart saddled his grey mare again—this time with a government grant of £2500. He crossed the Macdonnells once more, and came to a further line of springs. Rarely more than 40 miles (64 km) apart, they beckoned him onwards for 650 miles (1040 km). Newcastle Waters he named after the Colonial Secretary; then he turned west, hoping to reach the known country of the Victoria river. Here he was halted by the Murranji—a stifling, waterless scrub of thickets armed with murderous spikes. With his stores almost exhausted he was forced once more to return.

In December 1861 Stuart set out on his sixth journey. Beginning in the Flinders Ranges, the party rode for six months, passing waterholes and creeks, over salt-pans and stones, through canyons and swamps. By May they were once more at Newcastle Waters, and confronted by the dreaded Murranji. This time they forced their way due north, hacking a passage, mile after mile, slowly but surely. Weeks of toil brought them to a chain of pools, then to a lake full of fish, at Daly Waters. There followed a row of fine rivers, among them the King and the Waterhouse, named after members of the party. At last, on 24th July 1862, they reached the sea. Stuart had struck the coast about 40 miles (64 km) east of the spot where Darwin was later to be built; he named it Chambers Bay after the eldest daughter of one of his patrons.

The return journey of 2000 miles (3200 km) was an ordeal. The leader was smitten with scurvy and going blind. For three months he was carried in a stretcher slung between two horses. He died two years later, in England; but his mission was accomplished: he had demonstrated the existence of a practicable route from Adelaide to the northern sea—a route which offered drinking-water at suitable intervals for almost the whole of its course.

Stuart's explorations had two direct results: the first temporary, the second lasting. The Government of South Australia had given him official encouragement, and felt entitled to claim the new lands revealed by his journeys. Hitherto, though unexplored, they had theoretically formed part of New South Wales; but only seven months after the return of Stuart the Government at Westminster transferred the whole of the Northern Territory to South Australia, naming as its boundaries the 26th parallel and the 129th and 138th meridians. So, temporarily, South Australia more than doubled her area.

COMMUNICATION LINKS

THE OVERLAND TELEGRAPH

The permanent effect of Stuart's achievement was that it paved the way for the Overland Telegraph line. Stuart was confident that the construction of such a line was feasible, and Charles Todd, the Government Astronomer, heard this with interest; so that when in 1870 there was talk of a telegraph link between the United Kingdom and Australia, Todd offered to build an overland line from Darwin to Augusta.

In June 1870 Todd was appointed Postmaster-General and the work began. He planned the route from Stuart's maps, chose the sites of twelve repeating stations, ordered 2000 miles (3200 km) of wire and 36,000 telegraph poles. We cannot here recount the hardships endured by the working parties. It entailed the combined efforts of 500 men over more than two years; but at last, on the 23rd August 1872, the line was complete. At a stroke, Australian newspapers, instead of being three months behind with the news from England, became up to date.

The Overland Telegraph played an important part in the early days of the Northern Territory. By its side ran a rough track which for seventy years was the only north–south road across the continent. Strung along it at intervals of about 200 miles (320 km) were the repeating stations, which formed the only permanent habitations in the heart of Australia. For a generation they were the refuge of those lost in the Territory, providing rest, food, medicine, maps and news; and a traveller in distress would break the telegraph wire and wait for the repair party to rescue him. Sited near springs or creeks, a number of these stations have developed into settlements, among them: Alice Springs (named after Mrs Todd); Charlotte Waters, on the southern border of the Territory; Daly Waters, near the Murranji; Tennant Creek, in the centre; Barrow Creek, north of the Macdonnells; and Katherine River, in the north.

THE TRANSCONTINENTAL RAILWAY

As a logical successor of the Overland Telegraph the settlers of the Northern Territory were promised a Transcontinental Railway, following the same route. This dream has so far not been realised, for there are only two relatively short stretches of railway striking inwards from her northern shore and her southern border, separated by a gap of about 550 miles (880 km). The southern "feeler" from Oodnadatta to Alice Springs was completed in 1927, and a rectangular planned town was built a few miles south of the actual springs, on the "shores" of the Todd "river" (which only rarely contains water). Wells provide a good supply of water—for drinking, for stock, for the trees in the streets and for flourishing vegetable gardens.

The northern "feeler," reaching south from Darwin, was begun in 1886. Construction was very difficult, and it took four years to build the 150 miles (240 km) track to the gold mines of Pine Creek. By 1907 it was clear that South Australia had not the resources necessary to develop the Northern Territory, and four years later it passed formally under the administration of the Federal Government. Railway construction began again; and after three years another 60 miles (96 km) had been built, from Pine Creek to the Katherine river, ending in a fine bridge a quarter-mile long. By 1929 the railway had reached Birdum, about 50 miles (80 km) beyond Katherine, to end in a swamp. Birdum is now deserted, and trains do not run beyond Larrimah, a mile or two to the north.

This railway, on which the settlers have for so long pinned their hopes, is only a narrow (3-foot; 1-m) gauge single-track line. Both sections run at a loss, and there has been much discussion over the merits of the railway. Will the gap ever be closed? Will the existing lines remain open? Must a public service be self-supporting? Will the Northern Territory ever be developed without a transport network? A goods train can carry more cattle than a whole fleet of diesel lorries; and it may be that the railway is the only means of combating the recurrent droughts of the Territory, with their appalling loss of stock.

AIRCRAFT

Following the railway came the aeroplane. Ross-Smith pioneered the route to Australia in 1919, and by 1938 Darwin had become the air gateway to the continent, with 28 planes arriving each week. Darwin had

FIG. 115.—Northern Territory: the Stuart Highway. This road, constructed in 1943, is popularly known as "The Bitumen." It runs for almost a thousand miles (1600 km) to connect Darwin with Alice Springs and forms the sole overland traffic artery of the Northern Territory.

three airfields, large oil tanks, shops and offices, banks and hotels; and soon a regular air service was organised linking with all the State capitals.

Then in February 1942 Darwin was savagely bombed by 92 Japanese aircraft: the town was left ablaze and the harbour a port of wrecks. A Japanese invasion seemed imminent, and in reply the Federal Government built a modern motor road from Alice Springs to Darwin, with a link eastwards from a point near Tennant Creek to Cloncurry in Queensland. The north-to-south route forms the latest line of communication along the explorer's trail, and fittingly commemorates his deeds in its name, "Stuart Highway." Private cars and giant diesel lorries race along, stopping from time to time for petrol, stores and overnight accommodation. They accomplish in a few days what Stuart did in seven months. (*See* Fig. 115.)

THE TERRITORY'S DIFFICULTIES

The misfortune of the Northern Territory is that it lacks any region which is both well watered and temperate in climate. Queensland has its Darling Downs; Western Australia has its Swanland; but Northern Territory has no core of productive country which can act as the focus of white settlement.

Climatically the Territory resembles Queensland in that its rainfall is concentrated in the summer months, from December to March; it differs from that State in that the well-watered country, with permanent streams and a complete vegetation cover, is limited to a narrow strip following the coast.

The winds are true monsoons. In summer large tracts of the Great Sandy Desert, Gibson Desert and Simpson Desert experience temperatures of over 37·8° C (100° F) regularly each day; the heated air rises and is replaced from the Timor and Arafura Seas. The earth's rotation deflects the northerly stream of air to the left, and the summer monsoon is generally blowing from the north, west or north-west. In the southern half of the Territory the summer rain may fill the billabongs and cause temporary interruption to road traffic; but evaporation is intense and seepage rapid. In the north the rain falls in torrents, and large tracts become swamps.

In winter the thermometer drops regularly to below 1° C (35° F); a relatively high-pressure system develops and the air moves outwards in the form of the dry south-easterly or easterly monsoon. The existence of a definite dry season prevents the growth of true tropical forest; but the coasts are fringed with almost impenetrable mangroves, there are thickets of palms and a dense growth of tropical grasses which attain to a height of 6 or 7 feet (about 2 m). Eucalypts form a scattered woodland, particularly the stringybark: the bark of this tree peels off in sheets, and the aborigines use it to make simple huts, to construct canoes and for vessels to hold food and water. In favoured places the huge spreading banyan is to be seen: it can cover almost half an acre of land. The banyan is valued by the native, for birds and small game shelter there, and its aerial roots supply a useful brown fibre.

The rivers are rich in fish, but their lower reaches form the home of crocodiles, some of them man-eaters, 14–15 feet (up to 4·5 m) long. In the wet season the mosquito is a menace; systematic burning of the grass early in the dry season helps to keep the mosquito in check.

Equally vicious is the termite or white ant: it does not attack living creatures, but wreaks enormous damage to property. Within five years the white ant can reduce a house of timber to a mass of pulp. He eats his way through papers, books, furniture and trees, and has been known even to attack billiard balls, lead and sheet iron. As one travels northward on the Stuart Highway the anthills grow larger. They are about 2 feet (0·6 m) high near Tennant Creek, in the middle of the Territory, and stretch in their thousands to the horizon. At Katherine they are pinnacled and buttressed hills 8 feet (2·4 m) high; and at Pine Creek they are monstrous mounds 25 feet (7·5 m) in height. The mortar of which these hills are made is secreted from the body of the insect; and within these termite cities is an astonishing social organisation. One local timber is immune to the white ant: it is the cypress pine, which grows in belts along the coast. Its wood is tough, and it contains an unpalatable oil; and railway sleepers of cypress pine have resisted more than 50 years of damp and white ant.

The coastal belt of the Northern Territory is potentially extremely productive land. During the 1880s the botanist, Dr Maurice Holtz, cleared 30 acres (12 ha) of land near Darwin, poisoned the white ants with arsenic and grew choice bananas and pineapples; oranges, lemons, limes and peaches; maize, rice, millet and tobacco; coffee and cocoa; cotton and sugar cane—and many other crops. The climate and soil seem ideal: the difficulties are economic—there is no organised transport system and no nearby market.

In a few remote corners the pioneers are at work. On the Daly river, 100 miles (160 km) or so south-west of Darwin, a small farming community grows peanuts, tobacco, fruits and vegetables, and a large diesel lorry runs their nuts to Darwin, first along 60 miles (96 km) of rough track, and then along "The Bitumen." But for weeks at a time in the wet season the lonely road is impassable.

There is apparently excellent potential rice-growing land along the Daly, Darwin and Adelaide rivers, and on the left bank of the latter river a large-scale rice project was recently undertaken. Here, at Humpty Doo (the name is an Australian expression meaning "everything's fine") an organisation financed from the United States planted 2000 acres (800 ha) of rice, with the aid of aeroplanes. Unfortunately

[*Courtesy Australian News & Information Bureau.*

FIG. 116.—Northern Territory: Humpty Doo. This was an experimental area of rice cultivation, 60 miles (96 km) south of Darwin. A creek was dammed to provide irrigation water.

the venture proved a financial failure; the area under rice was reduced in 1962 to about 1000 acres (400 ha), and by 1968 had shrunk to only 40 acres (16 ha). Yet there appear to be no physical reasons why this region should not become a producer of high-quality rice, if only the problem of markets can be solved (Fig. 116).

The failure of rice projects in the past seems to have been due to underestimation of the hazards of floods, droughts and pests and diseases. Research is being carried out at the experimental station at Tortilla Flats, on the upper Adelaide river, into the prospects of rice growing in Northern Territory. It indicates that to be commercially viable, the yield would need to be between one and two tons per acre, and the costs less than about 100 dollars per ton. Applications of superphosphate can raise the yield per acre, and new varieties are becoming available from the International Rice Research Institute near Manila in the Philippines. These include the "miracle rice," which has yielded 4 tons (4064 kg) per acre. There will still remain, however, the problem of irrigation and the discovery of suitable markets.[1]

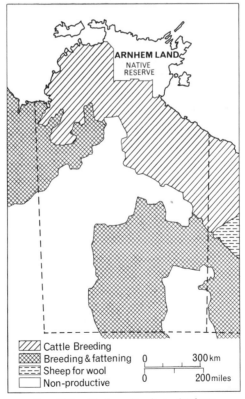

Fig. 117.—Northern Territory: land use.

South of the well-watered northern belt, with its permanent streams, lies a pastoral zone. It has been estimated that one-fifth of the Northern Territory (or about 100,000 square miles; 260,000 km²) consists of first-class pasture land, where vast grassy plains stretch to the horizon—plains of waving Flinders and Mitchell grasses, the best of the natural pastures (Fig. 117). The grazing lands extend north-west of Newcastle Waters and on into the Kimberleys of Western Australia; they lie to the south-east of Newcastle Waters in the Barkly Tableland, and they occupy considerable areas around Alice Springs. These are the domains of huge cattle stations, which we have already seen in the adjacent parts of Western Australia. The largest of them all (and probably the largest in the world) is Alexandra Station, which occupies 11,262 square miles (29,381 km²) and is almost as large as Belgium.

Northern Territory is essentially cattle land (Table 87 and Fig. 117).

TABLE 87
Northern Territory: number of stock, 1971

				Thousand head
Cattle	.	.	.	1145
Horses	.	.	.	41
Sheep	.	.	.	9
Pigs	.	.	.	3

Until recently the only way to bring the cattle to market was "on the hoof," along the drove roads.

"Every year between April and October, 70,000 to 90,000 head of cattle walk at least 800 miles into Queensland. There they are rested and pastured for a year or are trucked on the Queensland railway system."[2]

That was in 1948. Since that time droving has been virtually superseded by the road train, as we have seen in Queensland (p. 213).

Northern Territory has gained 900 miles (1440 km) of beef roads, which are tributary to the Stuart and Barkly Highways and the railway (*see* Fig. 81, p. 212). During the late 1950s and early 1960s a rapid increase took place in the use of road trains. In 1957 less than 4 per cent of the cattle of the Territory were moved by this method; but by 1962 the proportion had increased to 52 per cent.

The beef roads of Northern Territory are officially estimated to have raised the potential annual supply of cattle for the market from 166,000 to 378,000 head.[3]

We have already referred to the herds of wild buffalo in the better watered parts of Northern Territory (p. 54). They form an economic resource which in the past has been sadly misused and which is only now becoming properly appreciated.

From the early 1880s, when buffalo hunting was first recorded, till as late as the 1950s, the animal was valued only for its hide. The extent of the slaughter was related to the level of the price of buffalo hide. At its peak just before the First World War between 5000 and 8000 buffalo were being shot annually; and during the 1920s the rate of shooting rose again to reach a record of 16,549 in the season of 1937–38. During the late 1940s and early 1950s the price of buffalo hide was again high, and 12,000 animals were killed annually.

The economical utilisation of the buffalo has been hampered by the lack of knowledge of its numbers. In 1957 the Administration estimated that there were 500,000 in Northern Territory; yet the following year it doubted whether there were more than 100,000. Recent official estimates range between 150,000 and 200,000.

About 1958, when the price of hide was low, an important change of attitude became apparent, and for the first time the use of the meat was considered. A small number of buffalo, about 100 annually, were captured and shipped alive, mainly to Hong Kong. Other animals (about 500 annually) were killed and converted into pet food. At the same time came the first experiment in domestication, in which the Administration demonstrated that wild buffalo were easily tamed.

At last came the beginnings of the use of buffalo meat for human food within Australia. After a conference in 1960, abattoirs were licensed, the meat inspected and air transport organised. The number of buffalo killed for meat grew to over 17,000 annually. Nearly half the total was used in the form of sausages, other manufactured meat or buffalo beef; the rest was used for pet food.[4]

It seems clear that with careful management the buffalo could become a most valuable asset to the economy of Northern Territory. It is a good-tempered beast, easly handled; it produces almost twice as much meat as a cow and buffalo milk contains twice as much butter-fat as cow's milk. The buffalo will thrive on pasture where domestic cattle would be half starved; and its rate of breeding is higher and more certain.

In 1970 the first Buffalo Owners' Conference took place and the way appears open for further progress. This is likely to be slow rather than spectacular. The cattle stations are very large, and include many wild buffalo. Mudginberri, about 140 miles (224 km) east of Darwin, is a comparatively small station of 427 square miles (1110 km²), but is estimated to enclose 10,000 head of buffalo. Stapleton, 50 miles (80 km) south of Darwin, covers 770 square miles (1916 km²); Mountain Valley, 240 miles (384 km) south-east of Darwin has an area of 1000 square miles (2600 km²), while Mount Bundey, 60 miles (96 km) south-east of Darwin, covers 1200 square miles (3120 km²).

These stations include terrains of differing character and quality. On the higher land the pastures are capable of improvement, and these are the traditional cattle lands, grazed by Brahmin-cross animals. The wet flood plains nourish herds of buffalo in their natural state, and the conditions are ripe for the management of two parallel herds. This is the long-term plan for the American-owned Mount Bundey station, which aims to build up over fifteen years a herd of 60,000 Brahmin-cross cattle and one of 15,000 tame buffalo, with the aim of supplying markets in Europe. "It's good meat, leaner than steer beef, just as tasty and cheaper." [5]

What of the remainder of the Northern Territory? Another fifth may be classed as second-quality grassland—pasture which if well managed could support a stock-rearing industry. The rest is land which cannot obviously be made productive: it is rocky or swampy or deficient in water or true desert. Yet even here there are possibilities of mineral industries, for large tracts of the county have yet to be geologically surveyed.

MINERAL RESOURCES

Even now the Territory must be accounted rich in minerals, though the output is not to be compared in quantity with that of her neighbours. Gold has been produced since 1869, the chief centre being Tennant Creek, on the Stuart Highway. The same district produces copper too, and this for the first time in 1955 surpassed gold in the value of the output. High-grade mica—the only source of this mineral in the continent—is mined at Harts Range, about 60 miles (96 km) north-east of Alice Springs. Then in 1949 Jack White, a veteran prospector, recognised the ore of uranium in the old tin and copper workings at Rum Jungle, about 70 miles (112 km) from Darwin (the "Jungle" in fact is a monotonous, open scrub of eucalypts; and the origin of the name is uncertain).

Other important uranium strikes were made during the 1950s—in two localities near the Ferguson river—and the large deposits at Rum Jungle were confirmed as the most valuable in Australia, and among the greatest in the world (and the most accessible). In 1954 the first uranium treatment plant to be built in Australia was opened at Rum Jungle.

By 1962 the world production of uranium was in excess of the demand; mining ceased, but the production of uranium oxide from stock-piled ore continued until 1971. In 1970 and 1971 new discoveries of uranium were made in the area of the East Alligator river, about 150 miles (240 km) east of Darwin. They are considered to be of potentially world importance, and have been described as "breathtakingly rich."

The uranium discoveries are sufficiently important in themselves; but they have acted too as a stimulus to the mining industry in general. Gas has been found in commercial quantities near Lake Amadeus in the south-west corner of the Territory, and at two localities near Alice Springs. The deposits are estimated to contain 1,500,000 million cu. ft (42,500 million m^3).

Recently, two iron deposits have been opened up in the neighbourhood of Darwin. Production began at Frances Creek in 1967 and at Mount Bundey in the following year. The former is situated about 20 miles (32 km) north of Pine Creek and is linked to the railway by its own short spur; it is yielding 800,000 tons of ore annually. Mount Bundey lies south of Humpty Doo and produced 250,000 tons of ore annually until its closure in 1971. The surge in traffic has been met by renovation of the railway track and the introduction of new rolling stock. In common with developments elsewhere, the ore is being shipped to Japan.

On Groote Eylandt, off the western shore of the Gulf of Carpentaria, scrapers, bulldozers, power shovels and crushers are at work in connection with a large open-cast manganese mine. It already supplies all the national requirements of this mineral, essential in steel-making, and large quantities are exported to Japan, Europe and the United States. The annual target of 400,000 tons was soon surpassed; shipments during 1970–71 reached 737,000 tons and the output is being expanded to 1·6 million tons a year.

Currently, however, the most spectacular development in the Territory is the bauxite project of the Gove peninsula, in the northeastern tip of Arnhem Land. Here a 250 million ton deposit of highgrade bauxite has been proved, averaging 45 to 50 per cent alumina. The mineral layer is between 12 and 20 feet (3·6 and 6 m) thick, with an overburden of only 2 or 3 feet (0·6 to 0·9 m). Instead of a railway to link the mine with the dock, the company has constructed a conveyor belt system 12 miles (19 km) in length, and one of the longest in the world.

Exports of bauxite to Japan began in 1971. But it is a significant economy to convert bauxite to alumina, which is eight times as valuable; and a treatment plant was speedily constructed, with a capacity of a million tons annually. To service the project a completely new town has been built, with a hospital, school, hotel, shops, bungalows and flats. By the end of 1971 Nhulunbuy had reached a population of 3000 and had become the third town of Northern Territory, after Darwin and Alice Springs. Involving a total investment of $A375 million, this is one of the largest private business projects in Australia.[6]

DARWIN

Darwin is the smallest, the most tropical and the least developed of all the capitals in Australia. Its harbour was the chance discovery of Lieutenant J. L. Stokes when in September 1839 he was out in a boat from H.M.S. *Beagle*. His men surveyed the harbour; they climbed the cliffs and named a white headland Talc Head after the mineral exposed there. The new harbour Stokes named after his old friend and shipmate, Charles Darwin.

For a generation the harbour lay forgotten. Then, in 1869 a party landed in the mangrove-fringed bay, under the command of G. W. Goyder—the same Surveyor-General who had successfully delimited the crop region of South Australia. Their purpose was to choose and plan a capital for the Territory, lately incorporated in South Australia.

Overlooking the harbour was a diamond-shaped plateau with cliff-like edges, and here Goyder marked out the wide, straight streets, gardens and squares of his new town. The next year two shiploads of settlers arrived to begin their struggle with the forces of nature: with the scorching heat of September and October, the enervating, humid atmosphere of November and the torrential rains of December, January and February. But the Overland Telegraph was creeping inland, and Darwin knew it was not forgotten.

Darwin is still little more than an outpost of civilisation amid a tropical wilderness. It has no industries and practically no trade. In 1914, during a period of optimism, a £1,000,000 meat works was built by the beef concern of Vestey: it was intended to serve a vast area of 40,000 square miles (103,600 km²) stretching westwards to the Fitzroy river, in the Kimberleys. The plant worked at high speed during the First World War to provide food for the Allied services; but it was a premature venture: the works closed down in 1919, and by 1930 had become an empty shell. Darwin remains today a centre of administration (with a fine modern hospital) and a terminus of communications—by road, rail, sea, air and overland telegraph.

The population of Darwin is still small, but the town is growing steadily. From 1500 in 1933 it reached 2500 in 1947, and in 1971 totalled 35,281 people (including suburbs). The prospects of Darwin are closely interwoven with those of the Territory in general.

On Christmas Day 1974 the city was shattered by a cyclone whose winds reached 160 m.p.h. (256 km/h). At least 47 people were killed, 300 were injured and 10,000 homes were destroyed. In a massive airlift during the next four days half of Darwin's population was evacuated to southern cities. Yet no place on the monsoon coast of Australia is safe from cyclones: Darwin will be rebuilt on the same site, though the former timber-framed houses will be replaced by more substantial structures which can better withstand the ravages of cyclones.

THE FUTURE

It is clear that agriculture plays only a small part in the economy of Northern Territory. Cattle rearing is growing in importance as a result of the construction of "beef roads" and there is the beginning of a rational use of the buffalo. Tourism too is increasing, currently at the rate of about 12 per cent annually, and the 80,000 visitors of 1969–70 represented an industry estimated to be worth over 20 million dollars annually.

But the immediate future lies undoubtedly in the exploitation of minerals, which has shown a surprisingly rapid growth in recent years (Table 88).

TABLE 88

Northern Territory: growth in the value of mineral
production, excluding uranium

	Value of output at mine
Year	million dollars
1965 . . .	8·3
1966 . . .	13·3
1967 . . .	19·3
1968 . . .	23·4

The expansion that has taken place in the economy during only four years is well illustrated in Table 89, which indicates the changes that have taken place in the export trade during the period. Exports will be swollen further when the bauxite output is recorded in the statistics.

TABLE 89

Northern Territory: principal overseas exports, in $A thousand

	1965–66	1969–70
Iron ore and concentrates	—	9,124
Non-ferrous ores and concentrates . . .	173	9,091
Meats	3,348	4,807
Raw hides and skins	61	269
Copper ores and concentrates	2,044	116
Total exports	6,398	49,725

NOTES

1. D. S. Hamilton and M. T. Daly, "Recent developments in rice production in the Northern Territory," *Australian Geographer*, Vol. XI, No. 3 (1970).

2. Hon. C. L. A. Abbott, *Geographical Journal*, Vol. CXI, Nos. 1–3 (July 1948).

3. C. Duncan, "Beef roads of Northern Australia," *Australian Geographer*, Vol. IX, No. 4 (1964).

4. T. L. McNight, "Australia's Buffalo Dilemma," *Annals of the Assoc. of American Geographers*, Vol. 61 (1971).

5. K. Macleish and T. Nebbia, "The Top End of Down Under," *National Geographic Magazine*, February 1973.

6. *The Times*, 10th March 1971.

STUDY QUESTIONS

1. Draw a map to illustrate the journeys of J. M. Stuart.

2. Discuss the case for and against the completion of the north-to-south transcontinental railway.

3. Describe some of the problems which face the prospective settler in Northern Territory.

4. Do you expect to see any significant increase in the development of Northern Territory during the next twenty years?

Chapter XII

SHEEP, CATTLE AND WHEAT

SHEEP AND WOOL PRODUCTION

In this chapter we examine some of the major products of the Australian farmers. Outstanding among these is wool. The production of wool is the leading industry of Australia, and in the output of this commodity Australia leads the world, producing nearly one-third of the entire product (Table 90). In 1970 there were over 180 million sheep in Australia, representing 14 animals for every man, woman and child in the country. Of these, about 114 million were merinos, and only 39 million were of other recognised breeds.

TABLE 90

The World: number of sheep and production of wool, 1970–71

	Number of sheep (millions)	Wool production in terms of greasy wool (million lb)
U.S.S.R., China and Eastern Europe . .	243	1288
Australia	178	1952
New Zealand	59	736
Argentina	43	427
South Africa	30	257
United States	20	187
World	942	6022

By its nature the sheep is unsuited to tropical heat. In the north-west of Queensland sheep do not thrive; conversely, the cold, windy and rainy weather of the southern parts of the continent causes the death of many lambs and newly shorn sheep. Accordingly, there are practically no sheep in Northern Territory, and relatively few in Tasmania, while New South Wales and Victoria contain more than half the sheep in Australia (Table 91).

Within these temperature limits the distribution of sheep in a general way reflects the mean annual rainfall: most sheep are to be found where the rainfall is greater than 15 inches (375 mm) per annum, and there are very few where it drops below 10 inches (250 mm). Artesian wells reduce the dependence of the flocks on rainfall; but they are expensive: a 2000-foot bore costs about £1500—and many of them are much

TABLE 91

Australia: number of sheep, 1971

				Thousand head
New South Wales	.	.	.	70,605
Western Australia	.	.	.	34,709
Victoria	.	.	.	33,761
South Australia	.	.	.	19,166
Queensland	.	.	.	14,774
Tasmania	.	.	.	4,517
Australia	.	.	.	177,792

deeper. Nevertheless, over wide areas wells have doubled the stock-raising capacity of the land.

THE MERINO SHEEP

The success of the wool industry is based on the spread of the merino breed, which is particularly suited to warm, dry countries. Merino wool is of high quality: it is denser and more serrated than that from English breeds. The merino sheep is docile and hardy, and in particular can withstand drought conditions; it bears more wool in proportion to its size than any other breed of sheep; and it is found throughout the regions suitable for sheep, excepting only the well-watered coastal districts, where the main object is the production of fat lambs.

In the early days of the Australian colonies merino sheep were the monopoly of Spain, and only rarely did a Spanish monarch allow a few out of the country as a gift to a foreign favourite. By a fortunate chance, in 1796, when two ships from New South Wales were buying supplies at Cape Town, a small flock of merinos was available there for sale. The two naval officers, Captains Kent and Waterhouse, wisely purchased the entire flock of 26 merinos, and returning to Australia, distributed them to several landholders.

Captain John Macarthur, who already farmed 400–500 acres (162–202 ha) and possessed a flock of a thousand sheep, bought three of these merino rams and five ewes. In 1804 he was able to buy eight more merinos from King George's flock at Kew—almost the only merino flock in England. Macarthur kept some of his merinos apart and gradually built up a pure flock, whose wool fetched extremely high prices in England.

So, almost single-handed, Macarthur laid the foundation of the Australian wool industry. In 1807 he possessed 5400 sheep—one-fifth of all the sheep in New South Wales; but, naturally, only a few of these were merinos. In that year Australia exported 245 pounds (125 kg) of wool. By the early 1820s Macarthur's flocks contained more than 2000 pure merinos. He died in 1834; and in the following year the Australian wool clip amounted to 3,776,000 pounds (2,614,304 kg)—an eloquent testimony to his work.

By this time other breeders were at work, developing different strains of merino for special purposes. In the areas of good rainfall of Tasmania and Victoria they aimed at an increased weight of fleece; in the drier regions of South Australia and western New South Wales they produced a sheep whose wool was slightly longer and of lower quality, while the animal itself had longer legs and a larger frame, and was more resistant to drought. For the moderate-rainfall areas of northern Victoria and the western slopes in New South Wales the breeders reared an animal of intermediate type. About 1890 a variety of merino imported from the United States came into favour: the Vermont. Its heavy fleece hung from its body in great loose folds, but the extra weight consisted mainly of grease, and the Vermont was difficult to shear, so that the breed did not gain a permanent place in Australia.

As a result of the work of the breeders, an amazing improvement took place in the fleece. In Macarthur's flock of 1820 the average fleece weighed less than $2\frac{1}{2}$ pounds (1 kg), while his best merino rams yielded about 5 pounds (2 kg). By 1900 the average Australian fleece turned the scale at about 7 pounds (3 kg); today the average is more than 9 pounds (4 kg) (against a world average of $5\frac{1}{2}$ pounds ($2\frac{1}{2}$ kg)), and individual rams carry fleeces of up to 40 pounds (18 kg).

Mechanical shearing dates from 1885, when F. Y. Wolseley first demonstrated his machine in public. Hand shearing was found to be a little faster; but an immediate stir was caused when it was discovered that the machine cropped the animal more closely—to the extent of $\frac{3}{4}$ pound (340 g) per animal. The first large flock, consisting of 184,000 sheep at a station west of Bourke, was mechanically sheared in 1888; and by the end of the century machine shearing had become accepted as the general rule.

In contrast to the English breeds, the merino has no clearly defined mating season. The pioneers found that the autumn pastures of Australia were particularly nourishing, and so arranged for lambing to take place in March or April. They divided their sheep into flocks of about 300 or 400 and placed each in the charge of a shepherd by day, penning them at night under the care of a watchman. Until the 1850s the land was open and the shepherd guided his flock to the best pastures. But when gold was discovered at Bathurst, Ballarat and Bendigo, shepherds became scarce. To economise in labour the sheep farmers fenced their holdings and left the animals there all day and all night; and to their surprise the animals produced better wool when left alone. So arose the modern system of large fenced paddocks, ranging in size from tens to thousands of acres.

SHEEP SHEARING

The pioneers sheared their sheep about seven months after lambing time—that is, in November; today conditions are so varied throughout the sheep lands that shearing is in progress somewhere in Australia at any season. Queensland sheep are shorn in January; those of Western and South Australia in February; in March the shearers are in northern New South Wales, in June, the Riverina. In Victoria and Tasmania shearing takes place in September.

When shearing time approaches the flock is mustered and driven along the country roads at the rate of six to ten miles (9–16 km) a day. The one or two horsemen are aided by three able and faithful kelpies— sheepdogs of distinctive Australian strain, which appear to have evolved through crossing the Scottish collie with the dingo.

At the station sufficient ewes and lambs for one day's shearing are collected overnight and penned behind the shearing shed. Each pair of shearers is served by a catching pen, and it is the kelpie's task to maintain the flow of sheep in these pens. The station manager plans carefully to keep the sheep continually on the move: otherwise the paddocks near the shed will soon be eaten bare.

No one State can supply more than one-third of the shearers needed for its own flocks, and specialised parties of shearers travel about from station to station and from State to State. Two shearers using a semi-portable plant may be sufficient for the flock of a small holding, while a large sheep station may need the services of 48 shearers simultaneously. An average shearer handles about 100 sheep a day. A world record was set up in 1950 at Cloncurry by W. E. Rieck, who sheared 326 sheep in 7 hours, 49 minutes—a sheep every $1\frac{1}{2}$ minutes. Such feats, however, are fairly frequently surpassed and in 1964 the world record was held by a New Zealander who machine-sheared 565 ewes in 8 hours and 53 minutes.

Virtually all sheep are now sheared by machine. The principle is simple: motion is transmitted to each shearer from an overhead shaft through a set of jointed tubes to the handpiece, which is like a large version of a barber's clipper. The shearer dexterously removes the whole fleece in a single piece; a shed hand picks it up and throws it on to a slatted table, where it is skirted and inferior or stained portions are removed. It next passes to the classer, who examines it for fineness, length of staple and amount of grease, and grades it. The fleeces are then pressed and baled in jute packs and sent, first by lorry and then by rail, to the selling centre. Meanwhile the shorn animals have been branded and are now on their way back to the pastures.

WOOL PRODUCTION AND EXPORTS

Each year more than half a million tons of wool are produced in Australia, and 90 per cent of it is sold before being shipped. Wool, in contrast to most other raw materials, cannot be classified into a few distinct grades: more than 1500 types and sub-types have been recognised. Consequently it must be sold by sample, and wool auctions are held at fourteen centres in Australia. In New South Wales the wool markets are at Sydney, Goulburn, Newcastle and Albury; in Victoria they are at Melbourne, Geelong, Ballarat and Portland; in Queensland the market is at Brisbane and in South Australia at Adelaide. Western Australia has markets at Fremantle and Albany, and Tasmania at Hobart and Launceston.

Here the overseas buyers assemble and examine samples of the wool carefully to judge its fitness for their requirements. In recent years Japan has become the leading buyer, and in 1969–70 took well over one-third of the total output. The United Kingdom, Italy and France each bought about 9 per cent of the total, and there followed West Germany, Belgium and the U.S.S.R., in that order.

THE BEEF-CATTLE INDUSTRY

The beef-cattle industry of Australia has at least three distinctive features: its great distance from the European markets, the tropical climate in which it operates, and the sparse population of its producing regions.

Distance from the European market has meant that until recent times Australian beef carcasses had to be frozen, while those from Argentina might be merely chilled, and would consequently retain a better flavour. During the early 1930s, however, the University of Cambridge devised a method of chilling rather than freezing which would enable the carcasses to withstand the journey half-way round the world. The new process has benefited chiefly the producers of the highest-quality meat, for it is this which depends so much on its prime condition for a ready sale. Beef of the finest quality is produced on the pastures of Tasmania, Victoria, New South Wales and south-eastern Queensland, where the temperatures are equable and the rainfall reliable: here are the stud farms and the tender, young animals. Five-sixths of the beef cattle of Australia in fact are pastured in the temperate regions; nevertheless, the largest portion of the beef-cattle region (by area) lies north of the tropic.

This is the world's only major tropical beef-exporting region. English breeds are unsuited to tropical climates, but in 1933 English Shorthorns and Herefords were mated with Zebu cattle. To those familiar with English breeds the Zebu, a native of India, is an ugly beast (it has a hump on its shoulder and loose folds of skin on its neck); but it can withstand tropical heat and is not affected by insect pests. The crossbred animals are found to combine the most useful qualities of both breeds.

The tropical cattle lands are sparsely peopled, ill-served by modern means of transport, and subject to periods of drought. There is a large surplus of beef for export, but long overland journeys are usually necessary, the animals deteriorate on the way, and must be rested and fattened for a year in the better pastures.

THE EVOLUTION OF THE BEEF INDUSTRY

It was in these immense regions that the drover lived his hard and wandering life (*see* Fig. 118). Droving began after the rainy season: the

[Courtesy Australian News & Information Bureau.

FIG. 118.—Cattle droving in western Queensland. A mob of cattle is crossing the Cooper river near Windorah. It is 100 miles (161 km) to the nearest railway.

pastures were reviving and the water-courses shrinking, so that long-distance movement was less likely to be hampered by floods. During April the stockmen were busy mustering the cattle and branding them. At the appointed day the head stockman handed over the "mob" to the head drover. The head drover was a man of experience: he knew the waterholes, the camping sites and the pastures over thousands of square miles; he could manage cattle, horses and men—both black and white. He was responsible for delivering every beast to the railway yard perhaps a thousand miles away.

The head drover brought with him six or eight men (often aborigines, but always with a white cook) and up to 80 horses. Dogs were not used in cattle droving: they would be difficult to feed and could not resist the drought. A dozen of the horses were specially selected for night-riding; a score or more were pack animals, and the rest were day-riding horses or spares. So the mob of about 1250 plodded along the stock route, moving from water-hole to water-hole, fording or swimming the creeks, not less than the regulation ten miles an hour (16 km/hr) through the pastoral properties, fast indeed through a belt of poisonous red-flowered *gastrolobium*, fast too where there was a long gap between water-holes: then the cattle might be driven both day and night.

Normally the cattle were rested at night, under the care of a watchman. But stockmen slept lightly and were always ready for action. A sudden clap of thunder or any unusual noise might cause the cattle to stampede, and undo weeks of work. To soothe them the night watcher sang to them or lulled them with poetry.

From the open ranges to the coastal towns the cattle moved, generally along one of the three great stock routes: the Georgina in the east, the Great North Road in the centre, the Canning in the west (Fig. 119).

Most cattle moved by the Georgina. It drew beasts from the whole breadth of the Northern Territory, and many mobs had already travelled a thousand miles (1609 km) before joining the Georgina

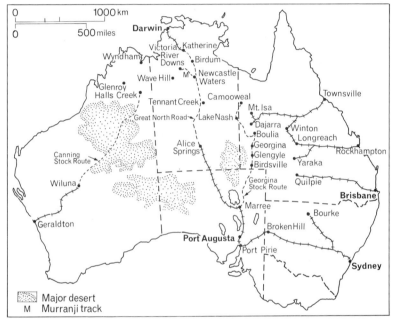

FIG. 119.—The chief stock routes, with their railway links.

proper at Camooweal, on the Queensland–Northern Territory border. From here they followed the creeks southwards, past Lake Nash, Boulia, Bedourie and Glengyle to Birdsville. At various points drovers would strike eastwards for the railheads at Dajarra or Quilpie or Bourke; others continued south to reach the railway at Marree.

The Great North Road was the shortest, the safest and the most straightforward. Essentially the route discovered by Stuart, it was improved by Government bores every 30 miles (48 km) or so. The mobs took three months to travel the thousand miles (1600 km) from Katherine to the railhead at Alice Springs, but only three days to move the next thousand miles from Alice Springs to Adelaide.

The Great North Road was fed from the west by the Murranji track, which joined it at Newcastle Waters. We have already seen (p. 302) how Stuart was forced to retreat from the spiky thickets of this area. In the early days, in 140 miles (224 km) there were only three waterholes, and in time of drought even these were dry. But the track provided a short cut, avoiding a thousand-mile journey to the north by way of Katherine. The first mob passed through in 1904. Later the Murranji was well supplied with Government boreholes, and a 70-yard (64-m) wide belt opened up through the thorny scrub. Today it is superseded by a "beef road".

The newest, the longest and the most remote of the stock routes is the Canning, named after A. W. Canning, the Government Surveyor of Western Australia. From Halls Creek near the north-eastern corner of Western Australia it stretches across the Great Sandy Desert to the nearest railhead, at Wiluna, from which there are connections to Geraldton and Perth.

Canning made a reconnaissance survey of the route in 1906. His map showed an immense blank. There were no known sources of water; but aboriginal tribesmen showed him their primitive wells, and by digging deeper he was able to demonstrate the existence of water every 20 miles (32 km) or so. So he went on, with camels for transport, noting that there was fodder for cattle; and after a journey of nearly a thousand miles (1609 km) he arrived at Wiluna.

Two years later Canning set out again, with a caravan of 62 camels: his object was to provide the new route with sufficient water. With 26

[*Courtesy Australian News & Information Bureau.*

FIG. 120.—The homestead buildings of Victoria River Downs, in the Northern Territory. Before recent subdivisions, this was the headquarters of the world's largest cattle holding, where 15,000 head grazed over 12,000 square miles (31,000 km^2).

men he dug 50 wells, at an average distance of 16 miles (26 km) apart. They lined each one with timber and provided it with buckets and cattle troughs. Two years more and the task was complete, and the stock route declared open. In 1930, when gold mining began at Wiluna, the Canning stock route proved invaluable as a means of supplying the camps with meat.

From Alexandra River Downs (11,000 square miles; 28,600 km²) in the Barkly Tableland, from Victoria River Downs (now reduced to 5500 square miles (14,300 km²)—*see* Fig. 120), and from dozens of other great cattle stations in the north, each of more than 5000 square miles (12,500 km²), came the mobs of cattle on their great annual trek to the ports. Each year 90,000–100,000 cattle were involved, divided into 70 or 80 mobs.

All this is changing fast. The construction of the Stuart Highway has rendered the Great North Road obsolete, and many of the other routes have been superseded by beef roads (*see* Fig. 81, p. 212). The Canning stock route, however, remains in use, and shorter droves are still needed to feed the new roads.

TABLE 92
Australia: Production of beef and veal, 1970–71

				Tons
Victoria	.	.	.	302,663
Queensland	.	.	.	297,412
New South Wales	.	.	.	277,910
Western Australia	.	.	.	63,318
South Australia	.	.	.	42,807
Tasmania	.	.	.	29,407
Northern Territory	.	.	.	14,092
Capital Territory	.	.	.	3,129
Australia	.	.	.	1,030,738

In 1970–71 there was a record production of beef and veal, amounting to more than a million tons (Table 92). A little less than half of this was used in the home market; but 491,000 tons were exported direct, and 44,000 tons were canned. The United States has become the greatest purchaser of exported Australian beef, and in 1970–71 took nearly three-quarters of it; there followed the United Kingdom and Canada.

DAIRY PRODUCTS

Dairy farming is the youngest of the four primary rural industries of Australia, and it is perhaps not yet fully established. A remarkable expansion in dairy farming has taken place since the beginning of the twentieth century: the number of dairy cattle has almost trebled, the production of butter almost quadrupled and the output of cheese multiplied by nearly nine. The average milk yield increased from 483 to

583 gallons (2196–2650 l) a year between 1965 and 1970, but is still low by world standards (a good English Friesian yields about 1000 gallons; 4546 l). More systematic fodder conservation and greater improvement of pasture appear to be necessary before the maximum efficiency of the industry is reached.

Dairy farming is more restricted in extent than beef production in Australia, since its requirements are more stringent. The pasture must be of much higher quality; since cattle must be milked twice a day, there must be a good labour supply; and since milk will not keep for long, there must be easy transport to a nearby population or, failing this, to a creamery. These conditions are satisfied chiefly in favoured coastal stretches of Victoria, New South Wales and south-eastern Queensland.

In 1969–70 there were over 4 million dairy cattle in Australia, almost a record number. They produced 1,661 million gallons (7551 million l) of milk, and of this the greater part (over 60 per cent) was converted into butter. About 20 per cent was drunk at home as fresh milk, nearly 10 per cent was made into cheese and 6 per cent was condensed or concentrated. In that year the United Kingdom received 85 per cent of the Australian exports of butter and 27 per cent of the exports of cheese.

WHEAT PRODUCTION

In 1969–70 Australia ranked third among the wheat exporting countries of the world, after the United States and Canada. She exported more than half her total crop, and this represented about 15 per cent of the wheat entering international trade. It is insufficient to affect greatly world wheat prices in general; but Australia is the major producer of soft white wheat, and prices in this section of the wheat market may reflect conditions in Australia.

Whether measured by area or by value, wheat is the one dominant crop of Australia. Its nearest competitor by value is orchard fruit; but the value of all the orchard fruits combined amounts to less than half that of wheat. In area the land sown to wheat amounts to 45 per cent of all the land under crops; and in two States (New South Wales and Western Australia) wheat occupies more than half the total crop land.

Wheat in Australia is grown on mixed farms in combination with wool production, and sometimes together with barley and oats, sorghum and linseed; consequently if wheat prices fall the farmer tends to reduce his wheat acreage and to pay more attention to other farm products. This happened in the late 1940s and early 1950s, when the area under wheat declined by nearly 30 per cent between 1947 and 1952. The remarkable thing is that the reduced acreage was offset by an increase in yields from 12 bushels an acre up to 17 bushels. Part of the improvement was due to exceptionally good weather; but good farming too is playing its part: the farmers are using improved rust-resistant strains of seed, they are making an increased use of machinery and are building up the fertility of the soil through better crop rotations.

All the mainland States have important shares in the wheat industry. Tasmania is too cold and damp to grow wheat on a large scale: this is the only State where the acreage of oats exceeds that of wheat. Tasmanian wheat is in fact found to be more suitable for biscuit-making rather than for bread: most of it is accordingly shipped to the mainland, and Tasmania "imports" wheat for her own needs.

The leading wheat-producing States are New South Wales and Western Australia, which together account for well over half the total crop. Queensland is a relatively small producer, but is generally self-sufficient in flour; otherwise, the mainland States produce far more than they need for bread-making, and ship large quantities overseas (Table 93).

TABLE 93
Australia: production of wheat

	Thousand acres		Thousand bushels	
	1969–70	*1970–71*	*1969–70*	*1970–71*
New South Wales . .	8,623	5,475	162,786	110,604
Western Australia . .	6,788	5,835	66,700	108,650
Victoria . . .	3,298	1,879	83,544	36,901
South Australia . .	3,210	1,983	59,159	29,028
Queensland . . .	1,504	825	14,898	4,401
Tasmania . . .	15	11	353	283
Capital Territory . .	3	1	73	28
Australia . . .	23,441	16,009	387,512	289,895

HISTORICAL DEVELOPMENT

In the colonial period there were frequent references to drought, flood and plant disease, suggesting that wheat was grown in spite of adverse conditions rather than because of a favourable climate and soils. Much of the credit for the later expansion of wheat growing is due to the local inventors and the plant breeders.

By the 1840s the chief need was to speed the harvest, for the crop ripened rapidly in the warm Australian summer. In contrast to the United Kingdom, there was no need to dry out the crop by standing it in stooks; and the straw was so much waste, for where the animals remained in the fields all the time there was no need for bedding. What was needed was a special form of harvester—a stripper, which would remove only the ears of corn and leave the straw standing.

A stripper was first successfully demonstrated in 1843, by John Ridley, a miller of South Australia, who seems to have been working on lines similar to those of J. W. Bull. Ridley's stripper included a comb to hold the ears of corn in place, while revolving beaters geared to the wheels removed the ripe heads. These fell into a box; they had then to be winnowed, sieved and bagged. The machine was pushed by two horses and operated by five (later four) men: it replaced the slow and tedious scythe or sickle and enormously speeded up the harvest.

The stripper remained the standard harvesting equipment until the 1890s, when it was replaced by H. V. McKay's combined harvester: this not only stripped but also threshed, winnowed, sieved and bagged the crop, reducing the number of men required from four to two.

Ploughing had its special problems, particularly in mallee country, where it was extremely difficult to rid the land completely of the stumps and roots of trees. Obstructions such as these would have soon ruined the normal type of plough; but two other South Australian inventors, the brothers R. B. and C. H. Smith, collaborated to produce the stump-jump plough, which was first used in 1876. This is a multiple-furrow plough, whose shares are so arranged that any one of them, as soon as it meets an obstruction, automatically rises and clears it, to re-enter the ground when it has passed. Large tracts of the wheat belt in South Australia, Victoria and Western Australia were thus quickly made ready for cultivation.

But mechanical aids are of little use without suitable varieties of seed, and this was the weakness of Australian wheat farming throughout the nineteenth century. The wheats in use had too long a growing season: before they could reach maturity they were dried up by the hot winds of summer; and many types were liable to rust.

In 1889 William Farrer, a surveyor, began growing different strains of wheat at his home in what is now Australian Capital Territory, combining cross-breeding with selection. Nine years later he was appointed official experimentalist to the newly formed New South Wales Department of Agriculture. Farrer produced many varieties for the wheat growers: high-yielding wheats, quick maturers and drought-resistant and rust-resistant strains. He is perhaps chiefly known for the variety Federation, which was released in 1901: it was the result of a cross between a high-yielding local wheat with one whose parents were a Canadian variety, on the one hand, and an Indian, on the other. Federation was a dark-brown grain, resistant to drought, easy to harvest and easy to bag, and it held the stage for a generation before even better varieties replaced it. Farrer was the first breeder of wheat in Australia, and most of the strains still in use are descendants of Farrer varieties.

CLIMATIC CONTROLS

In Australia, as in the United Kingdom, wheat is growing throughout the winter. But since the temperatures are higher than those in the United Kingdom, the harvest is correspondingly early. In Australia the farmer sows the seeds in May or June (corresponding to November or December) and he harvests in December (corresponding to the United Kingdom June). Where the rainfall is marginal the farmer leaves his land fallow one year in every three and knows that in this way the ground will store several inches of rain so that the following crop will germinate independently of the rainfall.

The wheat belt is limited broadly by the temperature and rainfall conditions which apply during its seven or eight months' growing period. Where the average temperature for these months is higher than 18° C (65° F), wheat is unimportant. This isotherm passes roughly parallel to and just south of the Tropic of Capricorn, so that about half the continent is unsuitable for wheat-growing on temperature grounds alone. Within this area, wheat is not grown widely where the rainfall during the growing period is more than 20 inches (500 mm) or less than 10 inches (250 mm). In New South Wales and Victoria the upper rainfall limit runs parallel with the coast but 80–100 miles (130–60 km) inland; no part of South Australia has too heavy a rainfall (excepting perhaps Kangaroo Island); but in Western Australia a coastal crescent extending from beyond Perth to beyond Albany is excluded on account of its heavy rainfall—this is the forest region of Western Australia (p. 267). The lower rainfall limit, the 10-inch (250-mm) isohyet, runs roughly parallel to the 20-inch (500-mm) line but about 250 miles (400 km) farther inland (considerably less in Western Australia).

REGIONAL PRODUCTION

Within these climatic limits the intensity of wheat growing depends upon local conditions. Australia does not possess the wide, open, fertile wheatlands of the Canadian prairies: her wheat belt is more restricted and more interrupted by unsuitable land. The rugged slopes of the Australian Alps are largely uncultivated. In Western Australia there is an extensive tract west of Esperance which is unfarmed, although climatically it seems to be ideal for wheat; but here flourish poisonous plants such as *gastrolobium* and *oxylobium*, which forbid the pasturing of animals; and without stock of some sort farming is impracticable. In Eyre's Peninsula (South Australia) and in parts of the mallee country of north-west Victoria the ground water is too salty for stock, and again, the land is practically unfarmed.

In the wheat belt, then, natural conditions, methods of farming and standards of living vary greatly from place to place. In Western Australia the shortness of the rainy season makes it difficult to rear sheep as an adjunct to wheat growing, and requires the use of quick-growing and early maturing varieties. Wheat begins to arrive at Geraldton for shipment before the end of October. This grain is of high quality. But the soils show wide variations in quality, from productive loams to sand, and all need dressing with superphosphate. To be economic, the farms must be large (about 3000 acres (1200 ha) in area). Shortage of water is a serious problem in the north; in the centre supplies are augmented from the goldfields' water main (p. 264); in the south water is more plentiful, and sheep may be reared with less risk of failure.

In South Australia wheat is grown as far west as Fowler's Bay, on the Great Australian Bight; but this is an area of erratic rainfall, and average yields are low. Conditions are rather better in Eyre's Peninsula, where many farms are supplied with piped water from the Tod river reservoir, north of Port Lincoln. Again, the soils are deficient in phosphate. The most productive wheatlands of the State are east of Spencer and St Vincent Gulfs. Yields are high (up to 27 bushels per acre). Progressive farmers rest the land between cereal crops and introduce a leguminous crops, such as peas or lucerne, reducing the acreage of wheat, but increasing the yield and improving the quantity and quality of the livestock.

In the south-east of the State are the mallee lands, which extend across the border into north-west Victoria. These are sandy areas whose natural water supply is deficient. It has been supplemented by boreholes, by pumping from the Murray river and from reservoirs at Lake Lonsdale and Rocklands, among the northern foothills of the Great Divide. Altogether about 8000 miles (12,800 km) of open channels conduct the water from river or reservoir to the farmers' earthen tanks.

South of the mallees of Victoria is the Wimmera, which forms the core of the wheat belt in Victoria. It includes greyish soils which, when suitably farmed, are among the most productive in Australia: they are clay-loams with a high lime content, and to yield good crops they are fallowed, kept free of weeds and are sown late in order to prevent a rank growth. The Wimmera is a region of large-scale farming with a generous use of machinery. The average yield is about 26 bushels to the acre.

New South Wales is the largest wheat-producing State, but yields are not as high as in the Wimmera of Victoria. In the whole of the wheat belt we have so far examined the maximum rainfall occurs in winter; but at Dubbo and Condobolin (respectively north and west of Bathurst) the rainfall is well distributed throughout the year. Farther north-east the maximum rainfall occurs in summer, and here the farmer meets difficulties which are absent from the rest of the wheat belt. Rain may interrupt the harvest; weeds become troublesome; a wet spring encourages rust; and erosion becomes a serious danger on sloping land.

From these varied sections of the wheat belt the grain is carried by road to the nearest railway siding and then by rail to the ports. Since Australia has a relatively small population, she is able to export between one-half and two-thirds of her total crop. Almost the whole of the exported wheat is in the form of bulk grain, and in 1969–70 more than a third of the total exports were shipped to China. The United Kingdom and Japan each received about 15 per cent, and there followed in order, Malaysia, Singapore and the Netherlands. About 6 per cent of the exported wheat was in the form of flour, and helped to feed the populations of Ceylon, Indonesia, Papua, New Guinea and Mauritius.

STUDY QUESTIONS

1. How does the sheep-rearing industry of Australia differ from that of Wales?

2. Assess the significance of "beef roads" to the beef-cattle industry of northern Australia.

3. Construct a map to illustrate the wheat belt of Australia. Explain the physical controls which limit the belt.

4. What are the distinctive features of: (*a*) wheat farming, and (*b*) beef production in Australia?

Chapter XIII

INDUSTRY, TRANSPORT AND TRADE

INDUSTRY

MINING AND MANUFACTURE

So long as Australia was a collection of separate colonies industry consisted chiefly of the production of goods for local use, such as foodstuffs, clothing, furniture and bricks, together with the preliminary treatment of raw materials in such processes as wool-scouring and saw-milling. When federation took place in 1901 trade barriers between the States were removed and a common protective tariff was introduced. Manufacturing industry accordingly expanded, and its growth was heightened by the First World War, which interrupted imports, yet created new demands for the Armed Forces. Many of the present-day industries, such as iron and steel, electrical engineering and textiles can trace back their establishment to this period.

During the depression of the 1930s there was a temporary setback, but the Second World War again had a stimulating effect on manufactures: shipbuilding yards and aircraft factories were established, and new forms of metal manufacture and chemical industries came into being.

Since the end of the war there has been a steady expansion in Australian manufactures. By 1948 the total value of the manufactured products (£A489·3 million) had overtaken that of the agricultural and pastoral products (£A479·8 million), and Australia had ceased to be predominantly a farming nation. During the 1950s and 1960s the number of factory employees rose from 969,000 (in 1951) to 1,331,000 (in 1968), while the value of the factory output actually quadrupled.

Let us consider these industries, noting first their distribution among the States, and then their rank in the Australian economy.

As in other advanced nations, the distribution of manufacture in Australia is linked with the distribution of sources of power; and since most of the coal and water-power resources are concentrated in the eastern and south-eastern coastal districts and in Tasmania, these are the areas of the major manufactures.

The Hunter valley coalfield feeds the iron and steel industry of Newcastle, and this district also manufactures bricks, tiles and pottery, foodstuffs, textiles, sulphur, cement and superphosphates. The coal of Illawarra supplies the iron and steel and copper industries of Port

Kembla, together with its cement and superphosphate manufactures. The industries of Victoria depend chiefly on electricity generated from the brown-coal deposits of the Latrobe valley, though some coal from New South Wales is received at Melbourne. The activities of the Melbourne district include clothing, the assembly and manufacture of motor cars, the processing of food and the production of agricultural machinery.

The industries of Tasmania are related to local supplies of hydro-electricity, and include two important metal refineries: those of the Australian Aluminium Production Commission at Bell Bay, near Launceston, and those of the Electrolytic Zinc Company at Risdon, near Hobart. In Queensland the industries cluster mainly in the Brisbane–Ipswich area, and are supplied with Ipswich coal. They include large railway works. Western Australia is short of high-grade coal, but, nevertheless, has developed large-scale industrial plants at Kwinana.

For statistical purposes Australian manufactures are grouped into sixteen categories with more or less arbitrary limits. This division does, however, afford some indication of the relative significance of various types of industry in the Australian economy.

Iron and steel and associated industries. Judged by the value of its output, one group dominates all others, and accounts for more than one-third of the total output: it comprises "metals, machines, implements and conveyances." It includes the mining and treatment of the metallic ores, the fabrication of steel and metal goods; engineering in all its branches; the production of vehicles, locomotives, ships and aircraft; and the manufacture of agricultural machinery. This group of industries, indeed, is the foundation on which Australian manufactures have been built; yet by United Kingdom standards its establishment is recent, for in 1900 it hardly existed; and in the post-war period its growth has been rapid.

In 1899 the Broken Hill Proprietary Company was mining ores of silver, lead and zinc in north-west New South Wales and smelting them at Port Pirie in South Australia. In search of flux for the smelters, the company acquired in passing the iron deposits of Iron Knob and Iron Monarch in the Middleback Ranges to the north-west of Spencer Gulf. After 1905, when it seemed possible that the ores of Broken Hill might become exhausted, the company turned its attention to the mining and smelting of the iron ores, which proved to be close to the surface, unusually pure (low in phosphorus) and exceptionally rich (with a 62–68 per cent iron content).

Soon the Broken Hill Company came to play a leading part in the Australian iron and steel industry. In 1915 it erected at Newcastle the first large-scale steel-making plant in the continent—more than 1500 miles (2400 km) from the ore supplies, but close to the Hunter valley, the site of the chief coalfield in Australia. The company then went on to develop a fleet of vessels so as to become independent in the transport of its materials.

In 1928 the Hoskins family succeeded in establishing a second iron and steel works on a virgin site at Port Kembla, and a later amalgamation brought these too under the control of the Broken Hill Company. The site has several advantages: close by is the Illawarra coalfield, where the company owns collieries which produce a high-quality coking coal; there are local sources of fluxing limestone and there is ample room for expansion. Recently a new blast furnace (Australia's largest) has been erected here, with a daily capacity of over 1700 tons of pig iron. New open-hearth furnace plant, plate and strip mills and tin-plate works have also been built; these are designed to increase the ingot capacity at Port Kembla to $2\frac{1}{2}$ million tons a year.

The annual capacity of the Newcastle works is now 2 million tons of steel ingots. Here too, in order to safeguard their fuel supplies, the Broken Hill Company has acquired four collieries in the Hunter valley, with the result that the Company is the largest producer of coal in Australia.

We have seen (p. 247) that in 1941 an iron industry was inaugurated in South Australia at Whyalla. On the adjoining site is the largest shipbuilding yard in the continent, where among other vessels, the company builds its own ore carriers. A compelling advantage of Whyalla is that it is less than 40 miles (64 km) by rail from the ore deposits of Iron Knob. Though there is coal at Leigh Creek (about 200 miles (322 km) to the north), this is unsuitable for coking, and the fuel for the Whyalla furnace is imported from New South Wales. In 1965 the Broken Hill Company installed a second blast furnace on the site and opened an integrated steel works, which now supplies girders and plates to the neighbouring shipyard.

There are assured reserves of ore for the Australian iron and steel industry, not only in the Middleback Ranges, where there are 200 million tons of high-grade hematite close to the surface but also in the neighbourhood of Yampi Sound, in the north of Western Australia, where there are a further 68 million tons of similarly high-grade ore close to tide water. Western Australia, too, had its first blast furnace in operation in 1968.

The most spectacular recent developments in the iron industry, however, have been in mining rather than manufacture. As we have seen, new towns, railways and ports have been constructed in areas that were hitherto almost uninhabited; the output of ore has soared, and a thriving export trade has begun, mainly to Japan. While the greatest impact is being felt in the Pilbara (pp. 281–91), new iron mines have been opened also in Tasmania (p. 75) and Northern Territory (p. 311). Table 94 indicates the rapid expansion that is taking place in the production of iron ore and also includes details of the non-ferrous metals.

TABLE 94
Australia: output of metallic minerals since 1965

	1965	1966	1967	1968	1968–69	1969–70	1970–71
Iron ore, metallic content in million tons	4·3	7·0	10·9	16·9	20·5	27·3	35·7
Lead ore, metallic content in thousand tons	24·9	19·2	18·2	51·5	52·4	40·7	—
Zinc ore, metallic content, thousand tons	—	0·3	0·2	2·7	11·2	—	—
Tin concentrate, thousand tons	6·2	7·6	8·6	10·4	13·8	18·7	—
Bauxite, million tons	0·6	0·9	2·3	2·6	3·2	4·3	5·8

Non-ferrous metal industries. We pass now to the non-ferrous industries. The gold strikes of 1851 at Bathurst and 1892 at Coolgardie and the many other discoveries had the effect of opening up the interior of the continent. Though gold is still produced on the "Golden Mile" at the rate of 800,000 ounces (22,680,000 g) a year, the precious metal no longer dominates the export list, and in 1968 accounted for only 2·6 per cent of the value of all the mineral exports. Its place as the leading mineral has in fact been taken by iron, which in 1968 accounted for 19 per cent of the total and was rapidly increasing.

Until the Second World War the chief mineral-bearing districts were the traditional centres of Broken Hill, Mount Morgan and Mount Lyell, with a newcomer in Mount Isa. These districts, which account for the bulk of the lead silver, zinc and copper production of Australia, are still thriving or expanding centres.

Since the Second World War, however, as we have seen, there have been dramatic discoveries of rich mineral fields, many of them in the hitherto largely undeveloped tropical zone. Uranium has been mined at Rum Jungle in Northern Territory, at Mary Kathleen in Queensland, and at Radium Hill in South Australia; but official statistics of output are not published. The production of bauxite in the Cape York and Gove peninsulas has become one of the major current developments. Mount Isa trebled its output of copper between 1955 and 1966, and a new copper refinery was built 700 miles (1120 km) away at Townsville.

Zinc is coming to play an increasingly important part in the economy, and in recognition of this a new zinc smelting and sulphuric acid plant (costing £A8 million) has been built at Cockle Creek, near Newcastle; this supplements the refinery at Risdon, Tasmania.

The total value of the mineral output in 1968–69 was $A980 million, and for the first time the value of all minerals exceeded that of wool, hitherto the leading product of Australia.

The motor-vehicle industry. Perhaps the most important of the industries based upon steel is the automobile industry. With two vehicles on the road for every five inhabitants, Australia now ranks as one of the most highly motorised nations in the world, and is now capable of supplying virtually all her requirements in this respect.

While motor body building and the manufacture of tyres and spare parts have been established in Australia for many years, the first locally assembled and mass-produced private car—the Holden—appeared only in 1948. The General Motors–Holden Company, which originated in Adelaide, now has plants in several centres, and in 1958 supplied half the vehicles newly registered in Australia.

The second place in the home market is held by the Ford Company, whose plants are at Geelong on Port Philip Bay, and at Broadmeadows, a northern suburb of Melbourne. Victoria, indeed, is the home of the Australian automobile industry.

The industry is expanding: by the late 1960s the annual number of new car registrations had risen to almost 500,000. The number of vehicles exported quadrupled during the 1960s, from 8000 in 1962 to almost 29,000 in 1968. About half of these are shipped to New Zealand. By the late 1960s the motor industry employed 115,000 people and contributed 11 per cent of the gross national product.

Food, drink and tobacco industry. No other group of manufactures approaches in importance the group we have just examined, but second on the list are the industries which process food, drink and tobacco. They include flour mills, freezing and chilling works for meat, canning plants for fruit and vegetables, wine and liquor establishments, creameries, cheese and butter factories and cigarette factories. Most of these works are located in the ports, where they can serve overseas markets. Fortunately most of the home consumers too can be reached easily from the coast owing to the peripheral distribution of the population. The canning industry of Australia is second only to that of the United States; and its supply of tinplate is now being augmented from the new mill at Port Kembla.

Chemicals and associated industries. Ranking third is the group of industries entitled "chemicals, dyes, explosives, paints, oils and grease." It has risen rapidly, for as late as 1952–53 it occupied fifth place in terms of the value of its output. Its growth is largely a matter of the expanding petroleum industry.

Since 1951 a chain of modern oil refineries has been established in Australia. They are all sited close to deep water, where ocean tankers can pump ashore their crude petroleum; they have access to large quantities of cooling water, and they are near centres of consumption, though sufficiently remote from habitation to satisfy safety requirements.

As a result, the capacity of the Australian refining industry soared from 1 million tons a year in 1951 to 8 million in 1959, to 14·8 million in 1962 and to 32·2 million in 1972. This is more than sufficient to supply the needs of the home market. The refineries draw their crude oil from the Persian Gulf, from North Borneo, and from western New Guinea. They provide a variety of petroleum products and in addition supply the raw materials for new chemical industries. A new superphosphate plant erected by the Shell group at Geelong was inaugurated in

1958, and four new petro-chemical factories were built next to the Altona refinery on the western outskirts of Melbourne: they produce plastics and synthetic rubber. In all there are about thirty major petro-chemical plants in Australia.

The relative sizes of the refineries, as indicated by their capacities, are shown in Table 95.

TABLE 95
Australia: capacities of oil refineries, 1972

	Throughput capacity (*million tons per annum*)
Geelong (Victoria)	5·3
Kwinana (Western Australia) . . .	5·2
Altona (Victoria)	4·3
Kurnell (New South Wales) . . .	4·1
Clyde (New South Wales) . . .	3·8
Brisbane, Ampol (Queensland) . . .	3·0
Adelaide (South Australia) . . .	2·2
Westernport (Victoria)	2·2
Brisbane, Amoco (Queensland) . . .	1·1
Total	32·1

Indigenous oil and natural gas. We have seen (p. 206) that the first commercial oilfield in Australia was at Moonie, in south-eastern Queensland. Discovered in 1961, it began producing in 1963; and the first supplies reached Brisbane in the following year, through a 200-mile (518-km) pipeline.

TABLE 96
Australia: production of indigenous oil, by oilfields

	1968 mil. barrels	1969 mil. barrels	1970 mil. barrels	1971 mil. barrels	1971 converted to mil. tons
Bass Strait .	—	0·5	47·0	95·7	12·9
Barrow Island .	10·8	13·4	16·7	16·2	2·2
Moonie/Alton .	3·1	1·9	1·4	1·0	0·1
Total . .	13·9	15·8	65·1	112·9	15·2

Source: *Petroleum Press Service*, June 1972

In the light of later discoveries, the Moonie field ranks as a very modest source of oil (Table 96). In 1966 there came the announcement of oil strikes at Barrow Island, off the north-west coast of Western Australia. Production here began in 1967. At first the reserves were estimated to be about four times as great as those of Moonie, but recent statistics indicate that Barrow is producing at sixteen times the rate of Moonie.

About the same time as the Barrow discoveries came the exciting news of oil strikes in offshore Victoria, in Bass Strait, where oil and gas were found in commercial quantities in nine out of the sixteen wells drilled. These oilfields are estimated to be by far the richest so far discovered in Australia, and their current output is about six times as great as that of Barrow Island.

Prospecting continues over extensive regions of the continent, and recently oil strikes have been made near Alice Springs in Northern Territory and in the Cooper Basin in north-eastern South Australia. By the end of 1971 Australia was already producing 58 per cent of her oil requirements and this proportion is expected to approach 70 per cent as the known fields come into full production.

Australia has been equally fortunate in the discovery of prolific fields of natural gas. Stimulated by success at Moonie, prospectors persevering in the sedimentary basins of Queensland were rewarded by the discovery of several gas fields in the neighbourhood of Roma, on the Brisbane to Charleville railway. Again, in the light of later discoveries, these are small fields; but it was nevertheless considered viable to build a pipeline 280 miles (450 km) long to supply Brisbane with natural gas: this was completed in 1969.

TABLE 97
Australia: production of natural gas, since 1965,
in million cubic feet

Year	Output
1965 . . .	143
1966 . . .	143
1967 . . .	152
1968 . . .	216
1969 . . .	9,375
1970 . . .	53,061
1971 . . .	79,049

TABLE 98
Australia: production of natural gas by fields, in million cubic feet

	1970	1971
Bass Strait (Victoria)	22,089	35,757
Moomba/Gidgealpa (South Australia)	23,001	33,328
Roma (Queensland)	7,564	8,155
Barrow and Dongara (Western Australia) . . .	406	1,801

In the meantime new and larger gas fields had been found at Gidgealpa (1964) and Moomba (1966), in the north-east of South Australia, and in the Bass Strait (1966 and 1967). Both districts proved to be rich sources, and their outputs are growing at about equal rates (Table 97). The Bass Strait fields supply natural gas to Melbourne, and the Moomba and Gidgealpa fields supply Adelaide through a pipeline 480 miles (600 km) long.

Drilling is currently in progress off the coast of Pilbara (Western Australia), in 400 feet (120 m) of water. This is an unprecedented depth of water for the industry, but there are five producing wells and it is believed that the reserves in this Pilbara field will prove to be as extensive as those of the North Sea. A spokesman for the company has envisaged the export by the late 1970s of substantial quantities of liquefied natural gas from this field to Japan.

TRANSPORT

ROAD TRANSPORT

In Fig. 121 are indicated some of the major highways of Australia. In contrast to the numbering of the United Kingdom roads, those of

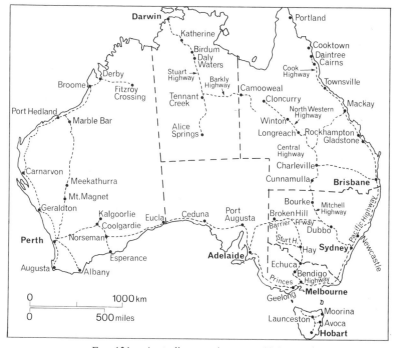

FIG. 121.—Australia: some important highways.

Australia are given names. No attempt has been made to map the extensive systems of first-class roads which focus upon all the State capitals; instead, some of the more important through routes have been shown, so as to indicate the extent to which the more remote regions can be served by motor traffic.

In Australia long-distance road transport has been developed to a fine pitch. Stock are moved by heavy duty vehicles known as road trains. In these a high-powered diesel road wagon (150 horse-power) draws two or three trailers whose compartments can accommodate 80 cattle or

800 sheep. This is the modern counterpart of droving; but there are extensive stock-rearing areas which the road has not yet reached.

Australian roads are classified by surface into four grades. In the highest the surface is of bitumen or concrete; and in the whole of Australia about 20 per cent of the total road mileage belongs to this grade. In the second grade the surface is of gravel or crushed stone; the third grade is "formed only" and the fourth is "cleared only." The last two classes account for about 55 per cent of all the road mileage of Australia. The proportions differ as between States. In Victoria the bitumen or concrete roads form 30 per cent of the total; in Western Australia the proportion is only 16 per cent. It is a comment on the lack of development in Northern Territory that, notwithstanding the Stuart and Barkly Highways, its length of first-class roads is below that of Tasmania—2320 miles (3712 km) compared with 3893 miles (6229 km) in 1970.

In Tasmania a first-class road links the north coast with Launceston and crosses the centre of the island to join with Hobart. On the mainland, apart from the Stuart and Barkly Highways, the longest continuous (or nearly continuous) stretch of concrete and bitumen highway is the coastal road from Port Augusta in South Australia to Rockhampton in Queensland. Between Adelaide and Sydney this is the Princes Highway, which we have noticed at Geelong (p. 119) and which threads the Latrobe valley. Through Brisbane to Rockhampton it is the Pacific Highway; farther north its surface becomes more primitive, but from Townsville as far as Daintree it is again well metalled: this is the Cook Highway. Beyond Daintree only fourth-grade roads link with Cooktown and Portland (p. 195).

A long road—about 1200 miles (1931 km) long or twice the distance between London and John O'Groats—joins Port Augusta and Perth. It is mainly of the second grade, but the last 200 miles (320 km) before Perth are of concrete or bitumen. First-class roads radiate from Perth, but the long "highway" which runs north-north-east to the mining centres of Meekathurra and Marble Bar ranks as "formed only." Road construction and improvement is proceeding rapidly in the Kimberleys, where about $A2 million are being spent annually. The existing, new and proposed roads in this "beef road scheme" are indicated in Fig. 81, p. 212.

RAIL TRANSPORT

In two ways the railway system of Australia is distinct: first, it is largely a coastal system, serving the capital cities (which are also major ports) and sending "feelers" inland to the mineral-producing districts; and secondly, it has inherited from the past three different gauges, which now constitute one of the most pressing problems in the Australian economic system.

The first short stretch of railway in Australia was opened in 1854 and consisted of $2\frac{1}{2}$ miles (4 km) of track linking Melbourne with Sandridge (now Port Melbourne). In just over sixty years there were 27,000 miles (43,452 km) of railways, but these included three main gauges, which arose in the following way.

In 1850 the Sydney Railroad and Tramway Company proposed 5 feet 3 inches (406 cm), and two years later an Act of Parliament made this gauge compulsory throughout New South Wales. At the same time the Governments of Victoria and South Australia were advised, and two railway companies in Victoria placed large orders for equipment on this, the broad gauge. Then the Sydney Company changed its views, secured the repeal of the earlier Act and the substitution for it of one prescribing the standard gauge of 4 feet $8\frac{1}{2}$ inches (365 cm). So arose the standard gauge in New South Wales and the broad gauge in its southern and western neighbours. Queensland and Western Australia, on the other hand, for reasons of economy adopted a narrow gauge—3 feet 6 inches (271 cm)—from the start, and South Australia too constructed its branch lines to the narrow gauge.

Australia is not the only nation to have experienced multiple gauges: in 1871 the United States had as many as twenty-three different gauges; but there a conference of 1885 decided to convert them all within a year to a standard gauge. In the United Kingdom standardisation took place between 1870 and 1892; but in Australia the problem lagged on: a muddle in the formative period of railway construction was never corrected and has become more and more difficult and expensive to rectify.

The losses which result from the breaks of gauge are immeasurable. At each State border goods and passengers must be transferred from one train to another, which causes delay and increases the cost of transport. In 1958 the Commonwealth Commissioner of Railways wrote: "Traffic from Sydney to Western Australia has to be transferred at three points, and goods which, on the distance involved, should be carried from, say, Sydney to Perth in not over five days, are usually fourteen days in transit and frequently even longer." In time of stress it is impossible to transfer locomotives and rolling stock from one State to another; in time of drought sheep and cattle die because it is too expensive to move them.

Before we look at the proposed improvements it will be useful to examine the railway system as it now is (Fig. 122).

In Western Australia there is a close network of narrow-gauge lines which focuses on Perth and extends around the capital in a semicircle of radius about 180 miles (288 km). In addition, there are two major lengths of line which extend eastwards to the inland gold-mining centres: from Geraldton to Wiluna and from Perth to Kalgoorlie.

From Kalgoorlie eastwards to Port Augusta in South Australia runs the longest stretch of railway ever constructed at one time in Australia: it is 1050 miles (1680 km) long, and it includes the world's longest straight run, of 330 miles (530 km) across the Nullarbor Plain. This

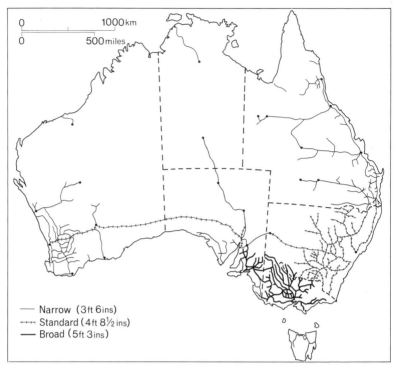

Narrow (3ft 6ins)
Standard (4ft 8½ ins)
Broad (5ft 3ins)

FIG. 122.—Australia: railways. Crossing a state border used to entail a change of trains. Recent extensions to the standard gauge track are described in the text.

line, built to the standard gauge, was promised to Western Australia as an inducement for her to join the Federation, and was built during the First World War. This is the "Trans-Australian Express" route, on which air-conditioned trains run, with observation car and sleeping accommodation.

Northward from Port Augusta runs 771 miles (1233 km) of what was intended as a second transcontinental line, which at present terminates at Alice Springs, in Northern Territory. In the north is its shorter counterpart, running 317 miles (510 km) from Darwin to Birdum. The stretch from Port Augusta to Marree is built on the standard gauge; the remainder is a narrow-gauge line.

Between Birdum and Alice Springs is a gap of 550 miles (880 km) as the crow flies (though there is motor transport by the Stuart Highway). Will the second transcontinental ever be built? It would be expensive to build and probably uneconomic to run through large stretches of desert or semi-desert. But the railway would be a boon to the cattle stations of the north; and when a nation is being knit together strategy may override economics.

For the rest, South Australia relies mainly on the broad gauge, which links conveniently with her easterly neighbour, Victoria. In Victoria the railway net focuses on Melbourne, and a trunk route leads northwards to Sydney. Common sense has prevailed in three extensions of the Victorian system across the Murray river into New South Wales: these were built on the broad gauge, and are operated by the Victorian Government.

In New South Wales there are coastal and inland routes between Sydney and Brisbane and a network of lines in the sheep–wheat belt. Two long westward extensions to the mineral fields of Broken Hill and Bourke provide a foretaste of the layout in Queensland. Since Brisbane is only 60 miles (96 km) from the border of New South Wales, it was clearly worth while to extend the standard gauge from Sydney over that distance to allow through trains between the two capitals. This, the Grafton-to-South Brisbane railway, was constructed in 1930 with the aid of Commonwealth funds.

The Queensland railway system is built almost entirely on the narrow gauge (3 feet 6 inches; 271 cm), and its backbone is the coastal line ("the Sunshine Route"), which extends for 1043 miles (1669 km) and links all the ports from Brisbane to Cairns. From this trunk route three lines extend westwards and tap the wealth of the pastoral and mineral industries: these are the Great Northern Line from Townsville to Cloncurry and Mount Isa (603 miles; 965 km); the Central Line, from Rockhampton to Longreach (427 miles; 683 km); and the Western Line, from Brisbane to Cunnamulla (about 600 miles; 960 km). The western railheads, as we have seen, form the terminals of stock routes and are invaluable to the beef-cattle industry.

To summarise, the trunk railways of Australia run from Perth to Cairns, a distance of 4351 miles (6962 km), and link all the mainland State capitals In case any reader should wish to undertake this journey, he should set aside a week for it.

For very many years discussions have been taking place on the vexed subject of unification of gauges. So far South Australia is the only State to ratify by legislation an agreement with the Commonwealth Government. It provides for a through standard-gauge railway linking Port Augusta with Darwin. A portion of this project is now complete: it runs from Stirling North (near Port Augusta) through Leigh Creek, the coal-mining centre in the north, and is open as far as Marree, the stock-route terminal It is only a small portion of the whole, but a beginning.

In 1956 the Rail Standardisation Committee made specific proposals designed to link all the mainland State capitals on the standard gauge, and steady progress is being made with the scheme. In 1962 Melbourne was joined with Sydney by the construction of 187 miles (300 km) of new standard-gauge line from Melbourne to connect with the New South Wales standard-gauge system at Albury. The next ambitious project was to lengthen the existing 1050-mile (1680-km) stretch of standard-gauge track between Port Pirie and Kalgoorlie. From Kalgoorlie it has been extended westwards for about 375 miles (600 km) to join with Perth, and from Port Pirie eastwards for about 250 miles (400 km) to join with Broken Hill. Both these lines were completed by 1969, and the first through trains between Fremantle and Sydney commenced early in 1970.

There is now a direct connection by standard gauge from Brisbane through Sydney and Broken Hill to Perth. The western extension is speeding the exploitation of the iron-ore deposits of Koolyanobbing (p. 296) and the establishment of an integrated iron and steel industry at Kwinana. The benefits of the new standard-gauge links are quickly becoming apparent.

AIR TRANSPORT

Australia is twenty-five times as large as Great Britain; her population is relatively small; half of her people live in or near the six capital cities, which are themselves hundreds of miles apart; and over a

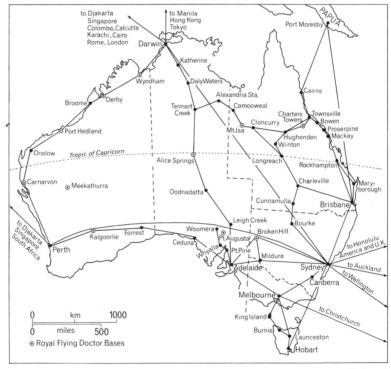

FIG. 123.—Australia: principal air routes. The air routes link all the state capitals and so provide quicker alternative routes to rail and road travel. They provide a vital service in joining together the railheads such as Mount Isa, Cunnamulla and Bourke, and they form the only alternative to road transport for the cattle stations of the north-west. Note the twelve flying doctor bases. In many isolated districts air transport has been the major factor in making normal settlement possible.

vast area of the centre and west are numerous isolated pastoral stations. To the problems of communication and transport which arise from these conditions the aeroplane provides the obvious solution, and in the terms of miles flown per head of population Australia is one of the leaders of the world in air transport.

The aeroplane is used not only for the carriage of passengers, mails and freight but also for survey and many other purposes. It sprays fields with fertilisers and orchards with insecticides. The helicopter has its special value: it hovers low to investigate the behaviour of water-courses and tidal creeks, and used in mineral prospecting it saves up to 70 per cent of the cost of a ground survey.

Two major airway companies operate within Australia. One, Trans-Australia Airlines, is Government controlled, while the other, Ansett/Australian National Airways, is privately owned; and the two compete harmoniously.

Darwin and the State capitals are joined by scheduled air services, as are also the ports of Queensland and Western Australia and the main cattle stations of Queensland Northern Territory. Services are most frequent between Sydney and Melbourne, where there are twenty-two flights daily in each direction for this 75 minute journey. The longest scheduled route is that between Perth and Darwin (almost 2000 miles; 3200 km), with calls at a string of ports on the way, such as Broome, Derby and Wyndham. There are two flights daily on this route, which takes about 17 hours (Fig. 123).

Air transport is one of the growth points of the Australian economy and all branches are expanding rapidly (Table 99); the passenger traffic handled by the State capitals and Canberra provides one criterion for establishing their relative economic status (Table 100).

TABLE 99

Australia: passengers, freight and mail carried on regular internal air services

	1965–66	1971–72
Passenger-miles (millions)	1831	3279
Freight, ton-miles (million short tons) . . .	37·6	52·4
Mail, ton-miles (million short tons) . . .	4·6	6·6

TABLE 100

Internal air services: passenger traffic in and out of the chief airports, in thousands

	1969–70	1970–71
Sydney . . .	3390	3515
Melbourne . . .	2603	2751
Brisbane . . .	1185	1347
Adelaide . . .	1017	1019
Canberra . . .	542	596
Perth . . .	421	510
Hobart . . .	201	222

Specifically Australian, however, is the Royal Flying Doctor Service, which is designed to serve the needs of remote settlers who cannot be reached easily by other forms of transport. The essential apparatus of the Service consists of the transceiver—a small wireless transmitting and receiving station, with which each isolated community is equipped. It transmits and receives messages in voice over a radius of 400 miles (640 km), yet is simple to operate and is sturdily built (in the Service's own factory). There are more than 1000 of these transceivers in use.

The Royal Flying Doctor Service operates from twelve bases: from Mount Isa, Charters Towers and Charleville in Queensland; from Broken Hill in New South Wales; from Alice Springs in Northern Territory; from Port Augusta in South Australia; and from Kalgoorlie, Port Hedland, Meekathurra, Wyndham, Derby and Carnarvon in Western Australia. A doctor has charge of each base, which includes a powerful radio station with an engineer; and an aircraft with pilot and ground staff.

A remote station which needs medical help speaks to the doctor of the nearest base. If the case is relatively simple the doctor diagnoses it from a distance and prescribes the treatment; and to simplify matters there are standard medical chests in which the drugs are named and

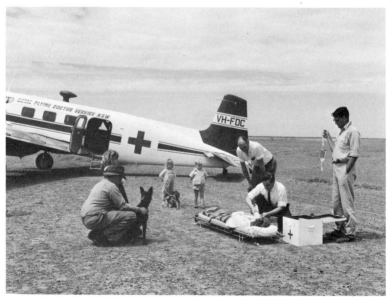

[*Courtesy Australian News & Information Bureau.*

FIG. 124.—The Royal Flying Doctor Service: a "house call." This service operates over two-thirds of the Australian continent from twelve bases. Here an emergency has occurred on a remote station; the family watches while the patient is fortified by a glucose solution before being flown into hospital.

[*Courtesy Australian News & Information Bureau.*

FIG. 125.—The school of the air. This school operates from the flying doctor headquarters at Mount Isa. The head teacher, left, confers with a member of her staff; note the map behind them illustrating the location of their radio-linked pupils.

numbered. In serious cases the doctor is flown in immediately, and if need be, the patient is placed on a stretcher and flown to the nearest hospital, which is advised by radio (Fig. 124).

The use of radio not only provides care for the remote farmer in sickness: it allows "neighbours" to hold friendly conversations though they may be hundreds of miles apart, and there are regular broadcast lessons for children in the "bush." (Fig. 125.) In this way it breaks down the barriers of isolation in a region twice the size of Europe.

TRADE

Australia still depends largely upon the export of primary produce for her income. Although manufactured goods are playing an increasingly important role in Australia's export trade, they are still of only minor account. In 1971–72 exports totalled $A4896 million. Wool continues, as it has for many decades now, to play an important part in the economy, and normally accounts for about 20 per cent of the total value of the exports. During recent years the value of the wool export has declined sharply in response to the drastic fall in wool prices. From a peak of $A961 million in 1963–64 it fell to $A643 million in 1967–68 and reached only $A583 million in 1971–72. This represented about 12 per cent of the total exports. Since that time the price of wool has made an equally dramatic recovery, and by mid-1973 had actually trebled within 18 months. Fluctuations of such magnitude, however, may do permanent damage to the industry.

Crops—mainly wheat, fruit and sugar cane—have been valued recently at about $A600 million; dairy products and meat are also substantial items.

The exports of ores, concentrates and metals doubled in value within six years to reach $A618 million in 1971–72, surpassing wool as the chief export of Australia. Of this total, iron ore represented well over half.

Since the Second World War Australian industry has undergone a rapid expansion, and Australia is now producing a very wide range of manufactured goods. At the present time Australia is making an intensive drive to capture a larger share of the world's secondary trade, and she is exploiting unusual manufactured products to capture markets which, hitherto, many have considered to be impregnable. Some of the unusual, even strange, products she is producing for export include crocodile skins (from Darwin); crayfish (from Western Australia), which finds a market in the United States; kangaroo pelts and frozen kangaroo meat; beer, both canned and bottled, to South-East Asia; and plastic and plywood boats, which find markets in the United States, Africa and Malaya. Such items, clearly, contribute little to the total export trade, but they show that Australian manufacturers realise the necessity of finding more export markets for this developing sector of the Australian economy.

During the past few years remarkable changes have taken place in the directions of Australian overseas commerce.

Before the Second World War nearly 55 per cent of the Australian exports were sent to the United Kingdom and less than 4 per cent to Japan. During the early 1950s the British share declined to 35 per cent, while the Japanese rose to $7\frac{1}{2}$ per cent; by 1966 the British share had shrunk to 17 per cent while the Japanese had risen to almost equal it; and by 1972 Japan had become the leading trading partner with Australia, taking 28 per cent of the exports. The United Kingdom, accounting for only 9 per cent, had been overtaken by the United States, with 12 per cent (Table 101).

TABLE 101
Australia: direction of exports, 1971–72

		Million dollars
Japan	. . . .	1360
United States	. . .	615
United Kingdom	. .	449
New Zealand	. . .	277
Papua New Guinea	. .	157
Western Germany	. .	148
Total exports	. . .	4896

Australia takes vigorous steps to promote new markets. Trade delegations visit China, South America and the Caribbean, the Middle East and West Africa, and a Dairy Development Company has been formed to establish contacts in Malaya, Thailand, Burma and the Philippines.

During recent years considerable increases have taken place in the Australian exports to Japan, the United States, China, India and Pakistan and the other countries of South-East Asia. Japan is now the leading customer for Australian wool, taking four times as much as Britain; she provides the chief market for copper concentrates and iron ore and receives virtually the whole of the export surplus of New South Wales coal. China is now the chief consumer of Australian wheat, taking three times as much as the United Kingdom; her imports of wool have greatly expanded and the Australian trade delegation has offered technical assistance in the establishment of textile manufacture in China. The United States dominates the market for Australian beef and veal and has begun to import Australian sugar.

It is not the geographer's province to speculate on the political implications of these changes, but there is little doubt that they are related to Britain's entry into the European Common Market.

STUDY QUESTIONS

1. Trace the development of the Australian iron and steel industry, paying special attention to the sources of the raw materials.

2. Relate the Australian railway network to the physical features of the continent. What are the chief disadvantages of the breaks in gauge?

3. Indicate on a map, and comment upon: (*a*) the distribution of existing standard-gauge railway lines, and (*b*) the additional standard-gauge lines recommended by the Rail Standardisation Committee in 1956.

4. Examine the geographical basis of the pattern of air communications in Australia.

Chapter XIV

POPULATION AND SETTLEMENTS

POPULATION

THE ABORIGINES

THE Australian aborigine has a dark (but not black) skin and straight or gently waving hair. He is lithe and strong in body; his hands are sensitive and slender. His jaw muscles are so tough that he can lift a large kangaroo in his teeth. He reached Australia in the distant past probably by means of the sea-going canoe, and he brought with him a domesticated dog and the material and social culture of the Old Stone Age. This culture he retains where he is remote from white civilisation: he uses no metal or pottery, plants no crops, builds no permanent dwelling and wears no clothes. Yet he has a complex social organisation, and a rich language, and (contrary to earlier beliefs) has a high intelligence.

The decline of the aborigine is a distressing story. When white settlement began in 1788 there were at least 300,000 aborigines living in many tribal groups. The latest estimate (1961, and admittedly unreliable) places the total number of full-blood aboriginals as 40,081, of whom fewer than half retain their tribal organisation. Full-blood aborigines are extinct in Tasmania and virtually so in Victoria and New South Wales. They remain only in the three tropical States: Western Australia has perhaps 15,000 in the tribal state, Queensland and Northern Territory, each about 3000.

The aborigine has a remarkable knowledge of the resources of his area at the different seasons; and he has managed to adapt his way of life both to the burning heat of the desert and to mangrove-fringed and crocodile-infested monsoon coast. In the desert he can trail a lizard across the dry earth and he knows where to dig for the honey-ant and for *cyclorana*, the frog which stores water in its body. In the northern forest the men with their dingoes leave camp on hunting expeditions each day, in search of lizards, snakes, opossums and bandicoots, and rejoice when they find wild honey.

The problem is that survival of the race seems possible only on a tribal basis, for without that organisation the aborigine seems to lack the will to live. Yet more protection and care on the part of the Government means a lessening of the influence of the tribe. Education of the children in particular results in a constant conflict between school and tribe.

Considerable areas of central and northern Australia are set aside as aboriginal reserves: the largest of them includes most of Arnhem Land,

and is about 150 miles (240 km) from north to south and 250 miles (400 km) from east to west. No non-aboriginal person may enter a reserve without Government permission; inside them are small groups of white administrators whose object is to safeguard the health of the aborigine, to distribute food where necessary, and to provide elementary education.

In principle, the reserve is thus dedicated to the aborigine. Conflict, however, arises where important deposits of minerals are known to exist in aboriginal land, as is the case in the Gove Peninsula (p. 312). At present, the mineral royalties are being paid into a trust fund for the benefit of the aborigines; but the whole question is under review, and in 1973 a judicial inquiry was instituted into aboriginal land rights. In the meantime no mining leases are being granted or renewed on aboriginal land, except to aborigines.

Until the early 1960s the aborigine was a ward of the State, and though he was protected he was not a full citizen. Since 1966 the aborigines have been declared to be British subjects and Australian citizens, equal in law with all other residents. The 57 special schools that were operating in Northern Territory in 1970 are regarded as temporary institutions, and ultimately all aboriginal children will be educated in the normal community schools.

Very few aborigines are fully nomadic. Most of them live a settled life, though with many traditional survivals. At the 1966 census the number of people describing themselves as 50 per cent or more aboriginal, or just "aboriginal," was 80,207; but an independent estimate by the Commonwealth Office of Aboriginal Affairs sets the aboriginal population (including those that are less than 50 per cent aboriginal) at about 140,000. Its number is increasing faster than the Australian average.

There seems little prospect that the full-blood aboriginal will find a niche in the white civilisation. He makes an excellent stockman, but there is no real outlet for him in a town. The half-caste, on the other hand, is readily accepted as a full Australian citizen, and his children attend the same school as those of white parents. Ultimately, it seems, the aborigine will be assimilated into a white Australia, and as a separate race will become extinct.

THE GROWTH OF AUSTRALIA'S POPULATION

The following table illustrates the small size of the population during the first half of the nineteenth century. The discovery of gold in the early fifties, however, led to a great influx of pioneers: within twelve months 100,000 immigrants arrived to search for gold. The gold rush provided the first major impetus to settlement. Since that time the population has steadily grown, owing partly to natural increase and partly to immigration.

TABLE 102
Australia: population growth (exclusive of full-blood aborigines)

December 1801 . . .	5,945
1851 . . .	437,665
1901 . . .	3,824,913
1921 . . .	5,510,944
1931 . . .	6,552,606
1941 . . .	7,143,598
1951 . . .	8,527,907
June 1961 . . .	10,508,191
September 1971 . . .	12,807,800

Yet in 1939 the population of Australia totalled only about 7 millions: a whole continent had fewer people than Greater London. When in 1942 the Japanese invaded New Guinea it became painfully clear that a sparsely peopled nation was ill fitted to resist aggression. Moreover, the Australian birth-rate was falling, and by 1940 the average number of children to a marriage was little more than two. In 1948 it was estimated that if unreinforced by immigration the population of Australia would still be less than 8 millions by the year A.D. 2000.

In fact, however, the most remarkable feature of the population in the present century has been its steady increase at the rate of a million every ten years. From 3,765,339 in 1900 it reached 6,500,751 in 1930, and by the end of 1959 it had passed the 10 million mark.

This rapid increase in recent decades is one of the results of an active immigration policy which was adopted by successive Australian governments over many years. Until recently one of its leading features was the principle of a "White Australia." As it was put in a semi-official handbook, "Those who are not of European descent may not enter Australia as permanent settlers." No other British Dominion had taken so firm a line on racial matters. Spokesmen in its support drew attention to the racial strife which occurred in South Africa, in the southern States of the United States and even from time to time in the United Kingdom.

Recently there has been a modification of this hitherto rigid policy, and in 1971 the official standpoint was stated as follows:

"Australia's immigration policy is directed towards the maintenance of a socially cohesive and homogeneous nation. It seeks to avoid the creation of permanent minority groups resistant to integration. ... The policy does not exclude persons of any ethnic origin; but it does exercise prudent caution in the matter of accepting large numbers of people with substantially different backgrounds, characteristics and customs who may resist general integration even in the long term." [1]

The effects of this more liberal attitude towards immigration will be watched with interest.

Since the war the character of the migration to Australia has changed. Formerly the immigrants were expected to become farmers in order to develop the primary industries of the continent; and some of the early mass-emigration schemes failed when the English factory worker found himself ill suited to the rigorous Australian outdoor life.

More lately, mechanisation on the farm has made such progress that the need for agricultural labour is far less urgent; at the same time new manufactures have been introduced and are expanding, so that the modern immigrant tends to move into industry. In its turn, the expansion of industry begets an increased demand for scientists and technologists, and these are prominent among the new immigrants.

The principle of "assisted passage" dates back to a decision at the Imperial Conference of 1921. The immigrant pays only a nominal sum, but agrees to remain in Australia for a reasonable length of time. In the early years of the scheme assisted migrants entered at the rate of about 25,000 a year; now the number is in the region of 50,000–60,000 a year. The total number of arrivals is much greater, but is offset by a substantial number of departures, so that the net increase by migration is about 100,000 a year. Assisted passages are granted to applicants from the United Kingdom and to about a dozen other countries of Europe; and British persons now form less than half the arrivals. A single instance illustrates the gain to Australia: "New Australians" form more than half the labour force of the Snowy Mountains scheme.

DISTRIBUTION OF POPULATION

The average density of population in Australia, as calculated from the totals in Table 103, is only four persons to the square mile. This figure emphasises the small size of the population in relation to the vast extent of the continent; but it needs to be qualified immediately, since the population is so unevenly distributed.

One might expect that in a nation so dependent on farm products a large proportion of the people would be living in the countryside. In fact (as we see below), more than half of the population of Australia lives in the metropolitan areas and only about one-fifth in the rural areas.

TABLE 103

Australia: area and population of States and Territories

				Area (sq. miles)	Population, at census of 30th September 1971
New South Wales	.	.	.	309,433	4,617,000
Victoria	.	.	.	87,884	3,514,600
Queensland	.	.	.	667,000	1,835,500
South Australia	.	.	.	380,070	1,178,900
Western Australia	.	.	.	975,920	1,036,100
Tasmania	.	.	.	26,215	391,300
Capital Territory	.	.	.	939	147,500
Northern Territory	.	.	.	523,620	86,900
Australia	.	.	.	2,971,081	12,807,800

At first sight the map of the distribution of population in Australia is quite startling (Fig. 126). Most of the people live on or near the coast between Cairns in Queensland and Adelaide in South Australia. This is the "fertile crescent" of Australia. Two other areas of close settlement occur: in Tasmania and in the south-west of Western Australia. No other part of the continent is even moderately populated: most of the interior, the north and the west are virtually uninhabited.

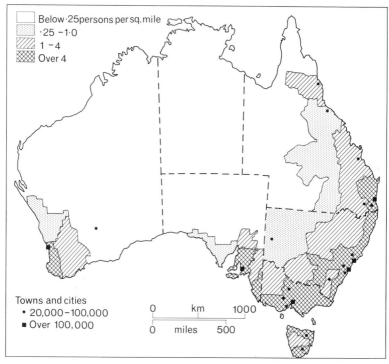

Fig. 126.—Australia: distribution of population. The density of population is indicated for normal statistical divisions according to the census of 1961. The shading represents a mathematical average and does not necessarily show the actual location of the population within the division.

This uneven pattern of population distribution is explained—one might almost say governed—by the physical conditions. The close settlement of the east, south-east and south-west is related to the adequate rainfall, the cultivable land, the timber resources and the deposits of coal. Farther inland the people are largely pastoral farmers and there is little need of or opportunity for close settlement: hence there are local concentrations of population only at mining or marketing centres.

Beyond, there is only desert or semi-desert. In such areas, which constitute about one-third of the continent, neither crops nor animals can be raised and population is negligible. In half a million square miles, shared among Western Australia, South Australia and Northern Territory, there are no sheep, no cattle and no white settlers.

URBANISM

It remains to notice the extraordinarily high proportion of the Australian population which dwells in the towns. It is a remarkable fact that more than half the people in the continent are congregated in the ten largest cities and towns.

The concentration of the population in a handful of large cities may seem surprising, but a number of factors help to explain the situation. First, in colonial times the early, and principal, settlements were ports. Penetration inland took place from these ports; hence, as the hinterlands developed, they became the natural focal points for commerce. Secondly, as the outback became developed and peopled, there grew up an ever-increasing demand for consumer goods, and the ports, linked with the interior on the one hand, and conveniently placed for the import of raw materials on the other hand, grew up as manufacturing centres. Thirdly, Australia's agricultural and pastoral activities are largely extensive in their nature and do not make heavy demands on labour. Indeed, relatively few people are engaged in primary production and increasing mechanisation is reducing still further the numbers required for agriculture. Fourthly, the amenities of city life act as a magnet, especially to the younger generation, who are less willing to tie themselves to a rural life, which in most cases is harder than that offered by the cities. Fifthly, most of the recent immigrants were urban dwellers, and there has been a natural tendency for them to settle in the cities which provided the sort of life to which they were accustomed (Table 104).

TABLE 104
Australia: population of the capital cities, 1971

Sydney	.	.	.	2,799,600
Melbourne	.	.	.	2,498,000
Brisbane	.	.	.	866,200
Adelaide	.	.	.	842,600
Perth	.	.	.	701,400
Hobart	.	.	.	153,000

Doubts have been expressed as to the wisdom of allowing so uneven a distribution of population. Should not the authorities encourage people to settle in the farming districts, which produce the wool, wheat, fruit and meat—Australia's staple exports?

In South Australia, at least, there is some concern to curb the growth of the capital city, and the first new town of the State will be built at Monarto, about 50 miles (80 km) east of Adelaide. Its planned population is about 250,000, and its proposed industries include glass making, ceramics and light engineering.[2]

Water supply and power-development schemes, which are so much the concern of government activity, have their effect on the distribution of population. In the meantime, the expansion of industry is sufficiently rapid to absorb the growing labour force of the towns. With a high standard of living both on the farms and in the factories, there seems little need to attempt any major redistribution of the Australian people.

NOTES

1. *Year Book of Australia, 1971.*
2. *The Times*, 1st June 1973.

STUDY QUESTIONS

1. Discuss the position of the aborigine in Australian society.

2. Examine the geographical and economic implications of: (*a*) assisted immigration, and (*b*) "White Australia."

3. How have geographical factors affected the distribution of population in Australia?

4. Professor Griffith Taylor suggested a maximum population of 20–30 millions for Australia. How far would you subscribe to his estimate?

PART TWO

NEW ZEALAND AND THE PACIFIC ISLANDS

Chapter XV

NEW ZEALAND: GENERAL

NEW ZEALAND lies 1200 miles (1900 km) to the south-east of Australia: that is, the same distance which separates Hull from Leningrad. The country spreads over almost the same latitudes in the southern hemisphere as does Italy in the northern hemisphere, and there are indeed many points of comparison in the physical environments of the two States. In area New Zealand approximates to that of the United Kingdom. Her population in 1972 totalled 2,910,000—well below that of Denmark and about the same as that of Wales. It is remarkable that a country with so few people should have achieved so much.

STRUCTURE AND GEOLOGY

For its size New Zealand possesses an extremely varied structure and a wide range of geological deposits. There are structural elements common to both islands; but South Island is composed largely of a mosaic of earth blocks, raised and tilted in Tertiary times, and extending its whole length, while the most characteristic feature of North Island is the varied landscape which results from volcanic activity.

In New Zealand the geological succession is virtually complete (Fig. 127). Archaean gneisses and schists form the mountainous core of South Island. They occupy almost its entire width in the south, where the island is widest; they shrink to a narrow band farther north to form the western slopes of the Southern Alps, and they reach the sea in the north on the shores of Golden Bay and in the neighbourhood of Queen Charlotte and Kenepuru Sounds. Farther north the Archaean base seems to have foundered, for it does not appear in North Island.

Cambrian strata have not been recognised in New Zealand; but Ordovician, Silurian and Devonian rocks form the Tasman Mountains at the extreme north-west of South Island.

More prominent are the folded Carboniferous deposits, which occupy considerable areas in both islands. Unlike strata of the same age in the northern hemisphere, they do not contain coal, but consist largely of thick deposits of sandstones and slates, sufficiently resistant to form striking mountain chains. In South Island they give rise to the main mass of the Southern Alps and to the Kaikoura Mountains to the

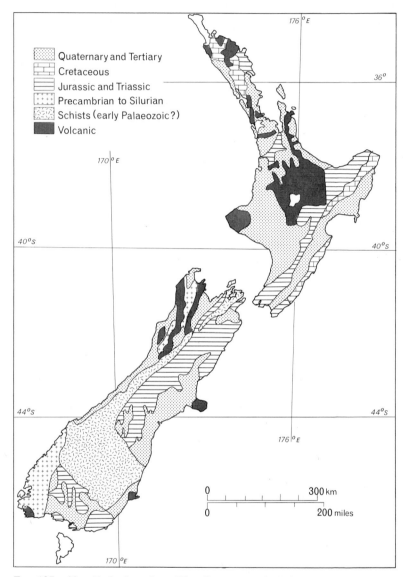

Quaternary and Tertiary
Cretaceous
Jurassic and Triassic
Precambrian to Silurian
Schists (early Palaeozoic?)
Volcanic

FIG. 127.—New Zealand: geology. Virtually every geological period is represented. Note how the volcanic rocks form headlands, while the soft Tertiary and Quaternary sediments form lowlands. In this map the Carboniferous deposits have been combined with the Jurassic and Triassic rocks. A portion of the schists is indicated on a larger scale in Fig. 128.

north-east. The line of the Kaikoura continues across Cook Strait into North Island, where Carboniferous rocks form the connected series of mountain chains which under various names (Tararua, Ruahine, Huiarau and Raukumara) stretch from Turakirae Head near Wellington to Cape Runaway (Figs 131 and 132).

Triassic and Jurassic beds strike north-east and south-west in narrow bands in both islands, forming the eastern flanks of the main ranges. Cretaceous sediments, more restricted in area, are nevertheless of great economic importance, since they contain the major coal deposits of the Dominion. In North Island they form much of the coastal lowland of the south-east; and they occur sporadically in the Auckland Peninsula, where coal has been worked on the shores of the Bay of Islands. In South Island the Cretaceous rocks are exposed at Cape Foulwind, and high-quality steam coal is shipped from Greymouth, Westport and Seddonville.

The Tertiary sediments are closely related to the physique of New Zealand in that they form lowlands or at least areas of mild relief. In South Island they floor the Canterbury Plains, the narrow coastal plain of Westland, the plains of the Invercargill district of Southland and the lowland fringe of Tasman Bay in the north. In North Island the Wanganui and Taranaki lowland of the south-west is composed of Tertiary material, as are the plains around Cambridge and those bordering the Bay of Plenty in the north; and it floors the remarkable trough which extends from Palliser Bay in the south to terminate in the Gisborne area in the north.

The Southern Alps of New Zealand, like the Alps of Europe, were elevated in Tertiary times; but they have little else in common. The folding and thrusting which is so evident in the European Alpine chains has played little part in moulding the landscape of New Zealand. There, as Professor Cotton has demonstrated,[1] the typical mountain structure is the raised or tilted block.

Two main periods of mountain building appear to have determined the physical features of South Island. In late Jurassic or early Cretaceous times the surface layers of the earth were crumpled to form a series of mountain ranges trending north and south; these were then subjected to a long period of erosion, and eventually reduced to quite moderate elevations. They are now represented by the resistant quartzites, crystalline limestones and intrusive granites of north Nelson; by the gneissic and plutonic rocks of western Otago; and by the schists of central Otago.

In Tertiary times the greater part of New Zealand was below the sea, and received deposits of mudstones, sandstones and thin limestones. But towards the end of the period, in Pliocene times, pressures were set up once more in the earth's surface, and as a result the older rocks, now peneplained, were broken into blocks and raised or tilted irregularly. The newly deposited Tertiary material emerged from the sea to form a more or less complete cover to the lower parts of the older rocks. Being relatively soft, they were quickly attacked by the rivers, and are now generally preserved only in the lowlands.

So arose the present landscape of South Island, where the relief and drainage closely reflect lines of faulting.

The most spectacular deformation is the Alpine Fault, whose surface indication takes the form of a great wall rising to over 3,000 feet (900 m) above sea-level and extending for about 300 miles (480 km): it forms the western edge of the Alps and separates the greywacke schist to the east from the younger rocks to the west. There has been horizontal as well as vertical displacement: the rocks along the north-west side have moved towards the north-east, while those on the opposite side have moved to the south-west. The total horizontal displacement is believed to have been of the order of 300 miles (480 km). No sudden movements have been recorded during the last century; but the fault is still active

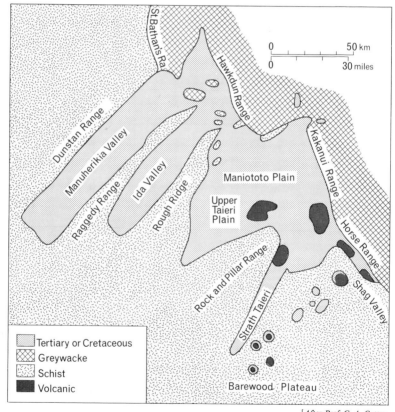

[*After Prof. C. A. Cotton.*

FIG. 128.—Central Otago: geology. The whole of this district lies in the region broadly shown as "schist" in Fig. 127.

in the geological sense, for the courses of rivers that cross it have been deflected, and terraces that lie astride it have been displaced.

A small area of central Otago, extending from the Dunstan Mountains to the Shag river, suitably illustrates some of the typical surface features. The ranges forming the north-eastern border, such as the Hawkdun Range, are of greywacke—a hard sandstone which has been formed of marine sediments and consolidated by earth movements. The parallel ranges which trend north-east and south-west are of schist, while the basins are floored by Tertiary rocks or alluvium (Fig. 128).

The chief element in the landscape is a series of elongated blocks which have been tilted down to the north. The most westerly of the group is the Dunstan Range, which rises 4000 feet (1200 m) above the Tertiary basin and overlooks it in a south-east-facing fault scarp. Its even crest is evidence that it has been peneplained. A broad trough (the Maniototo depression) separates it from its eastern neighbours, the Raggedy Range and the Rough Ridge: their names suggest the irregular skyline which has developed as a result of the erosion in a relatively dry climate of schists in which the foliation is nearly horizontal. "Tors" give a characteristic appearance to the landscape: they are castle-like residual rock masses which are bounded by joint planes. Rough Ridge is interesting on account of its discontinuous or "splintered" eastern fault scarp, where three relatively short faults are arranged in echelon. A broader block follows to the east, known as the Rock and Pillar block: it is about 8 miles (13 km) wide and presents an unusually regular fault scarp to the east, about 20 miles (32 km) long. Eastwards again is the long and narrow trough of Strath Tieri, whose sediments rest in an angle between fault planes.

In contrast to the tilted blocks of South Island, the core of North Island derives its character from the volcanic activity of Tertiary times. Viscose lava, slowly emerging from the depths, built up the great domes which form the Banks and Otago peninsulas of South Island, while masses of fluid lava issued west of the mountain chains of North Island and accumulated to form the Taupo Plateau, much of it between 2000 and 3000 feet (600 to 900 m) above sea-level. Its froth cooled to form the porous and infertile grey pumice which is found in many parts of the plateau.

Lava and ash, ejected more violently, cooled to form the series of fine cones which include Ruapehu (9100 feet; 2776 m), Ngauruhoe (7515 feet; 2292 m), and the most symmetrical of all, seagirt Egmont (8340 feet; 2544 m). Some of the volcanoes are still active, and other varied manifestations of volcanism are to be seen on the plateau. Here are geysers, hot pools; solfataras, quietly discharging sulphurous gases; fumaroles, hissing with super-heated steam; and small, conical mud volcanoes. The region extends north to the Bay of Plenty; and 35 miles (56 km) out to sea is the active volcano of White Island.

CLIMATE

Like the Mediterranean lands, New Zealand lies astride the junction of the tropical high-pressure zone and the belt of westerly winds. In winter the whole country lies in the path of the westerlies; but with the southward migration of the wind belts, North Island is brought under the influence of the high-pressure zone in summer.

If we examine this so-called high-pressure belt more closely we find that it breaks down into a series of cells of high pressure, or anti-cyclones, which usually traverse New Zealand in a steady stream from south-west to north-east, moving at a speed of about 12–20 miles (19–32 km) an hour, with their centres to the north of the Dominion. An anticyclone may be expected every seven days or so. Separating these cells of high pressure are troughs of low pressure, and it is these which characteristically bring the rainfall to New Zealand, and more par-ticularly, to the western regions of South Island.

Such a trough, showing the directions of the associated winds, ap-pears in Fig. 129. Those familiar with the weather maps of the United Kingdom will observe that in the southern hemisphere the rotation of the earth deflects moving air to the left, so that the circulation in an anti-cyclone is anti-clockwise, and not clockwise, as in Britain.

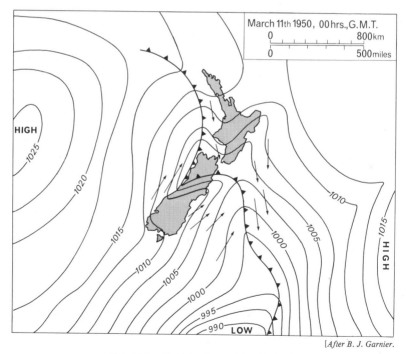

March 11th 1950, 00 hrs., G.M.T.

[After B. J. Garnier.

FIG. 129.—Cold front over New Zealand.

Hence the winds in the rear of a departing anticyclone are northerly in direction, and warm and dry in character, since they have resulted from descending air; by contrast, those in the front of the following anticyclone are southerly and cold. The plane which separates these two opposing streams of air may be designated a cold front; and when it passes there is a sudden change in wind direction from north-west to south-west and a fall in temperature. Along the front the cold, heavy air forces its way below the lighter, warm air, buffets it and forces it to rise: there are strong winds and a downpour of rain.

But as in the Mediterranean regions the storms are soon over, and parts of New Zealand enjoy totals of sunshine which are unknown in the United Kingdom.

THE MAORI

Into this land of wind, sunshine and rain; of grassy plains, wooded slopes and towering peaks; of glaciers and hot springs, of lava flows and vast volcanoes, came the Maori. Maoris are born seamen, and the main migration is believed to have taken place by canoe in the fourteenth century.

The Maori is of light-brown colour, tall and broad-shouldered, with dark hair and eyes and a dignified bearing. In the past they practised polygamy and indulged in cannibalism. There was incessant tribal warfare; but at home the Maori was (and is) hospitable and affectionate, a first-class farmer, and skilled at wood carving, weaving and dyeing (Fig. 130).

About 1800 there were 200,000 Maoris in New Zealand. During the wars of the 1860s the Maoris fought against the settlers with bravery and chivalry, sending in food and ammunition to a besieged enemy garrison on the grounds that they could not fight hungry men. But the Maori population was almost decimated during the course of the nineteenth century. Rum, tribal warfare, firearms and disease all played a part in reducing their numbers to 30,000 by 1900. Since that time, however, the Maoris have increased in numbers steadily and vigorously to reach 228,000 in 1971, equal to 8 per cent of the total population.

This rapid rate of growth is indeed a feature of the post-war Maori population. A high birth-rate has been accompanied by a steeply falling death-rate, so that the rate of natural increase of the Maori population is among the highest in the world.[2]

The Maori is accepted today as an equal to the New Zealander of European descent: there are Maori statesmen, doctors, teachers, lawyers and skilled tradesmen. The Maoris are concentrated largely in the Auckland and North Auckland districts of North Island, in which about 70 per cent of them are to be found. They prefer rural as opposed to urban life, tending their farms in the far north, in the Rotorua area, by the shores of the Bay of Plenty and in the coastal lowlands of the

[*Courtesy High Commissioner for New Zealand.*

FIG. 130.—A Maori village entrance. This richly carved gateway leads into a
Maori village at Rotorua. Now uninhabited, the village is preserved as a
specimen of Maori culture. It is not typical of modern Maori life.

north-east. When for economic reasons the Maori moves into the town,
he retains his link with the countryside and returns there when his
working days are over.

Yet Maori farming has its problems, which are revealed by disturbing
symptoms: overstocking, with the consequent depletion of pasture;
reversion to scrub; and the neglect and even abandonment of properties.
The causes are complex. After the wars of the 1860s the Europeans
grasped the best land, and many Maoris are now trying to survive on
inferior land. Elsewhere, Maori farms are too small to be economically
viable: some of these plots were considered sufficiently large when they
were allocated during the 1930s by the Department of Maori Affairs,

but are seen to be inadequate today. In other cases the holdings have become progressively smaller as a result of the Maori system of communal ownership: as the group becomes larger in number so the size of the individual plot becomes smaller. A further cause of deterioration is the leasing of land by Maoris to non-Maoris. The latter are aware that little or no compensation will be forthcoming for improvements to the land at the end of the lease and they accordingly wring as much as possible from the soil without any thought for the future.[3]

These are difficult problems which will require all the sympathy and technical knowledge that the Government can muster for their solution.

TRANSPORT

To see the road and railway systems of New Zealand in proper perspective we must first rid ourselves of ideas based on transport in the United Kingdom. New Zealand is as large as the United Kingdom and more mountainous: gradients are steeper and level land more scarce. The rainfall in most places is heavier, sudden downpours are more common, and there is a greater danger of flood. The country has been tamed in little more than a century by what was, at first, an exceedingly small population, and one which even now amounts to only one-twentieth of that of the United Kingdom. In designing her transport system, then, New Zealand has been forced to regard economy as a guiding principle.

The road and railway systems are very similar, with in most cases a road running next to the railway line. In South Island the trunk railway line keeps close to the east coast, and runs from Invercargill in the south to Picton in the north—a distance of 584 miles (934 km). From this line a number of branches penetrate westwards, but only one of them crosses the Southern Alps. This leaves the main line near Christchurch and uses the valley of the Waimakariri to take advantage of a narrowing of the mountain belt; even so, the engineers found it necessary to pierce the summits by means of the 5-mile (8-km) Otira Tunnel—the longest in the British Commonwealth. By this means the northern parts of Westland, including the coal-mining districts, are linked by rail to the rest of South Island, and can send coal to Christchurch.

In North Island the trunk railway is from Wellington in the south, traversing the western parts of the Taupo Plateau, through Auckland, to Opua on the Bay of Islands in the north—a distance of 626 miles (1000 km). Important secondary routes leave the main trunk for Gisborne in the north-east, Rotorua in the north of the plateau and New Plymouth in the west of the island.

The gauge adopted for the New Zealand railways is the narrow, 3 foot 6 inch (1·05 m) gauge: it is economical to construct and is suited to sharp curves and steep gradients, though it imposes a limiting speed of about 55 miles an hour. Almost the whole of the mileage—96 per cent of it—consists of single-track line, for the amount of traffic would not repay the cost of doubling the track.

The distinctive feature of New Zealand railways is the carriage of livestock. Store cattle are moved from the hills to the lowlands for fattening, and there is a busy traffic in young cattle through the dairy centres south of the Hauraki Gulf, such as Morrinsville and Matamata. In South Island store sheep move from the hills of the west, while fat lambs are transported from the lowlands of Southland and the Canterbury Plains to the freezing works at the ports.

The railways carry large quantities of fertilisers from the factories in the ports to the agricultural centres, and they transport timber from the interior to the four major cities.

Coal, however, forms the most important single cargo, and by tonnage accounts for about a quarter of all the goods traffic. It comprises both brown coal, from Waikato county (at the base of the Auckland peninsula) and from Southland; and bituminous coal from Westland. The latter is transported to Greymouth and Westport and from there shipped coastwise, or is carried eastwards through the Otira Tunnel to supply Christchurch and the neighbouring towns.

New Zealand produces over two million tons of coal annually: this is just sufficient to satisfy the nation's requirements. During the 1960s the railways virtually ceased to use coal, while the thermal power stations stepped up their demands, and by 1969 constituted the largest single coal user. Domestic consumers and dairy factories demand approximately equal quantities, and most of the remainder is utilised in other manufactures (Table 105).

TABLE 105

New Zealand: output and consumption of coal, in thousand tons

Consumption		1966	1969
Power stations		491	603
Domestic		344	279
Dairy factories		299	276
Cement works		233	205
Gasworks		241	169
Meatworks		121	127
Pulp and paper mills . . .		125	94
Railways		120	13
Total consumption . . .		2603	2275
Production		2595	2348

The future of coal mining will be governed by the interplay of the forces of supply and demand. It is difficult to forecast the shape of future demands, but the recoverable reserves of the different coalfields are known in some detail.

The only deposits of bituminous coal are near the west coast of South

Island. Here the Buller district possesses 31·1 million tons, the Greymouth district 2·6 million and the Reefton only 1·0 million tons. The chief known reserves of sub-bituminous coal are in the Huntly district of North Island, with 94·3 million tons; this is followed by Maramarua (15·7 million) and Rotowaro (13·3 million tons). Coal from Huntly, about 50 miles (80 km) south-east of Auckland, helps to supply the 180 MW power station at Mercer, while that from nearby Rotowaro is converted into briquettes and by-products.

New Zealand has not the vast distances of Australia; but she has remote areas of sparse settlement in Westland and North Auckland, while Cook Strait forms an irritating break in road and rail communications. New Zealand is therefore almost as air minded as Australia. In Australia approximately one in five of the population travels by air each year; in New Zealand the proportion is one in eight, while in the United Kingdom it is about one in 100.

The air services of New Zealand have made remarkable progress since 1950. The number of passengers carried between New Zealand and Australia has multiplied by five; the seating capacity of the aircraft has trebled, and the time required for the journey has been reduced from $6\frac{1}{2}$ to $2\frac{1}{2}$ hours.

Air transport has been stimulated further by the opening in 1965 of the international airport at Auckland: it has cost $A20 million and will accommodate the large jet aircraft that are now in use.[4]

INDUSTRY AND TRADE

New Zealand lacks the minerals and fuel which are necessary to establish large-scale heavy industries, but she engages in light engineering and foundry work of many kinds, builds locomotives, small ships, and coach bodies, and assembles imported motor vehicles. Electrical engineering in particular has made progress in recent years. Typical of New Zealand manufactures is the processing of primary materials, such as the production of leather goods, the canning and packing of fruit and vegetables and the production of phosphatic fertilisers for agriculture. The oil industry has recently made its appearance, for a large refinery, costing £20 million, has been built at Whangarei, about 100 miles north of Auckland. It was completed in 1964.

The largest single industrial enterprise is the new sawmill, wood-pulp and paper-making plant at Kawerau, near the Bay of Plenty and 25 miles (40 km) east of Rotorua in North Island. This establishment is the fourth largest of its kind in the world. To operate it the new town of Kawerau has been built, and the new port of Tauranga has been inaugurated on the shores of the Bay of Plenty.

The works are close to the 1000-square-mile (260 km^2) plantation of Kaingaroa (p. 373). Here the trees are chiefly of radiata pine, which grows quickly and produces high-quality newsprint, and now, after thirty years' growth, the timber is ready for cutting. Continuous replacement of the felled timber will provide a permanent supply for the mills. Both coal and hydro-electricity are used for power, but geo-thermal steam is now being tapped near by, and is supplementing the more conventional sources of energy (*see* p. 376).

Although New Zealand has large deposits of potential iron ore in the black beach sands of the west coasts of both islands, owing to the technical problems involved, it was not until 1969 that they were used for the production of steel.[5]

The iron-bearing sands extend from Westport southwards in South Island, and from Wanganui northwards in North Island; in addition to iron they contain titanium, and are estimated to represent about 800 million tons of titanomagnetite. A process has been developed by Canadian and West German companies to utilise these sands: the concentrates, mixed with coal and limestone, are heated in a rotary kiln instead of a blast furnace. The resulting sponge iron is then mixed with steel scrap and converted into steel in an electric furnace.

The steelworks are situated at Glenbrook, 36 miles (58 km) south of Auckland. The selection of this site in 1965 from 17 alternatives formed a practical exercise in the location of industry. It draws its iron sands from deposits only 12 miles (19 km) away on the Waikato river; its coal is derived from Huntly, less than 20 miles (32 km) away; its waterside site allows the works to benefit from the use of shipping; and it is close to the largest market for steel in New Zealand.

Production began in 1969, of ingots, billets, sheets and pipes. The works have provided a stimulus to the economy of the region: railways have been upgraded, water supplies have been extended and a house-building programme inaugurated. Nearby Waiuku has almost quad-rupled its population within six years to reach 6000 by 1970.

The consumption of electricity in a nation provides a fair indication of the progress of its economy. In 1950 the total electricity generated in New Zealand amounted to about 3000 million kWh; by 1960 it had doubled to reach over 6000 and by 1969 it had again doubled to reach 12,000 million kWh. The rate of advance continues, and in 1971 almost 14,000 million KWh were produced.

New Zealand is fortunate in the possession of abundant resources of water power, and this accounts for about 80 per cent of the total production of electricity. South Island, with a high and well-distributed rainfall, with natural lakes for storage and high altitudes, offers greater opportunities than North Island, and it is estimated that 75 per cent of the potential hydro-electricity is in South Island; yet 70 per cent of the demand for power originates in North Island. This was the justification for the construction of a power link between the two islands. The scheme, completed in 1965, was the largest of its kind outside the Soviet Union. It involved 345 miles (552 km) of transmission line to carry electricity at half a million volts, between Benmore in South Island and

Haywards in North Island, together with 25 miles (40 km) of submarine cable below Cook Strait.

There are twenty-five hydro-electric power stations in the public supply system of New Zealand, the largest of which is the 540 MW installation at Benmore. Eight hydro plants form a single system on the Waikato river in the volcanic plateau of North Island, and have a combined capacity of 1045 MW (p. 375). The hydro plants are supplemented by four thermal power stations, the largest of which is the oil-fired installation of 240 MW capacity at Marsden (p. 378). The most interesting of the thermal plants is that at Wairakei, whose generators are powered by subterranean heat: its capacity is 192·6 MW (p. 376).

New Zealand has exceptionally close trading links with the United Kingdom. In 1969–70 90 per cent of the nation's butter exports were shipped to Britain, together with 74 per cent of the cheese and 86 per cent of the lamb. In return the United Kingdom sent machinery for factories and farms, unassembled motor cars, aircraft, textiles and many other manufactured goods. Britain's negotiations for accession to the Common Market were therefore viewed in New Zealand with some concern. In June 1971, however, a special arrangement for New Zealand butter and cheese was negotiated by Britain with the Community, and was incorporated into the Treaty of Accession of 1972.

NOTES

1. C. A. Cotton, *New Zealand Geomorphology*, Wellington, 1955.

2. B. Heenan, "Recent Trends in New Zealand's Population," *New Zealand Geographer*, Vol. 22, No. 1 (1966).

3. *National Resources Survey Part II*, Bay of Plenty Region. Government Printer, Wellington, 1962.

4. G. T. Bloomfield, "The Auckland International Airport," *New Zealand Geographer*, Vol. 22, No. 1 (1966).

5. G. T. Bloomfield, "Progress in the New Zealand Steel Industry," *New Zealand Geographer*, Vol. 22, No. 1 (1966).

STUDY QUESTIONS

1. What are the physical similarities between New Zealand and Italy?

2. Describe some of the ways in which volcanic phenomena have influenced the landscape of New Zealand.

3. "In New Zealand the geological succession is virtually complete." Justify this statement.

4. Two anticyclones are moving east, their centres passing north of New Zealand. The trough of low pressure which separates them is passing over New Zealand. Explain the weather you would expect to experience at three different parts of the trough as it traverses New Zealand.

5. Compare and contrast the Maori with the Australian aborigine.

6. Describe the distinctive features of: (*a*) road and rail transport, and (*b*) manufacturing industry in New Zealand.

Chapter XVI

NEW ZEALAND: MOUNTAIN, PIONEER AND RANCHING REGIONS

NATURAL or Geographical Regions may be defined as areas which exhibit a relative uniformity of structure, climate, vegetation and human activities so that these elements combine to produce a distinct "personality," which marks the areas off from their neighbours. It is tempting when planning a regional description of New Zealand to separate the two main islands: North Island is the warm, volcanic, dairy region, the home of the Maoris; while South Island is the cooler, wetter, more mountainous land, where the farmer raises fat lambs and cultivates grain crops.

Our basis here is less simple. We distinguish twelve regions, using climate, structure and occupations as a guide (Figs 131 and 132), and we arrange them in order of the intensity of their economic development. We examine in this chapter the mountainous districts, where settlement is virtually absent; the pioneer regions, where settlement is advancing; and the ranching country, where the land is capable of supporting only a scattered population engaged in extensive farming. In the next chapter we describe the dairy regions, the fatstock and crop regions and the major cities.

MOUNTAIN REGIONS

The Southern Alps. Strictly speaking, the Southern Alps include only the highest portion of the mountainous masses of South Island, which form a chain of peaks whose summits range from about 700 feet (2100 m) above sea-level up to Mount Cook (12,349 feet; 3766 m), the highest in New Zealand. Here we use the term more loosely to include the whole complex of range and basin country which extends through the entire length of South Island. Its lower limit corresponds with the upper limit of sheep grazing or ranching lands, and may be placed at about 4500 feet (1380 m) above the sea.

The Southern Alps, as we have seen, are carved from Precambrian or early Palaeozoic rocks, which by Tertiary times had already been worn down almost to sea-level, but were then uplifted, tilted and fractured, and finally scoured by ice sheets. These have left their mark in several ways. First are the many parallel ribbon lakes to the east of the divide, such as Te Anau (33 miles; 53 km long) and Wanaka (30 miles; 48 km long). The heavy and well-distributed rainfall, together with these natural reservoirs, makes for a plentiful supply of potential hydro-electric power. The largest station at present operating has a capacity of

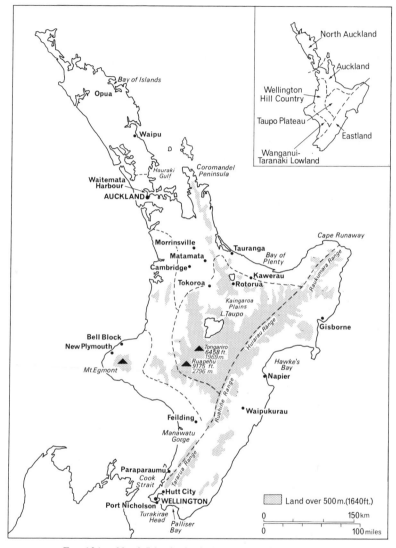

FIG. 131.—North Island: physical, natural regions and towns.

320,000 kw and is at Roxburgh, on the Clutha river, to which three major lakes contribute water (Fig. 133).

A second effect of the ice sheets is seen in the smooth lower slopes and the U-shaped valleys, which are particularly evident in the south-west. A third effect is the fifteen or so fiords (locally called "sounds") in the south-west coast, where a relatively recent submergence has drowned valleys which had already been deepened by glacial action. The

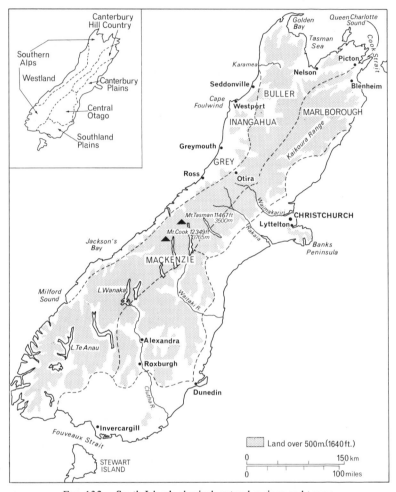

FIG. 132.—South Island: physical, natural regions and towns.

most northerly of them, Milford Sound, is perhaps the finest, with Mitre Peak rising almost sheer and towering to a height of 5560 feet (1696 m) above the water of the fiord (Fig. 134).

Shrunken remnants of the ice sheets survive in the Pembroke Glacier, near Milford Sound, and larger ice fields in the Mount Cook district feed the Tasman and Murchison Glaciers, which flow inland, and the Fox and Franz Josef Glaciers, which descend westwards to within 600 feet (180 m) above the sea. Farther north, the alpine core narrows and terminates in a series of finger-like ridges such as the Kaikoura and Seaward Kaikoura Ranges, which enclose among them deep, straight, longitudinal valleys.

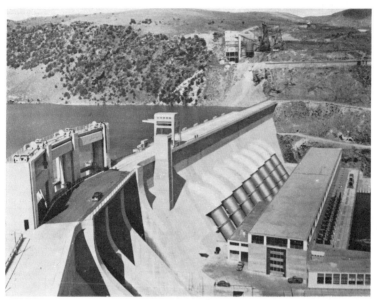

[*Courtesy High Commissioner for New Zealand.*

FIG. 133.—Roxburgh hydro-electric plant, South Island, New Zealand. This power plant, opened in 1956, has a capacity of 320,000 kw and is the third largest in New Zealand. It harnesses the Clutha river north of Roxburgh, central Otago.

[*Courtesy High Commissioner for New Zealand.*

FIG. 134.—Milford Sound. This deep inlet, bounded by wooded slopes which soar to rocky peaks, well illustrates the fiord coast of the south-west of South Island.

Climatically the Southern Alps are distinguished by their excessive rainfall, their low temperatures and their high insolation. Milford Sound, with a mean annual rainfall of 253 inches (6407 mm) is one of the world's wettest spots, and most of the region receives upwards of 150 inches (3750 mm) annually. The height of the mountains and their westerly aspect are sufficient to explain the high precipitation. But there are surprising differences over short distances, and sheltered valleys may be dry and dusty on summer days, while on still nights they become reservoirs in which the cold air, creeping downhill, collects.

The Southern Alps have their tourist value, but are otherwise almost uninhabited. The soils are thin and acid; and unlike the European Alps, there are few passes. A single railway crosses them, by the Otira Tunnel, and one or two roads complete the land communications. But there are reserves of timber for the future, and a rich store of potential water power.

In striking contrast to the Southern Alps yet enclosed by their continuations in the Tasman Mountains and Richmond Range is a small but fertile and flourishing lowland: this is the Nelson district, which fronts on the Tasman Sea.

In spite of a static or even declining crop area there have been substantial increases in output of all kinds. Pastures have been improved by aerial top-dressing, crop yields have been increased by irrigation, pests and diseases have been brought under control; selection by breeding has made the flocks and herds more productive. The region has a wide range of farming activities, but is noted specially for its intensive crops of fruit, vegetables and tobacco.

These are grown in the river valleys and along the coastal lowland, in particular on soils derived from early Pleistocene gravels, which have been strongly weathered to produce sands and clays. The most important of the special crops is tobacco, and this constitutes the only tobacco region of New Zealand. The plant grows best on well-drained land: it requires a high proportion of sunshine and absence of early and late frosts. During the 1950s and 1960s, area and output expanded substantially. The development of tobacco-picking machines represents an important technical triumph. Output in 1969–70 amounted to 7·2 million lb (3,265,820 kg), valued at $NZ4·6 million.

Second in importance to tobacco are apples and pears and here are produced more than 40 per cent of the nation's output. The industry dates from the period 1911–16, when a trial shipment to the United Kingdom demonstrated the viability of apple growing. The orchards benefit from research undertaken by Government institutions; surplus produce is absorbed in a canning factory that was opened in 1962.

In addition the region produced 40 per cent of the nation's raspberries and large quantities of hops, strawberries, tomatoes, peas, beans and other vegetables. There are local research stations for the hop- and tobacco-growers, and important food-preserving industries. These include a tomato juice cannery at Motueka, a quick freezing plant for peas, beans and other vegetables at Stoke (near Nelson) and a large canning and jam factory in Nelson itself.[1]

Nelson is New Zealand's chief fruit port: it handles about half the country's exports of fresh fruit. Its shipments are growing steadily, and almost quadrupled during the 1960s.

The Taupo Plateau. The Taupo volcanic plateau forms an elevated tract in the centre of North Island. Its average height is about 2000 feet (610 m), and from its undulating surface individual volcanoes rise to more than double that height (Tongariro, 6517 feet, 1988 m; Ngaurahoe, 7515 feet, 2292 m; Ruapehu, 9175 feet, 2798 m). These peaks have been built up from the quiet upwelling of thinly fluid, basic lava, while the plateau itself has been formed of the fragmental products which have resulted from explosive eruptions. Wind too has played its part in the latest stages, in spreading the lighter particles of "ash" and dust.

The Taupo Plateau is distinct on account of both climate and soils. By contrast to the rest of North Island, the Taupo Plateau has owing to its altitude a cool climate, and the highest peaks reach near or beyond the snow line. This is also the most inland portion of North Island, and as a result it has some of the marks of a continental climate. The winter maximum of rainfall, characteristic of North Island generally, is here less pronounced, and in one or two places, as at Chateau Tongariro, there is even a summer maximum. Open to the westerly influences, the Taupo Plateau is a wet region, receiving 60–80 inches (1500–2000 mm) of rain annually; and the low temperatures restrict evaporation and increase the humidity.

The soils, however, over large areas, consist of porous "ash" and pumice, and there is the peculiar spectacle of almost arid country of bracken and tussock grass (p. 399) in the setting of a humid atmosphere. Such soils are low in phosphates and other minerals, and formerly those farmers who ventured to pasture cattle there found them afflicted by a deficiency disease, "bush sickness."

More recently it has been shown that portions of the volcanic plateau can be improved for grazing purposes. The farmer applies liberal surface dressings of phosphatic fertilisers which contain a preparation of cobalt, to avoid bush sickness. He introduces cocksfoot and red-clover pastures, and grazes Hereford cattle on them for the production of beef. Only in the more accessible, sheltered and warmer lowlands is the dairy herd successful.

Elsewhere the Forest Service has planted large areas with quick-maturing pines (for the native timbers are slow-growing). The Kaingaroa State Forest, north-east of Lake Taupo, is the largest plantation in the world.

Forestry has impressed its stamp on the character of the region and is now an old established feature of the economy. In 1921, following the passing of the Forests Act, the State Forest Service was established. It carried out a rapid survey of the indigenous resources of timber, and in its report of 1925 adopted a major policy of planting softwoods. Experience had already shown that the radiata pine (*Pinus radiata*) was the most promising species, for it grew much faster than in its native California. The volcanic plateau was chosen as the main planting area: it contained large tracts of Crown land, was easily cleared and was considered unsuitable for farming. During the 1920s and 1930s the State planted 447,000 acres (179,000 ha) and private companies a further 372,000 acres (149,000 ha). In part forestry was seen as a means of relieving the unemployment that was rife during the Great Depression.[2]

Viewed more than a generation after the events, the planting programme must be judged excessive. So large an area was impossible to tend properly, and much of the timber is of poor quality: even so, the potential output of sawn timber is far greater than the nation requires or

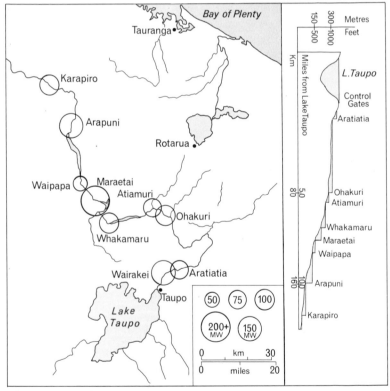

FIG. 135.—The Waikato Power Development Scheme, North Island. Lake Taupo is now a reservoir and the Waikato river a stairway of lakes. The eight power stations have a combined capacity of more than 1000 MW.

can export. In these circumstances an alternative use for the timber has been found in the pulp and paper industry, and virtually the whole of this form of activity is concentrated in the region. Saw-mills are dotted throughout the plateau and there are pulp and paper mills at Whakatane, Kawerau and Kinleith. The port of Tauranga, which forms the outlet for the industry, has become the nation's second exporting port by tonnage.

The Taupo Plateau contains 60 per cent of the exotic plantations of New Zealand. The most important overseas market for the pulp and newsprint is Australia: here there is insufficient softwood timber for the national requirements, and large quantities of softwood pulp are needed to mix with the local hardwood pulp. The Australian market is expanding, and there are good prospects of selling to Asia, so the New Zealand pulp and paper industry plans to expand. The mills do not compete among themselves, but specialise on particular branches of the industry: thus Whakatane manufactures cardboard, the Kawerau mills produce tissue paper and newsprint, while Kinleith makes brown paper and chipboard.

Forestry forms the background to the economy of the four main settlements of the Taupo Plateau—Rotorua, Putaruru, Whakatane and Tokoroa. It has given rise to the establishment of eight other specialised settlements, which range in population up to 1450; and it has brought into existence an efficient system of roads and railways.

Lake Taupo is drained by the Waikato river, and even in its natural state this was very suitable for the generation of hydro-electricity. Regulated by the lake, the river had an even flow. For much of its course it was entrenched in the volcanic rocks, offering a choice of sites for dams; and the substantial cover of vegetation reduced the risk of soil erosion.[3]

The civil engineers have been at work since the middle 1940s, and the task is now complete (Fig. 135). The lake has been converted into a reservoir by the erection of control gates at its outlet, and for 117 miles (188 km) the Waikato river has been transformed into a stairway of

TABLE 106

New Zealand: the Waikato Power Development Scheme, North Island

Installation	Dam height feet	Capacity in 1971 MW	Date of completion
Karapiro . . .	100	90	1946
Arapuni . . .	175	158	1946
Waipapa . . .	54	51	1961
Maraetai . . .	200	360	1951
Whakamaru . .	124	100	1956
Atiamuri . . .	82	84	1958
Ohakuri . . .	115	112	1961
Aratiatia . . .	109	90	1964
Total capacity		1045	

lakes, through the construction of eight dams. At each dam power is developed, and the total capacity reaches more than 1000 MW (Table 106).

To the north is the Rotorua district, famed as a tourist centre owing to its geysers, fumeroles, boiling springs and mud pools. Considerable use has already been made of the supplies of natural hot water. Bores tap the hot water, which is used for domestic heating. It is also used to supply heat for poultry and animal breeding and to warm glass-houses. These natural underground supplies of heat have even greater possibilities, however, as sources of geothermal power. At Wairakei, about 6 miles (10 km) north of Taupo, the first geothermal power station

[*Courtesy High Commissioner for New Zealand.*

FIG. 136.—The geothermal power station, Wairakei. The 20-inch (500-mm) diameter pipes, lagged with magnesium oxide wrapped in bitumen, are conducting geothermal steam to the Wairakei generating station situated on the Waikato river.

entered service in 1958 and was progressively enlarged to reach a capacity of 193 MW in 1963. The boreholes range in depth between 570 and 4000 feet (174 and 1200 m). It is estimated that the resources of subterranean heat here are sufficient to at least double the capacity of the station (Fig. 136).

THE PIONEER REGIONS

Only two pioneer regions are now left in New Zealand, those of North Auckland and Westland. But the country has a short history of European settlement, and a century ago virgin "bush" covered almost the whole of the present settled areas.

The New Zealand bush consists of majestic evergreen pines, red, white and black pines, towering 140 feet (42 m) above the ground. The finest of them all is the kauri, a tree of enormous girth. It has been known to have a diameter of 22 feet (6·6 m)—sufficient to allow two lorries side by side to pass through in comfort.

A Maori has given us his reminiscences of the methods of forest clearance used about 50 years ago.[4] Tree felling began in winter when the sap had ceased to rise. Below the forest giants was an undergrowth of saplings, fern and creeper, and this was cut first so that it would be thoroughly dry when the time for burning arrived. Then the bushwacker (the New Zealand axeman) began on the large trees. He carved out two segments near to the base of each tree, one on each side, so that the tree was delicately poised, yet did not fall. The bushwackers prepared hundreds of trees in this way; then they used the last two or three as battering rams to bring down the whole forest. A mighty crashing filled the air as three or four acres of timber fell headlong to the ground.

Nothing was done for the rest of the winter; then in January, in the heat of the summer, a match was applied and a great bush fire raced through the fallen timber. It left the ground black with ashes, and on this unpromising material the pioneer spread his grass seed. In the warm and damp New Zealand climate they quickly germinated, and the forest was replaced by pasture. Tents gave way to wooden huts; sheep and cattle moved in and a new farm was born.

So have 30 million acres (12 million ha) of virgin forest dwindled to the 8 million acres (2 million ha) of today.

North Auckland. The North Auckland pioneer region corresponds in extent with the Land District of that name, except that its southern boundary lies about 15 miles (24 km) north of the city of Auckland instead of 30 miles (48 km) to the south of that city.

Physically the Auckland Peninsula must be classed as lowland, since the greater part of it lies below 600 feet (180 m). But it is composed of an exceedingly complex series of rocks which range from Triassic to Recent in age and include considerable exposures of volcanic material. Its intricate eastern coastline bears the marks of recent sinking, and stands in sharp contrast to the western shoreline, with its succession of sandpits backed by lagoons and marshes.

The region shares a common climate with the neighbouring dairy region to the south. It is the warmest part of the Dominion and is noted for its particularly mild winters: this is the "winterless north," where grass will grow virtually throughout the year. More than any other region of New Zealand, it feels the effect of the annual migration of the wind belts: a train of alternate anticyclones and troughs from the west moves into the region for the winter, to be replaced by the tropical high-pressure systems in summer. As in the Mediterranean regions, there is therefore a winter rainfall maximum, with abundant sunshine through the year.

From the point of view of land use the distinctive feature of the region is its undeveloped or partially developed state. Swamp, tussock grass, ferny scrub and forest form a drab landscape, which is relieved only at intervals by the homestead and dairy herd of an enterprising farmer.

About 1952, for example, at Waipu, on the eastern shore in lat. 36° S., four young farmer brothers made a determined attack on 100 acres (4 ha) of bush. They crushed the scrub with the help of a tractor, burnt the timber, levelled the land with heavy harrows, spread a ton of lime to the acre, and later applied superphosphate and potash. Only then did they sow the seeds which would enable them to increase their existing herd of 120 dairy cattle and 100 young stock.

The region possesses one urban and industrial growth point at Whangerei, on the east coast.[5] With a 1971 population of 30,746, it has expanded by almost 50 per cent since the 1961 census. Here are an important cement works, the largest glass works in New Zealand and the nation's only oil refinery, which opened in 1964 with a capacity of $2\frac{1}{2}$ million tons per annum. The presence of the new source of energy has stimulated further development in the shape of the nation's largest thermal power station, close to the refinery at Marsden Point. This oil-fired plant has a capacity of 240 MW. The pocket of bustling activity seem strangely out of place in a region more than two-thirds of which consists of forest, scrub, swamp and sand, or low-density sheep pasture.

Westland. In official terminology Westland is both a county and a Land District, and provides the only example where the two coincide in area. Here we restrict the term to the coastal lowland west of the Southern Alps (whereas the county boundary extends eastwards as far as the mountain summits) and we extend the region northwards as far as the mouth of the Karamea river to include the lowland portions of Grey, Inangahua and Buller counties.

So defined, Westland forms a long and narrow, hummocky and gravel-strewn lowland about 200 miles (320 km) long and with a maximum width of about 20 miles (32 km). Largely formed of recent alluvium, it includes, however, in the north, tracts of Tertiary sediments: these are valuable in that they provide the chief bituminous coal deposits of New Zealand.

Numerous short and torrential streams cross this lowland, which, indeed, has been built up by the merging of their deltaic fans. North-to-south communications are therefore difficult. Bridges are few; a single north-to-south road links the heads of the estuaries, and rail transport is limited to the relatively short stretch in the north between Ross and Seddonville.

Climatically Westland is distinct in that it forms the only wet lowland of New Zealand. Its westerly exposure gives it heavy rainfall, high humidity and low ranges of temperature; yet, paradoxically, Westland enjoys abundant sunshine.

Everywhere except in the north of the region the mean annual rainfall is greater than 100 inches (2500 mm) and in places is much higher. At Jackson's Bay in the south it reaches 187 inches (4750 mm). The rain is brought both by north-westerly winds in the rear of a departing anticyclone and by south-westerly winds in the front of an approaching anticyclone; and, as we have seen, these systems cross New Zealand in continuous procession. While it lasts the rain is heavy; but soon the clouds roll away and the sun shines, so that parts of Westland have 2000 sunny hours in the year. Yet Eastbourne, the sunniest place in England, has about 1500 sunny hours.

The soils of Westland take their character not from the parent rock but from the excessively wet climate to which they are exposed. In many parts they are thoroughly leached, with a layer of hardpan 2 or 3 feet (0·6 to 0·9 m) below the surface. This, where it exists, forms an impermeable stratum so that the soils are waterlogged and acid, with semi-swamp conditions.

The mild winters coupled with a heavy rainfall encourage the growth of dense sub-tropical vegetation, and this remote region includes some of the largest tracts of virgin forest in the Dominion (Fig. 137).

Yet settlements do exist in Westland: in fact, this was one of the first parts to be occupied by Europeans. The attraction was gold, and the 1860s saw an influx of diggers, many of them from Australia. It is estimated that in 1860 there were 2500 gold diggers in the area. Mining towns mushroomed, but all the food was imported from outside. The gold deposits were soon exhausted, but one dredger still operates, on the Taramaukau gravels, south of Greymouth. This accounts for virtually the entire output of gold in New Zealand, which in 1970 amounted to 11,283 oz (320 kg), valued at $NZ420,000.

The gold seekers that remained turned their attention to coal and timber. Most of the coal deposits had been located by the 1880s; harbours were established at Westport and Greymouth, and by the 1890s were linked by rail to the chief mining centres. Mining, however, lacks the stability of farming, and the fortunes of mining towns wax and wane. In 1910 the Buller district supplied most of the coal, but by 1955

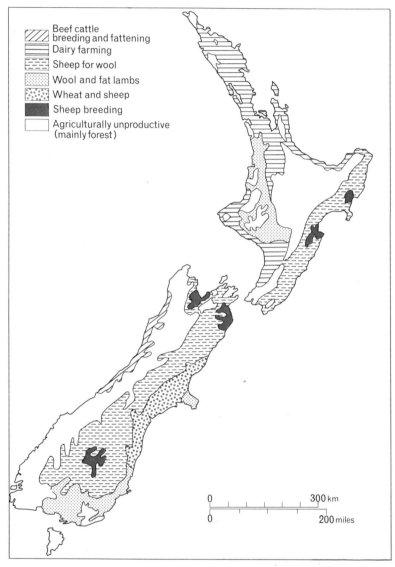

Beef cattle breeding and fattening
Dairy farming
Sheep for wool
Wool and fat lambs
Wheat and sheep
Sheep breeding
Agriculturally unproductive (mainly forest)

0   300 km
0   200 miles

[*After K. B. Cumberland, 1949.*

FIG. 137.—New Zealand: land use. The map, which illustrates the distribution of the different types of farming, should be compared with the insets in Figs 131 and 132. The solid black areas represent districts of intensive sheep breeding and fattening, based on the cultivation of fodder crops; they are also renowned for their orchards, vineyards and market gardens.

its contribution had shrunk to about a third of the total: Greymouth produced half, and Reefton about 14 per cent.

The coal output of New Zealand is declining: from a peak production of 3 million tons in 1960 it fell to 2·7 million in 1965 and 2·3 million in 1971. This is not to imply that the coal seams are exhausted: there are an estimated 32 million tons of recoverable bituminous coal in the Buller field alone. But changes in the pattern of demand are affecting the industry, and the railways in particular have virtually ceased to be in the market for coal.

Fig. 138.—South Island: the coal centres of the west coast.

The decline is particularly serious for the west coast, where whole clusters of settlements have been created by and are dependent on coal mining (Fig. 138). The fortunes of the mines affect not only those directly employed there, but also transport workers, labourers, clerical workers and shop keepers.[6]

In the long run the region will depend for its prosperity on farming. Essentially this is grassland country, with an emphasis on dairying. But only 8·6 per cent of the area of the region is considered suitable for agriculture, and even this is distributed in scattered strips of alluvial land flanking the middle courses of the streams. Owing to the heavy rainfall the soils are leached, and need phosphate and lime; but supplies are short and transport is expensive. Nevertheless, there has been a slow but steady increase in the number of cattle, and seven butter factories have been established.

THE RANCHING REGIONS

There are four ranching regions—two in each island. They differ in structure and in climate; but they are similar in that they comprise hill country, where the pastures are native or only slightly improved. The herbage is insufficiently rich to fatten stock, and so sheep are reared primarily for their wool and cattle for fattening elsewhere. Farms are large (up to 50,000 acres; 20,000 ha in area); the animals are relatively thinly scattered, and they range widely. Yet these regions perform an essential function in that they form a reservoir from which the flocks and herds of the lowland farms are replenished. They correspond to the hill pastures of Scotland and Wales, where the farmers rear but cannot fatten their stock.

Central Otago and the Mackenzie Country. Central Otago and the Mackenzie Country which lies to the north form a compact region of South Island. To the west it is bounded by the row of glacial lakes, and to the east by the lowland which fringes the east coast. Structurally the region is distinct in that here raised and tilted blocks separated by gravel-filled troughs are seen to perfection. It is a region of plateaus, gently inclined dip slopes, abrupt fault scarps and level plains.

Climatically this, the most inland region of New Zealand, is the most continental in character. The high mountain rim, which shelters it to the west, increases its effective distance from the sea. Here are found the greatest temperature extremes in New Zealand, and here too are the lowest rainfall totals. Rainfall is relatively high on the elevated blocks, but diminishes rapidly as one moves eastwards into the sheltered troughs. Most of the region receives less than 25 inches (635 mm) annually, and some parts far less. Thus Alexandra, in the valley of the Clutha river, has the phenomenally low total of 13·22 inches (336 mm) per annum.

In accordance with the true continental pattern there is a summer maximum of rainfall; but its efficiency is reduced by a high rate of evaporation; and there is the surprising spectacle of irrigation in the middle of this predominantly wet Dominion. The irrigation channels, introduced by the Government half a century ago, have brought about "islands" of orchard and market-garden land together with rich pastures for fattening lambs. These have little in common with the rest of the region and contrast strangely with the steep, barren and often eroded hills in the background.

Most of the hill country is utilised as extensive sheep pasture; but in the Clutha valley there are relatively small orchard areas whose value is out of all proportion to their size. Here the terraces in the neighbourhood of Roxburgh, Alexandra and Clyde in the middle reaches of the river produce 30 per cent of New Zealand's apricots and peaches, 8 per cent of her apples and pears and 8·5 per cent of her strawberries and raspberries.[7] The region is sheltered from the west by the Alps, and its low humidity and wide range of temperature render it largely free from fungus diseases and insect pests. Abundant sunshine helps to ripen the fruit, but the exceptionally low rainfall needs to be supplemented by irrigation. The sandy loams are ideal in texture, but they are poor in organic matter and lack certain trace elements, so that appropriate fertilisers need to be applied.

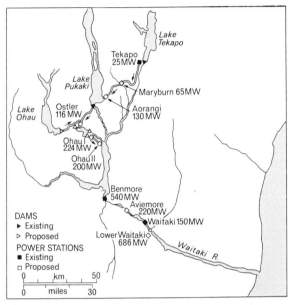

FIG. 139.—South Island: the Waitaki Power Development Scheme. This scheme includes the largest power station and the largest reservoir in New Zealand. When complete, there will be ten power stations with a total capacity of 2356 MW.

The Otago hill country is one of the major water power producers of New Zealand. Here are the country's two longest rivers—the Clutha and the Waitaki—and both are fed from large glacial lakes. They flow in deep and steep-sided valleys which are easily harnessed for the generation of power. The Waitaki, since it is closer to the main load centres, is the scene of the greatest development; and the flooding of parts of its valley has caused a minimum of disruption to property. Here is the Benmore station, the largest in New Zealand (capacity: 540 MW). Its dam, completed in 1964, has created the largest man-made lake in the nation, covering 30 square miles (78 km²) (Fig. 139). On the Clutha river is the Roxburgh station, which in 1970–71 was second only to Benmore in the production of power. New Zealand is fortunate in that her hydro-electric resources, developed and potential, are considered to be sufficient for the foreseeable future.

The Canterbury Hill Country. In the Canterbury Hill Country the mountain belt is narrower, the rocks are younger, structural troughs are less evident and the climate is colder and wetter. There is neither the need for irrigation nor the land suitable for it.

Here in the rugged country of the Southern Alps the native tussock grass is grazed by merino sheep. We may take as an example the Mount Algidu station, among the valleys and ranges at the head of the Rakaia river, near where it is joined by the Wilberforce. To bring in all stores and to take out all the wool, a four-horse dray must ford the treacherous Wilberforce river, for there is no bridge. With a merino flock numbering 8000 the musterers travel far from the homestead and work from portable prefabricated huts as bases. The remote farmstead is linked to its neighbours by radio telephone. In summer the rivers wander about in a maze of gravels; but the spring snow-melt brings great volumes of water: the river swells and may occupy the whole floor of its valley.

To the east conditions are easier and the Trias–Jura deposits sink below the newer sediments of the Canterbury Plains.

It is in the Canterbury Hill Country that the effects of the two major pests of New Zealand are most apparent: these are the rabbit and the red deer.

Rabbits had been introduced into New Zealand by 1838, and by 1870 they were recognised to be a pest. Where the settlers had burnt the tussock grass to promote new growth the rabbit quickly gained a hold. The immediate effect was to ruin the pastures, and in the economic depression of the 1880s many farmers went bankrupt. The more lasting and disastrous result was to lay bare the soil and so to prepare the way for erosion. The steeper, deforested hillsides have suffered the worst damage and now provide a desolate background to many a scene in Canterbury, Otago and Hawke's Bay.

It was found impossible to introduce myxomatosis into New Zealand owing to the absence of a suitable carrier, and the rabbit has been attacked by the "conventional" weapons of poison, guns, traps and dogs. In 1947 the Government established a Rabbit Destruction Council to encourage and supervise the pest-control work of the farmers. But so long as rabbit farming was profitable the rabbit would never be completely exterminated; and in 1954 the export of rabbit carcasses was declared illegal. The continued work of destruction has had its effects: between 1948 and 1956 the areas classed as "heavily infested" declined from 4·2 million to 375,000 acres (1·7 million to 150,000 ha); and where formerly the rabbit devoured all pasture the green tinge of spring is once more appearing.

The English red deer was introduced into New Zealand by the early colonists to augment their food supplies, and was later valued as a hunting and tourist attraction. Until about 1925, in fact, the deer was a protected animal. But it had no natural enemies in its new environment, and it multiplied rapidly to become a pest, destroying pasture and young trees, and accelerating soil erosion.

Government deer stalkers now spend months at a time in the remote hill country, such as the valley of the upper Hurunui in north Canterbury. Their supplies are dropped by aircraft, and they send out loads of deerskins by packhorse train. They are hardy mountaineers and expert riflemen; and with their aid in peak years more than 100,000 deer have been killed; but the control of the deer menace is not yet complete.

The Taranaki–Wellington Hill Country. This region, lying west and south of the Taupo Plateau, is distinguished from it by structure, relief and land use. In place of the volcanic rocks of the Taupo Plateau, here are marine sediments of late Tertiary age, which form the largest single exposure of their type in New Zealand. The rocks are varied in character, but include clayey and shaly limestones and are generally soft. They have not been greatly contorted, but were lifted as a single block and have since been subjected to active erosion by rivers. While the summits reach 2000 feet (609 m) the general level is well below that of the Taupo Plateau, and the Wanganui river and its tributaries have succeeded in excavating deep and wide valleys, which are separated by steep-sided ridges.

The region receives a relatively high rainfall, much of it having more than 70 inches (1750 mm) per annum; but the broken nature of the relief ensures a high proportion of runoff, and since much of the surface is porous, it is not excessively wet for sheep grazing. The Taranaki–Wellington Hill Country is a region of large, scattered and isolated farms, where it is a hard struggle to prevent the pastures from reverting first to scrub and then to forest.

Eastland. By its structure, climate and farming Eastland forms a clear-cut geographical region; and this unity is emphasised by the administrative boundaries of Hawke's Bay and Gisborne land districts, which correspond with the regional boundary. To the west is the narrow belt of Carboniferous deposits which extend the whole length of North Island from Cook Strait to the Bay of Plenty, forming the continuous series of mountain chains which we have already noticed (p. 357). To the east is the sea. The relief is varied: coastal lowlands and river plains alternate with hilly tracts which average about 1000 feet (300 m) above sea-level. The hilly districts are composed of Cretaceous and Tertiary sediments; the lowlands are formed of alluvium.

Climatically Eastland is noted for its erratic rainfall. Sheltered from westerly influences, it is more exposed to the irregular southerly and easterly winds, while occasional tropical cyclones bring sudden and heavy rain. In March 1924 Rissington (north-west of Napier) received 20 inches (500 mm) in 10 hours! The heavy rainfall of the exposed ridges contrasts strongly with the relatively dry climate of the sheltered valleys. Yet the winters are relatively mild and the sunshine is of Mediterranean frequency.

Sheep thrive in these conditions; but level land is scarce and the pastures are not sufficiently rich to fatten lambs. This is therefore primarily a rearing region, and one of the greatest reservoirs of store sheep in the land. Here are some of the highest concentrations of sheep in New Zealand. Almost every county in the region shows high densities, and one small one, Waipukurau (40 miles (64 km) south-west of Napier), with more than 2000 sheep per thousand occupied acres, has the highest sheep density in New Zealand. The exceptions are in two districts: three remote and hilly counties to the east of the Bay of Plenty have low densities, as do another three in the south, through which pass the main mountain ranges.

In nature Eastland was clothed largely in fern and scrub. New Zealand fern is evergreen and tall, and grows vigorously; but it is sufficiently dry for burning in a dry summer. The pioneer farmers did this, and then sowed the seeds of pasture grasses in the very ashes of the ferns. In the following months the grass grew quickly; then in the spring the young fronds of new fern began to uncurl. To conquer it the farmer grazed his land intensively for one or two months. He gave his animals no other food, for only half-starved stock will deign to eat fern. The thorough grazing and trampling killed off the fern in most areas, while the new grass was strong enough to assert itself.

Manuka scrub could not be attacked in this way: it will not burn when green, nor will the animals eat it even if starving. The pioneers waited till the seeds had ripened; then they cut down the scrub ready for burning. They allowed the seeds to germinate; then in the summer they set light to the old scrub, burning the new with it. Then they set the grass seeds, and in a few months sheep were grazing where formerly there had been scrub.

Farther inland the surface is more rugged, the rainfall is heavier and where the forest has been cleared soil erosion is a danger. Near the coast, by contrast, there are isolated districts of rich lowland with a sunny and dry climate. Here the land is intensively farmed: there are orchards and vineyards, market gardens and fields of maize, while roots and clover are grown as fodder crops. Such are the lowlands which focus on Napier, and on Gisborne, famous for its cultivation of rye-grass seed.

In general, Eastland is prosperous and well provided with communications. It is traversed by a main railway line, is supplied by a network of roads and is served by many market towns.

NOTES

1. *National Resources Survey*, Part IV, Nelson Region, Government Printer, Wellington, 1965.

2. E. Stokes, "Timber, Pulp and Paper," *New Zealand Geographer*, Vol. 22, No. 1 (1966).

3. *National Resources Survey*, Part II, Bay of Plenty Region, Government Printer, Wellington, 1962.

4. Tawera Moana, "Bushwacking in New Zealand," *The Listener*, 22nd August 1940.

5. *National Resources Survey*, Part III, Northland Region, Government Printer, Wellington, 1964.

6. *National Resources Survey*, Part I, West Coast Region, Government Printer, Wellington, 1959.

7. *National Resources Survey*, Part V, Otago Region, Government Printer, Wellington, 1967.

STUDY QUESTIONS

1. Consider the significance of the Southern Alps: (*a*) as a climatic barrier, and (*b*) as a gathering ground for water.

2. What is meant by the "winterless north"?

3. Compare and contrast Eastland with Westland.

4. Compare the stock-breeding industry of New Zealand with that of the Welsh hills.

5. Why is South Island more suited than North Island for the development of hydro-electricity?

6. To what extent has (*a*) relief and (*b*) climate influenced land use in New Zealand?

Chapter XVII

NEW ZEALAND: DAIRYING, FATSTOCK AND THE MAJOR CITIES

ANIMAL HUSBANDRY: DAIRYING

NEW ZEALAND operates what is probably the most efficient dairy industry in the world. It has achieved this status by advancing simultaneously along several fronts. It applies the latest technological improvements to the farms, to the factories and to the transport of the products. It reaps the economies of scale in all spheres. The Department of Agriculture exercises a strict control over quality, and New Zealand, in spite of her remoteness, competes successfully in the world's markets by reason of her low costs. The New Zealand Dairy Board, which centralises administration and marketing, constitutes the largest single exporter of dairy produce in the world.[1]

Mechanisation is such that the labour force involved is among the smallest in the world. Cheese and butter factories are larger than those in use in western Europe and the United States; thus, in little more than a decade the average output of the cheese factories has risen from 500 to 1200 tons annually, while that of the butter factories has doubled to reach more than 3000 tons annually.

Automatic packing and wrapping of butter is well established and in 1967–68 a new continuous process of butter-making was introduced to supersede the batch process. In cheese-making, the locally designed "Cheddar-master" machine replaces much laborious hand labour.

In transport the advances are equally striking. Bulk transport, which originated during the early 1950s, has spread to all the dairying areas. Water cooling has been introduced in the farm dairies, and the country roads have been improved to accommodate the larger vehicles. Farms have been amalgamated, herds have increased in size and the total number of dairy cattle has grown from 1·7 million head in 1948 to 2·2 million in 1971.

The dairy regions of New Zealand are almost entirely confined to North Island. Cows which spend their time climbing up and down steep slopes do not make good milkers; and the best dairy herds are found on level lowlands and rarely at altitudes greater than 600 feet (180 m). The dairy regions have mild winters, in which grass grows almost continuously throughout the year. Two things follow: first, that the herds spend nearly all their time in the paddocks; and second, that the farmer has little need to provide a stock of winter feed. He relies upon pasture

388

to an extent which is not possible, for example, in English Cheshire or Somerset.

The dairy pastures of North Island are artificial: this was in nature a region of forest, fern and scrub, and the farmers had a laborious task of clearing before the tidy landscape of today emerged. The introduced pastures consist chiefly of perennial rye-grass, white clover and paspalum. The last is a grass of South American origin: it grows rapidly in summer and provides abundant fodder, forming an excellent food for dairy cattle. But it must be grazed heavily, or it will soon grow rank; and the dairy farmer arranges his programme accordingly.

Dairying is particularly dependent on good transport. For cheese-making the milk must be sent to the factory each day; and this in practice means a journey rarely more than four miles. Cheese factories, then, are closely spaced throughout the region. For butter-making, however, only the cream is needed, and the New Zealand dairy farmer usually creams his own milk. Butter factories, then, are usually more distant from the majority of their suppliers—up to 30 miles (48 km) away; since they serve much wider areas than the cheese factories they are much larger. New Zealand butter factories have an average output which is five times as great as those of Denmark.

DAIRY REGIONS

The dairy regions of North Island comprise the lowlands which fringe the Taupo Plateau to the north, west and south (Fig. 131, p. 369). On climatic and geological grounds they may be divided into the Auckland dairy region and the Wanganui–Taranaki Lowland.

Auckland. This region, which includes the lowland portions of the Land District of that name, forms the heart of the dairy industry of New Zealand. It has a dense and prosperous rural population, huge cheese and butter factories and a highly developed town life which focuses on Auckland city. The network of road and railways is as close as any-where in the Dominion.

Here are the most intensively stocked dairy pastures in New Zealand; and on them graze nearly one-third of all her dairy cattle.

We have already seen that climatically this region is similar to its northerly neighbour, the pioneer region of North Auckland: it has high humidity coupled with abundant sunshine; winter warmth together with occasional torrential rain.

Geologically Auckland is a varied region—a patchwork or mosaic in which rocks ranging in age from Pleistocene to Trias and including basic and acid volcanic material are to be found side by side. The volcanic areas tend to be more elevated than those of younger rocks; but nowhere is the land excessively broken. The height of the Coromandel peninsula seems to be due to the elevation of an earth block rather than to the resistance of the volcanic material of which it is comprised; and conversely, the Hauraki Plains, to the west of the peninsula, represent a depressed block, whose northern portion is submerged to form the Firth of Thames and the Hauraki Gulf.

The concentrations of dairy cattle are greatest in these plains together with their extensions to the west and south. They are floored by Pleistocene and Recent sediments. But dairy farming is equally well established in the district of varied deposits west of the Firth of Thames and south of Auckland, and it extends too into the northern fringe of the Taupo Plateau. Climate and accessibility are here as important as soils, for the soils can be and are improved by fertilisers.

The deficiency is chiefly in phosphates. In part leaching is the cause. More important, perhaps, is the low phosphate content of much of the parent material of New Zealand soils; and an aggravating feature in the volcanic areas is the presence of iron compounds, which combine with phosphates to form an insoluble mass and actually reduce the amount of phosphate available for plants.

In consequence, 90 per cent of New Zealand fertilisers have a phos-

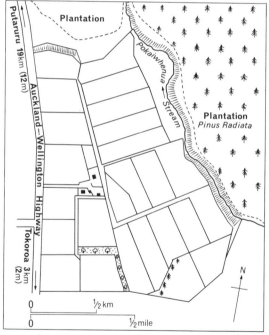

[Courtesy Association of Agriculture.

Fig. 140.—A dairy farm, South Auckland. Almost all the paddocks are under grass, which is grazed and cut for hay, or more usually turned into silage. The exceptions may be a crop of swedes and one of turnips, to interrupt a succession of several years of grass. The buildings comprise farmhouse, milking shed, implement shed and garage.

phate base, and there is a regular import of natural phosphates from Nauru and Ocean Islands, to the extent of about $1\frac{1}{4}$ million tons a year (p. 416).

We may illustrate some of these features from an actual dairy farm (Fig. 140), on the edge of the Taupo Plateau, two miles (3 km) from the small town of Tokoroa. It is bounded to the east by part of the great plantations of pines which we have already noticed (p. 374) and to the west by the highway between Wellington and Auckland.

The underlying rock is a hard volcanic material, rhyolite; and above this the soil-forming layer is derived from showers of "ash." The top five inches or so are dark in colour, and below this the soils are yellowish. They are classed as sandy silts: their natural fertility is low, but they respond well to fertilisers. The farmer treats all his pastures with at least 2 hundredweight (101 kg) of cobaltised superphosphates to the acre; and if they are used for new grass or for silage they receive up to 5 hundredweight (254 kg). The quantity of cobalt required to combat "bush sickness" is quite small—only about 5 ounces (142 g) to the acre. Yet before its introduction, about thirty years ago, this land could not be used for grazing in spite of what appeared to be good pasture.

The farmland is divided into twenty-five small, fenced paddocks, each of which occupies about $4\frac{1}{2}$ acres (2 ha). They are rectangular, and they are arranged on each side of a narrow grass track or corridor, and so are easily accessible. Subdivision of the farm in this way allows the farmer to graze his paddocks quickly and evenly in rotation; but the growth of grass in spring and early summer is so vigorous that there is a surplus, which he converts into silage.

While most farms in the dairy districts supply milk to the cheese factory or cream to the butter factory, this particular farm, being close to the growing town of Tokoroa, helps to supply the population there with fresh milk. For this reason the farmer is building up a herd of Friesians (noted for their high milk yield) as opposed to Jerseys (noted for their high yield of butter-fat), which are more typical of the New Zealand dairy districts. He has 84 milking cattle, no sheep or pigs, but 20–30 hens; and with the aid of his silage and a few acres of turnips, swedes or kale, he is self-sufficient in cattle food.

The Bay of Plenty coastal area has additional interests. On the narrow coastal strip is one of the major citrus and sub-tropical fruit regions of New Zealand. Sheltered by the Taupo Plateau and free from killing frosts, it possesses the mild conditions necessary to nourish the lemon. Here are grown 80 per cent of the nation's lemons and about 30 per cent of its grapefruits and oranges. The region also produces about half of the country's sub-tropical fruits: they include such delicacies as passion fruits, tree tomatoes and Chinese gooseberries. The main fruit districts are in the western portion of the Bay, around Te Puka, Katikati and Tauranga.

Tauranga is a port of more than local importance, and emphasises the close connection between the coastal belt and the Taupo Plateau to the south-west. Tauranga is the newly developed port for the timber and related industries of the plateau.[2] Its hinterland includes many sawmills and the pulp and paper mills at Kawerau, Kinleith, Whakatane and Rotorua. It is a highly specialised port, and ranks as the second exporting port of New Zealand by tonnage. But its import trade is fast developing: this includes phosphates for the local fertiliser works, grain for the local millers, petroleum products and cement. Tauranga ranks fourth among the import ports of New Zealand.

Auckland City. Situated to the north of this, the main dairy region of the Dominion, is the city of Auckland. It is the largest city in New Zealand, and one of the fastest growing in the country: since 1900 it has multiplied its population eightfold, to reach 698,400 people by 1971.

The site of Auckland is of unusual interest. Subsidence of the land has resulted in an intricate indented coastline, and as we have seen, the depression of an earth block has formed a major gulf (Hauraki Gulf). A drowned valley—that of the Waitemata river—leads eastwards into this gulf, and on its southern shore Auckland was founded.

To the south is a narrow isthmus, where only 6 miles (10 km) of dry land separate the Tasman Sea from the main Pacific Ocean, and across this neck of land the city has now spread itself. To the west, communication is possible with the North Auckland district, and here both road and railway crowd together to make use of the narrow land bridge. To the north a narrowing of the Waitemata estuary has aided ferry crossings to the opposite shore. Here is the growing residential suburb and pleasure resort of Northcote; and it is to improve communications in this direction that the striking harbour bridge has been built.

The whole district bears the signs of recent volcanism. There are many perfect craters, such as Mount Wellington, Mangere Mount and One Tree Hill (which now contains a golf course). Sheltering the harbour entrance is the comparatively large Rangitoto Island, whose volcano, rising to 854 feet (260 m) is the highest in the district. Among the old lava flows is one which results in a causeway that almost spans the harbour, in the neighbourhood of Kauri Point.

While volcanism is happily extinct in the Auckland district, there appears to be the possibility of earth tremors, and the designers of the new bridge have given it a firm anchorage (some of the foundations have been sunk to 90 feet (29 m) below water level) and have allowed a generous margin for expansion.

Auckland is thus a city of hills, which command extensive views over semi-tropical gulfs and mountainous islands; a city which adds luxuriant gardens to its two cathedrals, its university college, its museums and opera house, its gay shops and electric trams.

Auckland is one of the major ports of New Zealand, and one of its chief manufacturing centres. With a minimum depth of 33 feet (9·9 m) its harbour is used by the largest freighters, and the new bridge is sufficiently lofty to allow this traffic free access to the port. Auckland is chiefly concerned with the shipment of cheese, butter and chilled mutton from its rich hinterland; and prominent among its imports are oil, coal and phosphates for use in the manufacture of fertilisers.

The Wanganui–Taranaki Lowland. By contrast with the Auckland dairy region, the Wanganui–Taranaki Lowland has a relatively simple geological pattern. A magnificent volcanic cone, Mount Egmont, 25 miles (40 km) across, rises abruptly from a semicircular lowland; and

[*Courtesy High Commissioner for New Zealand.*

Fig. 141.—Mount Egmont (8250 feet; 2516 m). This majestic, isolated extinct volcanic cone dominates the Taranaki countryside. It is surrounded by a ring of productive dairy farms.

on the soils of its lower slopes a rich pasture flourishes and supports herds of dairy cattle (Fig. 141). This hollow ring of concentrated dairy farming is one of the most remarkable features of the distribution of livestock in New Zealand. To the north, the dairy herds occupy the narrow coastal lowland, here formed of Tertiary sediments, and then thin out; to the east, a stronger concentration of dairy cattle fringes Cook Strait, then turns south to reach the outskirts of Wellington. The coastal plain here is developed on Quaternary and Recent sediments.

Climatically the region may be considered typical of New Zealand. It has a high proportion of sunshine (about 2200 sunny hours in the year); a fairly heavy rainfall (most of the region has upwards of 40 inches (1000 mm) per annum), and a good deal of gusty weather.

This region, easily accessible, was early occupied, and the farms bear a mature appearance, with established hedges, red-tiled roofs and neat whitewashed wooden homesteads.

Mount Egmont is completely encircled by villages and farms; the district has a good road network and an even distribution of cheese factories. North of the volcano, on the road between New Plymouth and Waitara, is the Bell Block factory, one of the many co-operatively owned enterprises in North Island. It is a little unusual in that it combines both butter and cheese making under one roof. The equipment

[*Courtesy High Commissioner for New Zealand.*

FIG. 142.—A New Zealand butter factory. Each large churn, designed and manufactured in New Zealand, holds $2\frac{1}{2}$ tons of butter. The picture shows the removal of nearly one ton of butter.

is modern and spotless: the tubes and cylinders of the pasteurisation plant handle 3000 gallons (13,638 l) of milk an hour; the curds and whey in cheese-making are mechanically stirred in a huge tank; and the butter churn holds $2\frac{1}{2}$ tons at a time (Fig. 142). Bell Block factory is supplied by forty-eight farms and produces annually 300 tons of butter and 1000 tons of cheese. Most of it is shipped to the United Kingdom.

In Wellington Land District the plains widen to form a semicircular lowland with a radius of about 30 miles (48 km). This is a populous district, containing eight sizeable towns, and possessing a close net of roads and railways. The farming is less specialised here: in addition to his dairy herd the farmer rears sheep and cultivates grain.

We may illustrate from the area tributary to the town of Feilding. Though the small-scale map suggests a plain, in reality the surface forms a low plateau, in which several parallel streams flowing south-westwards have entrenched themselves. Destruction of the forests in the higher land to the north-east has loosened the soils and hastened erosion.

The farming activities differ over quite small areas. In the rough hillsides to the north-east of Feilding—the foothills of the Ruahine Range—the farmer concentrates on sheep for their wool and keeps store cattle to control the ferns and to improve the pastures. In the flood plains of the upper valleys the farming emphasis is on dairy cattle, while in the south the farms are mixed, with fat lambs as the chief source of income. A special enterprise is the breeding of Romney sheep, which takes place on the rolling country about 1000 feet (300 m) above sea-level north-west of the Orowe river, and about 10 miles (16 km) north-east of Feilding. This unusual specialisation cannot be explained solely on physical grounds: we must take also into account the enthusiasm and technical skill of the farmers who have developed here stud flocks containing many thousands of Romney ewes—a type of farming which is almost unique in the world.

Feilding itself, on which the district focuses, has become one of the largest fatstock market centres of New Zealand. It handles 8000 or 9000 animals each week, and its rectangular grid of pens can accommodate 50,000 sheep. The town did not exist until 1874, when the first settlers arrived, bringing with them the plan of a town modelled on that of Manchester, England. They chose their site wisely, for it has considerable nodality; and 12 miles (19 km) to the south-east is the Manawatu Gorge, forming the only easy east-and-west route in the southern half of North Island.

The industries of Feilding closely reflect the activities of its region. A freezing works handles half a million carcasses annually; and a large wool-scouring works and a bacon factory have more than local importance. A seed factory illustrates the local specialisation on the cultivation of grass seed; and there is one of the largest butter factories in the Dominion, with an annual output amounting to about 2000 tons.

ANIMAL HUSBANDRY: FATSTOCK

Meat production is widespread throughout New Zealand, as can be seen from the location of the meat freezing works (Fig. 143). These are almost equally divided between the two Islands (seventeen in North Island, sixteen in South Island). The North Island works are to be found in all the lowland areas and most, though not all, of them are coastal. The majority of them are capable of handling two or three hundred or more cattle daily during the season; as well as many thousands of sheep. The freezing works of South Island process mainly mutton and lamb. There are none on the West Coast, but there are concentrations in the

Christchurch and Canterbury Plains area and in the Invercargill area of Southland.

Employment is highly seasonal and the numbers are high. Four large works at Auckland have a peak labour force totalling 4000 people, of whom nearly 60 per cent are Maoris. The national total of employment in the meat works amounts to more than 20,000 so that the industry

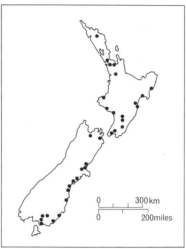

Fig. 143.—New Zealand: distribution of
meat-freezing works.

ranks high in the country's economy. Its products form a staple cargo at eight major ports, of which Auckland is the chief.[3]

The two chief fatstock regions, however, are both in South Island. Typically these are regions of mixed farming, where fat lambs and fat cattle are the chief concern of the farmer, but where the cultivation of grain crops also forms part of the farm enterprise.

FATSTOCK REGIONS

The Southland Plains. The core of this region is formed by the low-lying part of the large county of Southland; but it extends both eastwards and westwards to include the whole or parts of four or five other counties.

Geologically the region is distinct in that its lowland core is composed of Pleistocene and Recent sediments. Masses of the more resistant Triassic and Jurassic strata form the hills which flank the plains to the east, north and west, and rise to more than 1000 feet (300 m); farmers here rear sheep, but the pastures are insufficiently rich to fatten them.

Climatically the region is distinguished by what is by New Zealand standards a rather low rainfall—between 30 and 50 inches (750 and 1250 mm) per annum. The region has earned the title, "rainy Southland"; yet Southland is drier than most parts of North Island and bears no comparison with Westland. The rainfall is perhaps more obvious in that it is unusually reliable and is evenly distributed throughout the year. Temperatures are lower than in most other farming districts; this restricts the growing season of grasses to eight months of the year, and the farmer accordingly provides for winter feed by growing oats and root crops such as turnips, swedes and mangolds.

We may illustrate conditions in Southland from a sheep farm 15 miles (24 km) from Invercargill, where most of the farmers are of Scottish extraction. The farm is situated on flat land, and contains about 280 acres (112 ha), which are divided into sixteen paddocks. It carries 1000 sheep, and the farmer's main object is to produce fat lambs for the English market. Each year he cultivates about 40 acres (16 ha) (or two paddocks) of oats or turnips for winter fodder for the ewes; and each paddock in turn grows crops for two or three years before being sown again to grass.

There is always work to be done: harrowing, manuring, sowing or harvesting. Ditches are regularly cleaned; wool is baled after the shearing; fertiliser bags are sown together to cover the haystacks; lambs are drafted away to the freezing works. The sky is full of cloud; gulls wheel overhead and rain seems to beat incessantly on the corrugated-iron roof.

Dunedin. At the eastern edge of the Southland plain lies Dunedin, the smallest of the four main cities, with a population in 1971 of 117,740. It owes its foundation (in 1848) to a group of Scottish Free Churchmen, whose aim was to convey the ideals of Scottish life into New Zealand. They attached particular importance to education, and Otago University (now a college of the federal university of New Zealand) was the first institution of its kind in the country.

Styling themselves the "New Zealand Company," they employed a surveyor to explore and select a settlement site. He chose the Clutha–Taieri district, with Otaku (Otago) as its port. The harbour was long and sheltered, but divided into an inner and an outer portion by a chain of peninsulas and islands. The main direction of the inlet reflects the trend of the structural folding of the region, while the peninsulas and islands represent a subsidiary alignment almost at right angles to the main trend. The largest sailing vessels of the day could reach Port Chalmers, with 20 feet (6 m) of water at high tide; but the inner harbour offered only 6 feet (0·9 m) or less.

The chief attraction of the site was the sheltered harbour, which, like that of Port Lyttelton, has resulted from the drowning of a mass of volcanic material. Steep wooden slopes overlook the harbour and restrict the site; but the early settlers preserved the woodland, and it still stands as a green belt of great charm around the northern side of the city.

A plan was laid for the city, intended to reproduce as far as possible the special features of the Scottish capital. In fact a rigid straight-line pattern of streets was imposed almost regardless of the trend of spur and gulley in the ridges west of the harbour.

For two years the surveying went on; and then news came of the impending settlers less than a week before they actually arrived (March 1848). A number of frame houses had been shipped out from Britain, and within a year Dunedin had two hotels, a wooden church and many solid weather-board houses; while Port Chalmers had a customs house, the Post Office treasury, two stores, two inns and butchers' shops. There were also Maori-style grass huts and gypsy-like tents. As a contemporary newspaper put it, "a tent is very useful ... and will make capital trousers afterwards." [4]

The town was given the name of Edinburgh, and its main streets were named after those of the mother city. The accents of Scotland are still to be heard in the streets of Dunedin.

With the discovery of gold in central Otago in 1861 a rush set in, and Dunedin forged ahead to become temporarily the leading commercial centre of New Zealand. Roads and railways now focus on the city from three directions: from the plains and hills of Southland, from the basins of central Otago and from the southern portion of the Canterbury Plains. These supply its exports of wool, mutton, butter and cheese, fruit, hides and tallow; and they receive in exchange its imports of phosphates, oil, wheat and iron and steel goods.

The port lies at the head of Otago Harbour, 12 miles (19 km) from the open sea; and in the absence both of the current of a major river and tidal scour, silting takes place in the upper harbour. A retaining wall has been built, and with the aid of dredging, the wharves at Dunedin can accommodate vessels with a draft of 25 feet (3·8 m). Larger ships use the outport of Port Chalmers, where there is a minimum depth of 30 feet (4·6 m) of water.

The Canterbury Plains. With a maximum breadth of 45 miles (72 km) and a length of about 150 miles (240 km), the Canterbury Plains form the largest low-lying farming region in New Zealand.

Geologically it consists of Quaternary sediments, and the soils which have developed on them comprise rich loams, light and easy to work, sometimes gravelly, but well suited to machine farming.

Climatically the Canterbury Plains are distinct owing to their low rainfall and humidity and their high summer temperatures. Sheltered by the Southern Alps from westerly influences, they form the only large tract of land in the Dominion with a mean annual rainfall lower than 30 inches (750 mm). Deep trench-like valleys traverse the eastern flanks of the mountains, and air which finds its way from the west over the summits sweeps down the valleys, becomes warmer and has a desiccating effect on the land. These foehn-like winds bring the highest temperatures to be found anywhere in New Zealand, with maxima in the neighbourhood of 32° C (89° F).

The comparatively low rainfall is insufficient to support forest, and in a state of nature a large part of eastern South Island was clothed in tussock grass: this is a tough and wiry grass, adapted to withstand both drought and wind, which grows in clumps 2–4 feet (0·6 to 1·2 m) high. Tussock itself is not very palatable to sheep; but in the shelter of the individual clumps many smaller grasses and herbs can grow, and these do form useful pastures. In favourable conditions, as in the Canterbury Plains, the clumps were so close together that they gave the appearance of a complete cover. This native pasture was sometimes burnt to encourage new growth, for the animals eagerly graze young tussock for a short while; at other times the tussock land was ploughed and sown with introduced grasses or root crops. Today little tussock grass remains on the flat, cultivable land, though it is still to be seen on the steeper and less-accessible tracts.

Before the use of refrigeration, the aim of the farmer on the Canterbury Plains, as elsewhere, was to produce high-quality wool; and for this the merino was the most suitable breed. With its small, wiry frame, and its urge to explore the tops of ridges in search of food, the merino is still in its element in the broken, hilly districts. But the merino is bony and difficult to fatten; and when the quality of the meat became the chief consideration the farmer of the Canterbury Plains crossed merino ewes with imported British rams, and found that the resulting animal was a far better producer of meat. A recent tendency is to mate these cross-bred ewes with Southdown rams, in order to procure lambs which fatten rapidly. In this way the farmer makes the best use of the abundant spring fodder of the Canterbury Plains.

Today the Canterbury Plains farmer keeps up to a third of his land under permanent pasture. On the rest he operates a flexible rotation of cereals, root crops and grasses. All grow rapidly in this region of sunshine and reliable spring rains, and as well as being the chief fatstock region of the Dominion, the Canterbury Plains are also its most important arable region. Here are found two-thirds of all the grain crops of the country, including four-fifths of the wheat.

So prolific is the soil that sown grass can be grazed in spring, cut for hay in the summer and even then harvested for seed a month or two later. Wheat and oats, sown in the autumn, can be grazed in the winter without detriment to the following harvest. So all portions of the farm help to feed and fatten the sheep, and in addition may produce a saleable crop.

A farm example. We illustrate the region from a farm about 30 miles (48 km) north of Christchurch. It lies in the rolling downland which borders the flat land of the plains. There are nearly 800 acres (320 ha), which range from 300 to 680 feet (90 to 240 m) above sea-level. The farm comprises twenty paddocks, which average about 20–30 acres (8 to 12 ha) each, and there is in addition a 210-acre (84-ha) stretch of tussock grass which is too steep to cultivate and reseed. This tussock area is not as nature left it, for the farmer makes good use of the latest farming aid, the aircraft. Initially, he engaged a low-flying plane to broadcast clover seeds to the tussock grass, and each year this, together with the rest of the farm, receives a top dressing of superphosphate from the air, at the rate of $1\frac{1}{2}$ hundredweight (76 kg) to the acre.

The farm carries about 1600 ewes and 42 rams, and from every 100 ewes the farmer expects to rear 120–140 lambs. July, August and September are the lambing months. Shearing takes place in October, and with good weather the two hired workers complete the task in ten days. Each animal yields a fleece weighing 10 or 11 pounds (4·5 or 4·9 kg); about 40 fleeces go to the bale (which weighs nearly 3 hundredweight; 152 kg) and there are about 50 bales of wool to be sold. Early in November the first draft of fat lambs is ready for the freezing works. It numbers about 230 animals, and a large motor truck transports them either to the works at Islington or to those at Belfast (both places are close to Christchurch). There the carcasses are stored in freezing chambers until a refrigerator ship arrives at Lyttelton; then they are moved by insulated railway vans to the dockside. By the end of March the last of the 1300 lambs are on their way to the works, and the main task of the farmer is over.

Christchurch. The cultural, industrial and commercial centre of the Canterbury Plains is Christchurch—a city with an interesting "personality," which stems from its origin.

In 1848 the plans of Gibbon Wakefield and John Robert Godley in England bore fruit in the establishment of the Canterbury Association. It derived its name from the Archbishop who was its president, and its members included the Archbishop of York, seven bishops, three Cabinet Ministers and a dozen peers. The object of the society was to found a Church of England settlement in New Zealand based upon a cathedral and a college.

In December 1850, four shiploads of settlers, about 800 people in all, landed at Port Lyttelton (named after the Association's Chairman). Godley had preceded them, had surveyed the site of Christchurch, 6 miles (9·6 km) inland on the plains, and had organised the first jetty in the port.

Christchurch today bears the marks of its origins. It has been called the most English city outside England. A rectangular grid of wide streets lies astride a meandering stream, the Avon, which has been planted with gardens. The museum, cathedral, university college and Provincial Council Chamber are all built in Victorian Gothic style and could be matched in many an English provincial city.

Christchurch is the commercial centre for the wool, meat and grain of the fertile Caterbury Plains. It early felt the need for improved port communications, and the first railway in New Zealand spanned the 7 miles (11 km) separating it from Port Lyttelton. While Christchurch is built on the level plains, Lyttelton occupies the north-western edge of the volcanic Banks Peninsula, and the harbour itself is unusual in that it is formed of a submerged volcanic crater: the steep, curving slope which overlooks Port Lyttelton from the north and west represents the rim of the crater.

Christchurch is both a commercial and an industrial centre, and the woollen industry of Kaiapoi, a northern suburb, has an established reputation. Vessels drawing 34 feet (10·2 m) of water moor alongside the quays of Port Lyttelton, and discharge directly into railway trucks, then load with wool, grain, frozen meat, cheese and butter—the products of the Canterbury Plains. The population of the urban area in 1971 was 302,610.

WELLINGTON

It remains to examine the site of the capital. Wellington overlooks a deep, almost circular land-locked inlet known as Port Nicholson, which opens southwards into Cook Strait.

The land surface here has broken into fault-bounded blocks, and Wellington is built on the eastern side of one of these raised portions of the earth's surface. Its fault runs in a straight line for five miles to the north-east of the city, and it is this which accounts for the alignment of the shore in this direction. Earth movements along the fault have not ceased, and one night in 1855 the inhabitants awoke to find that the shore had risen 5 feet (15 m). This startling change had its value, for it provided a convenient terrace which was later used for the railway running eastwards. Other portions of Port Nicholson appear to be fault guided too, such as the shores of the rectangular Evans Bay.

Wellington is built round a semicircular bay in the west side of Port Nicholson (Lambton Harbour), where deep water approaches the shore. It has, however, been possible to reclaim a relatively narrow belt parallel with the shore, and here is now the commercial and industrial core of the city. Southwards and westwards the land rises steeply almost to 1000 feet (300 m), restricting expansion in these directions, but providing a fine scenic setting for the capital city.

Wellington is not the focus for any single natural region. It is in close touch with the dairy industry of the Wanganui–Taranaki district, and with the ranching of Eastland; and on the far side of Cook Strait are two districts of intensive agriculture, around Marlborough and Nelson. In the latter area apples, tomatoes, raspberries and peas are grown, together with hops and tobacco. But the real merit of Wellington lies in its fine harbour and its central position, from which all parts of New Zealand are accessible.

Like Auckland, Wellington has grown rapidly during this century, from 43,638 people in 1901 to 324,032 (including suburbs) in 1971. The expansion has taken place in two directions: to the south the city has extended across the neck of the peninsula which shelters the harbour, where the suburb of Melrose fronts Cook Strait; to the north-east the railway has aided settlement in the valley of the Hutt river (at the foot of the fault scarp), where Hutt City has grown to become a major centre in its own right, with a population more than twice the size of Wellington in 1910!

The commerce of Wellington has been aided by the depth of Port Nicholson and by the small tidal range (only 4 feet (1·2 m), even at spring tides). The approach channel has a minimum depth of 37 feet (11·4 m) of water, and large vessels can load and discharge at open quays, where there are several berths with a depth of 36 feet (11 m) at low water. Land locked though it is, the harbour cannot offer complete protection from the fierce south-westerly gales which occasionally race through Cook Strait, and ships' masters are warned to moor their vessels with care. The trade of the port is typical of New Zealand commerce: oil and coal, textiles and machinery move inwards; frozen meat, wool, cheese, butter, timber and grain move outwards, and there is a surplus of export tonnage.

With two cathedrals, the Parliament Building, the offices of Government Departments, museum, art gallery and University College, Wellington is one of the finest cities of the southern hemisphere.

TABLE 107

Some New Zealand statistics

Principal crops, 1969–70

	Thousand bushels	Thousand hectares
Wheat	9,417	115·6
Oats	2,812	49·5
Barley	6,786	63·3

Number of stock, 1972

	Thousand head
Sheep	60,883
Dairy cattle	3,425
Beef cattle	5,574
Pigs	603

Population of chief cities and towns, including suburbs, 1971

Auckland	698,400
Wellington	324,032
Christchurch	302,610
Hamilton	136,006
Dunedin	117,740
Palmerston North	80,732

Principal exports, 1971

	$ million
Meat and meat products	392·1
Wool	188·6
Butter	112·0
Hides, skins and pelts	50·6
Cheese	47·9
Casein	30·2
Pulp, paper and paper board	28·2
Fruit and vegetables	21·4

Trade with the United Kingdom, 1970

	$ million
Imports from the United Kingdom . . .	299·9
Total imports	944·3
Exports to the United Kingdom . . .	386·0
Total exports	1,086·7

Directions of trade, 1971

Exports from New Zealand	%	Imports to New Zealand	%
United Kingdom . .	34	United Kingdom . . .	29
United States	17	Australia	21
Australia	8	United States . . .	12
Other countries	41	Other countries . . .	38

Some major industries

Meat freezing and preserving

Year ended	Employment	Value of product $ mil.
1968 . . .	22,186	396
1969 . . .	23,630	457
1970 . . .	25,283	502

Butter, cheese and other milk products

1968 . . .	4,712	238
1969 . . .	4,530	243
1970 . . .	4,250	225

Fruit and vegetable preserving

1968 . . .	2,730	31
1969 . . .	2,643	33
1970 . . .	2,769	34

Pulp, paper and paperboard

1968 . . .	3,386	69
1969 . . .	3,421	76
1970 . . .	3,682	87

NOTES

1. J. K. Bewley, "A Survey of Changes in Production, Manufacturing and Marketing in the New Zealand Dairy Industry 1947–48 and 1967–68," *New Zealand Geographer*, Vol. 26 (1970).

2. J. F. Buckland and G. J. Fielding, "The Bay of Plenty Littoral," *New Zealand Geographer*, Vol. 21, No. 2 (1965).

3. G. J. Burridge, "The Location of Meat Freezing Works in New Zealand," *New Zealand Geographer*, Vol. 20, No. 1 (1964).

4. J. Forrest, "Dunedin and the Otago Block: Geographical Aspects of a Wakefield Settlement," *New Zealand Geographer*, Vol. 20, No. 1 (1964).

STUDY QUESTIONS

1. Examine the part played by fertilisers in the Auckland dairy region.

AUSTRALASIA

2. Compare and contrast the dairy industry of New Zealand with that of Denmark.

3. How do physical conditions in the Canterbury Plains aid the farmer in his work?

4. Describe the system of farming in the Canterbury Plains. How does it achieve its objects?

5. Write a short account of the site, origin and present functions of Christchurch.

6. Compare the modern development of Wellington with that of Auckland.

Chapter XVIII

THE PACIFIC ISLANDS

THE Pacific, the greatest of all the oceans, is larger than all the land masses put together. It is also the deepest of all the oceans, with an *average* depth of about 14,000 feet (4,200 m) (almost equal to the height of Mont Blanc) and a maximum depth of 35,000 feet (10,500 m) (much greater than the height of Mount Everest). Its eastern rim is formed by a regular and unbroken series of fold mountains which rise steeply from the depths of the ocean floor. Its central portion includes thousands of scattered volcanic and coral islands; its broken western rim is formed by festoons of mountainous islands which extend from the Aleutians, through Japan, New Guinea and the Solomons to New Zealand. These island arcs, which represent the real eastern edge of the continents of Asia and Australasia, overlook deep ocean trenches to the east, and earthquakes and volcanic eruptions testify that here is the most unstable portion of the whole of the earth's surface.

NEW GUINEA

The largest of the Pacific Islands is New Guinea, which, indeed, is considered to rank after Greenland as the second largest island in the world.

New Guinea is roughly three times as large as New Zealand. Much of it is still unmapped and large areas, especially in the mountainous interior of the island, still remain unexplored. Its total population is unknown, and estimates range between one and four millions. Its surface is exceedingly rugged, for its backbone consists of a mountainous mass whose summits rise to 16,000, 17,000 and 18,000 feet (4800, 5100 and 5400 m). Lying within 10 degrees of the Equator, New Guinea experiences a heavy rainfall, which is accentuated by the mountainous interior. It is estimated that more than half the island receives more than 100 inches (2500 mm) of rainfall annually and that the maximum exceeds 250 inches (6250 mm). The moisture and heat encourage the growth of dense forests, which clothe the mountains almost to their summits; and the rainfall feeds many torrents which race along the deep ravines that separate the mountain chains, and represent an abundant store of potential hydro-electricity.

Racially the people are varied, and include pygmy and negroid types, Malays and Polynesians. There are still primitive tribes which practise ritual murder and cannibalism, where the white man is unknown. No other land has remained so aloof from modern civilisation. In much of New Guinea the culture is still that of the Stone Age: the people hunt with the bow and arrow; the only implement in their shifting cultivation is the digging stick, by whose aid they grow beans, sweet potatoes or the sago palm. Any clearings they make in the forest are accomplished by the use of the stone adze. Among them the peoples of New Guinea speak 460 different languages—an apt comment on the natural barriers to communication in the island.

We have spoken so far of "geographical New Guinea," meaning the entire large island. Politically this is divided by a north-to-south boundary line into two almost equal portions. Until 1962 the western half was administered by the Netherlands and named Iriana, and formed the only portion of the former Netherlands East Indies to remain in Dutch hands. In August 1962 the Netherlands and Indonesia agreed that the United Nations should temporarily administer Western New Guinea, and on 1st May 1963 authority was transferred to Indonesia. Iriana appears to offer little scope for white settlement: it includes much thickly forested mountain country, and its lowlands are largely either jungle-clad or swamps where man is liable to disease.

The eastern half of the main island is further subdivided into a north-eastern and a south-eastern portion. The former, together with the islands to the east—New Britain, the Bismarck archipelago and Bougainville—constitute a Trust Territory of the United Nations, under Australian administration. It is known as the Territory of New Guinea. The latter, known as Papua, is a Territory of Australia. Since 1949 the two have been merged administratively, and are styled "the Territory of Papua and New Guinea."

Since information regarding West Irian is not readily available, our brief account is limited to eastern New Guinea. Geologically this is a young and unstable land, situated in a zone of crustal weakness. Volcanoes are still active and earthquakes are common. The highest peak, Mount Wilhelm, is just twice as high as Mount Kosciusko in New South Wales. Under a heavy rainfall, erosion is active, deep gorges have been excavated, landslips are common and the eroded material accumulates at the river mouths in the form of spreading deltas.

Structurally we may distinguish several well-defined regions, which are arranged broadly parallel with a north-west and south-east trend. North of the main island is a chain of smaller mountainous and volcanic islands, of which the largest are New Britain, New Ireland and Bougainville (Fig. 144). Along the north coast extends a series of mountain ranges, which thrust eastwards into the Solomon Sea; their partially submerged extension forms the Trobriand Islands. They are succeeded to the south by a structural depression which forms the swampy lowlands of the Sepik and Ramu rivers. Farther south the land rises to constitute the lofty mountainous spine of the main island: in the

FIG. 144.—New Guinea.

west it consists of a complex series of high plateaus and broad valleys; to the east it narrows and becomes less elevated in the Owen Stanley mountains, and its partly submerged peaks are seen in the Entrecasteaux and Lousiade island groups. Most of western Papua consists of a vast deltaic plain which extends into West Irian and forms one of the world's most extensive swamps. They are traversed by the Fly river, the largest in New Guinea.

This variety of terrain is matched by an equally varied climate and vegetation. Two narrow coastal strips on either side of Port Moresby receive less than 50 inches (1250 mm) of rainfall annually; the deltaic plain of western Papua experiences between 75 and 125 inches (1875 and 3175 mm); the Owen Stanley range has over 125 inches (3175 mm) and the mountain core to the west, more than 175 inches (4415 mm).

High temperatures and humidity in the lowlands speed up the process of leaching, and the soils deteriorate rapidly; hence the lowland peoples need to practise a shifting cultivation. In the hills the soils tend to be more stable, and a settled agriculture is possible. Over three-quarters of the main island, however, is forested, and the lowlands provide some of the most characteristic examples of equatorial forests, with their abundance of species of tall trees, often with buttressed trunks, laced together with lianes. The mangroves of the coastal swamps and tidal estuaries form barriers to penetration. Above 3000 feet (900 m) the trees are shorter, and oaks, pines and beeches become dominant. The actual tree line is as high as 12,000 feet (3600 m) and above are the shrubs, ferns and tussock grasses that constitute the only natural grasslands of New Guinea.

Typically the traditional lowland farmer lives in a rectangular house built on stilts and with a framework of saplings. Pitched roofs thatched with sago or nipa palm leaves throw off the rain. Below the house the domestic pigs scavenge the scraps that are dropped through the cracks in the floor. Around the houses are groves of coconuts, bread-fruit, bananas and pawpaws. But the lowlands in general are sparsely peopled: malaria is a deterrent and the soils are lacking in humus.

In the highlands the rainfall is more reliable and crop failure rare. An important event that attracted people into the highlands was the introduction about 350 years ago of the sweet potato, which can be grown up to 9000 feet (2700 m), and which, prepared in a variety of ways, forms the staple highland diet. The plant needs to grow in well-drained land, and the drainage ditches that separate the ridges planted with sweet potatoes form a characteristic rectangular pattern in the highlands. On steeply sloping land the cultivators build barriers of timber or rubble to prevent soil erosion.[1]

The highland house is circular or oval in plan; it is built on the ground, and in order to keep out the cold of the evening it has no windows and only a small doorway. It is framed in timber, thatched with grass and floored with bamboo; it needs to be rebuilt every four years or so.

New Guinea has never been very important for plantation crops, for several reasons. Transport is difficult; port facilities are inadequate; much of the territory was developed only recently, in a period in which economic depression was common. Concern by the government for native welfare made it reluctant to encourage the development of plantations. In 1965, of a total indigenous population of about 2,150,000, only about 40,000 were employed on plantations.

In Papua the chief plantation crop is rubber, all of which is shipped to Australia; the plantations are concentrated in the neighbourhood of the two settlements of Port Moresby and Popondetta, and around Milne Bay, in the eastern tip of the country. In the Trust Territory the chief plantation product is copra. Coconut plantations often serve more than one purpose: cocoa trees may be planted among and below the coconut palms, and cattle may be grazed on specially sown fodder crops. The coconut plantations are in the Madang district, on some of the larger offshore islands, and in scattered areas in the highlands.

The timber industry has a considerable potential. At present the Araucarian pine is the chief commercial species and is the basis of plywood manufacture; the Japanese, however, have shown interest in hardwood timber, and future development is likely in this direction.

New Guinea lacks coal and iron, and oil has so far not been found in quantity. Natural gas has been discovered in western Papua, and the reserves appear to be large, though they are far from any existing markets.

The most important mineral development is not on the main island, but to the east in Bougainville, the largest island of the Solomon group, which politically forms part of New Guinea. Here the Bougainville Copper Company in 1972 began to mine a large deposit of low-grade copper ore, which contains also small proportions of the precious metals. There are estimated to be 900 million tons of ore with a copper content of 0·48 per cent; the target is to dig 30 million tons annually, whose concentrates will contain about 150,000 tons of copper, a million ounces of silver and half a million ounces of gold.

The copper project is transforming the economy of the island, which hitherto has contained only village settlements. The largest centres in 1966 were Sohano and Kieta, with populations of 877 and 748 respectively, and the whole island contained only 72,490 people. An open-cast mine has been established near the source of the Jaba river, near the centre of the island; close by are the crushing and concentration plants. The tailings are being discharged into the river, where a belt up to 5 miles (8 km) wide at its mouth has been allocated for their disposal. The fish are dying. Villages are being resited and compensation paid to their inhabitants; new settlements are under construction: Panguna, near the mine, will be a "company" town of 3000 people (*see* Fig. 145), while Arawa, on the north-east coast, will be a business and trading centre, planned for an eventual population of 10,000.[2]

[*Courtesy Australian News & Information Bureau.*

FIG. 145.—Bougainville Island: Panguna. Camp site and mining operations of the Conzinc Rio Tinto of Australia Ltd.

[*Courtesy Australian News & Information Bureau.*

FIG. 146.—Bougainville Island: Mt Nautango. This deposit of volcanic rock on the site of the huge copper mining project at Bougainville is being used in the building of access roads to enable heavy mining equipment to be taken through the mountains.

Open-cast mining inevitably involves the devastation of extensive tracts of land (*see* Fig. 146). More reassuring on this score is an oil palm development project on New Britain, the largest of the offshore islands. It is taking place along a strip of coastland about 150 miles (240 km) long facing Kimbe Bay in the north of the island. This is a sparsely peopled area, yet it contains fertile and well-drained volcanic soils and is climatically suited to the oil palm. Roads, shipping facilities and airstrips are already in existence owing to the choice of Hoskins as an administrative centre, and as a result of nearby timber logging and milling operations.

The Hoskins oil palm scheme has a dual character: it combines plantation development with resettlement of indigenous people. A private company is developing a large oil palm plantation in 11,400 acres (4560 ha) of land, and in 1971 opened a processing plant capable of handling the fruit from 25,000 acres (10,000 ha). Concurrently the Administration is settling 1560 families on smallholdings: each plot comprises about 15 acres (4·5 ha), of which about half are planted to oil palm. The settlers have come mainly from the densely populated districts of the central highlands of New Guinea, and from the Gazelle peninsula of north-eastern New Britain. To forestall tension between the newcomers and the local villagers the Administration has promoted the planting of more than 600 acres (240 ha) of oil palm in the villages.

Oil palm is a commercially valuable crop: it is estimated to yield an income at least three times as great as that derived from copra, coffee or cocoa. The Hoskins scheme appears to be highly successful and the district is "well on the way to becoming one of the most developed agricultural areas of the country." [3]

The future of New Guinea seems hopeful. Local government councils were introduced in 1950 and there are now more than 100 of them distributed throughout the country. In 1964 universal suffrage was granted and a House of Assembly established, so that the territory is well on the way towards self-government.

TABLE 108

Papua New Guinea: chief exports in $A million

	1966–67	1970–71
Coffee beans	10·2	20·6
Copra	10·0	14·2
Cocoa beans	9·5	13·6
Other coconut products . . .	5·8	9·9
Logs and sawn timber . . .	2·3	6·4
Plywood and veneers . . .	2·2	2·5
Rubber	3·5	2·3
Total exports	46·1	77·4

THE PACIFIC ISLAND GROUPS

It is not possible to describe in a few words the many thousands of islands which break the waters of the Pacific, for a map of them resembles a chart of the heavens (Fig. 147). We can simplify the problem by making a threefold division into Melanesia, Micronesia and Polynesia.

"Melanesia" signifies "the black islands," from the dark skins of their inhabitants. The islands of Melanesia lie roughly parallel to the coast of Queensland but a thousand miles (1610 km) away to the east; they include the Solomons and the New Hebrides and extend as far east as Fiji; and they comprise almost all of the islands whose shape can be shown to scale on the atlas map.

A thousand miles beyond Melanesia lies Micronesia ("the small islands"); it includes the Gilberts (British) and the Marianas, the Marshalls and the Carolines (all American). Their inhabitants generally have copper-coloured skins, thin lips and straight hair, and are akin to the mongoloid races.

Away to the south-east lies a vast triangular region of the Pacific Ocean whose corners are formed by New Zealand in the west, Hawaii in the north and remote Easter Island in the east. This contains the islands of Polynesia ("the many islands"). The Polynesians are among the finest

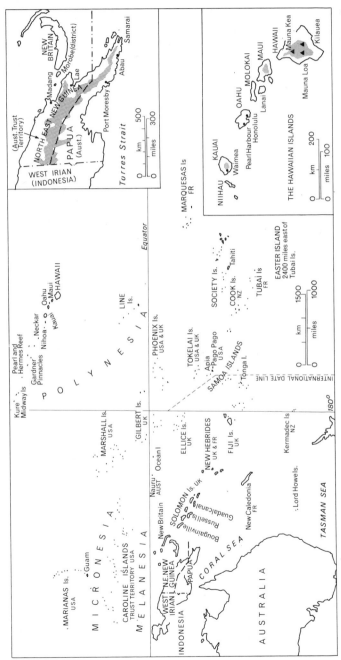

Fig. 147.—The Pacific Islands. The Pacific Ocean is larger than the combined area of all the land-masses of the world. The chief product of the Pacific islands is copra (dried coconut); but New Guinea in addition produces coffee, cocoa and rubber; Samoa produces cocoa and bananas; Fiji produces sugar and Hawaii pineapples, while Nauru and Ocean Island were important sources of phosphates. The insets show Eastern New Guinea and the main Hawaiian islands on a larger scale.

of the primitive races of the world—intelligent, cultured, well-mannered, handsome and of magnificent physique. We have already met some of them in the Maoris of New Zealand. The Polynesians performed amazing feats of seamanship and endurance, and in their long double canoes they spanned the entire Pacific.

MELANESIA

We must limit ourselves here to a brief glance at some of the island groups, and as an example of Melanesia we begin with the Solomons.

The Solomon Islands. The Solomon group consists of a double row of elongated, mountainous islands which extend northwards and eastwards of New Guinea and continue the general trend of its ranges. The larger islands are 100 miles (160 km) long, and their summits rise to several thousand feet (over 1000 m) above sea-level. As in all the Pacific islands, their core is composed of volcanic material, and in Bougainville, the largest of the group, there are two active volcanoes.

The Solomons have a continuously hot and moist climate and are therefore less attractive to white settlers than most other Pacific island groups. The inhabitants, moreover, have been more consistently hostile than elsewhere, and commercial development is accordingly slight. In the early days of the Queensland sugar plantations it was from the Solomons that many of the native workers were shipped. After this traffic was declared illegal, plantations of coconuts were established on the islands and today the firm of Lever Brothers operates 20,000 acres (8000 ha) of coconut plantations there. Most of these are in the central parts of the group, in Guadalcanal, in Ysabel and in the Russell Islands.

As in other types of plantation, the trees are arranged in orderly rows. Harvesting is easy: one simply waits until the nuts fall from the palm. A mature palm in good condition yields about 60 nuts each year: they are collected by lorry or cart every few weeks; the shells are split open and the white kernel removed. Drying is necessary to preserve the flesh and to reduce the weight for shipment; it may be carried out by the heat of the sun, or more quickly by the smoke from burning husks, or more effectively in a steam-heated kiln although the latter method is of course more expensive.

Usually the ocean vessel cannot approach close to the plantation wharf, and launches carry the copra over the surf to the waiting ship. Its destination is likely to be Port Sunlight or Liverpool, where its oil will be used in the manufacture of margarine and soaps.

The Fiji Islands. South-east of the Solomons and still in Melanesia lie the Fiji Islands, a group which alone includes 322 islands.

A century ago the Fijians were cannibals. The islands were annexed by the United Kingdom, and formed a Crown Colony until 1970, when Fiji became independent. Their inhabitants cultivate yams and sugar, or work in the coconut plantations. The natives are handsome and intelligent, and many of them qualify as doctors; they are fond of dancing and ceremony. But native Fijians are now outnumbered by Indians, who were transported to the islands to work in the sugar plantations; their numbers have increased rapidly, and, indeed, the Indian population threatens to double itself every 20–25 years. Fiji in fact has one of the highest rates of natural population increase in the world; yet less than one-fifth of the land is suitable for cropping or grazing, and the problem of supporting the population from the products of the soil is becoming more and more acute.

Copra is a staple product of Fiji, but by value it is outweighed by sugar, and the colony possesses one of the largest sugar mills in the southern hemisphere. The capital, Suva, has fine modern government buildings, and here is the Central Medical School, where doctors for the whole of the western Pacific are trained.

Fiji lies sufficiently far south to experience the belt of constant south-easterly winds, so that the south-east facing slopes receive the heaviest rainfall. Since all the islands are mountainous there are striking contrasts between the wetter south-east facing parts, where the mean annual rainfall is greater than 200 inches (5000 mm) and the drier north-west facing districts which in Vanua Levu receive less than 80 inches (2000 mm) in places and in Viti Levu less than 70 inches (1800 mm).

The wetter portions are clothed in forest, which extends as high as 3500 feet (1050 m) before becoming stunted; cultivation is almost entirely limited to the drier north-western coastal strips of both of the main islands. Sugar is by far the chief export of Fiji, and in 1969 was six times as valuable as the second export, coconut products (Table 109).

TABLE 109

Fiji: chief exports, 1969 (in million Fijian dollars)

Sugar	27·1
Coconut products . . .	4·5
Unrefined gold . . .	3·4
Molasses	0·6
Timber	0·3

In Fiji sugar is typically grown on smallholdings, each with an average of 9 acres (3·6 ha) under cane. Nearly a quarter of the economically active population is dependent on the industry; most of the cane is grown by the Indian section of the population, though the number of Fijians in the industry is growing.

Fiji faces serious problems. Only a small proportion of its area is potentially arable, and the average density of population on this land is 353 per square mile (136 per km²), rising in places in the north-west of Viti Levu as high as 900 per square mile (346 per km²).[4] Moreover the population is growing rapidly, transport costs are high from these remote islands and markets are insecure. In 1969 the United Kingdom was the chief customer of Fiji and took one-third of her exports; the remainder were shared by the United States, Australia, Canada, New Zealand and Japan, in that order.

The Tongan Islands. Four or five hundred miles east of Suva lie the Tongan Islands, which form the only remaining native kingdom in the Pacific. More than 150 islands are included in the group, though most of them are uninhabited. By a treaty of 1900 Tonga became a British Protectorate; but the Tongans retain their nationality, their language, their stamps and coins. They have, however, paid Britain the compliment of moulding their constitution on hers, and with Monarch, Parliament and Cabinet, Tonga has a Westminster in miniature.

Like most of the Pacific Islands, Tonga derives her chief wealth from the cultivation of the coconut, and she has successfully preserved her independence. There are no factories or mines on the islands, and all the plantations are native-owned.

MICRONESIA

The Gilbert and Ellice Islands. Scattered over a million square miles (1,600,000 km²) of the Pacific Ocean near the crossing point of the Equator and the International Date Line lie thirty-seven islands which form the British colony of the Gilbert and Ellice Islands. On their western outskirts lie the two islands of Nauru and Ocean Island, both of them renowned for their phosphate deposits. Part of Micronesia, they consist of two small, roughly circular coral islands 165 miles (264 km) apart, very close to the Equator, but 1500 miles (2400 km) from Australia and 2000 miles (3200 km) from New Zealand. Nauru is only $3\frac{1}{2}$ miles (5·6 km) across and Ocean Island is even smaller—$1\frac{1}{2}$ miles (2·4 km) across. They are therefore mere specks in the vast extent of the Pacific and represent the summits of submarine mountains.

But their small size bears no relation to their economic importance, for these two islands are estimated to contain 70 million tons of pinkish-brown phosphate rock, and form the fifth producer in the world of this vital mineral. Ocean Island forms part of the colony of the Gilbert and Ellice Islands, while Nauru is a Trust Territory administered by Australia; but in both islands the deposits are worked by the British Phosphate Commissioners by agreement of the Governments of the United Kingdom, Australia and New Zealand.

How did phosphate rock accumulate on these small islands? It is believed that they were once the breeding grounds of myriads of sea-birds, whose droppings were rich in phosphorus from the fish which formed their food. Rain-water, percolating through the deposits, dissolved out the phosphoric acid and converted the underlying coral limestone into phosphate rock.

The phosphate is dug in open quarries, and mobile grab cranes are used to load it into trucks on a narrow-gauge railway. It is crushed, dried in rotary kilns and is then ready for export. At both islands, however, special loading arrangements are necessary. Each is fringed by a coral reef, and beyond it the ocean floor drops steeply to great depths, well beyond the reach of the normal ship's anchor. Great 20-foot-long

(6-m) buoys have accordingly been provided, sufficiently large to support 1200 feet (366 m) of cable reaching down to the ocean floor; and to these moorings the ship makes fast.

From the storage bins conveyor belts carry the phosphate close to the edge of the reef, while swinging cantilevers span the deep water between the reef and the ship. They can be adjusted both in length and height to suit the position of the vessel. At Ocean Island a single cantilever loads one hatch at a time; but at Nauru there are two arms so that phosphate can be poured into the ship at the rate of up to 3000 tons an hour (almost a ton each second).

Cultivation is rarely possible on the thin soils of the phosphate plateaus of Nauru, and is limited to a narrow coastal fringe less than 300 yards (274 m) wide. Even drinking-water is scarce, and at times must be supplemented by the distillation of sea-water. The time is approaching when the phosphate deposits will be exhausted. In the case of Ocean Island it is estimated that this will occur during the late 1970s. The indigenous population have already migrated to Rabi, a fertile island in Fiji, which they were able to buy with the accumulated royalties from the sale of phosphates. The Gilbert and Ellice Islands colony will then, however, have lost its most lucrative resource, whose export in 1970 was valued at $A6 million—six times as valuable as copra, the second export. In addition alternative employment will need to be found for those employed in the phosphate quarries—currently 1325 people. These are serious problems, which are now exercising the mind of the administration.

In the meantime the two islands are exporting more than a million and a half tons of phosphates each year. Australia receives about 60 per cent of the total, New Zealand about 25 per cent, and the rest is shipped to the United Kingdom. So the farms of three nations are nourished from two specks of land in the middle of the Pacific Ocean.

POLYNESIA

As examples of Polynesia we may examine Easter Island, Samoa and the Hawaiian Islands.

Easter Island. Easter Island is a tiny outpost of Polynesia in the eastern Pacific. Triangular in shape, its longest side measures only 12 miles (19 km); yet its former cultural significance seems to have borne no relation to its small size.

The island received its name from the fact that it was discovered on Easter Day in 1722, by the Dutch explorer, Jacob Roggeveen. For nearly fifty years it lay forgotten; then in 1770 it was rediscovered by a Spanish expedition and annexed to Spain. When Spain was forced to relinquish her South American colonies Easter Island lay at the mercy of "black-birders"; and in one merciless raid in 1862 most of the able-bodied men of the island were transported to the Peruvian desert to work the guano deposits there. In one swoop the population of Easter

Island had been reduced from several thousands to about 100 souls; and this almost complete break with the past, in addition to its tragic cost in human suffering, has meant that the meaning and purpose of the ancient culture of the island has been lost.

The island is of volcanic origin, and from one of the cones in the east a fairly soft tuff was quarried and carved into huge human figures. They are grotesque half-length portraits; they range in height from 15 to 33 feet (4·5 to 10 m), and even the smallest weighs several tons. To heighten their fantastic appearance they were crowned with cylindrical hats of reddish stone quarried from a volcano in the west of the island. There are 600 of these remarkable statues in Easter Island. They were generally placed with their backs to the sea at the tribal burial places; but most of them were later thrown down during the course of tribal warfare.

Formerly almost every household possessed a wooden tablet inscribed with mysterious symbols, every alternate line being upside down: these are all now in museums, where they still puzzle the anthropologist. Abundant carvings relating to a sea-bird cult add to the mysteries of Easter Island, which, though forming the most remote fragment of Polynesia, seems to have been the scene of its greatest cultural development.

Today the island is a protectorate of Chile. Its population has risen to more than 700, and its mainstay is the rearing of merino sheep, of which there are about 35,000 head.

Samoa. Samoa consists of a group of volcanic islands, rugged and wooded and fringed with coral reefs; they lie about 1500 miles (2400 km) north-north-east of Auckland, New Zealand. Here is the largest branch of the pure Polynesian race apart from the New Zealand Maoris. Politically the group comprises Eastern Samoa, which is administered by the United States; and Western Samoa, which was formerly under the trusteeship of New Zealand, but in January 1962 achieved independence.

Eastern Samoa has a population of about 21,000; it consists of a single main island—Tutuila—which is about 20 miles (32 km) long from east to west; and it includes the only good harbour of the group—Pago-Pago. Western Samoa, with a population of about 130,000, contains two main islands; these are Savai'i and Opulu. Each is about 50 miles (80 km) long from east to west, and on the latter is the capital, Apia.

Samoan villages are almost without exception coastal, and are largely self-sufficient in foodstuffs: the inhabitants grow taro, bananas and coconuts, and engage in fishing. Export produce consists almost entirely of three commodities, namely copra, cocoa and bananas.

The Hawaiian Islands. The Hawaiian Islands, which are administered by the United States, are centrally placed in the north Pacific Ocean (*see* Fig. 147, inset). They were discovered in 1777 by Captain

Cook, who named them the Sandwich Islands after the Earl of Sandwich, who was then First Lord of the Admiralty. It was here that Cook met his death a year later in an unfortunate affray with the natives.

The islands extend in a narrow chain arranged from east-north-east to west-south-west and 1600 miles (2560 km) in length. They include eight large inhabited islands which are grouped together in the east, and ten or so small islands or reefs, for the most part uninhabited, which stretch far to the west, each one separated from its neighbour by about 150 miles (241 km) of sea. The whole chain presents the interesting phenomenon of a line of weakness in the earth's surface along which volcanic activity appears to have proceeded from west to east.

In the most westerly islands (Kure, Midway, Pearl and Hermes Reef, Lisianski, Laysan and Maro) the volcanoes have been completely destroyed by erosion, and coral has established itself on the submerged

[*Courtesy United States Information Service.*

FIG. 148.—Giant fern forests, Hawaii. These luxuriant fern forests grow on the lower slopes of Kilauea, the active volcano of Hawaii. They are now part of the 300-square mile (777-km²) Hawaii National Park.

platform. Farther east (in Gardner, the French Frigate Shoals, Necker and Nihoa) the islands, though almost eroded away, still preserve the evidence of their volcanic origin. From here, through the large islands from Niihau to Maui, one sees a succession of volcanoes becoming larger and more perfect as one moves eastwards, till finally, on Hawaii itself is Mauna Loa, the world's largest volcano by far, with a diameter of 60 miles (96·5 km) at sea-level. On its eastern flank the crater, Kilauea, is continuously active and contains a permanent lake of molten lava. (*See* Figs 148 and 149.)

Mauna Loa (the Great Mountain) rises to 13,680 feet (4172 m), but its northerly neighbour, Mauna Kea (the White Mountain) overtops it at 13,796 feet (4208 m). These are the two highest peaks in the Pacific, and by Alpine standards are lofty giants. More remarkable is the fact that they rise abruptly from the ocean floor at more than 16,000 feet (5000 m) below sea-level, so that in a real sense they are among the world's highest mountains.

The Hawaiian Islands lie in the track of the north-east trade winds, so that the summits and north-eastern slopes of the larger islands receive a constant and heavy rainfall, while the south-western flanks tend to be dry. There are thus usually sharp contrasts in precipitation over quite small distances. The summit of Mount Waiakeale on Kauai Island, in the west of the major group, has a mean annual rainfall of 489 inches (12,421 mm) (on a 28-year average) and so far as is known is the world's wettest place. In one recent year 624 inches (16,050 mm) of rain fell

[*Courtesy United States Information Service.*

Fig. 149.—The volcanic crater of Haleakala, Hawaii. Haleakala, 10,025 feet (3055 m), is the largest dormant volcano in the world. The crater, which is 21 miles (34 km) in circumference, is a major tourist attraction.

here; yet Waimea, a coastal town only 15 miles (24 km) away in the rain shadow to the south-west, receives as little as 20 inches (500 mm). A generally porous volcanic soil minimises the effect of rainfall, and about 100,000 acres (40,000 ha) largely under sugar cane, are irrigated.

The population of Hawaii is extremely mixed. Captain Cook estimated the number of natives to be about 300,000; but the introduction of diseases against which they had no resistance has decimated the indigenous population, and they now total only 90,000, including half-castes. The Polynesians are now quite outnumbered by immigrants from Japan, who total about 203,000. Other important racial elements include Filipinos, Chinese and thousands of American tourists, and the total population of the territory in 1970 was 769,913. This represents an increase of 22 per cent since 1960. The tourist industry is expanding rapidly. In 1955 109,798 people visted Hawaii; the corresponding figure for 1970 was 1,595,000.

The cultivation of coffee, rice and taro was formerly of importance, but these are now eclipsed by pineapple and sugar-cane plantations. The pineapple has been grown for more than a century, but rapid expansion came only after the introduction of canning in 1892. The crop now occupies about 50,000 acres (20,000 ha) of the higher land, and Hawaii has become one of the world's major producers of this fruit. The bulk of it is shipped to the United States. Sugar cane is a crop of the humid coastal lowlands, and the plantations cover about 240,000 acres (96,000 ha). This too is shipped to America.

Though Hawaii island is the largest of the group, its regular coastline has prevented the development of any major port. In contrast, Oahu, farther to the north-west, with greater dissection, coupled perhaps with slight sinking of the land, offers the sheltered harbour of Honolulu and the magnificent land-locked naval base of Pearl Harbour.

Honolulu is both the port and the cultural and administrative centre of the Hawaiian Islands. It is halfway house between the Pacific ports of the United States and the Far East, and it is an airport for the trans-Pacific services of Pan-American Airways. Its sheltered harbour is equipped to repair, refuel and provision ocean vessels; its canning industries reflect the farming activities of the archipelago. To the east are the renowned pleasure beaches of Waikiki. With a population of 324,871 (1970), Honolulu includes nearly half the inhabitants of the Territory, while its university and museum have made it the chief centre of learning in the Pacific.

NOTES

1. D. Howlett, *A Geography of Papua and New Guinea*, Melbourne, 1967.

2. L. P. Cummings, "The Bougainville Copper Industry Construction Phase," *Australian Geographer*, Vol. XII, No. 1 (1972).

3. W. J. A. Jonas, "The Hoskins Oil Palm Scheme," *Australian Geographer*, Vol. XII, No. 1 (1972).

4. R. Gerard Ward, *Land Use and Population in Fiji*, H.M.S.O., 1965.

STUDY QUESTIONS

1. What are the possibilities for the future economic development of New Guinea?

2. Explain the terms: Melanesia, Polynesia, Micronesia.

3. Examine the problems associated with phosphate mining in Nauru and Ocean Island.

4. How are human activities in Hawaii related to the physical environment?

Chapter XIX

ANTARCTICA

I⊤ is appropriate to conclude our study of Australasia with a brief reference to Antarctica, for between them, Australia and New Zealand administer well over half the continent; moreover, Antarctica has affinities with the three other southern continents, so that here may lie the solutions of problems which cannot be resolved in any one continent in isolation.

With an area of $5\frac{1}{2}$ million square miles (14·3 million km²), Antarctica is larger than the United States, larger than Europe, larger than Australia. It is placed almost centrally around the South Pole and almost centrally in the Southern Ocean; it is almost equidistant from Australia, South America and Africa; and it stands in sharp contrast to the Arctic region, where an ocean is almost completely surrounded by land.

Captain Cook on his second voyage (1772–75) circumnavigated Antarctica and disposed for ever of the notion of a supposedly fertile southern continent which stretched into temperate latitudes. A British expedition of 1898–1900 was the first to winter on the mainland; the first long sledging journeys were made under Scott in 1901–4; the magnetic pole was reached by Shackleton in 1909 and the geographical pole in 1912 by the Norwegian Amundsen. The first crossing of the continent was made by air in 1936, by the American, Lincoln Ellsworth. Not till the International Geophysical Year (I.G.Y.), in 1957–58, was an international concerted assault made upon the secrets of Antarctica: fifteen expeditions from eleven different countries then took the field, and the United States alone established and maintained six bases, one of them at the Pole itself.

Territorial claims in Antarctica are based largely on exploration, and take the convenient form of sectors which converge at the Pole (*see* Fig. 150). The first, the former Falkland Islands Dependency, was proclaimed by the United Kingdom in 1908; this was reconstituted as a colony ("British Antarctic Territory") in 1962. Australia and New Zealand administer the sectors which lie opposite their shores. Between Australian and United Kingdom territory is the Norwegian Queen Maud Land, and within the Australian sector is the small French territory of Adélie Land. There remains unclaimed a sector of 70°—the last remaining in the globe! Here the United States has been particularly

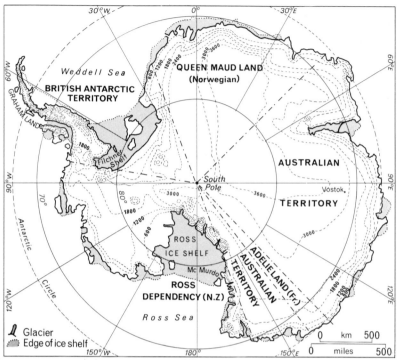

[*After A. P. Crary,* The Scientific American, *September 1962.*

FIG. 150.—Antarctica: ice shelves, main glaciers, relief and political divisions. The contours of inland Antarctica were virtually unknown before 1957; they indicate the surface of the ice and not the underlying rock. Heights are in metres.

active, but officially neither makes nor recognises any claims in the Antarctic. The Antarctic Treaty, which came into force in June 1961, "freezes" territorial claims for thirty years and preserves the Antarctic for peaceful purposes and scientific research. Signed by Argentina, Australia, Belgium, Chile, France, Japan, New Zealand, Norway, South Africa, the United Kingdom, the United States and the U.S.S.R., it records a real advance in international co-operation in this remote continent.

Antarctica contains more than 80 per cent of all the ice in the world, and this ice-cap in places reaches a thickness of $2\frac{1}{2}$ miles (4 km). Over most of the continent its surface lies at more than 6000 feet (1800 m) above sea-level. What of the rock surface below it? It had long been suspected that a hidden geosyncline connected the two major embayments in the continent—the Ross and Weddell seas. Seismic traverses during the I.G.Y. confirmed its existence and indicated that the rock surface for the whole distance lies below sea-level. This geosyncline divides the continent into two contrasting provinces: the larger is

formed by the stable block of East Antarctica and the smaller is West
Antarctica, which, apart from its cover of ice, would be a group of
islands (*see* Fig. 151).

East Antarctica is composed of a basement of Precambrian rocks,
overlain in places by Palaeozoic material. Devonian strata are known to
be covered by glacial drift; this in its turn is succeeded by Permo-
Triassic coal measures, which include potentially valuable coal seams
and are characterised by the long and slender fossil leaf, *Glossopteris*.
The sequence agrees closely with that found in South America, South
Africa, Australia and southern India. East Antarctica clearly has had at
times a temperate or even tropical climate, and is presumed then to have
formed part of a much larger, now dismembered continent.

West Antarctica stands in complete contrast. Its western fringe from
Graham Land to the Ross Sea consists of a mighty range of young fold
mountains, interspersed with volcanoes, and identical in structure to the
Andes of Patagonia: with these, indeed, it is connected by the loop of
banks and islands which encloses the Scotia Sea. To the east horizontal

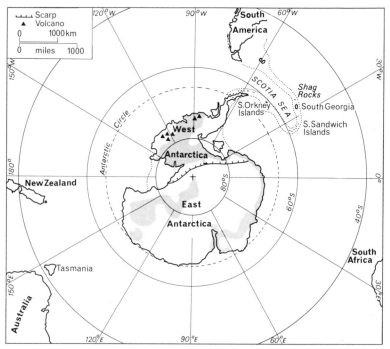

FIG. 151.—The setting and structure of Antarctica. East Antarctica appears to be a
    stable block, which overlooks West Antarctica in a bold scarp. West Antarctica is
    structurally similar to the South American Andes and is linked to them by a loop
    of banks and islands, including South Georgia and the South Sandwich and South
    Orkney Islands. Within the shaded areas, the rock surface beneath the ice is below
    sea-level.

Jurassic, Cretaceous and Tertiary strata match those of the Patagonian Pampas.

Climatically Antarctica is cold and dry. For the most part around the coast mean annual temperatures lie between −10° and −15° C (14° and 5° F), but decrease inland to reach −55° C (−67° F) over a wide area of the plateau. At the Pole, 9200 feet (2800 m) above sea-level, the mean January temperature is −41° C (−42° F) and the mean August temperature is −61° C (−78° F). At the Soviet base of Vostok, about 1000 miles (1600 km) from the Pole in longitude 97° E., and 11,200 feet (3360 m) above sea-level, on 24th August 1960, the appallingly low temperature of −88° C (−127° F) was experienced. This is the lowest temperature ever recorded in the world at ground level.

The prevailing winds are outward-blowing, and as a result of the earth's rotation are deflected to become south-easterly. The intensely cold air can hold little water-vapour, and most of the continent has a precipitation characteristic of the deserts. On the high plateau the annual precipitation is equivalent to less than 2 inches (51 mm) of rainfall; this increases to over 8 inches (200 mm) along the coasts and locally (in 90° W. long.) to over 22 inches (560 mm). Climatic changes in Antarctica could be of vital importance to the rest of the world: if the whole of its ice were to melt there would be a rise in sea-level throughout the world of the order of 200 feet (60 m) with disastrous consequences.

Antarctica is virtually lifeless, but its surrounding seas team with life: instead of salt water it may be regarded as broth! Mineral nutrients rising from below maintain its fertility and nourish minute single-celled marine plants; these form the food of the red shrimp-like crustacean known as krill. In its turn, krill is eaten wholesale by whales, seals, fish, sea birds and penguins. With the exception of the whale, few of these are hunted by man, for the Antarctic seal is not fur-bearing and the skin of the penguin is coated with blubber and is thus not marketable.

In an average year about twenty whale factory ships with over 200 whale catchers operate in the Antarctic. In the past Norway, the United Kingdom and Japan have been the chief participants, but in 1963 the last remaining British factory ship was sold to a Japanese concern. The Japanese hunt whales for their meat as well as their oil, and here certainly is a largely untapped source of human food, for a single whale can contain the equivalent of 300,000 portions of roast beef.

Antarctica is no longer deserted (see Figs 152, 153 and 154): in 1962 there were forty stations there, maintained by nine different nations. The United States has established a permanent station at the South Pole, and during the summer employs nearly 3000 men in the continent. The central supply base for the United States is at McMurdo Sound, and here 1000 men are supported with the help of a small nuclear power station, set up in 1962.

[*Courtesy Australian News & Information Bureau.*

FIG. 152.—Antarctica: transport by sledge. This party is based at Mawson, in the Australian sector, on the coast near long. 60° E, and is using the traditional dog-sledge for transport. In the background are the Prince Charles mountains, which rise from the Antarctic plateau.

[*Courtesy Australian News & Information Bureau.*

FIG. 153.—Antarctica: mechanical transport. This party, operating in a blizzard near Mawson, is using a small tracked vehicle. The initials indicate that it is an Australian National Antarctic Research Expedition.

[*Courtesy Australian News & Information Bureau.*

FIG. 154.—Antarctica: a seismic explosion. Most of the activity
is directed towards research. The shock waves recorded
from such an explosion provide information concerning the
thickness of the ice and the nature of the rocks below it.

SHORT GUIDE TO FURTHER READING

BOOKS

Oxford Survey of the British Empire, Vol. 5: Australasia. London, 1914. In spite of its date, this is still a valuable source, particularly on the physical side.

Geographie Universelle, Tome X: Oceanie, P. Privat-Deschanel.

Australia, G. Taylor, London, 7th edn., 1959.

The Romance of the Australian Land Industries, R. D. Watt, Sydney, 1955.

The Territory, Ernestine Hill, London, 1952.

Southwest Pacific, K. B. Cumberland, London, 1956.

The Climate of New Zealand, B. J. Garnier, London, 1957.

New Zealand Geomorphology, C. A. Cotton, Wellington, 1955.

The Pastoral Industries of New Zealand, R. O. Buchanan, Institute of British Geographers, Vols. 1–2, 1933–34.

The Crossing of Antarctica, Vivian Fuchs and Edmund Hillary, 1958.

Regional Landscapes of Australia, N. and A. Learmonth, 1971.

JOURNALS

Many valuable articles are to be found in the files of *Geography*, the *Geographical Journal*, the *Australian Geographer* and the *New Zealand Geographer*. A comprehensive summary of the I.G.Y. investigations was published in *The Scientific American*, September 1962. The references below supplement those listed in the notes to each chapter.

Geographical Journal

"Agricultural Regions of New Zealand," K. B. Cumberland, January 1949.

"Australia's Frontier Province," C. L. A. Abbott, January–March 1948.

"The Growth of the Australian Iron and Steel Industry," N. R. Wills, June 1950.

"Easter Island," Sir Harry Luke, December 1954.

Since 1957 there have been many articles on Antarctica. See in particular "The Commonwealth Trans-Antarctic Expedition," Sir Vivian Fuchs, December 1958.

Geography

"An Aluminium Industry in Tasmania," P. Scott, April 1955.

"The Petroleum Industry of Australia," P. Scott, January 1956.

"The Tasmanian Apple and Pear Industry," P. Scott, January 1959.

"The Build of West Antarctica," D. L. Linton, July 1960.

"The Alpine Fault, South Island, New Zealand," R. P. Suggate, January 1961.

"The Development of Port Kembla, N.S.W.," J. N. H. Britton, July 1961.

"Waitaki River Development," L. J. Stenhouse, April 1961.

"The Development of Geothermal Steam Power in New Zealand," B. H. Farrell, January 1962.

"Agricultural Experiments in N.W. Australia," R. G. Golledge, April 1962.
"The Australian Railway Gauge Question," J. H. Appleton, July 1962.
"Weipa—A new Bauxite Mining Area in North Queensland," E. M. Driscoll, July 1962.
"Queensland Ports and the Bulk Shipment of Australian Raw Sugar," E. C. Chapman, July 1962.
"Population Changes in the Sydney Metropolitan Area," M. I. Logan, November 1962.
"Trends in New Zealand's Population Distribution," R. D. Hill, November 1962.
"The Maori Today," Joan Metge, April 1963.
"Christchurch, New Zealand, and its Port," L. S. Suggate, July 1963.

New Zealand Geographer
"The Development of H.E. Power in New Zealand," L. F. Withers, April 1950.
"Phosphates in New Zealand Agriculture," M. M. Burns, October 1952.
"Railway Transport in New Zealand," J. W. Fox, October 1951.
"New Zealand Farms and the Phosphate Islands," A. Ellis, April 1948.

MAPS

The Times Atlas, Vol. I, London, 1958.
Australia, 1 : 5,000,000, J. Bartholomew, 1956.
New Zealand, 1 : 2,000,000, J. Bartholomew, 1957.
The maps comprising *The Atlas of Australian Resources* may be purchased separately at Australia House, London.
Antarctica, 1 : 7,000,000, supplement, *National Geographic Magazine*, Sept. 1957.

OFFICIAL LITERATURE

The year books of Australia and New Zealand are of great value; in addition descriptive literature may be obtained from the following agencies in London:

Tasmania: 458 Strand, W.C.2.
Victoria: Victoria House, Melbourne Place, Strand, W.C.2.
New South Wales: 65 Strand, W.C.2.
Queensland: 392 Strand, W.C.2.
South Australia: South Australia House, 50 Strand, W.C.2.
Western Australia: Savoy House, 115–16 Strand, W.C.2.
Australia: Australia House, Strand, W.C.2.
New Zealand: New Zealand House, Haymarket, S.W.1.

EXAMINATION QUESTIONS

The following questions are from Advanced Level General Certificate Examination papers set by the University of London.

1. Make a comparative study of the human geography of *either* Tasmania and South Island, New Zealand, *or* Western Australia and South Australia. (Summer, 1967)

2. Examine the extent to which climatic hazards affect the human geography of Australia. (Summer, 1967)

3. Compare the situation, site and functions of *one* major port on the east coast of Australia with *one* major port in New Zealand. (Summer, 1967)

4. *Australia*:

Total population, 1965—11 million.
Urban population—82 per cent.

With reference to the above statistics, discuss the effects of the concentration of population in urban areas on the future development of Australia. (Summer, 1967)

5. Review the significance of water in the geography of Victoria. (Summer, 1967)

6. Explain the contrasts in climate between the eastern coastlands and the western coastlands of Australia, *south* of the Tropic of Capricorn. (Summer, 1968)

7. Name *two* areas of contrasting human development in *either* Queensland or Western Australia. Outline the factors that explain the contrasts. (Summer, 1968)

8. With the aid of a sketch-map, discuss to what extent railway patterns are related to the distribution of mining centres in Australia. (Summer, 1968)

9. Explain the geographical bases of the manufacturing industries of *either* Victoria *or* South Australia. (Summer 1968)

10. Make a comparative study of the export trade of New Zealand and New South Wales. (Summer, 1968)

11. Write reasoned geographical accounts of *two* of the following: earthquakes in New Zealand, the Great Barrier Reef, fuel and power resources in Tasmania, beef production in northern Australia, farming in the Riverina. (Summer, 1968)

12. With the aid of a sketch-map, describe the distribution of the grasslands of Australia and outline their importance. (Summer, 1969)

13. Locate, and explain the geography of, the principal manufacturing industries of Australia. (Summer, 1969)

14. Relate arable farming in New Zealand to environmental factors. (Summer, 1969)

15. Describe the course, the regimes and the economic significance of the rivers of Australia. (Summer, 1969)

16. Outline the export and import trade of New Zealand and examine the trends in recent years in reciprocal trade with other countries. (Summer, 1969)

17. Select *two* contrasting areas of sparse population, *one* in Australia and *one* in New Zealand, and discuss the reasons for the low densities, emphasising the differences between the two areas. (Summer, 1969)

18. Describe and explain the main features of the relief and structure of New Zealand. (Summer, 1970)

19. Select *two* of the following cities and assess their functions in relation to their physical settings: Hobart, Perth, Brisbane, Melbourne. (Summer, 1970)

20. Discuss the factors (physical and human) which underlie the location and the development of the iron and steel industry in Australia. (Summer, 1970)

21. Write a geographical account of the Murray–Darling basin. (Summer, 1970)

22. Make a comparative study of the agriculture of North Island and South Island, New Zealand. (Summer, 1970)

23. Outline the development of the water resources of Queensland, the Northern Territories and Western Australia, taken together, and discuss the possibilities of further development. (Summer, 1970)

24. Assess the role of farming in the economy of *one* of the following States: Tasmania, South Australia, Victoria. (Summer, 1971)

25. Discuss the problems involved in the economic development of New Zealand. (Summer, 1971)

26. To what extent is the distribution of the manufacturing industries related to the distribution of population in New South Wales? (Summer, 1971)

27. Assess the effects of climate on the development of the Northern Territory. (Summer, 1971)

28. Make a comparative study of the location and functions of *either* Auckland and Wellington *or* Christchurch and Dunedin. (Summer, 1971)

29. Locate, and examine the development of, the main areas of mineral production in *either* Queensland *or* Western Australia. (Summer, 1971)

30. AUSTRALIA: *Crop production, 1967–68*

Wheat	.	.	.	277·3 million bushels
Oats and barley	.	.	.	74·8 ,, ,,
Rice	.	.	.	11·2 ,, ,,
Sorghum	.	.	.	9·9 ,, ,,
Maize	.	.	.	7·8 ,, ,,
Apples	.	.	.	19·1 ,, ,,
Pears	.	.	.	6·8 ,, ,,
Citrus Fruit	.	.	.	9·4 ,, ,,
Grapes	.	.	.	635,000 tons
Sugar-cane	.	.	.	16·8 million tons
Cotton	.	.	.	145,000 bales

Study the above statistics and, using them to supplement your own knowledge, describe and explain the distribution of crop production in Australia. (Summer, 1972)

31. Discuss the importance of the seaports of Queensland and the Northern Territory in relation to their hinterlands. (Summer, 1972)

32. Review the distribution of arable and pastoral farming in North

Island, New Zealand, and relate to physical and human factors. (Summer, 1972)

33. Assess the value to the economy of Western Australia of the exploitation of its natural resources. (Summer, 1972)

34. Give an explanatory account of the distribution of population in Victoria. (Summer, 1972)

35. Study the map on page 179, and in your answer book: (*a*) describe and account for the distribution of sheep; (*b*) discuss to what extent the distribution of cattle differs from that of sheep. (Summer, 1973) (*Note*: the map supplied was a dot map showing the distribution of sheep)

36. Locate and discuss the distribution of forests in Australia. Examine the exploitation of the forest resources and discuss their present and long-term development. (Summer, 1973)

37. "Diversification of the economy and of markets is of prime importance." Discuss this assertion in relation to New Zealand. (Summer, 1973)

38. Describe and account for the concentration of the population of New South Wales on the coastal plain. (Summer, 1973)

39. Assess to what extent the economy is related to the physical environment in Western Australia. (Summer, 1973)

40. Make a comparative study of the agricultural geography of the North Island of New Zealand and Victoria. (Summer, 1973)

CONVERSION TABLES

Temperature

°F	°C	°F	°C	°F	°C	°F	°C
100	37·8	55	12·8	10	−12·2	−35	−37·2
95	35·0	50	10·0	5	−15·0	−40	−40·0
90	32·2	45	7·2	0	−17·8	−45	−42·8
85	29·4	40	4·4	−5	−20·6	−50	−45·6
80	26·7	35	1·7	−10	−23·3	−55	−48·3
75	23·9	30	−1·1	−15	−26·1	−60	−51·1
70	21·1	25	−3·9	−20	−28·9	−65	−53·9
65	18·3	20	−6·7	−25	−31·7	−70	−56·7
60	15·6	15	−9·4	−30	−34·4	−75	−59·4

Precipitation

In.	Mm	In.	Mm	In.	Mm	In.	Mm
60	1524·0	20	508·0	4	101·6	0·5	12·7
55	1397·0	15	381·0	3	76·2	0·4	10·2
50	1270·0	10	254·0	2	50·8	0·3	7·6
45	1143·0	9	228·6	1	25·4	0·2	5·1
40	1016·0	8	203·2	0·9	22·9	0·1	2·5
35	889·0	7	177·8	0·8	20·3	0·05	1·3
30	762·0	6	152·4	0·7	17·8		
25	635·0	5	127·0	0·6	15·2		

Rough approximation 4 in. = 100 mm

Distance

Miles	Km	Km	Miles
1	1·609	1	0·62
10	16·1	10	6·2
15	24·1	15	9·3
20	32·2	20	12·4
25	40·2	25	15·5
30	48·3	30	18·6
35	56·3	35	21·7
40	64·4	40	24·9
45	72·4	45	28·0
50	80·5	50	31·1

Height

Ft	Metres
500	152
1000	305
1500	457
2000	610
2500	762
3000	914
3500	1067
4000	1219
4500	1372
5000	1524

Rough approximation 10 miles = 16 km

Rough approximation 1000 ft = 300 m

Area

1 acre = 0·404 hectares
1 hectare = 2·471 acres
1 sq. mile = 2·589 sq. kilometres
1 sq. km = 0·386 sq. miles

1 sq. yard = 0·836 sq. metres (m²), *roughly* 100 sq. yd. = 84 m².
1 sq. metre = 10·764 sq. yd., *roughly* 10 m² = 12 sq. yd.
1 acre = 0·404 hectares (ha), *roughly* 10 acres = 4 ha.
1 hectare = 2·471 acres, *roughly* 1 ha = 2·5 acres = 1200 sq. yd.
1 sq. mile = 2·589 sq. km (km²), *roughly* 10 sq. miles = 26 km².
1 sq. km = 0·386 sq. mile, *roughly* 100 km² = 40 sq. miles.

Mass

1 ton = 1·016 tonne (t)
1 tonne = 0·984 ton

Volume capacity

The direct metric equivalent of the bushel is the litre. This is not used as an equivalent in metric countries; instead the measurement used is the kilogram which, as a unit of mass, cannot be directly converted. Consequently no conversion factor is given.

Currency

The table below gives the available rates of exchange for the pound against various currencies referred to in the text as at 26th March, 1973. The floating of various exchange rates means that rates are only approximate.

Place and Local Units		Value of £ sterling
Australia	Australian $	£1·7488
Fiji Islands	Fiji $	£1·9875
Nauru	Australian $	£1·7488
New Guinea	Australian $	£1·7488
New Zealand	New Zealand $	£1.86965

Author's Note

The tables in the text have been derived almost entirely from the respective year books and have not been converted to metric measurement as it would prevent students from checking the facts and from adding later figures to keep the work up to date.

INDEX